Effective Reports

SECOND EDITION

Malra Treece

Memphis State University

ALLYN AND BACON, INC.

Boston   London   Sydney   Toronto

Portions of this book first appeared in *Communication for Business and the Professions*, by Malra Treece, copyright © 1978 by Allyn and Bacon, Inc.

Production Administrator: Jane Schulman
Editorial-Production Service   Superscript Associates
Cover Coordinator   Christy Rosso
Cover Designer: Harold Pattek

Library of Congress Cataloging in Publication Data

Treece, Malra.
  Effective reports.

  "Portions of this book first appeared in communication
for business and the professions, by Malra Treece,
c1978"—Verso of t.p.
  Bibliography: p
  Includes index.
  1. Business report writing.   2. Report writing.
3. Communication in management.   I. Title.
HF5719.T73   1985   658.4'5   84-24358
ISBN 0-205-08353-6

Printed in the United States of America.

10 9 8 7 6 5 4 3 2 1   90 89 88 87 86 85

Contents

iii

Preface

Effective Reports, Second Edition, is planned for use as a textbook in any class that has as its major emphasis the preparation of written and oral reports. It is also useful as a reference book for the home or office library.

APPROACH

Although much of the content is devoted to the preparation of written reports, oral presentations are also included. Two chapters, 16 and 17, describe the job-seeking process and illustrate resumes and letters of application.

The entire book is based on the premise that all elements of communication are interrelated. Principles of effective writing also apply to effective speech; and communication in any form, including reports of all kinds, is affected by the many and varied environmental and psychological influences that affect human behavior.

Although professional in approach, content, organization, examples, and problems, *Effective Reports* is planned for easy and interesting reading. Readability and interest are considered important from four major standpoints:

- To enable readers to understand and apply principles discussed throughout the seventeen chapters and three appendix sections.

- To enable readers to enjoy the book.
- To illustrate techniques of readable business and professional writing.
- To exemplify, by the textbook itself, one of the most important attributes of written or oral communication: consideration for the receiver of the message.

Successful writers and speakers must have an understanding of the process of communication and of the effects of different perceptions and emotions upon the reception of meaning. In addition, they are knowledgeable about their subject matter, and their messages are sincere. They are skillful technicians, using words as tools to bring about change.

NEW TO THE SECOND EDITION

1. A new chapter (Chapter 13) describes computer capabilities in relation to report preparation, including collection, organization, and analysis of data and writing as well as editing with the aid of a word processor. In addition, a list of commercial computerized databases has been added to Chapter 8, "Gathering Information from Secondary Sources."
2. The chapter on documentation (Chapter 12) illustrates footnotes and other elements of documentation in leading styles. Depending on available time and specific purposes of instruction, teachers may wish to focus attention on one particular style, leaving other methods for individual student reference.
3. Appendix C (formerly Appendix D) "A Brief Guide to English Usage," has been expanded somewhat with new illustrations, examples, and assignments.
4. Appendix B (formerly Appendix C) contains numerous new cases. New problems have been added throughout the book.
5. The section on short reports now consists of two chapters instead of one. These chapters (3 and 4) are presented early in the book to prepare students for assignments, perhaps from Appendix B, that can be used throughout the semester.
6. Chapter 11, "Interpreting with Graphic Aids," has been updated with new illustrations and somewhat expanded.

ACKNOWLEDGMENTS

Sincere appreciation is expressed to teachers and students at Memphis State University who contributed their ideas and words of encouragement during the preparation of this book and my previous books.

Valuable advice came from users of *Effective Reports*, First Edition, *Communication for Business and the Professions*, First and Second Editions, and *Successful Business Communication*, First and Second Editions. These users contributed particularly helpful ideas and suggestions because their advice was based on practical experience in the classroom. Their comments relate directly to *Effective Reports*, Second Edition, and to future editions of my other books on business communication. I deeply appreciate their continuing support.

The following firms and individuals provided material for *Effective Reports*, Second Edition. Thank you.

Fredna Vaughn and Memphis Area Vocational Technical School

Herman F. Patterson, Memphis State University

David R. Weigel and Energy Management Consultants

Tennessee Valley Authority

First Baptist Church, Memphis

David Bourland and Federal Express

Sanford Howard and John Bowman, partners, Pannel Kerr Forster

James N. Holm, Kent State University, for excerpts from *Productive Speaking for Business and the Professions*, Allyn and Bacon, 1967.

Sherry Clara Aldridge, Memphis State University

Ruth C. Batchelor, Associate Professor Emeritus, New York University

Barron Wells, Nelda Spinks, and Janine Hargrave, University of Southwestern Louisiana

Jean W. Vining, formerly of University of New Orleans

Ed Goodin, Associate Professor of Management, University of Nevada, Las Vegas

Michael L. Kamil, University of Illinois at Chicago Circle

Ann Denton, Memphis State University, provided assistance with information about library sources, as reported in Chapter 8. Thank you, Ann.

At various states in the development of the manuscript a number of dedicated teachers and scholars provided their advice and criticism and shared information with me:

Virginia Creighton, San Francisco State University
Carol Dreger, Edmonds Community College
Marie E. Flatley, San Diego State University
Stanley Gryde, Azusa Pacific University
James B. Robinson, Trenton State College
Ronald Schulz, Milwaukee Area Technical College
Charles L. Snowden, Sinclair Community College

Their valuable contributions, which influenced the content and approach of the book, are sincerely appreciated.

A further word of thanks goes to Marilyn Helms, who, as a graduate assistant, provided invaluable help in numerous ways. Thanks also to Wendy Ritger, Developmental Editor at Allyn and Bacon, and John Peters, Series Editor.

Further appreciation goes to members of the American Business Communication, who for many years have made valuable contributions to the field of business communication. My colleagues in this worthy organization have provided information, ideas, and inspiration that are reflected in *Effective Reports*, Second Edition.

M.T.

An Overview of Report Preparation

PART I

An Introduction to the Study of Reports

1

Welcome to your study of communication through reports. Your career, whatever your business or profession, will depend upon your success in communicating, perhaps more than upon any other ability. In addition, effective communication is essential to a satisfying personal life.

Your ability to excel in communicating is one of the most valuable assets you will ever have. Perhaps more than any other accomplishment, your knowledge and skill in communication demonstrate your intellectual capacity for advancement to responsible positions. As you move up the ladder of responsibility, communication becomes even more important. Lack of skill in communicating can act as a barrier to professional growth.

ALL ELEMENTS OF COMMUNICATION ARE INTERRELATED

The elements of communication are not separate ones at all, but parts of the whole. Principles of effective writing also apply to effective speech. Nonverbal communication enters into both oral and written messages. Communication in any form is affected by the many and varied influences that enter into human behavior. Although the emphasis in this book is on reports, all instruction in communication must be interdisciplinary. Thus your study will include instruction in language, research sources and methods, individual and organizational behavior, organizational management,

4

personnel management, business ethics, logic, public speaking, and several other areas of knowledge.

Most written messages are far more similar to other written messages than they are dissimilar. Competent writers learn to adapt from one format to another and to readers with differing needs and preferences. Regardless of your background and study in other areas of communication, however, you are not likely to excel in business research and report writing unless you have studied the subject and applied this knowledge to the preparation of reports.

COMMUNICATION IS ALWAYS IMPERFECT

Your communication efforts will always be less than perfect, as they are for all of us. Perhaps the most important principle to keep in mind, as you strive to speak and write effectively, is that all communication is imperfect. This truth applies to report writing or any other area of communication, including the many methods of nonverbal communication.

Perfect communication cannot occur because the transmission of a message depends on both the sender and the receiver. We can never be sure of the effect of our words or nonverbal messages on the receivers of these messages. We cannot predict an individual's reactions to our words because of such factors as his or her emotions of the moment, previous understandings, or unique connotations of words based on individual experiences. Many other factors act as barriers to understanding and acceptance of our intended messages. But we can do much to improve our skills in both sending and receiving communication. This learning must be a continuing process, based on a foundation of knowledge, understanding, and skills developed by concentrated study of communication theory and techniques.

COMMUNICATION MUST BE SINCERE

The term *communication* should not be used—as it sometimes seems to be—as merely a front, a facade, a glossing over. An accountant, physician, politician, teacher, or anyone else who covers up a lack of knowledge or conviction by the skillful use of words, or "packaging," is not really an effective communicator. *The most important quality of communication is sincerity.*

Techniques of effective writing and speech are vastly important, but mastery of these techniques is not enough. The thoughts we are trying to convey must be based on a sound background of information and understanding. A fuzzy and indecisive mind cannot send out clear, correct, and convincing words. In addition, readers and listeners must have confidence in the integrity and sincerity of the writer or speaker in order for information and ideas to be trusted and accepted. To communicate, we must be trustworthy and sincere. We must have meaningful messages to send forth, and we must have the ability to put these messages into words that will be believed, accepted, and acted upon by the receivers of the message.

REPORTS DIFFER IN NATURE AND PURPOSE

A report is a written or oral message planned to convey information or to present a solution to a problem. Using this broad and simple definition, many letters, memorandums, telephone calls, and personal conversations are forms of reports, as are notes on memorandum pads or the backs of envelopes. A report may consist of hundreds of pages, on which many persons have worked for months or years, or of a few paragraphs written in ten minutes.

Reports consist of written and spoken words, columns of figures, charts, computer printouts, or a combination of all these and of other forms. We speak of news reports, weather reports, stock market reports, accounting reports, and the very broad term, business reports. Although any kind of report conveying business information is a "business report," the definition must be narrowed.

In the definition that follows, the word *effective* has been inserted to describe what reports should be, not necessarily what they are. Even a poor report is still called by that name, and, thus, the wording of the exact definition of the term is complicated by semantic factors.

> An effective business report is an orderly, objective presentation of factual information, with or without analysis, interpretation, and recommendations, planned to serve some business purpose, usually that of making a decision.

Other descriptions of a report are that it

- is a management tool;
- may be described by many names and in varying ways according to purpose, format, subject matter, scope, length, readership, and other factors;

- varies widely in form, length, and content;
- may merely relate information, or may relate information and, in addition, analyze it and make recommendations;
- may be planned only to analyze existing information;
- is usually written for one reader or for a small group of readers;
- often moves up the chain of command;
- tends to be written in a more formal style than some other types of business communication;
- ordinarily is assigned;
- may be prepared at specified, regular intervals or only for a special need;
- requires careful planning and organization;
- answers a question or solves a problem.

The basic qualities of effective reports are the same, for the most part, as those of effective communication of any kind. Clarity, coherence, conciseness, a wise choice of arrangement in order to achieve readability and the desired psychological approach, correctness, neatness, consideration of the reader, exactness—these considerations apply to all types of communication.

When planning reports, however, we must give special attention to organization and to an objective, unbiased approach. Because reports are often longer than most letters or memorandums, they must be especially planned for readability and an orderly progression of thought.

REPORTS MUST BE SPECIFIC AND OBJECTIVE

We are especially concerned about *objectivity* in a report; that is, we must gather and analyze data without letting our preconceived opinions or personal biases influence our efforts in finding and presenting truthful and complete information and interpretations. Although, because we are human, it is impossible to be completely objective, we should strive to base conclusions on facts, not on emotions or desires. No other element in the report-writing process is more important.

We tend to see what we expect to see or what we want to see. The recognition of this natural human weakness, with an effort to avoid it, is essential to unbiased research and reporting. We also tend to overgeneralize and to interpret inferences and value judgments as facts. Although such "twisting of the truth," even though unconscious, is harmful in all facets of life, it is obviously a definite barrier to objective research and impartial interpretation of data.

Readers of reports are influenced by specific details that provide a complete answer to the stated problem, not by emotional, persuasive language planned to bring readers to the writer's point of view. The same considerations apply to oral reports and, to a great extent, to all other written or oral messages, even to sales presentations. The reader or listener is convinced by *evidence*, not by *persuasion*, as the term is ordinarily used. True persuasion consists of specific, factual evidence effectively presented in the light of the readers' or listeners' interests.

An objective approach, based on correct and concrete information, is emphasized throughout this textbook, especially in chapters on evaluating and presenting data. Such an approach is discussed in this introductory chapter because it forms the basis for true reporting of all kinds.

REPORTS ARE A FACT OF LIFE

Reports of some kind are necessary in all occupations. Whether you prepare them well or poorly, easily or with difficulty, almost surely you will prepare them. You will save much time if you learn to do them well.

Report preparation is not always stimulating, exciting, or entertaining. Dedicated researchers, however, consider the "search for truth" as one of their most exciting and fulfilling activities. Any kind of work is creative when we give it our best, approach it in our own way (there will always be restrictions), and carry it through to successful completion.

Your written and oral reports bring your ability and hard work to the attention of your superiors. Reports are not only responsibilities; they are opportunities!

In addition, your ability to write effective, readable reports will be an invaluable aid in many of your other classes, both at the undergraduate and the graduate level.

DETERMINING OBJECTIVES IS AN AID TO PROGRESS

At the beginning of your study, as in any endeavor, it is good to determine goals and to decide upon methods of reaching these goals. If you are enrolled in a class, no doubt your instructor's course outline includes specific objectives to be attained during the term or semester. To be worthwhile, these goals must truly be your own. You may wish to set goals for yourself that are higher than the required ones. Do you have objectives for this course in addition to the ones below?

1. To consider the ethics of communication in business situations and to develop an ethical approach to solving business problems.
2. To understand the theory and concepts of the communication process, particularly as they apply to business research and reporting.
3. To increase your ability to inform and convince through the use of language.
4. To learn the forms and purposes of frequently used business reports.
5. To improve your ability to make decisions involving the selection and organization of content, media, and format.
6. To learn to communicate information and ideas in written form by
   a. developing a clear, concise, convincing, and objective writing style that is adapted to the readers of the message.
   b. learning and applying high standards of physical presentation in preparing written messages.
7. To learn the basic techniques of report preparation, including how to collect, evaluate, analyze, organize, and interpret information and to present it in written and oral reports.
8. To strengthen your ability to analyze written and oral communications.
9. To develop an understanding of how computers and other technological developments can aid report preparation.

If you have specific objectives of your own, such as how to prepare special-purpose reports in your area of knowledge or for a particular job, no doubt these more specific objectives are included in the general ones listed above. If you do have specialized goals, let your instructor know about them, perhaps in the form suggested in the first problem at the end of this chapter.

ALL EFFECTIVE REPORTS CAN BE DESCRIBED BY THE FOLLOWING TERMS

Communication does not consist of one quality, but of several qualities woven together. Even when communication is limited to the medium of written business reports, many principles of effective communication enter into consideration throughout the process, from the beginning of the planning stage to the transmittal of the finished report.

Writing or speaking cannot be completely effective if it is weak in any area, regardless of how strong it is in other areas. For example, even though a report is carefully planned, researched, and objectively analyzed, it is less than effective if the writer does not know the principles of sentence construction or of correct language usage. On the other hand, correct language alone is far from enough, although it is extremely important.

Your work in the world is likely to be judged somewhat differently from the papers you prepare in school. If a report is not good from all standpoints, it will not be considered as fair or average, based on its strong points. If it is weak in one respect, it is weak overall.

The terms in the following list are not exclusive in meaning, and some are quite similar; for example, *clear* and *readable*. As these words apply to written material, they often are used synonymously, although *readable* is likely to mean *clear without reading effort*. Other terms with similar meanings are *courteous* and *considerate*. *Considerate is the broader term. Courteous* has more to do with phrasing, and, when applied to business research and report writing, effective communication throughout the report process. We cannot be considerate without also being courteous, but courteous phrasing does not guarantee true consideration.

Appropriate in Tone and Approach.   Communication differs in tone and approach according to the message, the listeners or readers, and the occasion. As much as possible, each message should be adapted to the individual reader. The tone of some reports differs from that of usual business letters. Writers must consider the purpose of the communication and, among other factors, organizational precedent for similar reports.

Attractive in Appearance.   Your business messages should be neatly typewritten and arranged attractively on the sheet. The typewriter keys must be clean. An electric typewriter with a film ribbon is best. Choose an appropriate format that is easily readable. Leave plenty of white space. Use good quality paper.

Businesslike.   The term *businesslike* does not mean that reports or other business messages are written in any specialized or particular language. Good business language is the same language that is correctly used elsewhere in life. You are not being businesslike, but old-fashioned, if you use such stereotyped phrasing as "Please find enclosed herewith," "in your hands," and "We beg to call your kind attention to . . ." Business writing should not be stuffy, stiff, or pompous, but simple, natural, and direct. It should be polite and matter-of-fact, much as you would address associates in your office, particularly those at a higher level.

Clear.   Business writing must be immediately clear. *Readability* is another term used in this book to mean clarity, especially from the standpoint of adaptation to varying groups of readers.

Clarity can be achieved by using: (1) concrete, specific words, including active verbs; (2) correct and appropriate sentence structure planned to convey the desired emphasis; (3) short, well-organized paragraphs, most of which begin with a topic sentence; (4) conventional punctuation, which is used not only to follow "accepted rules," but to convey meaning; (5) coherent phrasing and organization; and (6) readable formats.

Clear thinking must precede clear writing or speech. If the sender of the message does not know exactly what he or she wants to say, and does not keep the reader in mind, the message is likely to be inexact and ineffective.

Coherent.   Sentences and paragraphs should "hang together"; that is, the thought should flow naturally and freely from the beginning of the message to the end. If a message is well organized and contains well-chosen words, including necessary and appropriate transitional words, phrases, and paragraphs, it will be coherent.

Complete.   The message must be complete in that it answers fully all the reader's questions and gives all the needed or desired information. A report must fulfill its stated purpose which, in a report arranged in the inductive order, is stated early in the introduction.

Concise.   Conciseness means a written or oral message is no longer than it needs to be to accomplish its particular purpose or purposes. Conciseness is not necessarily brevity. A one hundred-page report and a ten-page letter are concise if every word is necessary to convey the information, to be considerate, and to be convincing. The lack of conciseness often occurs because of unnecessary repetition; rambling; wordy phrases, especially trite phrases of business jargon; and long, complicated words and phrases instead of simple, direct wording.

Considerate.   Consideration goes one step further than courtesy. The terms are not exactly synonymous. Consideration is the broader term and includes what you actually say in your message or the solution to your particular problem. Consideration is simply another name for one aspect of the *you-attitude*, which is often discussed in relation to business letters but is also applicable to business reports and all other business messages.

Constructive. Constructive writing is positive, specific, helpful, convincing, and effective.

Convincing. Convincing writing is written in specific, concrete words that lead logically to a reasonable conclusion. Readers are convinced by evidence, not by persuasion.

Correct. A message should be correct in information given, in the form and approach chosen, and in English usage. Being grammatically correct in every detail, as important as this feature is, is not enough for good business writing. A report that includes inaccurate, incomplete, or biased, nonobjective interpretations causes more havoc than erratic punctuation or misspelled words.

Courteous. All business writing and speech should be courteous. Good manners are necessary in all business and professional communication. When writing reports, you show courtesy by submitting them on or before scheduled deadlines. You are courteous when you exemplify all the characteristics of effective communication, as discussed in this summary and throughout the text; clarity, completeness, conciseness, correctness, objectivity, and all the rest. A cover, title sheet, and transmittal letter are other courteous, considerate touches to a formal report.

Creative. Business writing is not usually referred to as "creative writing," a term most often used to describe novels, poetry, short stories, and, perhaps, some advertising copy. All our work, however, is creative if we have put our best into it, if we have looked at the situation and tried to solve it in the best possible way, not necessarily in the way it has always been solved before.

Effective. Effective writing or speech accomplishes its particular purpose or purposes.

Emphatic. Emphasis should be used to call attention to the most important parts of the message. Proper use of the methods of emphasis is the most important aid to clarity. Methods of achieving proper emphasis and clarity are approximately the same: position, space, word choice, sentence construction, format, and mechanical means of emphasis.

Ethical. Business reports, like all other business communication, should be sincere, honest, and truthful. All communication should be based on a sincere interest in the reader and upon loyalty to the writer's employing organization.

Forceful. Good writing is not forceful from the standpoint that it is dictatorial or demanding. It is forceful in that it is strong and vivid, written mostly in the active voice. Forceful writing is usually concise, for it is not weighted down with unnecessary, wordy phrases. Because it moves, it is likely to have good sentence construction. Forceful writing is also emphatic writing, and it is likely to be convincing.

Formal. The word *formal*, when used to describe reports, describes both format and writing style. The word *formal*, like many other words, is relative and far from exact. As it concerns format, the greatest distinction between formal and informal reports is the inclusion of preliminary and appended parts. A formal writing style, as contrasted to an informal one, contains no contractions, casual, conversational expressions, or slang. All writing, regardless of formality, should be simple and natural.

Goodwill Building. In all business writing or speech, we must be concerned with goodwill, both with persons outside the organization and with other employees. In the case of reports, which are likely to move upward within the organization, the term *goodwill* is perhaps better expressed as recognition of your competence that you display by the overall quality of the finished report and your demonstrated ability throughout the report process. In addition, some reports are read by persons outside the organization; for example, annual reports are factual material to prospective employees or stockholders. For such reports, you must be concerned with building and maintaining goodwill toward your employing organization.

Interesting. Your business reports and other business writing will be interesting if they answer the reader's questions in an easily readable, concise form. Anecdotes and jokes, although suitable for a few kinds of business writing, are ordinarily out of place in factual reporting.

Objective. Business writing should be objective, or nonbiased, in that it is based upon facts. Objective writing is especially stressed in report writing, but it is important in all forms of communication. In reports, when opinions are stated, they should be clearly identified as opinion. Material expressed in the impersonal tone and formal writing style seems more objective to some readers than material written more informally with the use of personal pronouns, particularly *I* and *you*.

Original. Not every business report can be completely different from every other business report, for often the situations are the same or similar. Your reports should be original in that they are written in your own words, not copied from some manual or handbook. Reports and other kinds of writing often lack originality because they are worded in trite, stereotyped business jargon or other stale clichés.

Positive. The positive approach accents the pleasant aspects of a situation, not the unpleasant. It tells what *can* be done, not what *cannot* be done. Negative words such as *fail*, *criticize*, and *reject* are minimized, if not completely eliminated. The several methods of emphasis and subordination can be used to construct the message in a positive, pleasant, and diplomatic way.

Professional. Report writers make their work professional by continuing study of the use of language, research methods, logic, and the art and skill of writing.

Specific. Specific writing is the opposite of vague, general writing. It is concrete, not abstract or general. Specific writing is more forceful and vivid than general, abstract writing. Specific writing is usually the better choice. At times, however, in order to be tactful and courteous, you cannot be completely specific.

Tactful. Real courtesy and consideration, combined with careful word choice, should make all your messages tactful.

SUMMARY

Success in your professional and personal life depends to a great extent upon the ability to communicate, perhaps more so than upon any other ability. Oral and written communication, including reports, is a vital and frequent employment responsibility, whatever your specialization or employing organization.

The most important element of all communication is sincerity.

At the beginning of your study of report preparation or of any other subject, it is good to determine goals and to decide upon methods for reaching these goals.

A report is a written or oral message planned to convey information or to present a solution. Reports are essential in all businesses and professions. Basic principles and considerations are the same for all.

Because all elements of communication are interrelated, the most important qualities of effective reports are the same, for the most part, as those of all effective messages. When preparing reports, however, we must give special attention to organization and to an objective, factual evaluation and presentation. Recommendations must be based on evidence.

QUESTIONS AND PROBLEMS

1. Look back at the objectives listed for this course. Which ones interest you the most and the least? Why? In which areas referred to by these various objectives do you feel that you are now the strongest? The weakest? Express the answers to these questions in a letter or memorandum addressed to your instructor. (See Chapter 3 for suggested formats.)

2. Write a letter, memorandum, or other report to your instructor in which you give the following information:
   a. Your major and expected date of graduation.
   b. The kind of work you hope to enter or continue after you complete your college work.
   c. Whether you have a part-time job, and, if so, what you do, particularly as your work relates to report writing or other communication.
   d. Your previous work experience, especially your experience in communication of any kind.

3. Interview one or more persons who are working in your area of specialization. For example, if you are majoring in personnel management, interview one or more persons already employed in this field. Ask them for their advice about the skills and knowledge that you should try to obtain during your study of reports. Write a summary of the information you obtain in the format specified by your instructor. Be prepared to present this summary in the form of a short oral report to other class members.

4. Look in the *Business Periodical Index* under "Communication in Management" to find two articles that have been published within the past two years. Try to find articles that relate directly

to your major field of study. For example, if you are majoring in accounting, find articles about communication as it relates to accountants. Write a one-page summary of one or both of these articles in the format that your instructor suggests. Be prepared to present this summary, or these summaries, orally to the class.

5. Step to the front of the classroom. Introduce yourself to your instructor and to your classmates. Tell them about your major field of study and your career goals. Describe your present employment, if any, especially as it relates to written or oral communication. Tell them anything else about yourself that you wish, provided you keep your remarks to no more than the time limit set by your instructor.

6. This assignment can be substituted for the above. Form into groups of two. Meet with someone with whom you are not already acquainted, preferably someone you have never seen before entering this class. Spend five to ten minutes (or the time limit set by your instructor) in becoming acquainted with your classmate.

7. Introduce your friend (Problem 6) to your instructor and to your classmates, much as you would introduce a speaker at a conference or at another speaking engagement. Tell the class something about this person, perhaps some of the information described in Problem 2.

8. If you are now employed, describe your communication activities in relation to the discussion in this chapter. Examples of topics to be discussed or questions to be answered are these:

    a. Do you spend more time in written communication or in oral communication?
    b. What kinds of reports do you prepare?
    c. What kinds of reports do you receive?
    d. What other kinds of written messages do you prepare?
    e. By which methods (telephone, conversation, group discussion, or public speaking) do you communicate orally? What are the purposes of these forms of oral communication?

Classifications and Characteristics of Reports

2

Every oral or written report is different in some way from all others, yet in many ways similar to every other. Reports vary according to the reader, writer, subject matter, purpose, and many other factors. They are described by different terms in different organizations.

Although the terminology used elsewhere may differ from that in this book, understanding the report classifications given in this chapter will help you plan and prepare reports of various kinds because you will know the many ways in which they *can* be prepared. After learning basic principles, you can adapt to specialized and differing terminology, forms, and techniques.

In addition to the terms used in this chapter, reports are classified according to their specialized uses. Like individuals, they sometimes go by nicknames. For example, they may be called by special names, such as the "2001 Report," for which the descriptive term is only the number of the printed form on which data are recorded, or "the green sheet," to describe the color of the paper used for the report. Reports may also be classified according to product name or according to a company department or division or described by the purpose for which the report was prepared.

All these classifications you will learn on the job. Like other specialized terms you use in your daily work, they will soon become familiar to you. For example, Social Security claims representatives refer dozens of times a day to the "101" or the "201," which are the numbers given to special forms on which information is recorded. Accountants, as well as many other people at income-tax time, refer routinely to the "1040," as well as to other reports, by a number that serves as a name.

Reports are basically classified and arranged in the following ways, even if no one in a particular organization, including the writer, refers to them in this way. These terms describe factors common to all reports.

CLASSIFICATION BY READERSHIP

As is true with all effective communication, reports should be prepared and presented from the standpoint of the receiver or receivers of the message. Some reports differ from most letters and memorandums, however, in that you as the report writer cannot always be sure who your readers will be, even when the report is authorized and addressed to one individual.

For example, if you prepare a report for your supervisor, he or she may then use your report as a basis for a recommendation to someone higher in authority in the organization. In addition, your report may be filed away and referred to when other reports on the subject are prepared, perhaps years hence. In most instances, however, you *will* know who the principal readers of your report will be and can plan your approach accordingly.

If you believe that your report may be used in various ways, including publication, you will be wise to use a more traditional, formal approach than if you were writing routine memorandums to co-workers you know well. (See the terms *formal* and *informal* later in this chapter. Do not misinterpret the meaning of the word *formal*. All good writing, regardless of readership, should be simple, straightforward, and easy to read.)

Reports also are classified by readership in that they are *internal* or *external*. As the term indicates, internal reports are prepared for readers within your own organization, ordinarily someone higher in the chain of command. Many internal reports are prepared as memorandums. External reports go to someone outside an organization; for example, consultants submit reports to organizations other than their own. Another example of an external report is one to a government agency, perhaps to report the results of a research grant.

Although you will be guided by your expected readers, you can be sure that if your report is professionally written—that is, if it can be described by the characteristics of effective reports listed in Chapter 1—it will be well received by almost all readers, regardless of their background or position. A major consideration, however, is what your readers already know about the subject you plan to discuss. If at all possible, in the planning stage of your report, determine your readership and their needs and present knowledge of the subject.

CLASSIFICATION BY TIME INTERVALS

Periodic reports are prepared at regular intervals, such as daily, weekly, monthly, or annually. The annual corporate report is a periodic report, as is the daily sales report that consists only of rows of figures.

Special reports are not prepared at regular intervals, but only as the need arises. For example, a president of a bank with several branches learns that energy costs vary widely for the branches, which are located in buildings of similar size and construction. The president asks qualified bank personnel or an outside consulting firm to perform needed research and submit a report.

Progress reports, as the name indicates, relate the past and expected progress of an assigned project, often of a long, analytical report. These progress reports can also be described as periodic if, for example, a weekly progress report is expected until the project is completed. A consulting firm employed to find the reasons for the differing energy costs of the bank branches may be asked to make periodic reports to the president, perhaps weekly or as each branch bank is inspected. Progress reports are usually brief.

CLASSIFICATION BY AUTHORIZATION

Most reports are *assigned*. Even if the report writer wishes to initiate a project, it is ordinarily authorized by someone higher in authority, especially if the project is one that will necessitate much company time and expense. This authorization may be in written form and incorporated into the final report.

Justification reports usually are unassigned. Because they are usually, but not always, short and simply prepared, they seldom require written or oral authorization. As the name implies, they are prepared for the purpose of justifying a purchase, a procedure, or a change in the method of operation. Such reports are also prepared as *proposals* and described as such, as discussed in Chapter 7.

CLASSIFICATION BY SUBJECT MATTER

Classification by subject matter is obviously one that will apply to all reports. (As you have no doubt noticed, the same report can be classified in several different ways.) Reports can be classified according to their particular subject matter or on the basis of a grouping of subjects.

Such a grouping is also described as classification by departments, if, within an organization, we refer to accounting, sales, management, research and development, credit, and other similar subject fields. To classify more narrowly, each of these broad subject areas could be divided into more specific descriptions; for example, accounting reports may be described as cost, audit, tax, and finance reports.

CLASSIFICATION BY PURPOSE AND FUNCTION

Every report should fulfill one, two, or three of the following purposes:
> to inform,
> to analyze,
> to recommend.

Informational reports simply present data with no attempt to analyze or interpret the meaning of the data nor to make recommendations for action.

Analytical reports also provide information but, in addition, include analysis and interpretation.

Informational reports are usually, but not always, shorter than analytical ones. Informational reports can be of any length, depending upon the amount of information to convey. Conversely, an analytical report can be short. (Long and short are relative terms, in reports as well as in everything else.) We do, however, often hear the terms *long analytical report* and *complete analytical report*. *Complete*, when used as a descriptive term, may mean that the report contains various preliminary and supplementary parts, which are discussed in depth in Chapter 14. The word may also be used to signify that the report and the investigation that preceded it are broad in scope.

Analytical reports are sometimes further classified by such terms as *examination, recommendation,* or *improvement*. These distinctions are usually made between analytical reports that include stated recommendations and those that do not. An *examination* report includes an analysis of the data but no recommendations for improvement. Whether or not recommendations are definitely stated, an analysis of relevant data implies certain recommendations. For example, if a study of why a certain product is not selling well shows that customers do not like the color, obviously the report implies, or "recommends," that the color be changed.

The distinction between informational and analytical reports will be important to you as you consider a proposed project. One of your first steps, particularly if you are a new employee, will be to determine exactly what is expected, not only from the standpoint of whether to analyze the data but from all other aspects of the problem.

Another term that is sometimes used in connection with an analytical report is *research report* or *research study*. A definition of research is "to make a diligent and systematic inquiry or investigation into a subject in order to discover or revise facts, theories, applications, . . ."[1] Using this definition, we see that an analytical report is not necessarily based on data gathered by the report writer, who may prepare an analytical report from data already accumulated. In addition, a research report is not necessarily an analytical one, as research may be done only to gather information and to relay it, not to analyze the information and make recommendations.

An analytical report may consist of many combined informational reports from the standpoint that the data from these reports are combined and analyzed, often with the aid of a computer, and, from these combined data, analyses and recommendations are made for the solution of an existing problem.

CLASSIFICATION BY DEGREE OF FORMALITY

Purpose and readership determine the degree of formality. The words *formal* and *informal*, as when used elsewhere, are relative terms when applied to reports; there is no exact and distinct dividing line. Reports that are not definitely and conclusively formal are best described as informal, a description that fits most business and professional writing and speech. In written messages, the words *formal* and *informal* are used to describe format, writing style, or both.

Format

A completely formal written report includes preliminary and supplementary parts that are omitted from the more informal arrangements. Such a report, as previously mentioned, is also described as

1. *Random House Dictionary of the English Language* (New York: Random House, 1967), p. 1219.

a complete report. Some of these preliminary parts are *letter of transmittal, letter of acceptance, table of contents, list of tables,* and *synopsis.* Supplementary parts include a *bibliography, appendix section,* and perhaps an *index.*

Informal reports may be presented in letter or memorandum format or in the various other short-form arrangements illustrated in Chapter 4. In addition, informal reports are prepared on numerous kinds of preprinted forms in order to simplify preparation and reader comprehension.

A long report is likely to be arranged in the formal (complete) format, and a short report is likely to be presented as a memorandum or in some other informal report arrangement. This distinction, however, does not always apply. A fairly short report—six or seven pages, for example—may appropriately include preliminary and supplementary parts.

Writing Style

Formal writing includes no contractions, expressions that could be considered slang, or abbreviated sentences or sentence fragments. An informal writing style may include contractions and casual, conversational phrases or modes of expression.

Regardless of how the writing is described or how formal the situation, it should not appear unnatural, stilted, or pretentious. Some reports are written more formally than routine memorandums, but all business and professional writing should be interesting, natural, and easy to read. Both formal and informal writing should be grammatically correct, and both should be arranged and worded with the reader in mind.

Actually, neither classification, formal or informal, is completely exact as it pertains to most business and professional writing. "Semiformal" is more descriptive. *Ordinarily, you need not worry about degrees of formality but should merely write in a correct, natural, direct, simple, and respectful manner.* If you are not sure of the personality and the preference of your readers, and usually you won't be, you are wise to lean more toward the formal style than to be overly casual and familiar. Words that we put on paper, especially in the form of reports, are, at the least, semipermanent. We can never be sure how our written material will be used or when it will be used. A report that you write today could be filed away and used as a reference source ten or fifteen years from now.

The passages below are examples of formal writing, at least from the standpoint that they do not include contractions, colloquial language, or other evidences of an extremely informal approach.

They also illustrate the fact that a casual, colloquial approach is *not* required for easy readability or a natural style.

> The primary concern of American education today is not the development of the appreciation of the "good life" in young gentlemen born to the purple. . . . Our purpose is to cultivate in the largest possible number of our future citizens an appreciation of both the responsibilities and the benefits which come to them because they are Americans and are free.[2]

> Those who favor advertising make a strong argument when they say that the majority of lawyers will continue to abide by the Canons of Ethics and provide honest service. This argument becomes stronger when it is asserted that it is, and always will be, in the best interests of the members of the Bar who strive to uphold the honor and integrity of the profession to police their own members on this issue.[3]

An example of extremely informal writing, on the same subject as the second passage quoted, is as follows:

> Okay, fellow barristers, we've decided to advertise. That historic decision doesn't mean that we *have* to do so—it's up to you. But—please—no flashing neon signs, singing commercials, or half-price sales. It's not true, as some of you pessimists and idealists have bemoaned, that the legal profession has at last hit rock bottom. That happened a long time ago.

The following short business letter is also written in an informal style:

> Thank you, Joan, for your blow-by-blow account of the annual sales meeting. Before I received your letter, I was sorry that I was forced to remain here in the main office.

> Even so, I'm looking forward to seeing you at next year's meeting.

Your choice of writing style—light or serious, informal or formal—must be influenced by your relationship with the reader and

2. James Bryant Conant, Annual Report to the Board of Overseers, Harvard University, January 11, 1943. Quoted by John Bartlett in *Familiar Quotations*, 14th ed. (Boston: Little, Brown, 1968), p. 1026.

3. Jeffry A. Garrety, "The Advertising Decision Facing the Practicing Attorney" (unpublished report, 1977).

the subject matter of your message. A light, humorous tone, no matter how clever, is inappropriate in some situations. On the other hand, business and professional communications are often concerned with subjects of less than immortal impact—although they are desirable or necessary for whatever purpose they are planned to accomplish.

CLASSIFICATION BY PERSONAL OR IMPERSONAL WRITING STYLE

Most business writing, including many reports, is written in the *personal tone*; that is, the writer is free to use *I*, *we*, *you*, and other first- and second-person pronouns so long as they are not used to excess. The *impersonal tone* includes no first- or second-person pronouns. This style of writing is also referred to as the *third-person objective*.

An advantage of using the impersonal tone in reports is that it seems more objective and nonbiased. References are to facts and interpretations, not to the writer. The choice of writing style does not affect real objectivity; nevertheless, because it appears to do so, many writers and readers prefer the impersonal tone.

Another important advantage is that by using no first- or second-person pronouns, more emphasis is given to the facts and analyses being presented, where the emphasis should be. You should emphasize the results, not what you did as the researcher.

Some traditionally minded readers of business reports judge a report written in the impersonal tone to be more professional, more objective, more scientific, and more carefully prepared than one written in the personal tone. If you are likely to encounter this reaction, you are decreasing the likelihood of the acceptance of your ideas by using the personal tone. The use of *I*, *we*, and other first- and second-person pronouns may distract the reader's mind from whatever it is that you are trying to say.

The impersonal writing style is, in itself, more formal than the personal. It is ordinarily used when the report, according to format and wording, is described as formal. Written material, however, can convey formality even with the use of first- and second-person pronouns. Hence, the terms *formal writing style* and *impersonal tone* are not synonymous, although they are often used together in the same report.

Although opinions of the writer may be expressed, emphasis should be upon conclusions based upon the findings of the report, not upon what the researcher believes. The use of *I* and *we* in a formal report may lead readers' thoughts away from the information being reported to the person who did the reporting. This undue emphasis is often reason enough for wording some types of writing in the impersonal tone.

Opinions can be stated impersonally, without the use of *I*, as illustrated below:

```
The results of the study indicate that electricity
consumption could be reduced approximately 20
percent by the installation of fluorescent lights
throughout the plant and offices.

The study indicates that the company should install
fluorescent lights throughout the plant and offices.

Fluorescent lights should be installed throughout
the plant and offices.
```

That it is the report writer who is making the recommendation is apparent in most cases, since he or she has done the research and is writing the report.

The preceding sentences, if written in the personal tone, might read as follows:

```
We could decrease electricity consumption
approximately 20 percent by the installation of
fluorescent lights throughout the plant and offices.

The results of the study indicate that we should
install fluorescent lights throughout the plant and
offices in order to decrease electricity consumption
by approximately 20 percent.

I recommend that we install fluorescent lights
throughout the plant and offices.
```

Notice that the personal tone results in a more natural and informal approach. In the third example the words *I recommend* emphasize the writer of the report and not the recommendation, as these words are in the emphatic sentence beginning. The second sentence includes the word *we* but uses the important and emphatic first position to mention results and the emphatic closing position to state benefits of the recommendation. In the first example, as well as the third, *we* refers to the organization, not to the report writer.

You are likely to do much more writing in the personal tone than in the impersonal, and appropriately so. *The expert writer,*

however, can write well in either style and can choose wisely be-
tween the two for differing kinds of material, readership, and sit-
uations. Try to judge each bit of writing according to what you have
to say and who will read it.

CLASSIFICATION BY ARRANGEMENT OF IDEAS

Reports can be arranged in *direct* (or *deductive*) order or in *indirect*
(or *inductive*) order. They can also be arranged in chronological ("as-
it-happened") order.

Basically, the difference between direct and indirect order is
this: The direct arrangement begins with the most important part
of the message and then expands upon this central message by giving
details, examples, or added information or explanations. The indirect arrangement builds up to the most important part of the message by beginning with an introductory section, presenting findings,
and ending with conclusions and recommendations. These two arrangements can be used in written works of all lengths, including
letters, memorandums, and reports.

For the most part, basic considerations as to which order should
be chosen are the same for both writing and speech. Direct order is
usually the best choice unless there is a definite, obvious reason for
using indirect or chronological arrangement.

The direct arrangement of any written work is advantageous
in that it is easy to read because the most important part of the
message is presented first. The reader knows immediately what the
communication is about. The emphatic beginning is used as it
should be, to emphasize something important. The direct arrangement, however, has a psychological disadvantage in some instances.
The reader may not be prepared for "the answer," especially if it is
a disappointing one or something that the reader is not prepared to
believe or accept.

In such a situation, the indirect arrangement should be used
to prepare the reader to accept or to believe the conclusions of the
letter or report. For example, if reasons are given first or if information is included to show how the final decision was reached, the
reader is more likely to accept the decision. In addition, explanation
of circumstances and background material are often necessary to
make clear the most important part of the message, even though
the reader is willing to accept the message.

News stories and news releases are usually written in the direct
order; the main facts of the story are given in the first paragraph,
facts of lesser importance are given in the second, and so on. This

plan is used in news releases so that condensing, necessary sometimes because of limited space, can be done from the bottom up. Even when the article or release appears in its complete, original form, the direct arrangement of ideas, from the most important to the least, increases reader interest and understanding. Business letters, memorandums, and reports, like newspapers, are often read hurriedly; any arrangement that will increase quick and easy understanding should be used.

The inductive report arrangement, so traditional in some organizations in past years that it is sometimes described as the "traditional" arrangement, is no longer mandatory or routinely expected even for long analytical reports. Overall, the trend in report writing is toward informality and conciseness. Many readers prefer the "answer" at the beginning, even if this answer is not particularly pleasant. Other readers still prefer the inductive arrangement, saying it is more "logical" because it tells *why* (purpose) and *how* (methods) before presenting *what* (findings) and arriving at the *answer* (recommendations).

Not all material, including reports, can be written in the direct order, even when there is no psychological aspect to consider or precedent to follow. To do so would decrease, not increase, reader understanding. The reader (or listener) must have an idea of the subject to be discussed before understanding conclusions. You may need introductory paragraphs or sections to lead to comprehension of the most important facts.

A paragraph is also arranged in direct or indirect order, or perhaps in chronological order. A paragraph arranged in direct order begins with a topic sentence. A paragraph that builds up to the topic sentence is arranged in indirect order. The direct arrangement of paragraphs should ordinarily be preferred because of increased readability, although paragraphs, like sentences, should be varied in order to improve style, flow of thought, and the exact expression of ideas.

The two immediately preceding paragraphs illustrate the use of topic sentences as first sentences, resulting in the direct order of paragraph arrangement. The following paragraph illustrates the topic sentence at the end of the paragraph, as well as the informal writing style.

Are you thinking by this time that all these terms are just too much? Do you believe that the most important principle of writing is just to sit down and write—or, if you prefer, to stand up and write? (Thomas Wolfe, the six-foot-six-inch novelist, wrote while standing at his refrigerator, with the manuscript on top of the refrigerator.) You are at least partially right—it does no good whatsoever to talk about writing a report, or anything else, if you never get around to writing one. On the other hand, it's possible just to sit down and start writing, or dictating, and come out with a jumbled mess. Like other abilities, successful report writing is based on an understanding of principles and concepts that are best described by exact terminology.

Figures 2-1 and 2-2, excerpts from a report in letter form, illustrate the use of the direct and the indirect order of arrangement. For a short report similar to the one on Saladmix in these two figures, many readers and writers prefer the direct order. This letter as shown in these figures, however, could serve as a summarizing transmittal letter to accompany a long comprehensive report. The notation about accompanying charts and graphs would be omitted and reference would be made to the complete report. For this particular subject, many readers would prefer far more detailed analysis on such matters as competing brands, types of advertising, and other factors. The problem as stated should be discussed in far more detail unless the reader has complete confidence in the writer's decision. For a much longer report, on this subject or any other, the indirect order is often considered preferable.

> Saladmix should be introduced into the market during March of next year.
>
> This recommendation is based on marketing data that show seasonal sales of other salad dressings and mixes, ours and those of our competitors. The highest volume months are June and July, followed by April and May. February and March are the months with the lowest volume in sales, with only a slightly higher total reported for December and January, as shown on the attached tables and charts.
>
> Because we cannot get Saladmix on the market before September of this year, we will have missed the highest volume months. Although introduction in September would give Saladmix a possible advantage over potential competition, I do not believe such an advantage warrants the additional cost. Sales from October to March are only 31 percent of the total annual sales, while sales from March to October are 69 percent of the total.
>
> By introducing Saladmix in March, preferably during the first week, we can take advantage of the highest volume months and benefit most from the increased advertising that will be necessary whenever Saladmix is released.
>
> If you have any further questions about possible marketing strategies concerning Saladmix, please call my office.

Figure 2-1. *Illustration of contents of letter report presented in the direct order of arrangement. (Based on a report prepared by Al Lyons.)*

Here is the report on the introduction of Saladmix. Marketing data that show seasonal sales of other salad dressings and mixes, ours and those of our competitors, are shown on the attached tables and charts.

The highest volume months are June and July, followed by April and May. February and March are the months with the lowest volume in sales, with only a slightly higher total reported for December and January.

Because we cannot get Saladmix on the market before September of this year, we will have missed the highest volume months. Although introduction in September would give Saladmix a possible advantage over potential competition, I do not believe such an advantage warrants the additional cost. Sales from October to March are only 31 percent of the total annual sales, while sales from March to October are 69 percent of the total.

By introducing Saladmix in March, preferably during the first week, we can take advantage of the highest volume months and benefit most from the increased advertising that will be necessary whenever Saladmix is released.

I, therefore, recommend that Saladmix be introduced into the market during March of next year.

Figure 2-2. *Illustration of contents of letter report presented in the indirect order of arrangement. (Based on a report prepared by Al Lyons.)*

Compare these direct and indirect arrangements:

Indirect Arrangement	*Direct Arrangement*
Introduction (purpose, methods, scope, other introductory material)	Recommendations (if stated) or conclusions, based on detailed findings
Detailed presentation of findings, usually divided into several sections	Purpose, methods, scope, and other necessary explanatory material (Sometimes these sections follow findings.)
Conclusions (based on findings) and recommendations, either stated or implied	Detailed presentations of findings, usually divided into several sections

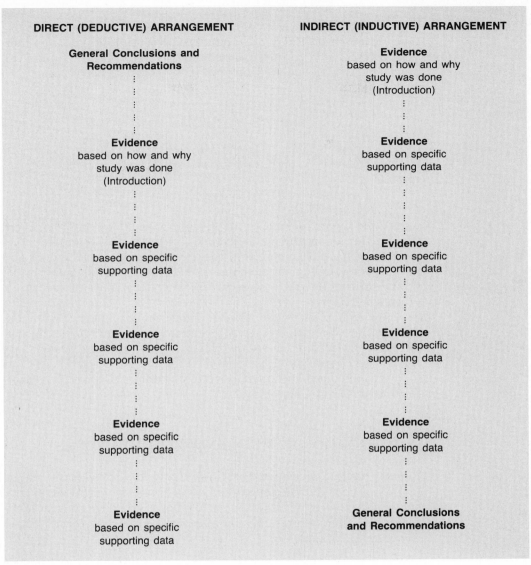

DIRECT (DEDUCTIVE) ARRANGEMENT

**General Conclusions and
Recommendations**

⋮

Evidence
based on how and why
study was done
(Introduction)

⋮

Evidence
based on specific
supporting data

⋮

Evidence
based on specific
supporting data

⋮

Evidence
based on specific
supporting data

⋮

Evidence
based on specific
supporting data

INDIRECT (INDUCTIVE) ARRANGEMENT

Evidence
based on how and why
study was done
(Introduction)

⋮

Evidence
based on specific
supporting data

⋮

Evidence
based on specific
supporting data

⋮

Evidence
based on specific
supporting data

⋮

Evidence
based on specific
supporting data

⋮

**General Conclusions
and Recommendations**

Figure 2-3. *Illustration of Direct and Indirect Arrangements.*

A more detailed illustration of the direct and indirect arrangements is shown in Figure 2-3.

As shown in Figure 2-3, the words *evidence* and *specific* describe requisites of all good reporting. The word *supporting*, however, includes both advantages and disadvantages of the recommendations. In a way, stated disadvantages are a form of "evidence," or proof, in that a thorough analysis of both advantages and disadvantages, with an objective and complete presentation, indicates that you have considered all aspects of the situation before coming to your conclusions and making your recommendations.

Even though a report itself is presented in the indirect order, the use of a synopsis, which may be included in a transmittal letter similar to Figure 2-1 or 2-2, or as a separate preliminary part, combines features of both the direct and indirect arrangements in the overall report "package." In the complete report format, the report package consists of preliminary parts, the report itself, and supplementary parts.

The synopsis is a greatly condensed version of the complete report. Because of the placement of the synopsis before the actual report, the report package is, in effect, arranged in direct order, even though the report proper is arranged in inductive order. In some reports we should prepare the reader to accept or to believe disappointing or startling conclusions. In such instances, the synopsis is better omitted unless to do so would be going against the expected or assigned format.

We realize, of course, that the reader of any message can look first at the conclusions and recommendations section no matter where it is placed. Even so, the reader is not immediately given an unwelcome message without explanation or justification.

The synopsis and other parts of a formal report are discussed in more detail in Chapter 14.

CLASSIFICATION BY METHOD OF PRESENTATION

Reports may be presented both in *oral* and in *written* form. Many reports of considerable length and scope, or those involving extensive research, are prepared first in written form, then presented in oral form. The oral presentation may include only the highlights of the complete report.

The written report is often condensed for distribution or for publication. The synopsis, which is prepared as a preliminary to a formal report, may be used for this purpose.

THE ROLE OF CLASSIFICATIONS IN REPORT PLANNING

The conventional classifications given above are useful in planning, evaluating, and describing reports. Your study of report preparation, however, should not be based on these differing classifications.

Instead, emphasis should be given to determining the problem, collecting and evaluating data, and presenting the report in oral or written form. Characteristics of all effective reports are similar, regardless of classification: readability; coherent organization; clear, concise, specific, diplomatic writing; correctness; and all the other attributes of effective written communication.

The following approaches to report writing are usually used together, although there can be exceptions:

1. Formal format WITH formal writing style WITH impersonal tone (third-person objective writing style) WITH the indirect (inductive) arrangement.
2. Informal format (letter, memorandum, or other short form; few if any preliminary or supplementary parts) WITH personal tone WITH direct arrangement (may be indirect, even if short, in order to attain a more persuasive psychological approach).

SUMMARY

Although terminology differs widely, reports may be classified according to readership, time intervals, authorization, subject matter, function, degree of formality, the use of personal or impersonal tone, order of arrangement, and method of presentation.

The following classifications of reports are often used together:

- Formal format and writing style, impersonal tone, indirect (inductive) arrangement.
- Informal format, formal or informal writing style, personal tone, direct arrangement.

Most business and professional writing, with the exception of formal reports, is written in a rather informal (actually, "semiformal") style, using the personal tone.

QUESTIONS AND PROBLEMS

1. Discuss the advantages and disadvantages of the personal and the impersonal tone; the formal and the informal writing styles; the direct and the indirect arrangements.

2. In what kinds of writing may *you* be used or implied, but not *I* or *we*? Explain.

3. Rewrite the following sentence, using the personal tone:

   ```
   The results of the study indicate that more men's
   business suits could be sold if they were
   manufactured in a wider range of colors.
   ```

4. Rewrite the following sentence, which is from the concluding section of an analytical research study, using the impersonal tone:

   ```
   I recommend that the instructional emphasis now
   given to the following types of written
   communication be increased.
   ```

5. Write a paragraph of at least four sentences on any subject. Use the personal tone and an informal (but grammatically correct) writing style. Write the paragraph in the direct order; that is, the first sentence is to serve as the topic sentence.

6. Write another paragraph of at least four sentences on any subject. Use the impersonal tone. Do not use contractions, slang, or anything else that is definitely informal, but write simply and naturally.

7. Assume that each of the following paragraphs is the first paragraph of a report planned to determine a suitable location for an addition to a chain of restaurants named Country Vittles. Consider all examples to be the first paragraph of the report body, not from any of the preliminary or supplementary parts.

   Example I: A Country Vittles restaurant should be built on Highway 20 West in Galena, Illinois.

   Example II: I recommend that a Country Vittles restaurant be built on Highway 20 West in Galena, Illinois.

   Example III: The purpose of this study is to determine possible locations for a Country Vittles restaurant and to determine which site should be chosen for the next addition to the Country Vittles chain.

   Example IV: I've completed the study of possible locations for Country Vittles. Because everybody likes country cooking, I'm convinced that we need to build restaurants all over the world. But because we don't have the bread (cornbread or otherwise) for all these, I've picked out the best bet for our next restaurant. You'll find my recommendation at the end of this report. Everybody is going to be surprised.

a. Which example(s) indicate(s) that the report is arranged in direct order? Indirect order?

b. Which example(s) indicate(s) that the report is written in the personal tone? In the impersonal (third-person objective) tone?

c. Which example(s) indicate(s) that the report is written in the informal writing style?

d. Which example(s) is (are) likely to be taken from a complete and formal analytical report?

e. Each of the four examples was taken from an analytical report. How can you tell?

f. From the paragraphs given, do you think the report is a periodic one? Why or why not?

g. Of the four passages, Example IV is likely to be the most undesirable. Why?

8. Assume that each of the following paragraphs is the first one of a report planned to determine which magazines, if any, should be added to those currently available in the teachers' reading room. Consider all examples to be the first one in the report body, not from any of the preliminary or supplementary parts.

Example A: Subscriptions to the *Journal of Business Education, Business Education Forum,* and *The Secretary* should be added to the collection currently available in the teachers' reading room.

Example B: I recommend that subscriptions to the *Journal of Business Education, Business Education Forum,* and *The Secretary* be added to the collection currently available in the teachers' reading room.

Example C: The purpose of this study is to determine which magazine subscriptions, if any, should be added to the present collection available in the teachers' reading room.

Example D: With the assistance of the members of the Library Committee, I have completed a study of the magazines in the teachers' reading room. Although deciding whether or not we need any more—and which ones—was quite a hassle, you'll find our recommendations at the end of this report.

a. Which example(s) indicate(s) that the report is arranged in the direct order? The indirect order?

b. Which example(s) indicate(s) that the report is written in the personal tone? In the impersonal (third-person objective) tone?

c. Which example(s) indicate(s) that the report is written in the informal writing style?

d. Which example(s) is (are) most likely to be taken from a complete and formal analytical report?

e. Each of the four examples was taken from an analytical report. How can you tell?

f. Can you determine from the four examples whether or not the study was authorized? If it was not authorized, by what special term could it be described?

g. From the paragraphs given, do you think the report is a periodic one? Why or why not?

9. Classify each of the following report situations according to the terms given in this chapter.

a. A teacher reports students' absences to the Veterans Administration by circling the names of students with poor attendance. The report is made each month.

b. An engineering consulting firm studies a church building and makes recommendations for the conservation of energy. The report is sixty pages long and includes various preliminary and supplementary parts. The last section of the report includes recommendations.

c. A vice president of a business organization interviews applicants for employment and chooses the three who seem to be the best qualified. He describes the three applicants in a memorandum to the president of the organization.

d. A university prepares a "self-study"—a comprehensive report of more than a thousand pages, prepared by many committees and revised by an editor. Self-studies are made every ten years. All aspects of the educational program are analyzed. The report is presented to an accrediting committee, which studies the university and presents its own report to officials of the university, with suggestions for improvement. University officials make the suggested improvements and report to the accrediting agency that they have done so.

e. At the end of each month, the manager of an apartment complex submits a report of activities and occurrences throughout the month. The monthly reports are prepared from daily reports.

Format and Arrangement of Short, Informal Reports

PART II

Letter and Memorandum Reports

3

Many letters and memorandums, widely used in business offices and organizations of all kinds, are, in effect, reports, although they are not always described as such.

The words *short* and *informal* are relative and inexact, as are many other words. A short report is not necessarily informal, and an informal report is not necessarily short.

A *short, informal* report, as it is considered in this book, is any reporting or analysis of information that is not presented in the complete, formal arrangement that includes preliminary and supplementary parts, as discussed and illustrated in Chapter 14. The report decreases in formality, as far as format is concerned, as each of the preliminary and supplementary parts is omitted.

Informal reports, whatever the format, are often presented in the direct order, but the choice of arrangement depends more upon the content of material to be conveyed than upon the degree of formality desired.

CHOOSING AN APPROPRIATE FORMAT

The formats used for reports differ in many ways among organizations, as they should. No particular format is suitable for every purpose or for every organization, and sometimes no particular format is specified, with the choice left to the judgment of the report writer.

You, as a beginning report writer, may be free to use the format
of your choice, although you are more likely to use a format already

established by other writers in your organization. If this is the situation, you should conform exactly to the established arrangement and presentation. To do otherwise results in distraction for the reader, who expects to find certain information in a certain place in the report.

If you are free to use an arrangement of your choice, the examples in this chapter and in Chapter 14, with necessary and appropriate modifications, will be suitable for almost any report. Use care and judgment in format selection. A wisely chosen format is an aid to readability, organization, conciseness, and the proper use of emphasis.

LETTER REPORTS

The term *letter report,* if used at all, refers only to a report presented in the form of a regular business letter. Using a broad interpretation of the definition of reports given in Chapter 1, "a report is a written or oral message planned to convey information or present a solution," many, if not most, of the millions of business letters written every day could be described as reports because they convey information. Although distinction is often made between factual and persuasive writing, such materials as sales letters and advertising copy must contain factual, specific information in order to be convincing and effective.

Illustrations of reports presented in letter form are shown in Figures 3-1 and 3-2. Figure 3-1 is an example of a letter written in direct order and arranged in the letter style described as the *modified block.*

Figure 3-2 is an example of a letter report written in indirect order. It is arranged in the letter style described as the *semiblock.* Both of these letters, as shown by the absence of an accounting firm's letterhead, are *personal business letters.* The Certified Public Accountant is acting as an individual consultant.

The information shown in Figures 3-1 and 3-2 could have been presented in various ways. In this particular instance, a letter seems to be the best choice because it is personal, friendly, and informal. Similar findings presented to another person within the writer's organization would ordinarily be in memorandum format. The material could have been presented to Mr. and Mrs. Hobbs in a short report accompanied by an individual letter transmitting the report, although such formality is not necessary in this instance.

Analyze these letters, Figure 3-1 and Figure 3-2, in relation to the terminology used earlier in Chapter 2. Notice that both letters

7900 Creek Bend
Houston, TX 77071
October 14, 198–

Mr. and Mrs. Melvin Hobbs
2157 Rolling Water Cove
Houston, TX 77069

Dear Mr. and Mrs. Hobbs:

I recommend that you trade your house on Voss Road for the equity in
Dungreen Townhouses. This recommendation is based on the following
factors:

1. By trading the house for the equity in the eight–unit townhouse
   complex, you will not be required to pay capital gains tax. If you
   sell the house, the difference between the purchase price and the
   selling price is taxable. Both the house and the townhouse complex
   are investment property.

2. Because of the greater overall value, the townhouse complex will
   appreciate more, in dollar value, than the single–family house.

3. Attractive, well–located rental property is becoming scarce.

4. The price of the townhouses is less than replacement costs.

5. The non–escalating interest rate of 8¼ percent is extremely low.

6. Because of allowable depreciation and other expenses, these
   townhouses will shelter some of your high taxable income.

Another factor, less advantageous, is the amount of time that must be
devoted to management. In addition, the complex could be hard to sell
quickly should you need to do so.

I was happy to make this study for you, as you requested. If you like,
I will investigate the possibility of part–time management services.

Figure 3-1. *Letter report presented in direct order. Letter style:* modified
block.

```
Further explanations and specifications are shown on the attached
sheets.

                                        Sincerely,

                                        Robert Hutchinson

                                        Robert Hutchinson, CPA

wht
Attachments
```

Figure 3-1 *continued*

illustrate these terms:

> *special,* in that similar reports are not made at periodic inter-
> vals;
> *assigned,* as indicated by the term "as you requested";
> *subject matter,* advice on real estate exchange;
> *function,* analytical;
> *degree of formality,* informal;
> *writing style,* personal, as indicated by inclusions of *you, your,*
> *we;*
> *format,* letter.

Even after you decide to use a letter format to transmit information, you still must determine the letter style to be used. The
modified block style shown in Figure 3-1 and the semiblock style
shown in Figure 3-2 are widely used letter arrangements. They are
considered somewhat conservative. These letter arrangements are
shown here for the purpose of illustration and to prepare you to use
these styles, if you wish to do so and if your instructor directs, for
assignments throughout the course.

These short letters, like Figures 2-1 and 2-2, illustrate in extremely abbreviated form the same principles as those of the much
longer recommendation reports discussed in following chapters. Except for more complicated and comprehensive research procedures
and more formal arrangements, the overall process of both these
short letters and the long reports is practically the same.

7900 Creek Bend
Houston, TX 77071
October 14, 198–

Mr. and Mrs. Melvin Hobbs
2157 Rolling Water Cove
Houston, TX 77069

Dear Mr. and Mrs. Hobbs:

As you requested, I have made a study of the advisability of trading your fully paid–for residence on Voss Road for the equity in Dungreen Townhouses. I was happy to make this study for you. Detailed explanations and specifications are given on the attached sheets.

Favorable factors are these:

1. By trading the house for the equity in the eight–unit townhouse complex, you will not be required to pay capital gains tax. If you sell the house, the difference between the purchase price and the selling price is taxable. Both the house and the townhouse complex are investment property.

2. Because of the greater overall value, the townhouse complex will appreciate more, in dollar value, than the single–family house.

3. Attractive, well–located rental property is becoming scarce.

4. The price of the townhouses is less than replacement costs.

5. The non–escalating interest rate of $8\frac{1}{4}$ percent is extremely low.

6. Because of allowable depreciation and other expenses, these townhouses will shelter some of your high taxable income.

Another factor, less advantageous, is the amount of time that must be devoted to management. In addition, the complex could be hard to sell quickly should you need to do so.

Figure 3-2. *Letter report presented in indirect order. Letter style:* semi-block.

The proposed real estate exchange is a sound financial decision.
Personal considerations must be left up to you, but I believe that
part-time management services would be economical and convenient.

Sincerely,

Robert Hutchinson

Robert Hutchinson, CPA

wht
Attachments

Figure 3-2 *continued*

The letters shown in Figures 3-3 and 3-4 illustrate two additional letter styles, the *full-block* and the *simplified* arrangements. These letters can also be considered informational reports, using the term in a broad context, as they supply information to Mrs. Holcombe about the letter arrangements used for the letters themselves. (She had requested advice about the choice of a letter style for her company.) Because both letters end with recommendations, they can be described as being in the indirect, or inductive, order.

The *subject line* shown in Figure 3-4 is a required part of the simplified letter style. A subject line can be correctly used with any letter arrangement, although its use is optional except with the simplified style. It is placed a double space below the salutation in letters that include a salutation. The triple space that precedes and follows the subject line in the simplified arrangement gives added emphasis to the subject line. In the full-block or simplified styles, the subject line should begin at the left margin. In other letter styles, the subject line may be centered.

The letter shown in Figure 3-5 is a variation of the simplified letter style. In fact, it could be described as a simplified version of the simplified letter style. This letter arrangement is not widely used for the same reasons that the arrangement shown in Figure 3-4 is not widely used: Many writers are reluctant to break with tradition by omitting the salutation and complimentary close.

Figure 3-5 is designated here as the *functional* letter style to

BOARD OF EDUCATION
Memphis City Schools
2597 Avery Avenue, Memphis, Tennessee 38112

Please reply to: Memphis Area Vocational
Technical School
620 Mosby Avenue
Memphis, Tn. 38105
Phone 901/527-8455

September 21, 198—

Mrs. Laura Holcombe, Office Manager
Holcome—Carr Insurance Agency
392 North Deer Creek Drive
Pikeville, KY 41501

Dear Mrs. Holcombe:

As you requested, I am sending you examples of letters that
illustrate two of the newer letter styles, the full—block and the
simplified arrangements. I am glad to help you in the preparation of
your new correspondence handbook.

This letter illustrates the full—block arrangement. Because of the
efficiency with which this letter style can be typewritten, it is
growing in popularity.

Some persons object to this arrangement because everything is at the
left; they believe that the date and the closing lines should be
centered or backspaced from the right margin in order to give balance
to the letter. Other persons prefer the crisp, businesslike
appearance of the full—block style.

This letter differs from the modified block style you are now using
only in the placement of the date and closing lines; they begin at the
left margin instead of the center of the page. (They can also be
backspaced from the left margin when using the modified block or
semiblock style, but this position requires even more typing time.)

The semiblock arrangement is the same as the modified except that the
paragraphs are indented.

46   ***Figure 3-3.*** *Example of letter arranged in* full-block *style.*

This full—block arrangement would be an appropriate one for your insurance agency. It is more efficient than either the modified block or the semiblock.

Sincerely,

Fredna Vaughn

Mrs. Fredna Vaughn, Supervisor
Business Education Department

sn

Figure 3-3 *continued*

connote practical simplicity. At the present time, this letter format has no official name in widespread use.

The functional arrangement is in many instances more desirable than the simplified style illustrated in Figure 3-4. Not all letters benefit from the use of a subject line, which is a requirement in the simplified style. For instance, a subject line would add nothing to the short, simple letter shown in Figure 3-5 and would result in a more impersonal approach. In addition, the writer's name and title are typed in capitals and lower case instead of in all capitals, as ordinarily used in the simplified style.

MEMORANDUM REPORTS

Memorandums are so frequently used that some writers apparently give little thought to their composition. No doubt some of the many thousands of memorandums written daily are unnecessary, as are many of the longer and more formal reports. On the other hand, too little internal communication results in inefficiency and poor morale. Employees want and need information in order to carry out their duties and to understand organizational strategy and purpose. They want to know what is going on and why. *Informed employees, who believe that they are valued and trusted by management personnel,*

BOARD OF EDUCATION
Memphis City Schools
2597 Avery Avenue, Memphis, Tennessee 38112

Please reply to: **Memphis Area Vocational
Technical School
620 Mosby Avenue
Memphis, Tn. 38105
Phone 901/527-8455**

21 September 198—

Mrs. Laura Holcombe, Office Manager
Holcome—Carr Insurance Agency
392 North Deer Creek Drive
Pikeville, KY 41501

THE SIMPLIFIED LETTER

Mrs. Holcombe, do you like this arrangement? It has several
advantages, but possibly some disadvantages, too. It is the easiest
letter of all to type. In addition, it has a businesslike, no—
nonsense look about it.

Another advantage, at least in most letters, is the use of the
subject line, which is always a part of the simplified style. Notice
that the subject line is preceded and followed by a triple space.

Some writers believe that this letter arrangement is unfriendly and
impersonal because the customary salutation and complimentary close
are omitted. These lines are unnecessary if the letter is worded as
it should be, so that the reader will understand it is "sincere,"
"cordial," and "very truly yours." Besides, many of the readers we
address as "dear" are not really dear to us, using the ordinary
meaning of the word.

Perhaps you will choose this letter arrangement to be the standard
one for your office. If not, I think the full—block would be a good
choice. Either the semiblock or the modified block is suitable for

48   ***Figure 3-4.*** *Example of letter arranged in* simplified *style.*

use in your office, but they are more expensive because they require more time.

Mrs. Holcombe, I have enjoyed advising you about selecting a letter arrangement. Will you let me know which one you choose for general office use?

Fredna Vaughn

Mrs. Fredna Vaughn, Supervisor
Business Education Department

sn

Figure 3-4 *continued*

are more likely to be cooperative and to devote their efforts to organizational goals.

Suggestions for Writing Memorandums

Because memorandums are used so frequently and are used between workers in the same organization, at times they are not given the attention they deserve. Memorandums should not be considered unimportant because they are such a routine communication medium in business offices. Your ability to write clear, convincing, and persuasive memorandums will be important to your career, perhaps extremely so.

All the principles of effective writing discussed in Part III, Chapters 5 and 6, apply to memorandums. You will study approaches such as the positive versus the negative and the reader other than the writer approach. Other considerations are organization, clarity, principles of emphasis, and readability.

As in most business writing, with the exception of some formal reports, you will speak directly to the reader. Some writers, when writing to their co-workers or people they supervise, refer vaguely to "all employees" or "employees." Although memorandums often go to a group of people, not to one individual alone, your memo-

MEMPHIS STATE UNIVERSITY
MEMPHIS, TENNESSEE 38152

Office Administration Department

4 June 198–

Miss Gladys Williams
4831 Firestone Road
Knoxville, TN 37916

Thank you, Miss Williams, for your letter of May 15 inquiring about
our doctoral program in business education. We are pleased to know of
your interest in Memphis State University and in this department.

With this letter I am enclosing a graduate catalog and an application
for admission. Admission to the doctoral program is based on a
minimum combined verbal and quantitative score of 1000 on the
Graduate Record Examination. You must also present a GRE score on the
Advanced Education section, although no minimum is required.

We hope that you will give our program serious consideration. If you
have questions after reading the catalog, please write me or call
901–454–2462.

Herman F. Patterson

Herman F. Patterson
Chairman

ls

Enclosure

Figure 3-5. *Example of letter arranged in* functional *style.*

randum will be read by *one reader at a time*. That is, by means of your written memorandum you interact *individually* with each reader. As each person reads your words, he or she responds positively or negatively. It is to your advantage that your readers understand your memorandums and respond in a positive way. As much as possible, address your readers, regardless of the number, as *you*.

One major weakness of many memorandums can be corrected by the simple procedure of shortening paragraphs. Memorandums are likely to be read hurriedly. Short paragraphs help the reader to quickly grasp your meaning, provided you have chosen exact, specific words, placed these words in well-constructed sentences, and arranged the sentences in logical order.

Your memorandums should build and maintain favorable relationships with your readers, as with all people with whom you communicate. These favorable human relationships, however, cannot be maintained indefinitely through words alone if these words are not sincere. Sincerity is the basis for all successful communication, or for real communication of any kind.

Illustrations of Memorandums

Memorandums are usually typewritten on forms printed with these headings: *DATE:*, *TO:*, *FROM:*, and *SUBJECT:*. Although the printed headings are not necessarily in this exact order, *TO:* usually precedes FROM: as a matter of courtesy.

Figure 3-6 is a memorandum about memorandums. Although you are not likely to have occasion to write a message on this particular subject matter, the example is used here for two purposes: to illustrate format and to present information that you will need as you prepare memorandums, including reports arranged in memorandum form.

The memorandum shown in Figure 3-7 illustrates how the information in Figure 3-6 could be presented in a slightly different format, using side headings.

The memorandums shown as Figures 3-8 and 3-9 are short analytical reports. Notice the careful organization of each of these reports. Also notice the displayed headings that are used as an aid to organization, readability, and emphasis.

The data shown in Figure 3-8 were gathered and reported by an electrical engineer employed as an energy consultant. (This illustration is an actual report.) The "answer" is given in the first sentence. In addition, the recommended choice is repeated with the discussion of Table 2, which provides the basis for the choice.

Date:　　November 19, 198-

　　To:　　All Office Employees

　From:　　Isabella Rogers, Office Manager

Subject:　　SUGGESTED FORMAT OF INTEROFFICE MEMORANDUMS

Please observe the following instructions when preparing memorandums. A consistent, uniform arrangement results in better organization, increased readability, and savings of time for both writer and reader.

1. Use single or double spacing. Choose single spacing unless the memorandum is extremely short. Always leave an extra space between paragraphs of single-spaced typewritten material.

2. Use your choice of blocked or indented paragraphs. Some writers believe that indented paragraphs make a typewritten message easier to read, but this factor is not nearly so important as keeping paragraphs fairly short. One-sentence or one-line paragraphs are acceptable and often desirable, especially in the emphatic opening position.

3. Use a long line (6 inches, 60 spaces pica, 70 or 72 spaces elite) for all memorandums, even short ones. This standard line length saves time in setting margins and estimating message length. It also allows space for tabulations, as illustrated in the memorandum you are reading. You need not attempt to center the message vertically.

4. Use headings as necessary or desirable, to introduce sections of the memorandum. Ordinarily you will need headings of only one degree, or "weight." They may be centered or placed at the left margin and typewritten in one of several forms, including ALL CAPITALS; Capitals and Lower Case; or <u>Capitals</u> and <u>Lower Case</u>, <u>Underlined</u>.

　　　　　Figure 3-6.　*Example of memorandum format.*

SUGGESTED FORMAT OF INTEROFFICE MEMORANDUMS, page 2, November 19, 198—

5. Sign or initial your memorandums to add authenticity and a personal touch. The signature or handwritten initials may be placed by the typewritten name or at the end of the last paragraph. A complimentary close (such as "Yours sincerely" or "Cordially yours") should not be used on a memorandum.

6. Show your title or position unless your readers are sure of it already. Even if your position is known to your readers, your title is necessary on important memorandums or on those that will be filed for later reference.

7. Make sure that your memorandums, like all written messages, are neatly typewritten and arranged. An attractive appearance is psychologically conducive to the acceptance of your ideas as well as being a matter of common courtesy.

8. Identify the second and subsequent pages of memorandums by subject, page number, and date. This heading may be shown in the method illustrated on this page or in various other ways. For example, if you wish to "stretch" a short second page, these items of information can be shown on three vertical lines at the left margin. (If many of your routine memorandums are longer than one page, make sure that they really need to be this long. Perhaps your writing can be more effective and economical by being more concise. But do not omit material necessary for the understanding or acceptance of your message.)

Your written messages to other employees in the organization are as important, if not more so, than those to readers outside the organization. Although format is only one element of effective writing, it must be considered as one of the many factors that work together for diplomatic, clear, and useful memorandums.

If you have further suggestions about the improvement of our interoffice communication or messages going outside the organization, please tell me about them. (Send me a memo.)

Figure 3-6 continued

```
          DATE:   November 19, 198—

           TO:   All Office Employees

         FROM:   James Brown

      SUBJECT:   YOUR INTEROFFICE MEMORANDUMS
```

The following suggestions should help you plan and prepare your
writings to other employees in this organization.

SPACING

Memorandums may be single or double spaced. If they are single
spaced, leave a double space between paragraphs, as you should do
when single spacing any typewritten material.

PARAGRAPHS

Paragraphs may be blocked on indented, as in letters. The blocked
style saves time and, to many persons, presents a more modern
appearance. Paragraphs in memorandums, as in letters, should be
fairly short. Long, unbroken paragraphs are hard to read.

MARGINS

The long length (6 inches, which is 60 spaces pica, 70 elite) is
ordinarily used in all memorandums, even short ones. The writing need
not be centered vertically. (A 6—inch line, elite, is 72 spaces, as
elite type contains 12 spaces per inch. For simplicity, this actual
line is ordinarily rounded to 70 spaces. The six—inch line length
allows side margins of slightly more than one inch.)

SIDE HEADINGS

Although side headings as shown here are not the only type that can be
used in the memorandum, this all—capital side heading is easy to see
and, if properly worded, immediately tells the reader something of

Figure 3-7. *Another example of memorandum format.*

the content of the following section. Compared to centered headings, side headings are quicker to type.

SECOND–PAGE IDENTIFICATION

The second page of a memorandum should be identified by subject, date, and page number. Instead of the illustration shown above, this identification may be shown in this order: subject, date, and page number.

SIGNATURE

No signature is required or expected on most memorandums, although they may be signed. They should be signed if the contents are of special importance or if the writer wants the reader to know that he or she personally wrote or dictated the message. A complimentary close is not ordinarily used on a memorandum. The signature may consist only of the writer's initials, placed at the end of the memorandum or by the writer's typewritten name at the top. The complete signature may also be placed in one of these two positions.

TITLES

The writer should show his or her title or position unless the readers are already sure of it. A woman does not usually show a <u>Miss</u>, <u>Mrs</u>., or <u>Ms</u>. before her name in a memorandum, although it is not considered incorrect to do so. <u>A man never shows Mr. before his name in a memorandum or elsewhere.</u> Often a courtesy title should appear before the name of the addressee, particularly if the addressee is in a position of higher authority than the writer. Although there is no rule to this effect, the writer is slightly discourteous to do otherwise.

NEATNESS

As in all written communications, an attractive appearance is psychologically conducive to the acceptance of ideas. In addition, neatness is a matter of common courtesy.

Figure 3-7 continued   **55**

May 1, 198–

TO: Tom Anderton
         Project Director

FROM: David R. Weigel
         Energy Consultant

SUBJECT: Recommendation for Gymnasium Lighting at Christian
         Brothers High School

RECOMMENDATION

The gymnasium should be illuminated with metal halide lamps and
luminaires, as my calculations show that these will provide the best
possible fit to the design criteria supplied by the client and chief
design engineer. Metal halide lighting will give the optimum mix of
economy and color rendition when compared with incandescent,
fluorescent, mercury vapor, high pressure sodium, and low pressure
sodium.

DESIGN CRITERIA

The design criteria arrived at by the client and the chief design
engineer are as follows, in order of assigned priority:

1.   Maintenance of 75 footcandles on the playing floor and at least
     30 footcandles on the bleacher seats,

2.   Minimum life cycle cost, assuming a 20–year life, and,

3.   Color rendition suitable for television broadcast.

The first of these is the illumination design, and cannot be changed.
I was told by the client that the second (life cycle cost) should be
weighted twice as heavily as the third (color).

Figure 3-8.   *Short recommendation report. (***NOTE:** *The same report is presented in a more formal format in Figure 14-8.)*

CALCULATION RESULTS

The following table depicts results of my calculations for six
different light sources. First cost is a function of the number of
lamps and luminaires required to achieve the specified light levels;
maintenance cost is related to the number of lamps, rated lamp life,
and cost per lamp replacement (including labor). Energy cost is
derived from the efficiency of the light scource, and the color
rendering index is taken from the IES standards. Life cycle cost
assumes a 12 percent energy inflation rate, a 10 percent capital
inflation rate, and zero percent discount rate.

Table 1
Calculation Results

Source	First Cost	Annual Energy Cost	Annual Maintenance	Life Cycle Cost	CRI*
Incandescent	$5,000	$9,800	$1,200	$780,000	100
Fluorescent	3,500	1,800	85	140,000	70
Mercury Vapor	6,000	2,500	180	195,000	65
Metal Halide	5,400	1,400	180	115,000	75
High Pressure Sodium	4,550	1,100	130	90,000	49
Low Pressure Sodium	6,600	800	250	78,000	12

* Color Rendering Index

Figure 3-8 continued

DECISION

For each light source, I have assigned points for cost and color.
Cost points are proportional to the life cycle cost as shown in Table
1, with the lowest receiving ten points and the highest receiving one
point. Color points are assigned according to the color rendering
index, with the highest receiving five points and the lowest
receiving one-half point. The source with the highest resulting
point total is the one which most closely complies with the design
criteria and client weighting, and it should be selected. Table 2
displays these point assignments and totals.

Table 2
Point Assignment

Source	Cost Points	Color Points	Total
Incandescent	1.0	5.0	6.0
Fluorescent	9.0	2.9	11.9
Mercury Vapor	8.3	2.7	11.0
Metal Halide	9.4	3.2	12.6
High Pressure Sodium	9.8	1.4	11.2
Low Pressure Sodium	10.0	0.5	10.5

Based on this table, I suggest illuminating the gymnasium with metal
halide lamps and luminaries, as they received the highest point
total.

After these results are approved by the client and chief design
engineer, please notify my office so that work on the necessary
drawings and specifications can begin.

58   *Figure 3-8* continued

TO: Mr. Lawrence Cole, Manager

FROM: William H. Ford, Jr., Assistant Manager

SUBJECT: REPORT, WITH RECOMMENDATIONS, OF TRUCK ACCIDENT

DATE: April 7, 198–

Mr. Cole, I have investigated this accident thoroughly and talked with everyone concerned. I shall be happy to discuss the matter with you or to assist in implementing the suggested policy changes.

RECOMMENDED ACTIONS

1. The Car–Wash Division should pay Milltown Ford $252.50 for charges incurred for the delivery truck wrecked by Hugh Jones.

2. Mr. Jones should be permanently removed from the payroll because of his negligence in causing the accident and because of previous traffic violations.

3. All employees should be informed of the company policy of not carrying collision insurance on fully depreciated (four–year–old) vehicles.

4. Only the assistant manager should be authorized to approve expenditures for damaged vehicles.

5. No charges of more than $500 should be incurred on fully depreciated vehicles.

6. The truck should be removed from Milltown Ford and sold for scrap.

Figure 3-9. *Short analytical report.*

INVESTIGATION OF ACCIDENT

On Friday, March 1, Hugh Jones, driver employed at the Delaware Street Car-Wash, skidded on wet pavement and struck a telephone pole at the Delaware and Third Avenue intersection. Mr. Jones was on the way to the Delaware Street Car-Wash to deliver supplies. He was not injured, but the truck, a 1971 Ford pickup, received extensive damage that left it inoperable.

Ray Cole, dispatcher, instructed a wrecker to take the truck to Milltown Ford for repairs. Mr. Cole, an employee for only eight weeks, was unaware of the policy of not insuring vehicles four or more years old. He is not to blame for authorizing the work.

By the time the insurance company claims adjuster notified us that the truck was not covered, expenses of $237.50 had been incurred. These charges are $200 for labor and $37.50 for wrecker service. Milltown Ford has now added $15.00 for storage fees so that the total amount owed is $252.50. This amount is increasing by $4.50 a day.

REASONS FOR RECOMMENDATIONS

The charges incurred must be paid to Milltown Ford, but the truck should not be further repaired, as about $1,500 would be needed to make it operable. It is already fully depreciated.

Mr. Jones has a poor driving record for the six months he has worked for the company. The police officer charged him with failure to keep the truck under control. He had already received a citation for speeding three months ago. On two other occasions, James Broom, his supervisor, warned him about speeding. The Car-Wash Division should not retain such a potential liability.

If the dispatcher had been aware of the policy of not insuring depreciated vehicles, the company would have saved $215, plus continuing storage fees. Further losses may occur if all employees are not notified.

Dispatchers and other personnel should not be forced to make decisions about expenditures for damaged vehicles, even if a definite policy of limiting costs to $500 for depreciated vehicles is established. Such decisions are outside their area of responsibility.

NOTE: Figure 3-8 is a variation of the same report shown in Figure 14-8, Chapter 14. The report is *intentionally* shown in two versions to illustrate different approaches for the same report situation.

Figure 3-9 also is arranged, basically, in the direct order, as recommendations are given early. The preliminary paragraph serves as a short introductory statement, much like short introductory remarks preceding a speech. This paragraph also serves the same function as a transmittal letter in a longer report arranged in the traditional format, as illustrated in Chapter 14.

Figures 3-8 and 3-9, as well as other illustrations throughout this book, are included to emphasize the variety of arrangements in which information and recommendations can be presented. Organization of information and recommendations, wording and arrangement of headings, and choice of format should be considered as aspects of the composing and reporting process.

Arrange your own reports in the most readable and attractive way you can, regardless of whether you find a similar format illustrated in a textbook. *Remember, however, to follow exactly a specified arrangement whenever you are instructed or expected to do so.*

SUMMARY

The term *short, informal report,* although relative and inexact, is ordinarily used to mean all reports that are not prepared in the complete formal arrangement that includes preliminary and supplementary parts. Many informal reports are presented in letter or memorandum format.

Informal reports are often, but not necessarily, arranged in the direct order, with recommendations given first. They frequently are worded in the personal tone, with the use of the pronouns *I* and *you.*

Frequently used letter styles are the modified block, semiblock, and full blocked. Less frequently used styles are the simplified and, as designated in this chapter, the functional.

Memorandums should be carefully written with the reader in mind. The writer must be concerned with building and maintaining favorable human relationships.

Paragraphs in memorandums should be fairly short. Readers should be addressed directly, not as members of a group.

CASES AND PROBLEMS

NOTE: When writing solutions to the following problems and all other problems and cases in this textbook, do *not* lift sentences or phrases from the problem itself. Write in your own words.

1. *Informing personnel of chosen letter style.* Assume that you are the owner of an insurance agency, a manufacturing company, or any other company of your choice. Letters from writers in your organization are arranged in several differing styles, including all those illustrated in Chapter 3, the indented style, and mixtures of arrangements that seem to be of no particular origin other than the writers' originality. (The indented style, now seldom used in the United States, includes indentations of each opening and closing line in the inside address and signature block, as well as indented paragraphs. This letter arrangement is extremely time-consuming, even with automated typewriters. Because it requires more typing time, it is more expensive.)

   Although you encourage freedom of thought and original thinking, you believe that efforts toward creativity should be directed into areas other than unusual letter styles, at least for routine letters. Choose one of the illustrations in Chapter 3 as the standard letter arrangement to be used throughout your organization. Write a letter to your employees asking that they use this style in all correspondence except direct sales messages or other specialized letters.

   Provide instructions above the specified letter style in your own letter. Mention that you are using your letter as an illustration of the desired format and arrangement. Explain that unconventional appearance is likely to attract the reader's attention to the format itself and, thus, away from the intended message. As when giving other instructions, readers are more likely to understand and to accept your ideas if adequate explanations and reasons for the change in procedure are given.

2. Look in *Business Periodicals Index* to find an article, or articles, about writing letters. Present your summary of data given in the article, or articles, in a letter addressed to your instructor, using one of the letter arrangements illustrated in this chapter.

3. Look in *Business Periodicals Index* to find an article, or articles, on writing business memorandums. Present your summary of information in a memorandum addressed to your instructor or to members of your class. Use headings as shown in Figure 3-7.

4. Assume that you are the personnel manager of an organization located near your college or university. Write a memorandum to your employees telling them of the availability of the course in business report writing (or business communication) in which you are presently enrolled. Assume that the company will pay all expenses and that the employees will be excused from work. Give all necessary details. You hope that all who receive the memorandum will attend during the next two terms or semester, provided that they have not previously completed this course or a similar one. You hope that about one-half the number will enroll during the coming term or semester, and the remainder during the following term or semester, as you do not want them all to be away from the office at the same time.

5. Obtain copies of actual business memorandums. Analyze them to determine whether they can be described by the classifications of reports given in Chapter 2. Analyze them further as to clarity, consideration of reader, and attractive appearance. Present your analysis in a memorandum addressed to your instructor. Be prepared to present your analysis in a short oral report to your class.

6. Obtain one or more actual business letters; evaluate and present your findings as instructed in Problem 5.

7. In a memorandum addressed to your instructor, describe a hobby, extracurricular activity, or area of interest or study that is of greatest interest to you, in addition to your present job, if you have one. Include information about the length of time you have been interested in this activity, the accomplishments you have made or the awards you have won, and anything that describes the activity or your involvement in it. Do you believe that this outside interest could result in a full-time career? Does this interest relate to your major field of college instruction or to your present employment?

8. Assume that you are Laura Holcombe, to whom the letters shown in Figures 3-3 and 3-4 are addressed. You have decided to adopt the full-block letter arrangement for use in your insurance agency. Write to Mrs. Vaughn. Tell her that you have made your choice and thank her for her assistance.

9. As chairperson of the committee to arrange a retirement dinner for Mrs. Margaret Lee, write a memorandum to all other employees of your organization. Tell them that Mrs. Lee is retiring on December 31, after thirty years with your organization. Your committee has planned a dinner party to be held at the Knick-

erbocker Inn, 1917 East Hudson Road, at 7:30 P.M., Saturday, December 11. (It is now November 17.) Cost for each person is $17.50, which includes the price of the dinner (menu is not yet chosen), wine, and a $2.50 contribution for a gift (also not yet chosen) for Mrs. Lee.

Mrs. Lee recently donated $5,000 for recreational facilities, including a jogging path, to be made available to all employees.

Employees are urged to bring their spouses and friends as guests. The cost for each additional person is $15. Reservations, with checks, must be received by November 27. Tell your readers where and how to make their reservations.

10. It is now December 10. Reservations for the dinner party of problem 9 total 217, about one-third of all employees, plus 152 guests. Your city is covered with eighteen inches of new snow. Write a memorandum to employees who have reservations and tell them that because of the snow you will cancel the banquet. Ask their permission to hold their checks and reservations for a dinner to be scheduled later. Explain you could not even buy the gift because of the snow.

11. It is now Monday morning. The Knickerbocker Inn refuses to return your $500 deposit for the dinner of problems 9 and 10, saying that major thoroughfares were cleared of snow by Saturday evening.

Mrs. Lee, you learned this morning, is using her accumulated sick leave to retire on December 15. She is leaving for Spain on December 16, and she will be busy all remaining evenings with preparations for her trip, according to her secretary. What should you do? What will you tell employees? Decide, and write a memorandum to those who have made reservations.

NOTE: Additional problems which pertain particularly to this chapter are given in Appendix B. Problem numbers 6, 7, 8, and 9 are based on Figures 3-1 and 3-2.

Short Reports in Manuscript Form

4

Reports described and illustrated in Chapter 4 are very much like the longer ones described and illustrated in Chapter 14. Short reports are included here, early in the text, to provide a basis for your own reports throughout the term or semester.

The most important difference between short reports illustrated in this chapter and the longer "complete" report described in Chapter 14 is the omission or inclusion of preliminary and supplementary parts. Many short reports, however, may require some preliminary and supplementary parts. Figure 4-2 includes a title page, a page of reference sources, and an appendix. (The appendix is not illustrated because of space limitations in this book.) In addition, a table of contents is helpful in many short reports.

Short reports and long reports, apart from their relative length, are quite similar. Nevertheless, long, "complete" reports by their very nature require more planning, research, and interpretation. Thus Chapter 14 is placed after the intervening chapters on business research.

ILLUSTRATIONS OF SHORT REPORT ARRANGEMENTS

Figure 4-1 is the first page of a short, informal report in manuscript form. Its subject is report format and arrangement, for which more discussion is given in a following section of this chapter.

The information in the report illustrated in Figure 4-2 could have been presented in various other ways, including the formal report arrangement illustrated in Chapter 14. In a more formal ar-

The format illustrated here is a good choice for informal reports, term papers, and other similar manuscripts unless you are expected to follow differing instructions because of company precedent or a specified style manual.

Headings

When you need only one or two levels of division, you need not take them in the order that would be necessary if your work required greater division. Other variations of the underlined side heading shown here are centered underlined headings, and headings in all capitals.

Spacing

Double-space the body of the manuscript unless cost and time considerations indicate that it should be single-spaced, or unless the format you are expected to follow is in the single-space arrangement. Triple-space (leave two blank lines) after the main title and before each side heading.

Paragraph Division

Leave at least two lines of a paragraph at the bottom of the page and carry over at least two lines.

Figure 4-1. *Format of first page of manuscript report.*

RECOMMENDATIONS FOR USING THE TAXAMATIC SYSTEM
OF PREPARING TAX RETURNS

Prepared for

John Robert Williams
Public Accountant

by

Geraldine Cone
Tax Preparer

May 30, 198_

Figure 4-2. *A report prepared for a firm of public accountants.*

RECOMMENDATIONS FOR USING THE TAXAMATIC SYSTEM
OF PREPARING 1040 TAX RETURNS

Summary

I recommend that the Taxamatic system be used in the Williams
Accounting Firm for preparing 1040 tax returns. This recommendation
is based on information obtained from tax preparers for the firm
(7,9), secretaries employed by the firm (11,12), representatives of
the Taxamatic Publishing Company (5,10), three present users of the
Taxamatic system (4,6,8), and secondary sources (1,2,3). In
addition, time studies were done of manual and Taxamatic
preparations of tax returns.

Purpose of Study

The purpose of the study was to determine the cost and time
required to prepare income tax returns with the Taxamatic Publishing
Company System (TPC) and to compare them to the cost and time of
preparing returns manually. This study is necessary because of
rising costs of labor, the difficulty of finding dependable and
efficient tax preparers and clerical workers, and the need to accept
more clients than in previous years. For the past several years,
numerous potential clients have been turned away because no
employees were available to help them (7,9).

Findings

1. Using the Taxamatic system of preparing returns, the preparer
enters information collected from the client on the forms provided.
These forms are then picked up or mailed to the computer center,

Figure 4-2 continued   **69** which determines the tax and returns the completed forms for the client's signature (3,5,10).

2. TPC was one of the first companies to computer process a tax return. Over one million Federal tax returns were processed in 1983 by Taxamatic (3). According to company representatives, the system is widely used in this geographic area, as well as throughout the country (5,10).

3. The system provides two forms: one for present clients and one for new clients. For previous clients, the preparer is not required to re-enter names, addresses, social security numbers, dependents, or other year-to-year entries. The total number of entries made on Taxamatic interview forms are usually half than on manually prepared forms (3,5,10).

4. TPC provides numerous training aids at no extra charge. Local representatives provide individual assistance in accounting offices (5,10).

5. The benefits of computerization have been explained in accounting literature for more than fifteen years. Saul Berkowitz, in his article published in THE CPA JOURNAL in 1972, made this statement:

> The variety of services offered by companies doing income tax returns by computer makes one of them beneficial to almost every accountant who does any amount of tax preparation. (1:933)

The use of computers in preparing tax returns has continued to increase since 1972, and, according to Taxamatic representatives, forms and procedures have become more simplified and useful each year

Figure 4-2 continued

(5,10). Computerized tax systems were recommended in a recent edition of West Falls Accountants' Newsletter(3:2).

6. Under the present system of 1040 preparation, the firm finds it necessary to hire part–time checkers and typists during the tax season. These positions would be totally eliminated through the use of Taxamatic, as each return comes back fully printed, ready for the client's signature (5,10).

7. Representatives from three accounting firms that presently use the Taxamatic system were interviewed to determine whether they agree with statements of TPC representatives and material in sales literature. All agreed that the system has been beneficial to their companies (4,6,8).

8. About one hour of a tax preparer's time and one–half hour of secretarial time are saved on each return by using the Taxamatic system. Labor costs, plus copying and paper, total $11.40 for a manually prepared return. Cost of a Taxamatic prepared return is $10.58, which includes the time of a preparer and the charge for each return paid to Taxamatic. No secretarial time is required. Complete calculations showing the amount of time saved, based on experimental studies with five of our tax preparers, are included as an appendix to this report.

9. Total cost savings, with a resulting increase in net profit, cannot be determined because preparers will be released for more productive work, such as discretionary and decision–making functions for clients. They can examine the clients' entire tax picture and give advice about changes that could be made in the coming year to reduce taxes.

Figure 4-2 continued

Published Material

1. Berkowitz, Saul. "Computer Prepared Income Tax Returns." The CPA
   Journal 42 (1972): pp. 933–935.

2. "Have You Considered Computerized Tax Systems?" West Falls
   Accounting Newsletter, November, 1984. (Four-page newsletter.)

3. "Taxamatic, the Tax Return Processing System." Chicago:
   Taxamatic Publishing Company, 1984. (Twelve-page booklet)

Interviews

4. Blair, Clarence E., Public Accountant, 6433 Lincolnia Road,
   Alexandria, Virginia 22312. Telephone interview, 2 May 1985.

5. Dixon, James, Sales Representative, TPC. Personal and telephone
   interviews, February 10 to May 15, 1985.

6. Lloyd, Kenneth, Manager of Tax Associates, 7537 Lee Highway,
   Falls Church, Virginia 22202. Telephone interview, 3 May 1985.

7. Morris, Lee, Tax Preparer, Williams Accounting Firm. Personal
   interviews, February through May 15, 1985.

8. Sandbrook, Violet, Certified Public Accountant, 306 Glendale
   Avenue, Arlington, Virginia 22202. Telephone interview, 2 May
   1985.

9. Saliba, Jo, Tax Preparer, Williams Accounting Firm. Personal
   interviews, February through May 15, 1985.

10. Williamson, Elaine. Sales Manager, TPC. Personal interview, 31
    March 1981.

11. Word, Kathy, Secretary, Williams Accounting Firm. Personal
    interviews, February through May 15, 1985.

12. Yearout, Martha, Secretary, Williams Accounting Firm. Personal
    interviews, February through May 15, 1985.

Figure 4-2 continued

rangement, the supporting evidence now included as an appendix, referred to in the report but not illustrated in Figure 4-2, would have been presented as a part of the report itself. Some traditionally minded readers would prefer that all supporting information be in the report itself and that the report include the expected preliminary and supplementary parts.

Geraldine Cone, the writer of the report shown in Figure 4-2, is obviously an employee of a rather small accounting firm. The reader of the report can be assumed to have confidence in the writer's judgment and not be overly influenced by an informal report arrangement.

The method of documentation illustrated in Figure 4-2 is also appropriate for other kinds of reports, including those described as "formal." As when deciding upon other facets of report presentation, you should consider any stated or implied preferences of the reader or readers, the format of similar reports prepared in the particular organization, and the kind and complexity of data to be discussed and analyzed. (Documentation is discussed further in Chapter 12.)

The method of documentation shown in Figure 4-2 is convenient in reports in which you wish to refer to more than one source to support individual statements. For example, the (3,5,10) notation after Item 3 refers the reader to Numbers 3, 5, and 10 as they are numbered on the list of references. These three notations include one published source and two interviews. With Item 5, the (1:933) notation refers to Item 1, page 933.

This method of documentation is also convenient when you are using a great number of published sources that require rather lengthy descriptions, such as census reports and other government documents. Complete information need be given only once, in the bibliography—or on the corresponding page headed with *References*, *Sources*, or similar wording.

In addition, this illustrated method of documentation is far more convenient for the typist than the traditional bottom-of-page footnoting system. For many reports, however, bottom-of-page footnotes are preferable.

Compare the method of documentation used in Figure 4-2 with the methods illustrated in Figures 14-7 and 14-10, Chapter 14. Figure 14-7 is documented by bottom-of-page footnotes and followed by a bibliography. Figure 14-10 is prepared by the same method of documentation as Figure 4-2.

The report shown in Figure 4-3 is similar to that shown in Figure 4-2 in that attachments convey some of the supporting evidence. This report has no documentation presented in the form of footnotes or other methods of reference. The attachments include further evidence, including excerpts from journal articles. Complete information about the author, journal, place of publication, date,

RECOMMENDATIONS FOR REPLACING PRESENTLY OWNED
TYPEWRITERS WITH SELF—CORRECTING MODELS

Prepared for

James T. Buchanahan
Administrative Director

Countrywide Insurance Company

by

Mary Duncan
Office Manager

Chickasaw Branch Office

August 20, 198_

Figure 4-3.   *Short recommendation report.*

RECOMMENDATIONS FOR REPLACING PRESENTLY OWNED
TYPEWRITERS WITH SELF-CORRECTING MODELS

Purpose and Scope of Study

The purpose of this study was to determine whether the typewriters owned by Countrywide Insurance Company should be replaced by self-correcting models. Factors considered were costs, appearance of typewritten work, time to be saved, and typists' efficiency and morale. Not considered in this study were offices outside the United States and Canada or word processing centers now in use in the home office and seventeen major cities. Another question, to be considered in a separate study, is the choice of brand and model most suitable for the needs of Countrywide Insurance Company.

Also excluded from this study is the question of whether memory capacities should be included in typewriters to be purchased to replace presently owned typewriters. This question will be considered along with the investigation of the best available brand and model of self-correcting typewriters.

Findings

1. Except for twenty-four self-correcting typewriters used in executive offices in Cincinnati, all presently owned typewriters do not include the self-correcting feature. (Word processing centers are excluded from consideration.)

2. An experiment conducted by Ms. Rita Richards, a secretary in the Chickasaw office, indicated that typewritten work is more attractive when done on a self-correcting typewriter, even if

Figure 4-3 continued

the typist makes few mistakes. In addition to almost invisible corrections, the ribbon, which is used only once, is always sharp and clear. (This type of ribbon is also available for typewriters without the self-correcting feature.) See examples of letters typed by a presently owned typewriter and the demonstration self-correcting model, which was furnished by IBM. These letters are attached to this report. (Attachment A)

3. According to Ms. Richards' experiment, one-fifth to one-fourth of a typist's time is saved by the use of a self-correcting typewriter. According to journal articles, time saved averages about 15 percent. (See excerpts from journal articles in Attachment B.)

4. According to Inventory Control, Countrywide Insurance Company owns 5,120 electric typewriters without a self-correcting feature and 27 manual typewriters.

5. Self-correcting typewriters average about $200 more per unit than the least expensive full-sized electric model without the self-correcting feature. Additional costs include ribbons, which are about $1 more expensive than the best quality ribbons for present typewriters. Correction tapes are $2.75, although their price is expected to increase soon. (A breakdown of cost figures is shown in Attachment C, based on the IBM Selectric III.)

Figure 4-3 continued

6. According to information reported by two equipment sales
   representatives and three recent journal articles
   (Attachment D), within five years 90 percent of all
   typewriters manufactured will include a self-correcting
   feature.

<u>Recommendations</u>

I recommend that self-correcting typewriters be purchased to
replace typewriters in all offices of Countrywide Insurance Company
in the United States and Canada. These are to be purchased on the
regular five-year replacement plan. Self-correcting typewriters,
although more expensive than typewriters without this feature,
greatly increase the attractiveness of typewritten work. They save
the typist's time, resulting in a decrease in labor costs, and make
typewriting duties easier and less frustrating.

The benefits of self-correcting typewriters far exceed
additional costs of machines, ribbons, and correction tapes. With
rapidly increasing salary costs, cost savings will far exceed
equipment costs, even if no more than 10 percent of the typists' time
is saved by the use of self-correcting models. Additional benefits
are more attractive typewritten materials, and, most important,
increased employee morale.

Figure 4-3 continued

and page numbers should be given with the excerpts, as with other methods of documentation, for "giving credit where credit is due."

PHYSICAL PRESENTATION OF REPORTS

The physical presentation of a report or manuscript of any kind will depend upon these factors:

1. The expected or required form and arrangement, based on organizational precedent or a specified handbook. Footnotes, headings, indentions, and other kinds of format and arrangement differ from authority to authority. If you have no specified handbook or guide to follow, use readability, simplicity, and consistency as your guides.
2. The complexity of the material and the need for breakdown into various divisions. For example, if a report outline includes headings to correspond to *I*, *A*, *1*, and *a*, the text of the report must include four types of headings. But if the report contains only the main heading (the title) and one level of division, only one form of heading is necessary in addition to the title.
3. The readers of the material, with their known or likely preferences.

Headings

Headings, which are also referred to as *captions,* are useful in reports of any length, even letter, memorandum, and one-page manuscript reports. The longer the written message, the more essential headings become. Regardless of the length of the communication in which they are used, exactly worded and arranged headings show immediately the organization of the writing, the weight of each heading, and its relationship to all the other headings and the entire content of the message.

Headings act as "dividers" of written communication and serve as titles for the material given below. *Each heading describes and includes the contents of all subheadings that come below it; for example, "A," "B," and "C" headings combine to equal the heading above them.*

Word headings carefully, not only from the standpoints of readability and organization, but to direct the flow of thought and the exact progression of ideas. Try to word headings so that they provide information instead of merely indicating the kind of information that is below them.

⚹ *No single arrangement and format of headings can be said to be the only correct one.* If you are using a particular reference manual as a guide, follow its specific instructions exactly. Most reference books, however, provide for a choice of style and arrangement, as does this textbook.

Headings can be varied by both typestyle and position. Headings may be typed in the following ways:

<u>SOLID CAPITALS UNDERSCORED</u>

SOLID CAPITALS

<u>Capitals and Lowercase Underscored</u>

Capitals and Lowercase

Headings may be positioned:

CENTERED

AT THE LEFT MARGIN, FREE-STANDING

<u>At the Paragraph Indentation, Run-In and Underlined</u>. The first sentence follows.

<u>At the Paragraph Indentation, Underlined,</u> in which the heading begins the sentence.

Headings can be set up in several other ways, especially in print or with the use of special typewriter elements. Headings are most likely to be centered or placed in a freestanding position at the left margin.

The traditional outline arrangement includes headings preceded by roman and arabic numerals and by alphabetic letters in capitals and lower case, as shown below.

FIRST-DEGREE HEADING (TITLE)

I. Second-Degree Heading
  A. Third-Degree Heading
  B. Third-Degree Heading
    1. Fourth-Degree Heading
    2. Fourth-Degree Heading
      a. Fifth-Degree Heading
      b. Fifth-Degree Heading
II. Second-Degree Heading

These divisions of the report outline, which are also shown in the table of contents (often in revised form), can be shown in the report according to the method shown below.

80

PART II
FORMAT AND
ARRANGEMENT
OF SHORT,
INFORMAL REPORTS

FIRST-DEGREE HEADING

The first-degree heading (title) is centered and typed in all capitals. When the title consists of more than one line, usually these lines are double spaced; the first line is longer than the second, and the second is longer than the third. (Titles should be as short as possible, but they should also be exact and descriptive.)

Second-Degree Headings

Second-degree headings, using the arrangement shown here, are centered and underlined. They describe the major sections of the report and correspond to the headings preceded by roman numerals, as shown in the report outline.

Third-Degree Headings

Third-degree headings correspond to A, B, C, and following letters, as shown in the report outline. In this plan of arrangement, they are placed at the left margin, typed in capitals and lower case, and underscored.

Fourth-degree headings. Placement at the paragraph indentation on the same line with the text distinguishes fourth-degree headings from third-degree ones. The underscore and the period separate the heading from the remainder of the paragraph.

Fifth-degree headings are also placed at the paragraph indentation, on the same line as the text. These headings, however, are integral parts of beginning sentences.

The alternate plans described below, as well as other variations, may be used for headings within the text of a report.

Type the title as a spread heading, like this:

TITLE OF REPORT

One space is left between each two letters, and three spaces are left between words. Thus the first-degree heading is a spread heading, second-degree headings are centered in all capitals, third-degree headings are centered and underscored, and following headings of decreasing importance are moved up one level throughout the report.

When you need fewer divisions than those shown here, you need not follow exactly this suggested order of arrangement—unless a variation would consist of a departure from instructions in the handbook you are using as a guide. For example, if your report requires only one level of division, you might choose to use side headings instead of the centered ones described here as second-degree headings. And, as in the preceding example of a well-designed memorandum, these side headings may be displayed in all capitals. (See Figure 3-7, Chapter 3.)

Another widely used arrangement of headings is shown below:

MAIN HEADING (TITLE)
SECOND-DEGREE HEADINGS

Third-Degree Headings

Fourth-Degree Headings. These headings begin at the paragraph indentation.

See the examples of reports shown in Chapter 14 for other arrangements of headings.

A portion of a table of contents, shown in Figure 4-4, illustrates that headings should be grammatically parallel within each category. For example, the three major headings shown here (Parts III, IV, and V) are parallel in that they are noun phrases. Headings A, B, and C under Part III are complete sentences. Headings A, B, and C under Part IV are noun phrases. Headings A, B, and C under Part V are complete sentences in question form. The rest of the table of contents has headings that are similarly parallel.

```
III.  BENEFITS OF CREDIT UNIONS TO PEOPLE UNDER AGE 22
      A.  Young People Are Interested in Security, Especially
          Insurance
      B.  Young People Want to Build Substantial Savings
          Accounts
      C.  Young People Need to Borrow Money

 IV.  DEMOGRAPHICS OF MAT CREDIT UNION ACCOUNTS
      A.  Share Accounts, Classified by Age Groups Under 22
      B.  Certificates of Deposit, Classified by Age Groups
          Under 22
      C.  Loan Accounts, Classified by Age Groups Under 22

  V.  MARKETING EFFORTS TOWARD BIRTH-TO-FIVE-YEAR-OLD GROUP
      A.  How Can We Attract New Accounts?
      B.  How Should We Promote These Accounts?
      C.  How Should We Service These Accounts?
```

Figure 4-4. *Portion of table of contents*

These headings are from the table of contents of a report on how to promote the services of a teachers' credit union to eligible young people. These headings are numbered here, for the purpose of discussion, with roman numerals and capital letters. They may be shown in this way in the table of contents, as in a tentative outline. These numbers and letters of the alphabet are also correctly omitted from a table of contents, as illustrated in Chapter 14.

Figure 4-4 is an illustration of an *acceptable* arrangement and wording of headings. Do not think that you *must* vary the grammatical construction of headings in the same report. Some writers and readers prefer that headings be consistent throughout, although most people consider headings to be sufficiently parallel if they are in the same form as others in the same group, as illustrated in Figure 4-4. The "requirement" that every heading in a report be grammatically consistent with every other heading throughout the report may prevent the best possible expression of ideas to be conveyed through headings.

If you use a table of contents, which can be helpful even in short, informal reports, make sure that the headings in the table of contents agree exactly with the headings in the text of the report itself.

An example of a complete report, including a table of contents with corresponding headings within the text, is shown in Chapter 14. In addition, wording of headings is considered with report organization in Chapter 10.

Margins

If the manuscript is to remain unbound, use a six-inch line (60 spaces pica, 70 spaces elite). These line lengths provide side margins of slightly more than one inch. Exceptions to this general rule include material to be published, for which you ordinarily should leave an additional half inch on each side. Another exception is that in some situations you should consider using a longer line in order to save duplicating expense, filing space, and paper.

For manuscripts to be bound on the left, move side margins an additional one-half inch to the right.

On the first page of a report manuscript, leave a two-inch top margin. On following pages, leave a top margin of approximately one inch. On all pages, leave a bottom margin of one to one and one-half inches.

Spacing

Formal reports are traditionally double spaced, but many organizations are now preparing all typewritten work in single-space form to economize. Your choice will depend on organizational policy, purpose and readership of the report, and cost considerations.

Pagination

The first page of the report itself (the "report proper") is considered as page 1. This page number is centered at the bottom of the page or omitted. Page numbers of following pages are placed in the upper right-hand corner, on line 5 to 7 from the top. Thus the "approximately one inch" top margin refers to the "white space" above the page number. Triple space after the page number before beginning the first line of type.

Additional Guides to Report Appearance

1. Use sturdy bond paper.
2. Use standard-size paper, 8½ by 11 inches.
3. Use a self-correcting typewriter or word processing equipment, if available.
4. If a self-correcting typewriter or word processing equipment is not available, make all corrections neatly with an eraser, correction tape, or correction liquid. Do not leave strikeovers, obvious erasures, or white spots made with correcting tape or liquid.
5. If a self-correcting typewriter or word processing equipment is not available, prefer an electric model equipped with a film ribbon that turns through the typewriter and is used only once. (Self-correcting typewriters also are equipped with film ribbons.) If your typewriter is not equipped with a film ribbon, replace ribbons regularly so that they do not become worn.
6. Make sure that typewriter keys are completely clean.
7. Leave at least two lines of a paragraph at the bottom of each page and carry over at least two lines to the next page. Thus, three-line paragraphs cannot be divided. The minimum bottom margin of at least one inch can be increased by enough lines to allow for appropriate paragraph division.
8. A subheading (caption) near the bottom of a page should be followed by at least two lines of type, preferably more. A wider-than-average bottom margin is preferable to a subheading with insufficient following material.
9. Indent paragraphs in all double-spaced material. Paragraphs are usually indented five spaces, but they may be indented eight or ten spaces. Single-spaced material may also be in-

dented. Leave a blank line between paragraphs of all typewritten material.

10. Avoid long paragraphs; they are hard to read.

SUMMARY

Memorandums and reports typewritten in manuscript form may be single spaced or double spaced. Ordinarily double spacing is preferred, but single spacing is being used more frequently because it saves paper and copying costs.

Subheadings, also referred to as captions, are useful in reports of any length or format. The longer the report, the more essential subheadings become. They should be worded and arranged in a format that shows the organization of the entire written work. They should indicate the importance of each part in relation to the whole.

Short reports, in comparison to longer ones, are less likely to include preliminary and supplementary parts, although some preliminary and supplementary parts are desirable or necessary in reports of any length.

The physical format and arrangement of a report will depend on the expected or required form and arrangement, plus the purpose and complexity of the material.

Headings in a table of contents should agree exactly with headings in the text of a report itself.

CASES AND PROBLEMS

NOTE: No cases or problems are given with this chapter because of the numerous ones in Appendix B. According to the directions of the instructor, students may prepare solutions to the cases in Appendix B in various report formats and arrangements, including those illustrated in Chapters 3, 4, and 14. Chapters 3 and 4 are presented early in the text to provide illustrations for reports to be prepared throughout the course. (Naturally, students and teachers may choose to study textbook chapters in some other order than the one in which they are presented.)

The Language of Reports

PART III

Choosing the Proper Emphasis and Approach

5

Regardless of the changing methods of recording, reproducing, and transmitting information, words will remain of prime importance, as they have been since the beginning of civilization. We shall continue to use spoken and written language because we must.

Although you may not be a professional writer or speaker, as the terms are ordinarily used, language is essential to your profession, whatever it is. In this sense the use of words is a professional knowledge and skill, even more important than specialized education in accounting, management, engineering, law, or any other field. Aside from its benefits to your career and social life, growth in language ability will be a source of personal pride and accomplishment, perhaps your most worthwhile goal.

Appendix C, "A Brief Guide to English Usage," relates to this chapter. If you have not already done so, study it with this chapter.

ACCURACY AND KNOWLEDGE: THE VITAL INGREDIENTS

The techniques of communication are vastly important, but mere mastery of these techniques does not ensure effective communication. If the thoughts we are trying to communicate are not based on a sound background of information and understanding, expert expression is of little value. A fuzzy and indecisive mind cannot send clear, correct, convincing messages. In addition, the confidence of the writer or speaker is affected by the knowledge, or the lack of it, of company policies and procedures and of the particular situation.

Obtaining the necessary knowledge and understanding upon which to prepare effective reports can be a tedious process. To a certain extent, it depends on your entire background. If you are knowledgeable in many areas because of an inquiring mind, varied experiences, and wide reading, you are already far better informed about many specialized business problems than you may think. Even without an excellent background of general knowledge, you can become well informed in your field by consistent and dedicated effort.

Because data are copied and transmitted by computers and other forms of mass reproduction, one error can become thousands of errors. Incorrect information in a letter, memorandum, or report sent to one reader is bad enough, but a message sent to thousands of people greatly multiplies whatever difficulties will be encountered because of the error.

The overall amount of information available in all fields is increasing at a tremendous rate. Much of what you learn in school will be at least partially obsolete in a few years or months. In your business or profession, by the time you have learned one procedure, set of instructions, or group of "facts," they are likely to be supplanted by others, and then more and more. To be a good leader (or even a good follower) you must be aware of change, expect it, accept it, and use it to your advantage and that of your employing organization. To be a good report writer requires even more knowledge, judgment, and decisiveness.

CONSERVATIVE, BUSINESSLIKE STANDARDS OF CORRECTNESS

Correct writing and speech, from the standpoints of grammatical correctness and accuracy of information, is not necessarily effective communication, nor is it necessarily easily understood, interesting, or diplomatic. Correctness is only one of the many components of effective communication, but reports and other business and professional communications cannot be completely effective if they are not correct grammatically, as well as in supplying correct information.

Although grammatical errors do not always result in misunderstanding, they are likely to weaken the reader's confidence in the writer's overall competence. At times, also, the wrong word and omitted or misplaced punctuation changes the intended meaning.

Notice the differences in meaning in these sentences:

```
All salesmen who have exceeded their quotas will
receive a 10 percent bonus.
```

```
All salesmen, who have exceeded their quotas, will
receive a 10 percent bonus.
```

```
The old publications which originally sold for $2 or
less are to be destroyed.
```

```
The old publications, which originally sold for $2
or less, are to be destroyed.
```

When a writer does not follow the accepted "rules" shown in English handbooks, meaning is inexact or completely in error. In the preceding examples, the first sentence in each pair contains a restrictive dependent clause that points out *which* salesmen and *which* publications; not all salesmen have met their quota, and not all old publications originally sold for $2 or less. The same clauses in the second sentence of each pair are nonrestrictive, and are correctly set off by commas. The second sentences in each pair state that all salesmen have met their quotas and all the old publications sold for $2 or less.

A misplaced apostrophe can also cause misinterpretation. Like the comma and other marks of punctuation, the apostrophe is sometimes used to convey meaning, not merely to make the meaning expressed by words more readily understood. In the following sentence

```
The customers' orders were promptly filled
```

the meaning is not the same as in the sentence

```
The customer's orders were promptly filled
```

The first sentence indicates that there are at least two customers; the second sentence indicates that there is only one customer.

The misuse of words similar in meaning or spelling can also cause misreading and misrepresentation. Usually the words "affect" and "effect," although often confused, do not change the intended meaning. They can do so, however, as in these sentences:

```
Will the increase in total sales affect the expected
salary increase?
```

Will the increase in total sales effect the expected salary increase?

91

**CHAPTER 5
CHOOSING THE
PROPER EMPHASIS
AND APPROACH**

Although these words are similar in spelling and pronunciation, the questions differ in meaning: the first question asks whether the increase will influence (have an effect on) the expected salary increase; the second question asks whether the increase in sales will bring about a salary increase.

We should adhere, for the most part, to established conventions, because to do otherwise is distracting. For example, the reader of a report may be distracted from the intended meaning by unusual phrasing or punctuation. In addition, we need to be adept in the use of language for the pragmatic purpose of saving time. When we *know*, we do not spend time in trying to decide upon grammatical usage or trying to find exact examples or instructions in an English handbook. Although all writers should keep reference sources readily available and refer to them when it is necessary to do so, the truly efficient writer will have no need to put them to constant use.

Improving your language ability—correctness, word choice, sentence construction, conciseness, coherence, and direct, simple writing and speech—should be your first and most important step toward becoming an effective communicator, provided you do not at this time feel confident of your ability in all these areas.

English handbooks and other reference books are listed in the bibliography at the end of this book. Every writer needs a shelf of reference books, including a comprehensive dictionary. Appendix C also can be used as a handy guide to English usage.

BASIC PRINCIPLES OF EMPHASIS

The report writer must understand the principles of emphasis, which contribute to readability, credibility, a psychological approach, and other attributes of effective communication. The qualities of excellent communication exist only in connection with other qualities.

Emphatic Positions

Position is one of the most important means of achieving emphasis. The beginning section of any kind of writing is the most emphatic position, provided that the writer has used this position advantageously. In most communications, this beginning position should be used to present the most important idea. This arrangement is referred to as the direct arrangement.

The first paragraph is the most emphatic section of a memorandum, a letter, or any other short written message. In a long report, the first paragraph is still an emphatic one, but because of the comparative length, the first section, often titled *Introduction*, becomes especially important because of its position, as well as for other reasons. The first sentence in a paragraph is the most emphatic one—hence the use of a topic sentence, as the first sentence, increases readability and emphasizes the principal meaning intended for that paragraph.

The first word of a sentence is in an emphatic position, except for sentences beginning with *a, an,* and *the* where the emphasis shifts to the immediately following words. Because the first position of the sentence is emphatic, do not start several sentences on the same page with *I;* the *I* becomes overemphasized and does not convey the desired you-attitude, or at least the impression of the you-attitude.

The closing word, sentence, paragraph, or section of a written message is also emphatic, next in importance to the opening word, sentence, paragraph, or section. The last word of a sentence is second in emphasis to the first word of a sentence; or, in periodic sentences, the last words are most emphatic because the preceding words build up to the conclusion. Thus, to subordinate an idea or statement, do not place it in the opening or the closing of a written work.

This principle applies throughout business writing; for example, the idea to be de-emphasized should be somewhere within the body of a letter or memorandum, not in the opening or the closing paragraph. In addition, an idea can be subordinated by sentence structure so that it is within a sentence instead of being expressed in the emphatic opening or closing position.

Emphatic Sentence and Paragraph Construction

The most emphatic way to present an idea is in a paragraph that consists of only one short, simple sentence. Because the most emphatic position is the first position, the greatest emphasis is achieved by a short, one-sentence paragraph at the beginning of a letter, memorandum, or other message.

In a complex sentence, the idea to be emphasized should be placed in the main clause, with the subordinate idea in a dependent clause. A phrase can also contain an idea to be de-emphasized.

Sentences written with the verb in the active voice emphasize the "actor"; that is, the subject of the sentence is the originator of the action expressed by the verb. Sentences written with the verb in the passive voice place emphasis on the receiver of the action. Sentences should be constructed according to the desired emphasis. The active construction results in more forceful, direct, and concise statements, as discussed in more detail in Chapter 6.

For a review of sentence construction, refer to the first section of Appendix C.

Word Choice to Emphasize or to Subordinate

Specific, concrete language is more emphatic, as well as more descriptive and readable, than vague, abstract wording. Try to emphasize positive, pleasant ideas and to de-emphasize unpleasant ones. At times the general word, not the specific, is more diplomatic, although less emphatic and forceful.

An abstract word describes ideas or concepts that cannot be easily visualized. Examples of abstract words are *conception, democracy, abstractness, charity*. Examples of concrete words are *blackbird, plaid, crunch, dawn, rain, saxophone, automobile*—particular objects which can be seen, heard, felt, touched, smelled. These words are more vivid than abstract ones. Specific words are more emphatic than general words. An example of a general word is *music*; a more specific term is *piano solo*; a still more descriptive phrase is *Chopin's "Polonaise in A-Flat" played by Vladimir Horowitz*.

Fresh, natural words are more emphatic than stale, stereotyped expressions. Avoid trite phrases such as "spring is just around the corner" and "last but not least." These trite expressions also violate the principles of conciseness.

Attention to One Idea

Giving more space emphasizes one idea over the remaining parts of the message. Notice that this is just the opposite of the method discussed previously, in which the main idea is quickly and bluntly stated in a sentence alone. Ordinarily the writer does not think—"Well, I will just give this more space because it is important"—but writes the message giving the necessary details, which require more space. Repetition may be used with discretion in order to emphasize, but much repetition is unintentional. Repetition, even of the same words, can sometimes be effective, but the writer must be skillful and the message must be carefully planned. Repetition often is used for sales writing or advertising, especially radio and television commercials, but not always to the best advantage.

Because the main idea of a message often requires more space in order to be complete and clear, using more space is considered a method of emphasis.

Visual Display Means of Emphasis

Mechanical means are such methods as underlining or the use of all capitals, dashes, special or unusual means of letter arrangement or indenting, and lists and tabulations. Different colors of ink, especially red, are often used in sales messages. Setting off lines with plenty of white space calls attention to these lines. The visual display means of emphasis are similar to those of readability, except that at times the methods used for emphasis are more unusual and extreme.

Subheads emphasize and display the organization of material. A postscript can be used to emphasize an important idea, but the postscript should not be used for something that should have gone into the letter itself.

Mechanical means of emphasis should not be overused or they lose any emphatic value that they might otherwise possess. If many points are emphasized, then the final result is that nothing is emphasized. In addition, some persons object to a message filled with underlining, all capitals, or portions typed in red, feeling that such an approach is unbusinesslike, too emotional, or scatterbrained.

Summarizing for Emphasis

Summarizing can be used to emphasize important points, particularly in longer works. In some reports or books, each section or chapter is summarized and then the entire work is summarized, perhaps through the use of a synopsis that is attached to the report itself. Summarizing, like the other means of emphasizing, contributes to readability.

A listing of points, such as those below, makes the items stand out and imply that they are important. They are easy to read and quickly understood.

Emphasis is achieved by:

1. Position
2. Sentence and paragraph construction

3. Word choice
4. Space
5. Visual display means of emphasis
6. Summarizing

OBJECTIVE WORDING AND WRITING STYLE

The term *objectivity* is applied to the planning and process of research and also to writing style. As discussed in Chapter 2, material written in the impersonal tone (third-person writing style) seems more objective than material that includes first- and second-person pronouns, although true objectivity consists of far more than the use or omission of pronouns.

Word all reports specifically, objectively, and exactly. *Emphasize facts.* Support with concrete, convincing details. When preparing an analytical report, analyze the data in order to reach conclusions and recommendations. These conclusions and recommendations must be supported by *evidence* instead of being based merely on beliefs, assumptions, and desires. Although at times you must state what you believe about a situation, or what the data seem to indicate, make sure that your reader understands that such a statement is an opinion. On the other hand, avoid an appearance of hedging and timidity. The conclusions and recommendations, like all other parts of the report, should be stated in specific, concrete terms, not in general, vague, abstract wording.

Anderson, Saunders, and Weeks, authors of an early textbook in report writing, use this illustration:

> There should be no hint of bias or emotional involvement in your subject. For example, in writing a report on stream pollution in a university community, an engineer presented facts, conclusive and irrefutable, presented them impartially and objectively for seventeen pages. Then he wrote: "At the very doorstep of the university is a grossly contaminated stream visible to students and visitors from all over the world. While not necessarily pertinent to this survey, it is ironic that the fundamentals of modern sanitation are taught in buildings located on the very banks of an odoriferous creek typical of antiquated methods of waste disposal."

> The newspapers quoted him; his superior reprimanded him. Yet in the whole report these were the only sentences which failed to reflect the required impartial and objective tone. Note the phrase which should have warned the writer that he was making a mistake,

"While not necessarily pertinent to this survey . . ." Opinion and emotional writing are dangerous in reports.[1]

These sentences from an engineering report illustrate the fact that emotional, opinionated writing is not confined to material that includes the words *I* or *we* but can occur just as readily in the third-person writing style. Notice the emotional and nonrelevant terms: *grossly contaminated, ironic, odoriferous, antiquated,* and *visible to students and visitors from all over the world.* Although the writer should not have attempted to disguise the condition of the stream, he greatly weakened the strength of his report by the addition of the two unnecessary sentences that so clearly indicated his personal opinions of the situation. The facts alone, summarized with recommendations for cleaning the stream, would have been far more convincing and professional.

Avoid using a great number of adjectives and adverbs in report writing or, for the most part, in writing of any kind. Modifiers, or qualifiers, are less direct and forceful than well-chosen, exact, and vivid nouns and verbs. The wise choice of nouns decreases the need for adjectives; the wise choice of verbs decreases the need for adverbs. Too many adjectives and adverbs tend to slow the flow of writing. They also tend to sound effusive and exaggerated.

An objective writing style is essential to all business writing, but the approach is slightly different for effective reports than for some business letters, particularly sales material. Even in sales writing or other persuasive messages, however, conviction is built by the presentation of specific, factual material, not by a mere appeal to the reader's emotions. The direct presentation of specific, factual material is essential for reports. Other ways in which reports differ from many letters, apart from the fact that first- and second-person pronouns are more likely to be omitted, are slight differences in tone. Reports tend to be less personal and casual than many letters, although no business message should be overly casual and familiar. As mentioned in Chapter 2 and elsewhere, many letters *are* reports.

CONNOTATIVE AND DENOTATIVE MEANINGS

Words have *connotative* meanings apart from their *denotative* meanings. The denotative meaning is the relation between a word and its referent, the object to which the word refers. For example,

1. Chester Reed Anderson, Alta Gwinn Saunders, and Francis W. Weeks, *Business Reports*, 3rd ed. (New York: McGraw-Hill, 1957), p. 105.

you can point to a desk instead of saying *desk* and to your shoe instead of saying *shoe*. As you speak or write these words, they stand for specific, tangible objects. Even these concrete words, however, or words like *post office* or *oak tree*, can be misunderstood because of the great variety of desks, shoes, post offices, and oak trees. In addition, many words that have a specific referent in one sense also have other meanings, and the same word can function as several parts of speech.

Connotative meanings are based on experiences, attitudes, beliefs, and emotions. Denotative meanings are said to be informative, while connotative meanings have affective results. To many minds, the word *home* brings thoughts of a fireside, good food, family, friends, comfort, and security; the word *house* has a more neutral meaning.

Words that usually have unpleasant connotations beyond their actual denotative meanings are *criticize, you claim*, and *cheap*. Although the word *criticize* means to evaluate, either positively or negatively, the word connotes a derogatory description, which is one dictionary meaning. *Cheap* is now considered as a cheap synonym for *inexpensive*, but far more derogatory and with an implication of poor quality. *You claim* indicates disbelief.

These words and similar ones with unpleasant general connotations should be used with caution, if at all. Other words to avoid are the negative and unpleasant words *fail, reject, turn down*, and *blame*.

We cannot know and control individual connotations based upon the personal experiences of the reader or listener. For example, if the receiver of the written or spoken message has had an automobile accident on Perkins Road, the name alone will elicit unpleasant memories and feelings. If a young man is in love with a girl named Linda, another girl with the same name may seem more attractive than a girl named Anna Lou.

Aside from their emotional effect, words have their own particular shades of meaning. Although words are described as being synonyms for other words, there are few real synonyms. Words are often similar in meaning to other words, but because of their particular connotations or the context in which they are ordinarily used, they cannot be substituted for their near-synonyms without some slight change in meaning.

A real mastery of words consists of far more than the memorization of dictionary meanings or of near-synonyms, although a good dictionary is a vital tool in learning the use of the language. You will never outgrow your need for a good dictionary regardless of how knowledgeable or professional you become. But learning the true nature of words consists of far more than looking them up in a dictionary, as is shown by the humorous misuse of words that sometimes occurs in the translation of passages from one language to another. As an example, the "body" of an automobile has been translated as the "corpse."

Words have connotations of high and low status. Garbage collectors are becoming sanitation engineers; janitors are called maintenance engineers, building engineers, or managers. Salespeople are referred to as representatives, special representatives, or registered representatives. Secretaries want to be referred to as private secretaries or administrative assistants. In our status-conscious society, perhaps titles are important. The mere change of title can be a morale booster and an asset to a person moving to another department or organization.

In department stores, what was once referred to as the complaint department became the adjustment department and then the customer service department. The credit card is now often called a courtesy card.

Words pertaining to liquor are avoided by some individuals, corporations, and government agencies. Funds for cocktail parties are referred to as "entertainment" or "public relations." The State Department has drawn money for liquor for a "representation fund." Bars are often called lounges, in which you can buy your favorite beverage and become, according to your choice of words and the amount of your favorite beverage consumed (or tippled, guzzled, swizzled, quaffed, sipped, tossed down, swigged, or wet one's whistle with), tipsy, giddy, glorious, dizzy, mellow, merry, fuddled, groggy, high, lit up, tight, high as a kite, three sheets to the wind, inebriated, intoxicated, loaded, plastered, or rip-roaring drunk.

Consider the implications of the following words:

- scheme—plan—program of action
- proposition—proposal—presentation
- gamble—speculation—calculated risk
- scrawny or skinny—slim—slender
- Stupid—unsound—unadvised
- favoritism—leaning—undetachment

You could make long lists of similar words. Do you recognize that words have differing and definite personalities of their own?

As much as possible, communicate with specific, concrete words with tangible referents, such as the *Mid-City Branch of First Connecticut Bank, Report Form 1281, the northeast corner of Main Street and Adams Avenue, or a bluepoint Siamese cat.* Even the most specific wording, however, will not result in exact images in the minds of the receiver and the sender of the message. For example, all bluepoint Siamese cats are not the same. Some have a crooked tail and crossed eyes, some have a straight tail and crossed eyes, some are large, some small, and on and on. Your reader or listener will think of a particular cat on the basis of individual experience— or not know the meaning of the term. Images formed on the basis of personal, individual experiences are a form of word connotations that we cannot control.

As another example, a pin oak tree may be associated with an important occurrence in the life of an individual or listener. Mention of a pin oak tree may distract from the intended written or spoken message, even though the receiver of the message may not consciously recognize the reason for the distraction.

To summarize, we should consider possible effects of our words on the minds of others. We can avoid words that have generally unpleasant connotations. We can choose words that are likely to have positive, pleasant connotations, but we can never be sure of their effect on individual readers or listeners.

CONSIDERATION FOR THE READER OR LISTENER

Pleasant, positive attitudes toward ourselves, other people, and the organizations for which we work will be reflected in our writing and other communication. If we do not have positive attitudes, our writing and speech, if not blunt and unpleasant, are likely to sound strained and forced.

Although we may not agree with another's viewpoint, we should try to understand it. This ability is one of the most important factors of communication of all kinds, including report writing.

What Is Meant by the You-Attitude?

The you-attitude, or the you-approach, is a term often used in the discussion of business letters, but it also applies to memorandums and reports, even formal ones written in the third-person writing style. You consider the reader by presenting complete, accurate information; arranging the material in an easy-to-read format; organizing material for coherence and clear understanding; objectively interpreting data; and presenting conclusions and recommendations in concrete, specific words.

The you-approach, according to the preceding interpretation of the term, does not decrease or limit objectivity. Instead, it strengthens an impartial approach because emphasis is away from you, the writer, and toward the reader—or, especially, toward the information being reported. Such writing is also persuasive in that the reader is more likely to accept your ideas and recommendations than if they were presented in a jumbled arrangement and interpreted in the light of your own personal bias—an approach that is usually obvious. Although the terms *objective* and *persuasive* are often thought of as being contradictory, in this sense they are complementary and interrelated.

The you-approach is similar in meaning to the word *empathy*. Through the you-approach, we consider the receiver of our written or spoken words.

Consideration for others, although extremely important, does not guarantee proficiency in communication. Certain techniques and skills must be acquired in order to achieve all desirable qualities of effective communication, including the you-approach.

Wording that violates the you-approach is illustrated in these sentences:

1. I am pleased to announce the opening of my new office [from a letter written by a CPA to a client].
2. We are very happy that our firm is now expanding [from a letter written to customers of a marketing research organization].
3. I am very happy that my recommendations have been accepted [from a report writer to the executive who authorized the report].
4. All of us here at Planning, Inc. are delighted that you have signed a contract with us [from a letter sent from a consulting firm to a client].

Notice that each of these four sentences, when read alone, seems only to show self-confidence or pride in one's employing organization, which are worthy attitudes. But if the reader does not interpret these statements in the light of personal benefits or consideration, the passages connote writer interest, not reader interest.

You should recognize, however, that sentences such as the preceding ones are difficult to judge out of context. Provided the overall tone and content of the letters or memorandums from which the sentences were taken are considerate and positive, the passages as given could possibly be acceptable. Even so, the sentences shown above would be more effective if they were reworded:

1. You are cordially invited to the opening of my new office at 5417 Quince.

2. The addition of another specialist in marketing research will provide you with more comprehensive, up-to-date information.
3. Let me know when I can be of help in implementing the recommended changes.
4. We will soon begin the research you requested. [The original version of Sentence 4, in addition to being writer-centered, implied that Planning, Inc. did not expect the contract, with the further implications that they do not deserve the contract but need the business.]

Frequent use of the name of your organization results in an I-approach, not a you-approach. In letters or other material going outside the organization, some writers include the company name several times on each page. This is not a good practice. To do so is unnecessary, in most instances, because the company name is given in the letterhead. In addition, emphasis is away from the reader, away from the information being conveyed, and toward the writer and the organization from which the letter comes.

Another disadvantage of frequent use of a company name is that the letter, memorandum, or report sounds stuffy and formal instead of personal, natural, and friendly. The reader knows that the letter comes not from the company (companies cannot read or write) but from someone at the company. *I* and *we* should be used when to do otherwise seems awkward and unnatural.

Some writers routinely use *we* instead of *I*, even when they obviously mean *I*. Such usage is undesirable and unnecessary. If the writer means himself or herself as an individual company representative—as often occurs even though the you-attitude is used throughout—the word to use is *I*, not *we*. If the writer is speaking of a group of employees or the company as an organization of individuals, *we* is appropriate. At times *we* is appropriately used to refer to the reader and the writer.

Although almost all letters and memorandums, as well as many reports, are written in the personal tone, an abundance of *I*'s and *we*'s gives the impression that the message does not exemplify the you-approach. Avoid starting numerous paragraphs with *I* because the first position of the paragraph gives added emphasis to the word that is placed there.

At times the you-attitude is achieved by using neutral, impersonal wording. In addition, such wording is often more appropriate, especially in many reports, including those in which *I*, *we*, and *you* are acceptable. If the idea to be expressed is a disappointing one, a neutral, matter-of-fact tone may be the best choice. For example, the sentence

> Your sales have drastically decreased.

does not include the you-attitude, even though the word *your* is used. It may be necessary to convey this disappointing information to the reader. Some ideas, because of their nature, cannot be made pleasant or positive regardless of skill in word choice. In this sentence, too, the word *drastically* contributes to the overall negative effect of the sentence. Probably there is no way to make this information sound like good news, and we wouldn't want it to appear so. Merely stating the facts is preferable, as in the following sentence:

> Sales during last May were $92,300; during May of
> this year they were $43,250.

This sentence becomes more diplomatic by the omission of the word *you*. (The assumption is that the salesperson will know that the sales referred to are in his or her territory. If not, you have other problems.)

In summary, the you-attitude is genuine consideration for the reader or listener. Although the word *you* may appear to be more *considerate* than *I*, the entire content of the message is more important than the choice of pronouns. If the word *I* is used to an excessive and obvious extent, however, probably the emphasis is actually upon the writer, not the reader. *In disappointing or sensitive situations, the neutral approach may be more diplomatic than either the you-approach or the I-approach.*

The You-Attitude—Can It Be Real?

The interpretation of the you-attitude should not be that it is a manipulation of the readers or listeners, a way of ingratiating ourselves into their favor so that we can sell our goods or convince them to do as we wish. Even if this is the attitude of the communicator (and every person does and must determine his or her own system of values), it is difficult to simulate a concern that we do not feel. A reader or listener does not need to be completely alert to realize that the wording sounds "fishy" or that the writer or speaker is trying for a "snow job." A message that provokes these reactions is worse than one that is harshly direct, but there is no reason for either of these two extremes.

The you-attitude has been described as being nonexistent, that our concern must be for ourselves and for our own company. Much of the controversy over the application of the you-attitude stems from an inexact understanding of the meaning that the term should convey. Although using the you-approach, we must continue to be concerned with the needs of our own company and of ourselves. You as a human being are more interested in your own welfare than that of some person to whom you are writing or speaking. The recognition of these realities, however, does not preclude genuine concern for others or the desire to serve, to play fair, and to understand the reader's point of view.

Is Honesty the Best Policy?

A sound and workable system of communication is based upon openness and honesty. The old-fashioned virtues of dependability, sincerity, and loyalty still build a lasting foundation for business organizations, governments, and individuals. Without trust and confidence, there can be no real communication.

The ancient adage, "honesty is the best policy," is definitely true, overall and in the long run. But look at the meaning of this sentence, or at least the meaning that the words imply. Are we to be honest because it's the best policy—because it will bring more profit for our company and a raise for ourselves? If this motivation is our reason for being "honest," are we necessarily honest at all? Is an admirable course of action "honestly" a virtue if we are following this course of action for personal gain? Probably not. Nevertheless, honest and ethical business practices are essential for an enduring and successful business or professional organization, and for an enduring and satisfying career.

A two-year study into the problems of communication resulted in the conclusion that the approach to communication should be based on an honest "leveling" by management and employees as to their feelings, attitudes, and motivations. This approach is based on several assumptions, all of which include the precepts of sincere, nonmanipulative relationships. One assumption is quoted as follows:

> The old values of honesty, sincerity, and trust, sometimes dismissed as Sunday school sentimentality, are actually Monday morning business realism in the quest for better communications. They create the climate in which communication grows. Where they do not exist, communication will be faulty, no matter how they are fertilized with

methods and techniques. A man's character seems to have more influence than his personality in improving communications.[2]

No thinking, ethical person disputes the premise that messages should be sincere, honest, and truthful. Without sincerity, all the techniques of skillful writing and speech become only cleverness, a quality far less desirable than wisdom or genuine goodwill. Being honest and sincere, however, does not require bluntness and curtness, whether the communication is a factual report or a persuasive letter. Certain basic principles of effective communication—diplomacy, the you-attitude, the positive approach, and a psychological arrangement of ideas and information—are sometimes viewed with skepticism, as if all these principles should be disregarded in order to avoid hypocrisy. With this outlook, writing and speech becomes unnecessarily direct, blunt, and harsh.

An organization, as well as an individual, builds and maintains goodwill by ethical business practices and by a sincere interest in the customers or clients it serves.

A POSITIVE, PLEASANT, AND DIPLOMATIC APPROACH

A positive approach includes several aspects. One is the pleasant approach, which stresses the pleasant and not the unpleasant elements of a situation and states what can be done instead of what cannot be done. Another aspect of the positive approach is eliminating, as much as possible, grammatically negative expressions such as *no, cannot, will not,* and *can't,* as well as other negative words and phrases, including *criticize, reject, fail, turn down, must, blame,* and *force.*

Success oriented is a description of another aspect of the positive approach; the opposite term is called the *doubtful tone.* Success consciousness implies acceptance or favorable action on the part of the reader or listener. Words to watch are *if, hope,* and *trust,* in addition to any other words or phrases that suggest doubt or weakness.

Notice the doubtful tone in these sentence beginnings:

```
If you want to follow these instructions . . .
```

2. A. W. Lindh, "Plain Talk About Communicating in Business," in *Readings in Impersonal and Organizational Communication,* ed. Richard C. Huseman, Cal M. Logue, and Dwight L. Freshley (Boston; Holbrook Press, 1973), p. 10.

```
If you should decide to adopt these recommendations
. . .
Although you may not want to put these suggestions
into effect . . .
We hope this meets your approval . . .
We trust this is a satisfactory arrangement . . .
I know this is less than you expected, but . . .
This is the best we can do because . . .
I know you will be disappointed in us, but . . .
I hope that this unfortunate occurrence will not
adversely affect my future report assignments . . .
```

All these expressions imply that the reader may not, or probably will not, agree to the suggested opinions or actions or continue to hold the writer in esteem. More persuasive wordings are shown below. *Some of the preceding statements should be omitted entirely.*

```
In order to put these instructions into effect . . .
After adoption of these recommendations . . .
I believe you will find these suggestions helpful
because . . .
We are glad to make the necessary arrangements . . .
```

To achieve the positive, pleasant, diplomatic tone, we should use the techniques of emphasis and subordination. These techniques include the direct and indirect arrangements discussed in Chapter 2.

NONDISCRIMINATORY LANGUAGE

Speech or writing can be inconsiderate and undiplomatic because of words that are considered sexist by the reader or listener. Although the speaker or writer may be absolutely fair and nondiscriminatory in thought and actions, language alone can build distrust and cause communication to be ineffective.

Avoid Masculine Pronouns Except When Referring Specifically to Males

The English language has no singular pronoun to represent either sex, except for the inappropriate *it*. Because of this lack, for centuries masculine pronouns (*he, him, his, himself*) were used with the understanding that they represented either sex.

Although masculine pronouns are still widely used as a generic word to indicate either sex, by both men and women, you are wiser to avoid such usage. It is offensive to many people. Regardless of the you-approach from other standpoints, language that is considered sexist can destroy goodwill. Another reason for avoiding such usage, although less important, is that it is a bit old-fashioned. Knowledgeable writers and speakers are aware of the disadvantages of the older, discriminatory language and make every effort to avoid it.

In past years, use of masculine pronouns occurred in such sentences as

```
An engineer must know how to use his slide rule.
```

At that time the word *his* was more logical than it is today, but it is still likely to occur in such sentences as

```
An engineer must know how to use his computer.
```

The idea that only men can be engineers is now as outdated as the slide rule. All occupations are open to women, but language is slow to reflect this change. Apart from the consideration of the number of men or women in an occupation, neither masculine or feminine pronouns should be used to describe a person whose sex is unknown. For example, do not refer to a secretary or a nurse as *she* unless you are referring to a particular woman who is a secretary or nurse. To do so is to imply that only women are secretaries or nurses, or that only women should be secretaries or nurses.

In the sentences used above as examples, *his* is unnecessary in reference to either the slide rule or the computer. The simple word *a* is sufficient, whether or not the engineer actually owns the slide rule or the computer. A masculine pronoun is often used in sentences such as these, in which the use of a pronoun is not at all necessary. Substituting *a* or *the* or reconstructing the sentence in some other way to avoid using a pronoun is one of the most appropriate and convenient ways of avoiding *he, his,* or *him*.

Another method of attaining nondiscriminatory writing is to use plural nouns. For example, instead of

```
An accountant can update his knowledge by attending
seminars
```

change *an accountant* to *accountants* and *his* to *their*.

Another method of avoiding masculine or feminine pronouns is to repeat the noun, although this method should be used with discretion in order to avoid obvious repetition. Also avoid frequent use of *he or she*—although the term may be used occasionally when there is no other way to avoid sexist wording and make your meaning clear. Overuse of *he or she* is distracting and results in awkward writing.

Sometimes the passive voice can be used to avoid pronouns, although this method should also be used sparingly because the active voice is often more direct, concise, and forceful, as discussed in Chapter 6.

For example, instead of writing

```
Each employee should sign and return his approved
vacation request form
```

say

```
Approved vacation request forms should be signed and
returned.
```

In this particular illustration, the sentence with the verb in the passive voice is shorter than the previous one. Apart from the elimination of *his*, the second sentence is preferable because emphasis is upon *approved vacation request forms*, where the emphasis should ordinarily be placed. If the writer wants to emphasize *each employee* and leave the sentence in approximately the first arrangement, *their* can be used to replace *his*.

This sentence could be expressed with a plural noun, as

```
All employees should sign and return their approved
vacation request forms.
```

Still another method of avoiding masculine pronouns is to use *you*, as discussed in preceding portions of this chapter.

In the preceding example, if you are writing *to* the employees instead of *about* them, *you* should be used because it is more direct, friendly, and interesting, in addition to being a method of avoiding *his*. To make the preceding sentence more tactful and diplomatic, omit *should* and word the sentence in this way:

```
Please sign and return the approved vacation request
form.
```

Avoid Other Forms of Discriminatory Writing and Speech

In addition to masculine pronouns used to designate either sex, several other kinds of writing are viewed as sexist.

Do not use such terms as *woman attorney, male nurse, woman doctor,* or *poetess.* Use *attorney, nurse, doctor,* and *poet.*

Do not say *girl* or *my girl* when referring to an assistant. Instead, call her your assistant or, preferably, refer to her by name.

Do not use the term *businessman* unless you are referring to a particular man. Prefer *executive, business manager, businessperson,* or some other descriptive and accurate term. A *businesswoman* may be described by this term, but prefer *executive, business manager, vice president,* or another word that accurately and fairly describes her position.

Instead of *salesman,* when the sex is unknown, use *sales representative, sales clerk,* or *salesperson.*

Instead of *foreman,* use *supervisor.*

The word *chairman* is still used by many men and women, and some women prefer the term from the standpoint that it is the name of a position, not a sexist term. (Many others don't like it.) Unless you are sure that the woman to whom you are referring chooses to be addressed as *chairman,* use some other word, such as *chairperson, chairwoman, presiding officer, coordinator,* or *department head.* In all instances, follow known preferences. If, for example, the head of a college department refers, to herself as chairman of the department and shows her title on letters in this way, you are being discourteous if you address her as *Chairperson* or *Chairwoman.*

From the same standpoint, address women as *Ms., Mrs.,* or *Miss* according to their preferences, if you know these preferences. If you do not know, use *Ms.* (In examples of letters in this textbook, the use of a title other than *Ms.* is based on the assumption that the writer of the letter knew that the woman to whom the letter was addressed prefers *Mrs.* or *Miss.*) Women have the right to use the title they prefer, just as they have the right to spell or pronounce their names any way they wish. Writers are being discourteous when they do not accede to these wishes, regardless of their own opinions about language that they consider sexist. *Ms.,* however, is frequently used to refer to a woman.

SUMMARY

Effective communication must be based on sound knowledge and understanding of the material being communicated, as well as upon proficiency in language. Writers and speakers should adhere, for the most part, to established conventions of language usage. To do otherwise is distracting and may lead to misunderstanding or lack of confidence in the writer's ability.

Emphasis is achieved by position, overall arrangement, sentence and paragraph construction, word choice, the use of space, mechanical methods, and summarizing.

An objective writing style is desirable in all business and professional writing, but it is essential in reports. Conviction is built by the presentation of specific, factual material, not by a statement of the writer's opinions or by an appeal to the reader's emotions.

Connotative meanings are based on experiences, attitudes, beliefs, and emotions. Denotative meanings are dictionary or dictionary-like definitions. Denotative meanings are said to be informative, while connotative meanings have affective results.

The you-approach is genuine consideration for the reader or listener. Pleasant, positive attitudes toward ourselves, other people, and the organizations for which we work will be reflected in our writing and speech.

A positive approach stresses the pleasant and not the unpleasant elements of a situation and states what can be done instead of what cannot be done. Negative expressions such as *fail, reject, blame,* and *turn down,* in addition to grammatical negatives, are decreased in number, or, preferably, omitted entirely. Wording should imply expected success; it should not indicate doubt. The positive approach is achieved by the wise use of methods of emphasis and subordination.

QUESTIONS AND PROBLEMS

1. Have you observed examples of reports, advertising material, speeches, or other forms of communication in which the truth was definitely and intentionally distorted—according to your sincere observation? (In analyzing this question, you are faced with another question: What is truth? To most of us, other communicators distort the truth when they disagree with us.) Explain.

2. Prepare a list of words of high and low status, such as sanitation engineer versus garbage collector; administrator versus clerk; maintenance engineer versus janitor.

3. Thing of a word or phrase with a more favorable connotation for each of the following expressions. For some of the words you can think of at least two more favorable expressions—one or

more somewhat neutral and one or more so favorable that it would be considered a euphemism. For example, *scheme* can be replaced by *plan*; even more favorable is *program of action*. Another example is *bogus* (negative), *artificial* (more neutral), and *simulated* (still not completely positive but more so than either of the preceding).

chore	scrawny	stupid
deal	poverty	stuffed shirt (cliché)
cheap	racket	gross (slang)
affair	blemish	drunk
liar	blunder	fired
stubborn	long-winded	a dictator
bookworm	ridiculous	cheat
smart aleck	fat	you're crazy!

When making negative terms more pleasant, you should remember that in actual communication often the best approach is to omit them entirely. In addition, you will notice that you often need more words to express negative terms in a more positive way, although they will never be completely pleasant and positive unless you change the meaning entirely. These words shown above are examples of "opinion" words instead of factual words, an approach inappropriate to business, technical, and professional writing, particularly to report writing.

4. Do certain words have particularly pleasant or unpleasant connotations to you because of your individual experiences? Explain.

5. Can you think of words, in addition to those mentioned in this chapter, that have been replaced by higher status words?

6. Improve the following passages from the standpoint of the you-attitude, diplomacy, and the positive approach. Assume any necessary and reasonable details. Omit details that seem unnecessary and undesirable.

   a. We are pleased to inform you that we have completed your study [opening sentence of letter transmitting report].
   b. It's against our policy, so we must reject your suggestions for the improvements of our products. Our engineers have already considered everything that people think are new ideas.
   c. This packaging material is not the kind that gets holes in it at the slightest touch.
   d. Your research is completely unscientific, and your writing style is at the third-grade level.

   e. Do not fail to finish the project by the end of the week.

   f. I have not had any experience except for summer work in a small library in my home town, where I was hired because my mother works there.

   g. We cannot complete the bridge until the transportation strike is over.

   h. Your memorandum indicates that you are ignorant of policies in our research department.

   i. If you are interested in this plan, you might let me know sometime.

   j. We trust that you won't let this unfortunate occurrence cause you to disbelieve us.

   k. You have neglected to reply to my memorandum of August 8 and telephone call of August 9.

   l. It will be impossible to do as you request; you should know that.

   m. The applicant is not shy or timid, and he doesn't seem to be stupid.

   n. If you can manage to complete your work on time, we can move on with the project.

   o. We hope that our mistake will not adversely affect our business relationship [used as last paragraph in letter].

   p. I am pleased to announce that our company, the Success Planners, is expanding and will begin classes for executives in organizations all over town, including yours, beginning on August 1.

   q. We are sorry that we must reject your request [last paragraph of letter or memorandum].

   r. I am sorry to take up so much of your valuable time, but I really need this information [from letter sent with questionnaire].

   s. We beg to extend to you our humble apologies.

   t. The instructions are plainly stated, as you can see for yourself by turning to page 5.

7. Improve the following sentences, taken from reports, from the standpoint of objective wording. A point to remember is that objective wording (unbiased) is likely to be attained by being specific. That is, you are striving for factual information, not your judgment of the matter—denotative words instead of connotative ones. Objectivity may be reached in some sentences simply by the omission of judgmental words; for example, instead of saying that costs have increased by the enormous figure of 45.2 percent say that they have increased 45.2 percent—and be specific as to which costs and which period of time.

a. The XYZ equipment is shamefully over-priced. In comparison, competing models sell at bargain-basement prices.
b. The tremendous increase in paperwork in our offices proves that it is foolish to tolerate the old copier any longer.
c. The oppressive income tax awards sluggards and incompetents and penalizes those who are competent and hardworking.
d. I can't believe that we have fallen so disgracefully behind last year's quota.
e. The amazing increase in profits—72 percent—is unquestionably due to the superb leadership of our outstanding management team.
f. Enormous difficulties in production contributed to a startling increase in costs.
g. The unbelievable increase in defects—27 percent—is undoubtedly the result of lax supervision.

8. Summarize a lecture from some other course in which you are enrolled, or summarize a lecture or discussion that you heard on radio, television, or elsewhere. You are concerned with applying the principles of emphasis to stress important points. Summarize in one short paragraph the entire lecture or discussion, then use three or four paragraphs to list other points or to expand on the topic summarized in the first paragraph. Conclude with an appropriate ending paragraph. (See the discussion in this chapter on the methods of emphasis and subordination, including the mechanical means of emphasis.)

9. This problem is based on the discussion of emphasis in Chapter 5, the explanation of the direct and indirect order in Chapter 2, the memorandum format as described and illustrated in Chapter 3, and the you-attitude and positive approach discussed in Chapter 5.

a. CONVEYING GOOD NEWS. You are the personnel manager. Write a memorandum to all office and plant employees conveying the following information:
   - Each employee will receive a small increase in take-home pay.
   - Employees have been paying all costs of dental insurance, although they have received a low rate of group insurance. The company has been paying one-half the cost of medical insurance, but not one-half the cost of dental insurance. Now the company is treating dental care as part of overall medical coverage and assuming one-half the cost of employees' insurance premiums.

- The effective date of these changes is January 1; the difference will first appear in paychecks received on January 31.
- Employees have been paying an average of $18 a month for family coverage for dental care. Thus, the average premium will now be $9, resulting in a $9 increase in take-home pay. (Make sure that employees realize this figure is an average one. Single employees and married ones with no children have been paying less than $18.)

b. CONVEYING BAD NEWS. You are the personnel manager. Write a memorandum to all employees. Instead of the information given in the preceding case, you must report an increase in medical and dental insurance. Costs of medical insurance, other than dental, will increase by 22.2 percent a month beginning January 1. Costs of dental insurance remain the same. (Employees will continue to pay the entire costs of dental insurance, and the company will continue to pay one-half the costs of medical insurance.) Reasons for the increase, as stated by officials of the insurance company, are rapidly rising hospital costs and physicians' fees.

10. Write instructions for using an electrical appliance, such as a blender, tape recorder, or clock radio. Assume that your reader has never seen the appliance. Include the purpose of the appliance in your instructions.

11. Think of some area of responsibility in your present or former job. Tell a new employee exactly how to perform this task or how to handle the responsibility. Put these instructions in memorandum form. Be prepared to present these instructions orally to the class.

Additional questions and problems suitable for use at this time are given in Appendix B and at the end of Appendix C.

A Clear and Forceful Writing Style

6

Clear and forceful writing is concise, simple, natural, and direct. It is unpretentious and calls attention not to itself, but to the ideas being expressed. Far more knowledge and skill are required for a forceful, simple style than for a complex, involved one.

BE CONCISE, COMPLETE, CONSIDERATE, COURTEOUS, AND CLEAR

Conciseness is not a synonym for brevity. *Brevity*, like *short*, *informal*, and other nonspecific words, is relative. Although a report of one hundred pages is not usually described as brief, it is concise if it is no longer than it needs to be to accomplish its particular purpose. Conversely, a one-page report, although brief, is not concise if it contains wordy phrases or unnecessary repetition.

Conciseness is a desirable quality of business communication of all kinds. Brevity is not necessarily desirable. Many writers and speakers are overly concerned with what they consider to be conciseness to the extent that their communications lack completeness, consideration, courtesy, or clarity.

Some competent letter writers, who realize the importance of building goodwill to customers and the general public, seem to think that the tone they use in their letters must be completely changed in their written or oral reports. It is true that reports ordinarily do not, and should not, contain the kind of paragraphs described in letters as "sales promotion." Nevertheless, we must continue to be concerned with goodwill in all forms of communication, including written and oral reports.

Omission of only a few words decreases understanding if these words are needed to show relationships from one thought to another or from one part of a report to another. Hasty discussion of necessary explanations and examples can delay or prevent the acceptance of recommendations.

As an extreme example of emphasis on brevity alone, suppose that after completing a comprehensive research project, you write a report that consists only of these words:

```
We should build a factory in Brazil.
```

Such a report is indeed brief, and it is the recommendation that has resulted from your research. Nevertheless, it is far from enough. The immediate questions in the mind of the reader are these: Why? How? When? Who will be responsible for this major undertaking? How much will it cost? When will this expenditure be regained? Upon what information is the recommendation based? How do I know that the research was capably done?

The report writer must provide specific, convincing answers to all these questions, and others. To do otherwise is to ensure that readers will not immediately begin work on a factory in Brazil.

The reader or listener does not want needless or irrelevant details, but enough material must be included to make the report, or other communication, understandable, convincing, courteous, and considerate. Although a communication that is unnecessarily long is expensive and annoying, one that is so brief as to be incomplete is even more expensive and annoying.

ELIMINATE BUSINESS JARGON

Phrases described as business jargon are used not only in business, but by many other writers in all occupations. Such jargon consists of unnecessary, trite, wordy phrases, included because the writer has seen them in other letters, memorandums, and reports. Some of these phrases are:

- at this point in time
- enclosed herewith please find
- we beg to call your kind attention to
- kindly be advised
- in reply to your recent favor (letter) we wish to state

- thanking you for your kind attention
- the same being at hand, I wish to state
- thank you in advance
- thanking you in advance
- I remain (at end of letter)
- do not hesitate (when used routinely, unnecessarily, or insincerely)
- this is to inform you

Yes, these phrases are still used occasionally, but, fortunately, their use is decreasing. Clichés and other stereotyped, stale expressions creep into our writing or speech because we do not take the time to think of our own words instead of using worn-out ones.

Almost always, the wordy phrases and trite business jargon listed below should be omitted or simplified. Those marked with a star can safely be put into a "never" category for use in business writing, but all should ordinarily be avoided, for they are slow, wordy, and old-fashioned.

- it has come to my attention
- in the amount of (for)
- to the amount of (for)
- for the amount of (for)
- amounting to (for)
- totalling the sum of (for)
- be assured, rest assured
- *be advised, *be informed, *consider yourself informed, *this is to inform you, *this is for your information
- herewith, herein, attached herewith, attached hereto, enclosed herewith, *enclosed please find
- *beg to state, wish to state, regret to state
- *reference to same, *compliance with same, *consideration of same
- *we beg to call your attention to the fact that
- *thank you in advance, *thanking you in advance, *thanking you for your kind attention, *thanking you for your time, *thanking you for your consideration
- *we wish to remain, yours truly
- as of this date, as of this writing, as of the present time
- be kind enough
- due to the fact that, in view of the fact that
- *thank you kindly, *kindly, *we kindly thank you for
- at an early date
- along this line
- *we beg to remain
- *pursuant to your request

- *the undersigned (except in legal papers)
- pending receipt of
- for the purpose of, for the reason that, due to the fact that (for, to, because)
- in spite of the fact that (because)
- evident and apparent
- take the liberty of
- regret to advise, regret to inform, regret to state
- *your esteemed favor
- AND MANY, MANY MORE

CHOOSE SHORT, FAMILIAR, EXACT WORDS

A simple writing style consisting of short, everyday words and fairly short sentences is far from being juvenile; the opposite is true. The Gettysburg Address and the Lord's Prayer are two examples of great works that are in simple, direct language. Simple writing does not limit the wise use of the infinite variety of language. Instead, it requires careful phrasing for the most exact expression of specific ideas, with language and approach especially adapted to the particular readers of the message.

Short words, if they are the exact words to express the desired meaning, should be preferred to long words. Business or professional writing is no medium for showing off a vocabulary of unusual or "intellectual" words. This statement does not mean that a capable writer in any field should be unconcerned about the development of an extensive vocabulary. We must know a great many words in order to write well—to know which simple words to choose and, in some instances, which long words are appropriate and exact.

We should consider our readers, especially their background and probable knowledge of the subject about which we are writing. If material is technical and specialized, some words must be defined for the reader outside the particular area of specialization, or simple words should be substituted for technical, unusual ones. We should never, however, give the appearance of writing down to the level of our readers. Nothing is more offensive than to indicate that the writer feels superior in knowledge to the reader. The purpose of communication is to express facts and ideas, not to impress the reader with a fancy style or an extensive vocabulary.

Short words, appropriately chosen, not only increase readability but also help to form a vivid and forceful writing style. Compare the simplicity of the words in the second column to those in the first:

Instead of	*Prefer*
Affix a signature	sign
approbation	approval
ameliorate	improve
causative factor	cause
engrossment	attention
expectancy	hope
finalize	end
inaugurate	begin
incorporate	include
interrogate	question (or ask)
peruse	read
prior to	before
promulgate	publish
salience	importance
utilizable	useful
utilize	use

Short words are not always the ones that are most clear. An unusual short word that the reader is not likely to understand is less desirable than a more familiar longer word. In addition, many words in ordinary, everyday use are quite long.

When we are writing to specialists in our own field, as often occurs in report writing, a technical, specialized word is likely to be more understandable than a shorter one that is substituted with the mistaken purpose of making the report clear, simple, and easy to read. To an accountant, accounting terms are easily and quickly understood; to a reader unfamiliar with accounting, specialized terms interpreted in layman's language may result in completely different meanings. The same principle is true for writers and readers in the medical field and in many other occupations and professions.

The most important consideration is the precise and appropriate choice of words according to meaning, context, and readers. Few words, long or short, have exact synonyms. Use the word that is most likely to express your exact meaning to the mind of the individual reader. This word is most often a short, familiar one. *Before you can choose words to express your exact meaning, that meaning must be clear in your mind.*

CONSTRUCT SHORT, READABLE SENTENCES

Sentences need not and should not be the same length. In order to avoid monotony, if for no other reason, both short and fairly long sentences should be used. Most important, sentences should be of the length and construction that best convey the ideas and information so closely related that they belong in the same sentence.

Average sentence length ordinarily should not exceed seventeen to twenty words, although an experienced, skillful writer can use longer sentences and achieve a readable style. Also remember that seventeen to twenty is an *average* number. Some sentences are longer and some are shorter. A series of short, simple sentences similar to those in a first-grade reader is monotonous and unprofessional. In addition, not all ideas and relationships can be effectively expressed in short, simple sentences. (Brevity and short sentences are not the most important elements of successful business and professional writing. At times these qualities have been given too much emphasis in the teaching of business writing.)

A thorough and automatic knowledge of sentence construction is essential to the expert writer, not only from the standpoint of readability but also from the standpoints of emphasis and correctness. The type of sentence chosen for a particular idea depends upon the idea to be expressed. Experienced writers do not consciously think of sentence construction as the material is written or dictated. As they revise, they change sentence structure. The revision most often necessary is that of cutting sentence length.

Check your work to make sure that only complete sentences are used and that they vary in form. In most business writing, simple sentences should outnumber complex sentences and compound sentences. In almost all writing, compound sentences should be the fewest of the three. Complex sentences are useful to subordinate or to emphasize ideas. An idea can be subordinated, also, by placement as a phrase within a sentence of any construction.

A review of sentence structure is included in Appendix C.

CONSTRUCT SHORT, READABLE PARAGRAPHS

Short paragraphs are useful in achieving readability. A paragraph of many lines is hard to read and discouraging to the reader, especially when time is short—as it usually is. Paragraphs in a letter, memorandum, or short report are often broken arbitrarily to increase readability

Some writers believe that a paragraph must have more than one sentence. The belief may have originated in a class in English composition, although in all kinds of writing one-sentence paragraphs are quite acceptable to most readers. A short, one-sentence paragraph can be used for attention, interest, and emphasis. It is particularly effective in the emphatic opening or closing position of a letter or memorandum. It can be correctly used in any position—for emphasis, attention, transition, or simply for the reason that nothing else is needed in the paragraph.

Although no exact rule can be given about maximum paragraph length, you should regard with suspicion any typewritten paragraph of more than ten or eleven lines. The average number should be fewer, particularly in short reports, letters, or memorandums. If your paragraphs tend to be unusually long, perhaps the entire organization of your report or other written material could be improved. Use topic sentences to begin paragraphs. If these topic sentences are exact, each forms a summary of the individual paragraph, and all topic sentences, read in sequence, provide a summary of the entire written message. Topic sentences, however, do not always appear at the beginning of a paragraph; for emphasis and variety, some paragraphs may end with a summarizing sentence, or the main idea may be somewhere within the paragraph. In addition, an exact topic sentence is not always apparent in short written messages. (If all paragraphs in this chapter were as long as the one you are now reading, they would be too long.)

Just as skillful, experienced writers do not consciously think of sentence construction as they compose, neither do they continuously ponder paragraph construction and the use of topic sentences. When they revise written material, their knowledge of sentence and paragraph construction enables them to achieve the desired emphasis and to increase clarity and coherence.

Notice the first paragraph in this section of this chapter. The beginning sentence, *Short paragraphs are useful in achieving readability*, serves as the topic sentence. In the second paragraph of this section, the main idea is expressed in the second clause of the second sentence: *although in all kinds of writing one-sentence paragraphs are quite acceptable.* In the third and fourth paragraphs, the first sentence expresses the main idea. In the paragraph you are now reading, the topic sentence is the closing one. Although most topic sentences are used to begin the paragraph, they can also be placed in other positions.

Paragraph construction, in relation to emphasis and approach, has been previously discussed in Chapter 5.

DESIGN READABLE FORMATS

A letter, memorandum, report or other bit of writing should be arranged attractively, leaving plenty of white space. A minimum of one inch at the side, top, and bottom margins should be left on all work. For short and average-length letters, wider margins are better.

Subheads are essential to readability if the written message is long, and *long* usually should be considered to apply to any communication of more than one page. Subheads can also be used in material of one page or less. They add readability in several ways.

Subheads force the writer to organize the material in meaningful units. If the subhead does not include a reference to the information under it, and only to that information, it is not well chosen. Poor subheads are worse than none at all.

Lists and tabulations make ideas stand out and present ideas in a logical order. The arrangement of each statement, question, or idea on a separate line (as illustrated in the list below) makes each of the items easier to understand than if all were crowded together into a paragraph.

To illustrate the use of a listing, as well as to summarize, the following information is repeated.

Readable formats should include:

1. Plenty of white space
2. An overall attractive appearance
3. Subheads
4. Lists and tabulations.

USE COHERENT PHRASING AND ORGANIZATION

Coherence is the logical, easy-to-understand flow of thought from the beginning to the end of a message, and is an essential element of readability. The term comes from the word *cohesion*; it literally means a *sticking together* of ideas so that the communication is unified, without abrupt shifts in arrangement or subject matter.

To be coherent, writing must also have unity. Unity and coherence are achieved by overall organization so that the message flows naturally and smoothly according to a plan decided upon before the writing or dictation is begun. (As we proceed with writing or dictation, we often see needed changes in the original plan. These changes should be made, and then the organization should follow the revised plan.)

If the message is truly coherent, the reader's mind grasps the relationships of words, sentences, and paragraphs and recognizes the overall progression of meaning. Transitional words and phrases and the repetition of key words, used with discretion, aid in the transfer of thought from one idea to another.

After you complete a letter, memorandum, report, or other communication, proofread it for abrupt changes in subject matter. The overall meaning may be perfectly clear to you, the writer, only because you knew from the beginning what you were trying to say; your reader will not have this advantage.

PREFER THE ACTIVE VOICE

Verbs are the strongest and the most vivid of the parts of speech. They are stronger in the active voice than in the passive. The active voice is more direct, forceful, and concise; it should ordinarily be preferred unless, as often occurs, there is a specific reason to use the passive voice. Only transitive verbs (those that have or imply an object) can be passive.

The following sentences illustrate the difference between active and passive verbs:

```
Active:    The decorator rearranged the office
           furniture.
Passive:   The office furniture was (has been)
           rearranged by the decorator.
```

In the second sentence, if the phrase *by the decorator* were omitted, the verb would still be passive. Of the two illustrated sentences, the first is more direct, forceful, and concise. At times, however, the person who acts, or has acted, is irrelevant or unknown. In such cases, the best sentence is the passive construction: The office furniture has been rearranged. An additional illustration is:

```
Active:    We should include more colors in our line
           of denim slacks.
Passive:   More colors should be included in our line
           of denim slacks.
```

The passive voice in this illustration emphasizes *More colors* by placement in the emphatic first position of the sentence. This may be the desired emphasis. In the following sentences, however, the active voice is the better choice:

```
Active:    Ruth asked many questions.
Passive:   Many questions were asked by Ruth.
```

Active: The committee approved two changes in the
         constitution.
Passive: Two changes in the constitution were
         approved by the committee.

The following sentences do not include verbs in the passive voice, but the construction results in the same slow, weak effect.

It is desirable to include more colors in our line
of denim slacks.

There should be increased production of our denim
slacks.

The words *there* and *it* are function words or "structural fillers" that replace true subjects. They are usually referred to as *expletives.* They are weaker than tangible, specific subjects.

The passive voice is in no way incorrect; neither are sentences beginning with *there* or *it.* They are discussed here because many writers use the passive voice and *it* and *there* unnecessarily, especially when writing in the impersonal tone. Regardless of the choice of personal or impersonal tone, most sentences can be and should be written with "real" subjects and active verbs.

Notice the differences in emphasis in the following sentences:

Active: A woman drove the truck.
Passive: The truck was driven by a woman.

A *woman* receives the most emphasis in the last position, as shown by the second sentence.

The most important consideration as to active and passive verbs, as with all word choice and sentence construction, is to express your intended meaning exactly. The desired emphasis is an aspect of meaning.

UNDERSTAND READABILITY AND READABILITY FORMULAS

Readability, as the word implies, means the ease with which the reader can obtain the desired message. As the term is used in written communication, it means immediate clearness. When written material is planned to achieve the desired emphasis, it is likely to be readable.

Readability and emphasis are influenced by word choice, sentence length, paragraph length, length of the entire message, subheads, listings, other aspects of format, organization, unity, coherence, and an attractive physical appearance.

Several formulas, or "indexes," have been developed that supposedly measure readability. Two of these are the Flesch Reading Ease Formula and the Gunning Fog Index. Rudolf Flesch's formula is presented in his book, *The Art of Readable Writing*, published in 1949.[1] Robert Gunning's formula appears in his book, *The Technique of Clear Writing*. (This book first appeared in 1952; this reference is to a revised edition.)[2]

Both the Flesch formula and the Gunning Fog Index rely heavily on sentence and word lengths to determine reading levels. Although Gunning recognizes that factors other than sentence and word length determine readability—such as percentage of verbs expressing forceful action, proportion of familiar words, proportion of abstract words—only sentence and word length are considered in his easy-to-use plan.

The readability score obtained through the use of the Gunning formula is expressed in terms of the general educational level of the reader, which may have little relationship to the actual grade completed in school. If, for example, the readability score is 17, this indicates that the material could be read easily by someone who has completed college. A score of 16 is used to mean that a person completing the sixteenth year of schooling, a college senior, could easily read the material.

Most effective writing of all kinds, however, has a lower readability score than 16 or 17, even if the material is planned for graduate students. Material may have a readability score lower than high school level and still be suitable for adults.

An important point to remember is that formulas cannot measure the quality of writing, only its complexity, and that to a limited extent. An expert writer can use long words and sentences and make a work more interesting and readable than a writer with less ability, although the expert's work has a higher readability score.

The formulas make no distinction between exact, well-chosen words and vague, confusing words, or between familiar words and rare ones. They measure only word length. They also do not distinguish sentences that are constructed wisely in order to exactly ex-

1. Rudolph Flesch, *The Art of Readable Writing* (New York: Harper & Row, 1949), pp. 213–216.

2. Robert Gunning, *The Technique of Clear Writing* (New York: McGraw-Hill, 1968), pp. 30–45.

press the intended ideas. Excellent writing cannot be measured by any formula, but an average reader can usually recognize its quality and understand its meaning.

These cautions about using readability formulas are not given to disparage their worth, for their admittedly limited purposes are valid ones. They measure sentence and word length and express this measurement in a score that is likely to apply to different groups of readers. The formulas can be dangerous, however, if they are misused. An appropriate readability score should not be accepted without question as an indication that the writing needs no improvement. Writing with a score higher than the expected "norms" should not be automatically classified as lacking in readability, although it should be reexamined.

The Gunning Fog Index is as follows:

1. Select a sample of writing of at least 100 words. Divide the total number of words by the number of sentences. This is the average sentence length. [Using several samples will result in a more reliable score. The independent clauses of a compound sentence are counted as separate sentences.]
2. Count the number of words of three syllables or more. Don't count proper names; combinations of short, easy words, such as bookkeeper or teenager; or verb forms made into three syllables by adding *ed* or *es*. This figure is the number of "hard" words in the passage. Divide this figure by the total number of words to find the percentage of "hard" words.
3. Add the average sentence length to the percentage of hard words and multiply by .4. The figure obtained through these calculations is the Gunning Fog Index, or readability score, expressed in grade-reading level.[3]

This readability formula is not the method used by writers of material for use in many textbooks, especially those for use at the elementary school level, for in these books the vocabulary, or the actual words to be included, must be considered. In readability formulas for adult use, only the length of words is considered, along with sentence length, although some methods include the consideration of "personal interest" words.

Let's find the readability score for the following paragraph from *The Mature Mind* by H. A. Overstreet, written in 1949. This book is much more readable than many other books on psychological subjects, but the 12.2 score is higher than an ideal score for short,

3. Gunning, *The Technique of Clear Writing*, p. 39.

nontechnical business communications. The example paragraph is well written: even with a higher percentage of long words, provided they were no more unusual than those actually used, the passage would be easily understandable. Another passage with a similar score could be much less understandable, according to the skill in sentence construction and word choice. (Overstreet does not mention television because in the year in which this paragraph was written, television was in its infancy.)

> Newspapers, radio, movies, and advertising—these might be called the "big four" of communication. These are the four great money-making enterprises of mind-making. It would be pleasant to report that they all make for the fine maturing of human character. But the report must be otherwise. In spite of what each has contributed to our growth, each has, through its own formula, found it profitable to keep us from full psychological maturing. Or, to put the best possible face upon the matter, each has found in us some immaturity that waited to be tapped. Engaged in the tapping process, each of these powerful forces has been too busy to think about the long-range consequences of its formula.[4]

The paragraph contains 120 words and 7 sentences. The words of three or more syllables (those not excluded by the formula) total 16. "Newspapers" and "otherwise" are excluded because they are combinations of short, easy words, like "bookkeeper," mentioned in the formula.

To find the sentence length, divide 120 by 7, which gives an average sentence length of 17.1. To find the percentage of hard words, divide 16 by 120; the percentage is 13.3. Add 17.1 to 13.3; the result is 30.4. Multiply by .4 to obtain the readability score of 12.16 or 12.2.

This reading-level score means that the material should be easily read by someone in the twelfth grade, or approximately so. This is similar to the reading level of such magazines as *The Atlantic* and *Harper's*, although articles by different authors vary somewhat in difficulty. Other popular magazines, especially *Reader's Digest*, are written at a level two or three grades below this twelfth-grade score. To obtain an accurate average score of writing of considerable length, we should use far more material than the paragraph we have considered here.

Although you should check passages of your own writing occasionally, most college students do not write in an extremely complex style—unless they are trying to impress their professor. Twenty

4. H. A. Overstreet, *The Mature Mind* (New York: W. W. Norton, 1949), pp. 225–226.

or thirty years from now, when you are a business executive, a politician, or a high-ranking government official, check your writing by the use of the Gunning Fog Index or a similar formula. If you resemble your present-day counterparts, you will need to simplify.

Robert Gunning and his associates have used the Fog Index in an attempt to simplify writing coming from the Army, Navy, Air Force, and the Department of Agriculture. It has also been used in many industries and with writers for newspapers and magazines. For Gunning's description of the use of this formula, its advantages and disadvantages, see his article, "The Fog Index After Twenty Years," which he wrote in 1968. In it he states:

> My feelings are mixed about this readability yardstick that I developed back in the 1940's; but they are much more positive than negative. The wide use the Fog Index has received is gratifying. On the other hand, occasional misunderstanding and misuse of it have been disturbing.[5]

REVISE FOR PROFESSIONAL QUALITY

Good writing is achieved by rewriting and then perhaps rewriting again and again. Even skillful professional writers revise their work, one reason why they are skillful professional writers.

In a busy office, however, there is little time or opportunity for extensive rewriting of routine letters, memorandums, or reports. Because of pressure to meet deadlines, which seems to be common to almost every occupation, you must be able to produce acceptable work without revising extensively. Whatever your knowledge and skill, however, and regardless of the lack of time, some revision is often necessary.

When revising a communication:

1. Check organization and the flow of thought.
2. Notice the length of sentences and paragraphs. Often they could be shortened.
3. Watch for unnecessary repetition of words or ideas.
4. Make sure that no essential material is omitted.
5. Check for subject-verb agreement and pronoun-antecedent agreement.
6. Watch for misplaced or dangling modifiers.

5. Robert Gunning, "The Fog Index after Twenty Years," *Journal of Business Communication* 6 (Winter 1968):3.

7. Make sure that necessary transitional phrases or words have been included. Make sure that there is no abrupt change in the flow of thought.
8. Decide whether the entire message can be made more concise without making it less understandable or convincing.

SUMMARY

1. Write simply. Don't try to impress your readers with an extensive vocabulary of five-syllable words, but don't give the impression of over-simplification or "writing down." Prefer short words to longer words, provided they are the *exact* ones to express your intended meaning. Consider the connotative meanings of words as well as dictionary definitions.

2. Express your ideas exactly. To do so you must have an extensive vocabulary. Be specific. Do not state vague generalities.

3. Write clearly, concisely, coherently, and correctly. Give all necessary information convincingly.

4. Write objectively. Base your interpretations and decisions upon facts, not upon your personal desires or unsupported beliefs. Although at times you must state what you believe about a situation or what the data seem to indicate, make sure that the reader understands that this statement is an opinion. Give concrete details to support your opinion. On the other hand, avoid an appearance of hedging and timidity. Nobody expects you to have positive and definite answers to everything. If you pretend to do so, nobody will believe you.

5. Avoid using an unnecessary number of *I's*, even when you are writing in the personal tone.

6. Write in an interesting and vivid style. Keep sentences fairly short, but vary sentence length. Avoid using many sentences that begin with slow expletive openings, such as *there are* and *it is*.

7. Use the active voice to emphasize the actor, the passive voice to emphasize the receiver of the action. Do not use the passive voice when the active voice will exactly express your idea in more vivid terms, as it often will.

8. Remember techniques of achieving readability through arrangement and format. Use an attractive arrangement with plenty of white space, listings, headings, and summaries. Use special arrangements, underlining, or other special methods of mechanical emphasis, but do not use them to excess.

QUESTIONS AND PROBLEMS

131
CHAPTER 6
A CLEAR AND
FORCEFUL WRITING
STYLE

1. Rewrite the following passages for conciseness. Retain the complete meaning.

   a. We are in receipt of your communication of recent date and in reply wish to inform you that we thank you for your communication and the prompt submission of your report which we had assigned to you and for your kind letter that was attached thereto.

   b. This is the machine that makes the most noise of all those in the room.

   c. Graduates who are the ones with the highest grade-point average will be the ones who will be interviewed.

   d. This memorandum is in reply to your telephone call of October. In reply to this memorandum I wish to advise that in reference to your question about specifications for the Anderson contract they have not at the present time been drawn up but they will be finished and completed sometime in the very near future.

   e. Will you let us know by any means, telephone or letter or otherwise, sometime soon, in a month or two but hopefully within a month, just what to do about the situation we conversed about and discussed pursuant to the changing of the method in which the beneficiary, that is the former beneficiary, is notified and informed that he or she is no longer the beneficiary, and that the policyholder has named and designated a new person to become the beneficiary. Or is this method and procedure mandatory, necessary, or even desirable?

   f. Eschew polysyllabic verbosity.

2. Rewrite the following sentences in the passive voice in order to increase diplomacy.

   a. You delivered the package to the wrong office.

   b. All your past employers told me something different about you.

   c. You know the instructions that I distributed to all personnel.

   d. You did not complete the investigation.

3. Rewrite the following sentences using the active voice instead of the passive voice or sentences beginning with *there* or *it*.

   a. Students were shown by the instructor how to weld the sides of the airplane.

   b. Implementation of the proposed procedure was delayed because of Leslie Brown's decision not to move ahead at this time.

c. There has been a brief period during which our office manager closed the word processing center.

d. It is interesting to notice from the attached statements that the exact balance of last month's account is the same as the exact balance of this month's account.

e. Four more houses were sold by Mr. Johns, and three more contracts were drawn up.

4. Rewrite the following letter to eliminate business jargon. Also eliminate or change words that carry unpleasant or confusing connotations. You may add an inside address and closing lines and arrange your letter in your choice of the styles shown in Chapter 3. (Of *course* you wouldn't write a letter like this. But if you can turn this one into a good one, you're on your way to professionalism.) Consider conciseness, sentence structure, and all other elements of effective communication.

> Dear Mrs. James:
>
> We are in receipt of your letter of recent date and in reply wish to state we shall be jubilant to submit to your claim to send cheaper merchandise than the items you previously and heretofore ordered us to send.
>
> Attached please find a new invoice for this cheaper merchandise which you claim will sell better in your store, that anything will sell better if it sells at all, which the present merchandise isn't doing much of. Your customers must be low class and down and out but are your salesmen really trying and have you thought about advertising?
>
> Reports from manufacturers about consumers' preference, and we contributed to information shown in these reports, reports are of the nature to suggest that consumers are trying to save money so you could possibly be right.
>
> Thanking you in advance for your esteemed favor, although I don't suppose it really is, please send your check posthaste and immediately. I am yours truly.

5. Discuss these statements:

a. A short word can be less readable than a long one.

b. Readability formulas can be misleading if used in the wrong way.

c. Specific words are more emphatic and more forceful than general words, but at times the general word is the better choice.

d. The writer may find it easier to write a long letter, memorandum, or report than to write a short one.

e. A thorough and automatic knowledge of sentence structure is essential or helpful to the expert writer, although it is true that some writers seem to write well without knowing what they are doing.

f. It is impossible to be completely objective.

g. Prefer not to start several paragraphs on the same page with *I.*

h. The use of business jargon can possibly save time, at least for the experienced writer, but the writer should work for a more original approach.

i. The salutation and complimentary close used on most business letters (are, are not) forms of stereotyped business jargon.

j. We can never be "completely complete," as it is impossible to say everything about anything. Thus, all communication is a form of abstracting—choosing exactly what to communicate and what to omit.

6. Write specific, complete, and detailed instructions for one or more of the following procedures:

a. How to change the ribbon on your typewriter.
b. How to change a tire on your automobile.
c. How to put film into your camera.
d. How to tie your shoe.
e. How to draw a paper clip.
f. How to operate a can opener.
g. How to calculate the number of rolls of wallpaper needed to paper a room.
h. How to brush your teeth.
i. How to check out a book in your school library.
j. How to check out a book in your public library.

7. Explaining Readability Formulas

You are the vice-president of Strong, Incorporated. Your company recently hired a communications supervisor because another vice-president learned that a competing company had done so. (Communications supervisors are becoming fashionable.)

The new communications supervisor, Noah Little, studied readability formulas in college. One of his first memorandums, addressed to all writers in the organization, contained the following instructions:

1. No written message going from the organization or used within the organization should score less than 10 or more than 12 when measured by the Gunning Fog Index, with the exception of material going to a group of college professors. These professors work with Strong, Incorporated, as consultants and with certain officials of Strong, Incorporated, on an advisory board set up to solve community problems.

   Because these people have doctoral degrees, indicating at least 19 years of formal education, letters directed to them should score at least 19 and preferably 20 on the Gunning Fog Index, or they will feel insulted. (When you asked Mr. Little why he included the figure 20, he replied that this group of professors seems to be unusually intelligent.)

2. Every writer is to check the readability score of every letter and memorandum during the next three months and prepare a report on his findings. If all written material scores within the recommended limitations, Mr. Little will assume that writers are doing a good job. He will also assume that writers who often exceed the recommended score of 12 are doing a poor job and will ask for their dismissal.

   The president of the organization, Sam Strong, describes himself as a "self-made man." Although he did not finish high school, within the last 30 years he has built a multinational organization with thousands of employees. He started the business with $10,000 inherited from his grandfather.

   Mr. Strong, who received a copy of Mr. Little's memorandum, has never heard of readability formulas. He asked you to explain the whole situation to him. You go into his office to do so, but you are interrupted by Mr. Strong's secretary, who tells him about an important telephone call. He is to leave immediately for London. Because you plan to be on vacation when he returns, he asks you to put your explanation of Noah Little's memorandum in your own memorandum to him. He seems unsure of Mr. Little's policies.

   Prepare the memorandum to Mr. Strong. He has asked you to explain the meaning of the Gunning Fog Index and to include your evaluation of Mr. Little's policies. Is there other information that you should include? How should you go about writing the memorandum? Write it.

The Report Process | PART IV

Planning the Report

7

The basis for a report is a problem. The research process, which ends with a written or oral presentation of research results, is the application of the scientific method of inquiry, or the scientific approach, to the solution of a problem.

THE SCIENTIFIC METHOD OF INQUIRY

The scientific method of inquiry, as it applies to the preparation of reports, consists of the following steps:

1. Determine the problem and define it in specific terms.
2. Collect essential facts pertaining to the problem.
3. Classify and organize data, with emphasis on processes, causes, and results.
4. Evaluate and interpret data in order to form generalizations toward the solution of the problem.
5. Select the most likely solution to the problem as indicated by factual evidence.

After completing the five general stages of the research process, present the solution, with reasons, explanations, and recommendations, in appropriate report form.

Plan the Research Study

The five steps given above are appropriate, valid, and necessary for research of any length and scope, resulting in a short memorandum report or a formal one of book length. For a comprehensive research study that is to result in a report of considerable length and importance, each of these steps should be thoroughly planned at the beginning of the research process and stated in a detailed written proposal, which is also described as the report plan or the research design.

Although a proposal, or a report plan, is of necessity only tentative, it serves as a guide from the beginning to the end of the report process. In addition, it is essential to the person or persons who authorize the report and keep track of the researcher's progress, often from short periodic reports during the completion of the major project.

A written plan of procedure can be helpful when planning a short, informal study, even one that will result in a one- or two-page memorandum report. Although a preliminary written plan is not routinely required or expected for short reports, you save time and decrease errors by having a guide to the steps of the overall report process as they apply to the particular situation and the problem being investigated. A great deal of time can be saved by thinking through the process before beginning the study.

Be Objective and Decisive

In all situations, regardless of the complexity of the report, strive for objective analysis and interpretation of information. You should in no way be guided by the proposal or report plan to the extent that you interpret data in the light of expected findings and conclusions, a weakness that is all too common in research of any kind. Even if the problem statement is in the form of a hypothesis (to be discussed later in this chapter), do not set out to find facts to prove or disprove the hypothesis. Although this type of research occurs more often than it should, it by no means meets the standards of the scientific method of inquiry. The competent researcher finds all available facts, within the scope of the definition of the report problem, and interprets these facts without regard to expected or desired outcomes.

The solutions, wise or unwise, to many of the problems we face in our personal and business lives are reached without formal research resulting in a report. At times, we think about a problem without making a decision; that is, we stop somewhere in our scientific approach before reaching a solution. Refusing to make a decision is in effect making one—that the decision is to be postponed. This may be the best solution at the particular time. Like all other decisions, it should be preceded by adequate and objective investigation and analysis. More often, an inability to reach a reasonable conclusion and solution is due to weaknesses somewhere in the preceding phases of research.

Be Specific

The first step, determining and defining the problem in specific terms, is essential to the success of the remaining steps of the research process. If the problem cannot be stated in descriptive, specific, written words, it is not yet clearly in mind.

A PROBLEM-SOLVING SITUATION

The word *research*, like the even broader term *communication*, applies to almost everything we do. As we attempt to solve ever-occurring problems, large and small, we engage in a form of research, although much of it is far from objective and scientific.

Suppose, for example, that you are driving to work and find that there is a severe traffic jam on the street you usually travel. Under ordinary conditions this street is the most direct route to your office. You have an important appointment at 9:15, and it is now 8:15. If normal traffic conditions prevailed, you could reach your office in half an hour.

Your problem is—what to do? Should you wait here and hope that the stalled automobiles will move on, or should you detour, provided you can work yourself onto a side street? (A comparable business problem would be to decide whether an organization should continue with the present and heretofore successful method of operation or, because of unexpected difficulties, change the method of operation.) Will the more indirect route, which is ordinarily slower because of school zones, residential areas, and stop lights, provide a quicker method of reaching the office?

You do not put this statement into written form, but, on a simple level, this situation compares to a problem you face when you undertake a business research project: You state the problem, choose a method of solution, collect and organize data, evaluate and interpret its meaning, and arrive at a solution to the problem, whether or not this solution is the best one.

Using this example, however, you usually undertake the action and find the data at the same time—that is, you embark on the assumed solution and collect and organize the data in your mind as you move along. Then your report is presented orally to your employer or associates when you arrive at the office. As you meander through the side streets or wait in your automobile in the traffic jam, you are collecting data as you keep track of the time. This may be unfavorable data, but you made your choice when you turned off the main thoroughfare or decided to wait.

Some business, professional, and government organizations seem to make their decisions in just this way; they go ahead and turn, or remain immobile on a jammed street, and figure out as time passes whether or not they made the right decision.

When you have more time and a serious problem, you cannot afford to operate in this way. Assuming you do have the time, what kind of research could you do? You could study the maps and determine the mileage by both routes. You could turn your automobile radio to the station that reports traffic conditions; perhaps you can learn the extent of the traffic blockage and when the street can be expected to be back to normal. Perhaps the radio voice could tell you something of the traffic conditions on the side streets you are considering. If you have telephone or radio contact with your office, you could find out how important it is that you arrive at the regular time, for perhaps the important appointment you are hurrying to has been cancelled for some reason, or perhaps it could be delayed.

This question, however, is not relevant to your subquestion of which route will provide the quickest trip to the office; it does apply to the question that you started with—what to do. These questions should not be analyzed together, but ones such as these tend to become jumbled as we find ourselves entangled in a problem or, especially, when putting the report into written form.

In the problem-solving situation, you would collect all this information, analyze it for its validity and applicability, and arrive at a conclusion upon which you would make your recommendation of the better choice of the two courses of action.

Your conclusion has been based partly upon inferences. If the radio voice has told you of a three-car accident that is blocking all lanes of traffic, you infer that it will be some time before your regular route is ready for travel. Your calculations of the mileage by both routes can be considered a fact if you are sure that the mapmakers were accurate—but then this assumption is also an inference. (Even though we can never be completely sure of most things, we must treat some inferences as if they were facts, at least until we have time to investigate them further.)

Reasonable inferences supported by sufficient facts may serve as a basis for recommendations, although at times these recommendations will be incorrect. Your value judgments, unsupported by facts, should not be used as a basis for recommendations. From a practical business standpoint, the fact that the side streets that make up the indirect route are more picturesque is not relevant to your question of which way to drive to the office. Your appreciation of flowering trees and clumps of daffodils is a value judgment, although many people would agree with you.

A form of secondary research would be for you to call to a person in the next car: "Sir, have you ever driven down Flamingo Street to Cherry, then to Rhodes and Barron, and then on Lamar to downtown?" If he has driven this route recently, his advice would be similar to that you might find in a business journal, located through *Business Periodicals Index*, of how another business organization solved a problem similar to the one you are now trying to solve. In all instances, you should use secondary research sources if they are available in order to take advantage of the experiences of other persons. To do otherwise is the same as reinventing the wheel each time we need a new wheelbarrow.

As you may have realized, much of successful business research and report writing is the application of mere common sense. But then common sense should not be qualified as "mere."

DETERMINING AND DEFINING THE PROBLEM

A problem exactly stated is a problem well on the way to being solved. Determining that a problem exists is not difficult from the standpoint of knowing that something is wrong or needs improvement. Stating in specific terms exactly what you wish to determine in a particular research study, as an aid to the solution of the problem, is more difficult.

Perhaps several studies of a problem within an organization will be necessary before a major issue is resolved, and perhaps your particular report is planned to cover only one factor of a major question. Or your study may be a comprehensive one with several contributing factors: if this is the case, you are in effect investigating a number of questions and combining the answers into a solution of the larger problem.

If the research project has been assigned to you, as ordinarily it will be, make sure that you and the person who authorized the report are in complete agreement about the purpose of the report, including limitations and boundaries of the study—exactly what you are and are not attempting to find out. You will also need to discuss cost considerations.

Other items of information that you must have before proceeding with the research process are these:

- What has been done in the past on this problem? Have previous reports been prepared? If so, where are they? Were recommendations, if any, put into effect? If so, were they successful? If not, why not? If they were not put into effect, why not?
- In addition to previous reports, if any, what other internal data are available?
- Who is likely to have more information on this particular subject?
- What use is to be made of this report? How the report will be used is not the same as your stated purpose; the purpose, or problem, is the question you are trying to solve by finding relevant information and interpreting that information. The report may be filed away, or it may be presented to a committee for further consideration, or recommended changes may be put into effect.
- When is the report needed?
- What limitations apply as to time, money, and facilities?
- What are the exact terms of the contract or assignment? If the study is a part of your regular employment responsibilities, the agreement is not likely to be referred to as a contract. A letter of authorization, followed by the researcher's letter of acceptance, serves as a written agreement as to what is to be done. If you are working as a consultant for a firm other than your own, you should have a written contract. Written specifications should be complete and exact.

Problem Statements: Informational Reports

Statements of purpose, described in preceding sections of this chapter, apply to analytical reports; they are planned to solve problems by analyzing information provided by research.

Definitely worded statements of purpose are also necessary for comprehensive reports that are merely informational; for example:

Problem Statement: To present a summary of outside employment activities of teachers in the College of

Business Administration, Washington University,
during the school year 1980–81.

The wording of the statement of purpose for any report can be presented in slightly different forms, as:

The purpose of this report is to present a summary
of outside . . .

or

This report will summarize outside employment
activities of teachers . . .

Notice that *This report will summarize . . .* is appropriate for a proposal, or report plan, prepared at the beginning of the report process. In the final report, the sentence should read: *This report summarizes . . .*

As for analytical reports, subtopics are necessary for comprehensive informational reports. For example, a breakdown into factors of the preceding statement of purpose might include:

Teaching in other institutions
Seminars and conferences
Speaking engagements
Consulting
Writing
Other self-employment
Other paid activities

Other statements of purpose for informational reports will include those that are used for presenting results of historical research and descriptive research. *Historical research*, as the term indicates, presents information about the past; *descriptive research* ordinarily depicts present conditions, situations, activities, facilities, or circumstances.

Hypotheses: Analytical Reports

A hypothesis is a statement to be proved or disproved as a result of research; for example:

Employee morale will be strengthened and absenteeism

decreased by providing career apparel at company expense.

A null hypothesis would be worded in this way:

No significant difference in employee morale or absenteeism will occur by providing career apparel at company expense.

The use of a null hypothesis is sometimes considered more scientific than the positive because a positive statement supposedly indicates that the researcher has already decided upon what the results will be. Nevertheless, bias can occur regardless of the wording of a hypothesis.

The declarative hypothesis states that a relationship exists between stated variables. A null hypothesis states that no relationship exists between stated variables. By stating a hypothesis, a researcher makes an assumption about the final answer, or solution, to the problem statement. Through the research process of gathering and analyzing data, the assumption stated in the hypothesis may be proved correct or incorrect, or the data may be inconclusive so that the hypothesis must be rejected.

Not all research is of the type that can be exactly formulated in terms of hypotheses. Notice that in the illustration given above, judging employee morale is a task difficult to prove or disprove to the extent that a hypothesis can be definitely tested. This business problem can be "solved," however, to the extent that the person or persons responsible for putting the research results into effect are reasonably sure that the recommended course of action is advisable. Other kinds of problems, particularly those that can be tested for a statistical significant difference, are suitable for statements of purpose in the form of a hypothesis.

Other Problem Statements: Analytical Reports

If the report is assigned, as it ordinarily will be, the report writer must know exactly what is wanted.

The questions that newspaper reporters are taught to ask—*who, what, where, when, why, and how*—apply to business report writing. Why is the report requested? Who will read it? When is this information needed? How will this information be used? Where can this information be obtained? And, most important of all, exactly what am I trying to find out?

Your answer to this last problem is your starting point, the statement of the problem. This statement of the problem may be broken into subquestions to include the answers to who, what, why, when, where, or how. All these questions must be considered together when determining and putting into an exactly written statement the problem you are trying to solve.

We face major and minor problems in all phases of our work and personal life; the difficulty arises in knowing what to include in the particular research study, for problems tend to overlap. If the statement of the problem cannot be put into definite words and stated in question form, it is not yet clearly defined. If the problem remains vague, general, and undetermined, planning helpful research, finding a solution, and reporting the solution will be difficult indeed.

This initial step of defining the problem should be discussed with whomever assigns the report. The exact purpose must be agreed upon by the person or persons who authorize the report and the person who undertakes the completion of the report.

Often the statement of the problem is used as the first sentence of the introductory section of the report itself. Notice the specific wording of the following problem statements:

> The purpose of this report is to examine all costs and revenues in the movement of sugar from the South Coast Sugar Mill in Matthews, Louisiana, and to determine whether it is profitable for the Kroger Company to transport it with its own equipment.[1]

Although this statement is not now worded in question form, notice that it could be: "Is it profitable for the Kroger Company to initiate a self-haul program for sugar from. . . ."

> Should Countrywide Insurance Company purchase career apparel for its women employees?
>
> Should Marketing Consultants, Inc. move from their present location in Commerce Square to the office building in Dillard Square?
>
> Should Countrywide Insurance Company replace presently owned typewriters, on the established

---

1. Stephen A. Wiggs, "Why the Kroger Company Should Initiate a Self-Haul Program for Sugar" (unpublished report, 1973).

three-year trade-in basis, for self-correcting Selectric III's?

Should the Seligman Realty Company continue the present method of door-to-door rent collection or establish a system of collection by mail?

Are the services and purposes of the local Chamber of Commerce well known to the citizens of the city?

Which kinds of books (recent fiction, older fiction, classics, general nonfiction, textbooks) are most widely circulated in the Whitehaven Branch Library?

Should the Advance Business School offer a course to prepare presently employed secretaries to work in the legal profession?

Why are the sales of the Xtra-Ezy lawnmowers 56 percent less in District I, on the average, than in District II?

All the questions given above are overall statements of the problem, which should be broken down into subcategories near the beginning of the report process. For example, the question about career apparel could be detailed in this way. (We know from the wording of the title that the report is limited to women employees. Perhaps male employees are already in uniform or they have voted not to wear uniforms—or perhaps this study is to be left until later.)

Should Countrywide Insurance Company purchase career apparel for its women employees?

- What are the benefits
    to the employer?
    to the employees?
    to the customer?
- What are the disadvantages?
- What is the approximate cost?
- Do the benefits to be derived outweigh the cost consideration and any other disadvantages?
- Where can this apparel be purchased?
- If this change in procedure is put into effect, how should it be administered?

As much as possible, think through the complete problem-solving process before you begin. Although the outline you draw up will be a tentative one, it is far better than none at all.

LIMITING THE PROBLEM

The boundaries of a research problem are referred to as the *scope*. *Delimitations*, another term used instead of scope, describes specifically excluded factors which might have been expected in the report.

The term *limitations* is used to refer to situations or handicaps, such as the lack of time or money, that prevented a complete research study or a thorough presentation.

These considerations, especially as they are presented in the introductory section of a formal report, are discussed further in Chapter 14. In this book, the term *scope* is used to indicate boundaries; *limitations*, at least as the word is used as a description of a part of the final report, indicates limiting or detrimental factors.

However these terms are used as headings of a report, the scope of a report problem must be limited by exact and definite boundaries. We consider the scope in order to state the problem in definite and specific wording, as well as to plan research procedures.

Look back at some of the preceding problem statements. Notice that these statements also include boundaries. For example, the problem statement about Xtra-Ezy lawnmowers indicates that the study will be concerned only with District I and District II, not with other districts. We are concerned only with sales, not with other aspects of the two districts, unless these other aspects influence sales in some way, as they may. Only the one product is to be considered.

This problem statement would be improved if it also included an indication of the time span; for example, why have sales for the last year been 56 percent less? If this time element is not specified in the general problem statement, it must be included early in the report along with such information as the description of methods and sources of information.

In this report situation, you are trying to find the *why*; you are also looking for the *how*, or how the sales can be increased in the slow district. You have the *what* and the *where*: the product and the two districts. The *who* consists of the personnel in the two districts, or perhaps in the general management or in the home office. The *when* is the span of time being studied. The problem is not clearly stated until the scope is definitely and specifically defined.

A TENTATIVE REPORT PLAN

Before beginning research to find the answer to a predetermined business problem, consider preparing a report plan, even though it must be a tentative one. Such an outline of procedure, although it will perhaps be changed during the research process, provides a far more efficient method of approach than having no plan at all. This preliminary plan, which should be specifically worded and prepared in written form, is often referred to as a proposal if it is to be presented to another person or persons for approval. A similar report plan is useful for informational reports, as well as for analytical ones.

This preliminary step to the research and reporting process is referred to here as a report plan, not a proposal, for you will need such a plan whether or not it is presented for the approval of others. When preparing proposals, which may be for business, government, professional, or educational research, you may find that a specified format and arrangement are required, including an estimate of cost.

When a specified format is expected, it is most important that you follow it exactly, just as you adhere to a particular and specified format for the reporting itself. Basically, though, a report plan or proposal is likely to consist of the types of information discussed here, which are in turn based on the steps to a solution of a research problem.

The report plan should include the following sections:

1. A specific statement of the purpose of the report, including, if necessary, subcategories. (See the report problem used earlier: Should Countrywide Insurance Company provide career apparel for its women employees?) Try to word the statement of purpose so that the scope (or boundary) of your research is apparent. If you cannot do so, include a separate statement—or paragraphs, as needed—to make clear exactly what you intend to do.

2. Methods of finding information to lead to a solution to the problem. A tentative bibliography may be included in this section.

3. Methods of organizing, evaluating, and interpreting the data in order to reach a solution. Although this step will not be necessary for all report plans and proposals, it is essential in some situations. If the methods consist only of looking at the data, determining what they mean, and putting them into report form, then these duties can logically be assumed without a definite statement in the report plan. If the data are to be analyzed statistically, or in any special or unusual manner, these methods should be stated.

4. A tentative presentation of the report. This step, like the one preceding, will not be required of many proposals or report plans, but it is helpful to you for your own planning and is also useful in class assignments. Although you cannot determine the exact outline until you have completed the

research or even later, a beginning outline keeps you from going too far astray in your thinking or in working toward a solution.

This tentative outline is also a tentative table of contents, with the headings of the main divisions of the report based upon the subdivisions of the problem statement. In the report about Countrywide Insurance and career apparel, the divisions of the problem statement (benefits, disadvantages, cost, etc.) are logical divisions of the final report.

In addition to the preceding items to be included in the report plan, state specifically in written form, if only for your own use, the answer to these questions:

- Is this report to be analytical or merely informational?
- Is it to be formal or informal, considering both the format and the writing style?
- Is it to be written in the personal or the impersonal tone?

The example shown in Figure 7-1 should not be considered as the only possible report plan or proposal. In some instances certain of the items shown here may be omitted, and others not shown here may be needed. In all instances, include purpose, methods, and sources of data.

An introduction to a formal report, containing similar information to that shown in Figure 7-1, is included in Chapter 14 with the discussion of the arrangement and content of a completed report.

A TENTATIVE TABLE OF CONTENTS

A tentative table of contents is shown in Figure 7-2. If you prefer, refer to such an outline *as* an outline, as you have done when planning papers for other purposes. Regardless of how you describe it, such a written plan for the material to be included and the order of presentation will aid throughout the research, interpretation, and writing processes.

A complete report plan, including a tentative table of contents, facilitates the preparation of the introduction (often described by another title) of a formal report arranged in the inductive (or indirect) order. A complete report plan *becomes* the introductory section of the report itself, after appropriate modifications in wording and changes to reflect any final deviations from the original plan.

Read the headings of the tentative table of contents shown in Figure 7-2. Notice that the researcher has, in effect, stated a hy-

PLAN OF PROPOSED REPORT

<u>Tentative title:</u> SHOULD THE CHICKASAW BRANCH OF
COUNTRYWIDE INSURANCE COMPANY
CONVERT FROM GENERALIST SECRETARIES
TO A WORD PROCESSING AND
ADMINISTRATIVE SUPPORT CENTER?

<u>Author:</u> Herbert L. Collins, Director of Personnel and Training

<u>Statement of Purpose:</u> The purpose of this report is to explore the possibilities of word processing and administrative support operations for the Chickasaw Branch of Countrywide Insurance Company and to determine the feasibility of converting to a word processing system. The study is necessary because of rapidly increasing costs in administrative operations and an increased volume of typewriting and related printing.

<u>Scope:</u> This study deals primarily with the potential for a word processing system to cut secretarial administrative costs by increasing the productivity of each secretary through specialization. Not included in this research is a complete analysis of the most desirable equipment, as presently owned equipment will be adequate at the beginning of the operation and possibly for some time to come. Another aspect of the problem not considered is the exact nature of the training to be provided to secretaries and executives. Also excluded is consideration of the increase or decrease in morale because of the conversion to word processing. A basic premise that cannot be considered in this research study is that efficiency and economy are achieved, more so than by any other element, through capable, efficient, and dedicated personnel.

<u>Limitations:</u> Professional consultation on word processing needs is not available in this city except from vendors of equipment. The cost of consultation with professionals from outside the city would exceed the amount considered reasonable for this preliminary study.

<u>Readers:</u> Anna Rose Tatum, President of Countrywide Insurance Company, and Lynn G. Bertagna, Manager of Chickasaw Branch.

<u>Sources and Methods of Collecting Data:</u> Secondary sources will be used to provide information about word processing systems used in other firms, types of equipment available as compared to present

Figure 7-1. *Example of a tentative report plan.*   **151**

equipment at Chickasaw Branch, and costs of typewriting by present
and proposed systems. A tentative bibliography is attached to this
report plan.

Interviews with management and secretarial personnel will be
conducted in order to learn the general functions now being performed
and the percentage of time spent in each function.

Sales representatives from IBM, Lanier, Xerox, and Exxon will be
consulted as to the advisability of establishing a word processing
center, although no further equipment is to be purchased
immediately. Telephone or on-site interviews will be conducted with
office managers and supervisors in local companies that now use word
processing systems similar to the proposed one.

Tentative Table of Contents of Report: (see attached outline)

Figure 7-1. *continued*

TENTATIVE TABLE OF CONTENTS

(An Outline of Possible Divisions of Completed Report)

PURPOSE, SOURCES, AND METHODS OF RESEARCH
    Purpose
    Scope
    Limitations
    Sources and Methods of Collecting Data
    Basic Plan of Presentation

WHY WORD PROCESSING SHOULD BE CONSIDERED
    What Is Word Processing?
    What Has Word Processing Done for Other Firms?

PROPOSED PERSONNEL CHANGES WITH WORD PROCESSING
    Secretarial Staff Can Be Reduced from Ten to Eight
    Career Patterns Can Be Established for Secretaries

ECONOMY AND EFFICIENCY THROUGH WORD PROCESSING
    Functions and Costs Prior to Word Processing
    Functions and Costs with Word Processing

WHY COUNTRYWIDE INSURANCE COMPANY SHOULD INSTALL A
    WORD PROCESSING CENTER

152   **Figure 7-2.** *Sample tentative table of contents.*

pothesis, a prediction of the results of the study. The competent and conscientious researcher will not be influenced by these statements, just as stating a hypothesis, or a null hypothesis, has no bearing on thorough and objective research and analysis. Some readers of such preliminary statements, however, would interpret them to mean that the researcher's mind is already made up, regardless of findings, and that the results of the research are likely to reflect this non-objective attitude. Headings as shown could be easily changed so that they would not predict the outcome; for example, in the third major section the heading "Secretarial Staff Can Be Reduced from Ten to Eight" could be changed to "Can the Secretarial Staff Be Reduced?"

If you are preparing a tentative table of contents as a class assignment preliminary to a research project, ask for your instructor's advice as to whether wordings of headings should reflect outcomes. In any event, it is not necessary that headings do so, even in the finished report, although they are an aid to readability and serve as a summary of the entire report. Your instructor may also ask that you prepare a tentative introduction at this time, although, for the most part, it is merely a repetition of the report plan. As you complete the introduction of the final report, remember to make appropriate changes in wording from the report plan or introduction prepared early in the research process.

A PROPOSAL

As previously mentioned in this chapter, a *report plan*, such as the one illustrated in Figure 7-1, is a proposal for a research project. The terms *proposal, research proposal*, and *proposal report*, however, are ordinarily used to denote a longer and more formal written presentation than what is ordinarily described as a *report plan*, particularly a plan for a class report or a short, informal business report.

The parts of a report plan discussed and illustrated earlier in this chapter are also parts of a research proposal (using the term in its more formal sense), but the proposal usually requires further information in addition to that shown in Figure 7-1. The word *proposal* is used not only as an offer to supply services as a researcher, but also as an offer of other services, such as consultation, or as a bid on a contract.

A statement of purpose and a description of proposed methodology are essential in the written presentation of any report project. Other categories of information that are likely to be necessary for complete research proposals include an estimate of costs, perhaps with a long, detailed budget; qualifications of researchers and other personnel involved in the work; necessary equipment and facilities; a summary of previous research in the area to be studied, including a bibliography and perhaps a summary of all previous investigation; a detailed work schedule, including a date when the project is to be finished; provision for evaluation of the entire project; and suggestions for continuing research.

The physical appearance of many proposals is somewhere between the simple report plan illustrated in Figure 7-1 and a complete formal report illustrated in Chapter 14. Proposals may be presented in letter, memorandum, or manuscript format, as illustrated by the short reports shown in Chapters 3 and 4. A long proposal should begin with an abstract, which is similar to the synopsis discussed in Chapter 14 and shown with a formal report. Like a synopsis (sometimes the terms are used interchangeably), an abstract summarizes the main idea of the report or proposal, with emphasis on the overall purpose and expected results. An abstract provides an immediate answer as to what the longer proposal is about and thus increases readability.

Solicited and Unsolicited Proposals

Proposals are *solicited* or *unsolicited*. Solicited proposals are submitted in response to requests for such proposals, which are often in the form of printed announcements. Unsolicited proposals are originated by the person or persons who submit them.

Requests for proposals come from government agencies, educational institutions, foundations, business and professional organizations, many other groups, and from individuals. Announcements that request proposals may include detailed, specific instructions on how the proposals are to be submitted, arranged, and written. These instructions should be followed exactly.

Unsolicited proposals differ little from solicited ones, although they may be more difficult to prepare because of the lack of guidelines. If no information is provided, the proposal should be prepared in the most easily read format and in the arrangement that seems most likely to obtain the desired results because of the proper use of emphasis.

All the attributes of effective writing apply to the preparation of proposals of any kind. Organization, conciseness, and readability are of particular importance. As in all communication, your ideas are most likely to be accepted if your readers are convinced that what you propose will meet their needs and desires.

Suggested Content of a Proposal

The sequence of information shown in Figure 7-1 can be adapted and expanded to serve as a research proposal. Such a proposal might contain the following areas of content:

1. A *cover sheet* that shows the following items:
   a. title of the proposal;
   b. name of the person, with position and organization, to whom the proposal is submitted;
   c. any necessary identifying numbers or phrasing to show that the proposal is in response to a particular announcement or set of specifications;
   d. person or persons submitting the proposal, with name, position, employing organization, address, and telephone number;
   e. date the report is submitted.
2. An *abstract* that summarizes the entire proposal.
3. A *table of contents* if one would be helpful.
4. An *introductory or background section*, provided that such information is necessary before going directly to the statement of purpose.
5. A specifically worded *statement of purpose* with necessary subcategories.
6. A *summary of related research.*
7. *Procedures*, which may also be described as *Methodology, Methods and Sources*, or *Sources of Data.*
8. *Personnel* to be involved in the project, with a summary of their background and qualifications.
9. *Facilities* and *equipment* to be used in the project.
10. *Cost estimate*, which may necessitate a long, detailed budget and a firm contractual maximum.
11. *Provision for reporting results.*
12. *Provision for evaluation of research.*
13. Provision for putting results into effect.
14. *Suggestions* for probable further research.

The suggested sections of a proposal can be modified in various ways according to the purpose of the research, readers, overall length, and specified format.

SUMMARY

The scientific method of inquiry, or the scientific approach, as it applies to the preparation of reports, consists of the following steps: (1) Determining the problem and stating it in specific terms; (2) Collecting data; (3) Classifying and organizing data; (4) Evaluating and interpreting data; and (5) Determining the most likely solution to the stated problem as indicated by factual evidence.

After completing the five general stages of the research process, the researcher presents the solution, with reasons, explanations, and recommendations, in appropriate report form.

The basis of a report is a problem. The first and most important step in the report process is determining what the problem is and stating it exactly, with necessary and helpful subcategories.

The report writer should think through the complete problem-solving process before beginning the research project, even though the plans will be somewhat tentative. As a guide to further steps, a written report plan saves time and keeps the researcher on track. A report plan, or proposal, is often submitted to another person, or to a group, for approval.

QUESTIONS AND PROBLEMS

1. For each of the following problem situations, state the problem (purpose), either in the form of a question or as an infinitive phrase. For example, a report planned to study the advisability of providing career apparel can be stated as:

> Should the Countrywide Insurance Company provide career apparel for its women employees? (*Question*)
> Purpose: To determine whether the Countrywide Insurance Company should provide career apparel for its women employees. (*Infinitive phrase*)

Be specific, but omit subcategories of the problem. Assume necessary and reasonable details, including names.

   a. A restaurant manager wants to know how to improve crowded conditions at the midday meal.
   b. A restaurant manager wants to know how to increase profits on the midday meal.
   c. A restaurant manager wants to know the choices most often made from the luncheon menu.
   d. A college professor is trying to decide whether to authorize monthly deductions from his paycheck for deposit in a tax-sheltered annuity fund.
   e. The professor has decided to invest in a tax-sheltered annuity fund, but he does not know which one to choose.
   f. An officer manager must choose a copying machine.
   g. A business education teacher must choose typewriters for a classroom to be used for beginning typists.

   h. A Chamber of Commerce wants to know what local citizens think of the Chamber's services and purposes.

   i. A dean of a college of business administration wants to determine the business course or courses that alumni believe to have been the most beneficial.

   j. A discount department store wants to know something of its "image."

   k. A large construction company is considering adopting a pension plan.

   l. The Park Commission is thinking of piping in music to all offices.

   m. A manufacturer needs to know how to market a new product, a compact refrigerator-icemaker.

2. For one or more of the problem situations listed in Question 1, state the problem in the form of a null hypothesis.

3. Choose a question that you wish to investigate in order to report the results in the formal business report. Prepare a tentative report plan, as shown in this chapter. Include a tentative title, statement of purpose, scope (or scope and limitations), readers, and sources and methods of collecting data.

4. Prepare a tentative table of contents for the research you planned in Question 3.

Gathering Information from Secondary Sources

8

In the preceding chapter, emphasis was upon the first steps of the report process: determining the problem, defining it in specific terms, and deciding upon the methods of finding a solution to the problem. This chapter moves to what is ordinarily the next step in the report process: gathering information from secondary sources.

THE IMPORTANCE OF SECONDARY RESEARCH

Sources of data are described as being *secondary* or *primary*. The word *secondary* is used to mean that data have already been gathered and recorded by someone else. Because much of this information is in published form and available in libraries, secondary research is often referred to as library research. Secondary data, however, include unpublished material and can be found in places other than a library, often in the files of your own company. Unpublished sources include reports of various kinds, dissertations, brochures, booklets, operating and procedures manuals, and texts of public speeches.

Primary is the term used to describe data that have not already been gathered and recorded by someone else. Primary data are obtained through observation, experimentation, and surveys. Surveys employ the use of questionnaires and formal or informal interviews done in person or by telephone.

Distinguish Between Primary and Secondary Data

161

CHAPTER 8
GATHERING
INFORMATION FROM
SECONDARY SOURCES

Distinguishing between primary and secondary data is far more important than merely knowing the meaning of the terms. Whenever you use another's material in any way, you are professionally and ethically obligated to give credit to the originator of that material. Customary methods of documentation, along with a brief discussion of copyright laws with their "fair use" provisions, are given in Chapter 12. No other consideration in research and report writing is more vital than the precept of giving credit where credit is due.

Begin with Secondary Research

Secondary research should ordinarily be the starting point in the data-gathering process. Regardless of the problem you are trying to solve, similar ones are likely to have occurred in other organizations or with other individuals. The solutions to these problems may be reported in business periodicals or elsewhere. Although these problems will be at least slightly different from your own, your knowledge of what other individuals and organizations have concluded in similar situations can help to answer your own questions.

We must build on the experience of others because there is no time to do otherwise. You should not spend time in completing a research project that has already been done unless you want to check the validity and reliability of the previous research study, expand upon it in some way, or update it.

For example, if a construction company needs to know the rate of increase or decrease in housing starts or in the price of an average new house in a given city, the researcher will find that recent studies have already been made of these questions, as well as of many others that often arise when a company plans its operations. Chambers of Commerce, government agencies, colleges and universities, and professional organizations are engaged continuously in such research and in reporting their findings for the benefit of business organizations and the public in general.

Library research should not be thought of as only supplemental, even for reports to be based mostly on primary data of one kind or another. In addition to finding specific information that applies directly to your problem, you may be able to obtain a general overview of the entire question you are investigating. Secondary research at the beginning of the report-writing process provides ideas for other methods of investigation. In addition, as you examine what seem to be the most relevant library sources, you are likely to be referred to other references, often better ones.

FINDING SPECIALIZED INFORMATION

A large library can be confusing and frustrating even to experienced researchers. You may feel that you are surrounded by billions of words, all of which have absolutely nothing to do with the problem you are investigating. Although it is quite possible that the exact information for which you are searching is unavailable, it is more likely that helpful information is somewhere in the library—if you can only find it. Because of the rapidly increasing numbers of books, periodicals, and other reference and reading sources, developing skills in locating information is absolutely essential.

Do you know how to find specialized information? Suppose, for example, that you want to read recent articles on communication as it applies to management, especially communication from employees to management. Or, more specifically, suppose that you are investigating the question of whether to have fifteen-minute meetings of all employees at the beginning of each work day. Where would you go to find out what benefits other organizations have derived from such meetings? Do you know the names of government publications that supply data about retail and wholesale trade, construction, agriculture, employment, and many other kinds of business information?

Can you find a list of all books on report writing that have been published during the past two years? Can you quickly determine the names of books written by any particular writer and whether or not these books are still available for purchase? Can you find out whether your particular library owns these books? Do you know how to locate articles that have appeared in business journals about the organization to which you are submitting an employment application? Can you find the names of articles that have appeared in *Reader's Digest* in 1973 on the subject of inflation, without having the 1973 magazines available?

Do you know the leading business periodicals in your particular field of study? Does your school library subscribe to these periodicals? Where are past issues stored, and have they been bound or reproduced on microfilm? Which method of classification does your library use, the Library of Congress system or the Dewey decimal system, or both? Where is the reference room? Does the library have open stacks? In addition to printed material, what other library sources are available, such as sound cassettes, films, film strips, and transparencies?

What is the *Business Periodicals Index*? What information will you find in *Moody's Manuals*? In addition to your school library, how many other libraries are available in your city or community for your use? Does your own company have a library? What information is made available by your local Chamber of Commerce?

Answers to some of the preceding questions are given below.

BASIC REFERENCE SOURCES

Only a few of the thousands of reference sources available can be listed in this book, but the following ones are likely to be most beneficial to you.

Bibliographies

The term *bibliography*, as used here to describe a reference source, means a complete or selective list of readings on a particular subject. Bibliographies have been prepared in many subject fields. They will be useful if they are specific enough for your particular purpose and are up to date. Bibliographies frequently accompany articles, books, master's theses and doctoral dissertations, research reports, and publications from trade and professional organizations.

One general source of bibliographies is:

> *Bibliographic Index: A Cumulative Bibliography of Bibliographies*. New York: H. W. Wilson Company, 1937 to date.

This index is organized by subject. It is a guide to books, articles, and other published sources that include a bibliography.

Investment Information Sources, *Public Finance Information Sources*, *Real Estate Information Sources*, and *Textile Industry Information Sources* are publications of Gale Research Company, which provides various other services to business.

General Guides to Business Research and Reference Materials

The following guides to business research and reference materials are helpful in finding or constructing bibliographies on business topics. They provide an overview of the process of finding secondary information and basic reference sources.

> *Encyclopedia of Business Information Sources*, 5th ed. Paul Wasserman, ed. Detroit: Gale Research Company, 1983.
>
> *How to Use the Business Library*, 4th ed. Herbert Webster Johnson. Cincinnati: South-Western Publishing Company, 1972.
>
> *Where to Find Business Information: A Worldwide Guide for Everyone Who Needs Answers to Business Questions*, 2d ed. David M. Brownstone and Gordon Carruth. New York: John Wiley and Sons, 1982.
>
> *Canadian Business and Economics: A Guide to Sources of Information*. Ottawa: Canadian Library Association, 1975.
>
> *A Business Information Guidebook*. Oscar Fiqueroa and Charles Winkler. New York: AMACOM, 1980.
>
> *Directory of Business and Finance Services*, 7th ed. New York: Special Libraries Association, 1976.
>
> *Materials and Methods for Business Research*. Linda J. Piele, John C. Tyson, and Michael B. Sheffey. New York: Neal-Schuman, 1980.

In addition to the general guides to information listed above, many other reference sources are helpful to the researcher. *Libraries issue brochures or other printed guides to material on their own shelves and in other libraries.*

The Card Catalog

The card catalog (also referred to as the public catalog) of a library lists the material available at that particular library. Some libraries have a dictionary catalog where all authors, titles, and subjects are interfiled in one alphabet. Other libraries use divided catalogs where authors, titles, and subjects are alphabetized in two or three separate catalogs.

Catalogs in libraries may not be in card form at all. Libraries that have automated their cataloging records produce their catalog in book form or in a microformat, such as microfilm or microfiche. Some libraries now have fully automated systems with computer terminals for users to access the cataloging records.

Libraries usually catalog books by either the Dewey decimal system or the Library of Congress system. The Library of Congress system provides for a larger number of divisions and is more suitable for large libraries than is the Dewey system.

The major classifications of the Dewey system are:

000—General Works
100—Philosophy
200—Religion
300—Social Sciences—Sociology
400—Philology
500—Pure Science
600—Useful Arts—Applied Science
700—Fine Arts—Recreation
800—Literature
900—History

The major classifications of the Library of Congress system are:

A—General Works
B—Philosophy and Religion
C—History—Auxiliary Sciences
D—Universal and Old World History
E,F—America
G—Geography, Anthropology, Folklore, Manners and Customs, Sports and Games
H—Social Sciences
J—Political Science
K—Law
L—Education
M—Music
N—Fine Arts
P—Language and Literature
Q—Science
R—Medicine
S—Agriculture
T—Technology
U—Military Science
V—Naval Science
Z—Bibliography and Library Science

WIthin the categories of both the Library of Congress system and the Dewey system, further divisions allow for more specific classifications. For example, books on business subjects are numbered 650–659 in the Dewey system and classified under HF (Commerce, General) in the Library of Congress system.

Knowing the subject classification of a topic you are investigating helps you find useful books simply by browsing the shelves of a library with open stacks. Although this method is admittedly casual and disorganized, it may provide information that you would not find otherwise. In addition, the books you discover, through their own bibliographies, indicate other relevant books.

Books shown in a card catalog in any one library obviously do not make up the same list of books as those shown in the *Cumulative* (International) *Book Index, Books in Print,* or similar indexes. Even the largest library is not likely to own all published books in any area or all that are currently available from publishers. In addition, the card catalog may show books, particularly old ones, that are not listed in the indexes. (These indexes and other sources are discussed in a following section of this chapter.)

If you are unsure of the most applicable subject heading, you may wish to refer to

> *Library of Congress Subject Headings,* 8th ed. Washington: U.S. Government Printing Office, 1975.

The typical catalog card lists the classification number, author's name, title of publication, place of publication, date of publication, pagination, notes on special features such as bibliographies, and sometimes comments on contents of the book. The card also shows the other subject headings under which the book is filed; these headings serve as a guide to the most important content areas of the book.

Guides to Books

A major guide to books, whether or not they are in your particular library, is

> *Cumulative Book Index: A World List of Books in the English Language.* New York: H. W. Wilson, 1928–present.

Before 1928, this index was referred to as the *United States Catalog.* The *Cumulative Book Index* includes books published in the English language all over the world, recorded by author, title, and subject. Monthly indexes are bound into annual indexes.

Two guides to books on a particular topic are

> *Subject Guide to Books in Print.* New York: R. R. Bowker, 1957–present. This index, which also classifies books according to author and title, includes books currently available for purchase in the United States.

> *Canadian Books in Print.* Toronto: University of Toronto Press, 1975–present.

Encyclopedias

Although the scope of your research must include much more than information given in encyclopedias, they are a good place to begin because they give an overall view of a particular field or of supplementary aspects of a report project. Encyclopedias are useful for general background information. They may also include a list of supplementary reading materials for your particular topic.

In addition to general encyclopedias, a number of specialized ones are available for coverage of specialized areas of knowledge. Some of these are the *Encyclopedia of Social Science, Exporter's Encyclopedia, Accountant's Encyclopedia,* and *Encyclopedia of Banking and Finance.*

Dictionaries

Dictionaries remain an important library source. In addition to general dictionaries, there are many specialized ones, just as there are specialized encyclopedias. In fact, the terms are overlapping; one book described as an encyclopedia may be similar to another described as a specialized dictionary. Some books use *both dictionary and encyclopedia* in their titles.

Specialized business dictionaries are especially good for definitions of business terms. Two such books are listed below:

> *Concise Dictionary of Business Terminology.* Albert Giordana. Englewood Cliffs, N.J.: Prentice-Hall, 1981
> *Dictionary of Business and Management.* Jerry Rosenberg. New York: John Wiley and Sons, 1978.

Handbooks and Manuals

Handbooks are similar to specialized encyclopedias and dictionaries, although they tend to be more complete than dictionaries. A business handbook presents a condensed picture of an entire field of business.

These handbooks, which are frequently revised in order to retain only accurate information, include the *Handbook of Auditing Methods, Industrial Accountant's Handbook, Handbook of Business Administration, Handbook of Insurance, Management Handbook, Marketing Handbook, Sales Executives' Handbook,* and *Real Estate Handbook.* Many other manuals and handbooks are also available, such as the *United States Postal Manual* and the *United States Government Organizations Manual.*

Yearbooks and Almanacs

Yearbooks, in addition to those that supplement encyclopedias, are published by various countries, trades, and professions. One important one is the *Statistical Abstract of the United States.*

Almanacs, such as the widely available *World Almanac and Book of Facts,* contain a wealth of information on many subjects.

Canada Yearbook, published by Statistics, Canada, provides economic data about many facets of Canadian business and government, as does *The Corpus Almanac of Canada.*

Biographical Directories

Biographical directories provide information about leaders or well-known persons, living or dead. The best known is *Who's Who in America,* which summarizes the lives of living Americans who have achieved prominence in any field. A similar reference source is *Canadian Who's Who.* Specialized directories include *Who's Who in Insurance, Who's Who in Education,* and *American Men of Science,* as well as many other occupational fields. In addition to those that are specialized according to profession, directories are also specialized according to sections of the U.S.; for example, *Who's Who in the South and Southwest.*

Who's Who in Finance and Industry is a directory of prominent business people. Another directory is *Who's Who in Finance and Industry (Canada). Poor's Register of Corporations, Directors and Executives* is a similar publication but more exclusive. *The Biography Index,* published quarterly, is a guide to biographical material in books and magazines.

Business Services

Business services provide business information of many kinds. Some of these publications and service organizations are listed and described below.

Moody's Manuals summarize data for all major companies. These manuals include five divisions: Industrials, Banks and Finance, Public Utilities, Transportation, and Municipals and Government. Although much of the information is planned for the investor or for investors' advisors, much is meaningful to the business researcher in areas other than investments.

These manuals are issued annually in bound volumes. They include the history of each company, a description of products or services, locations of home office and most important plants, a list of officers and directors, and financial data. An indexed loose-leaf service, issued every two weeks, keeps the service up to date.

Corporation Records, a loose-leaf publication of financial information and other facts about the corporations described, is published by Standard and Poor's Corporation.

Federal Taxes, published by Prentice-Hall, Inc., reprints U.S. government tax laws, rulings, and decisions, along with editorial comments.

Another well-known service organization is Predicasts, Inc., which provides various services in addition to forecasts and market data, classified by company, product, and service.

Guides to Periodicals and Pamphlets

Periodicals, sometimes referred to as magazines, journals, or serials, are often more helpful than books for use in business research. Thousands of publications in all fields cover every subject imaginable. Like information from books, data found in periodicals must be evaluated for appropriateness, reliability, and current value. Various indexes serve as a guide to the contents of general and specialized periodicals. Some of these indexes are listed and described below.

The *Reader's Guide to Periodical Literature* is a guide to articles in approximately 160 general-interest magazines such as *Reader's Digest, Good Housekeeping, Time, Newsweek, Business Week, Fortune, Atlantic Monthly*, and *Harper's*.

The *Business Periodicals Index* is a guide to articles in business, industrial, and trade magazines, including English language periodicals printed in Canada and elsewhere outside the United States. This index is one of the most useful in business research, particularly for the practical phases of business operations and for solutions to problems in specific industries. The *Business Periodicals Index* dates from 1958; its predecessor, the *Industrial Arts Index*, began publication in 1913. About 165 titles are indexed, including periodicals in accounting, advertising, banking, and all other major business and economic fields. The *Canadian Business Periodicals Index* has been published since 1975.

The *Applied Science and Technology Index* is a guide to articles in about 200 English language publications on scientific and technological subjects.

The Public Affairs Information Service Bulletin, referred to as PAIS, is an index, classified by subject, of periodicals, government publications, and pamphlets, especially in the area of economics and social conditions, public administration, and international affairs.

The F & S Index of Corporations and Industries (Predicasts, 1962 to date) covers company, product, and industry information from more than 750 financial publications, business-oriented newspapers, trade magazines, and special reports. The European edition and the International edition provide similar information about countries outside the United States, including U.S. company operations abroad.

Other indexes of interest are the *Engineering Index, Education Index, Business Education Index, Biological and Agriculture Index, New York Times Index, Wall Street Journal Index*, and the index to *Fortune*. In addition, most large newspapers are indexed in guides available in local and regional libraries.

Even with the numerous indexes to periodicals, including others not listed here, some periodicals are not indexed, particularly regional and highly specialized ones. To find lists of publications in all fields, consult the *Ayer Directory of Publications, Standard Periodical Directory, Union List of Serials in Libraries of the United States and Canada, Ulrich's International Periodical Directory*, and other directories of publications.

Trade Directories

Trade directories are lists of organizations giving products, officers, and other data. Guides to these directories include *Trade Directories of the World and Guide to American Directories*.

Thomas' Register of American Manufacturers and *Thomas' Register Catalog File* list thousands of products, with the names of companies that manufacture each product. *Encyclopedia of Associations*, the *Million Dollar Directory*, and *Middle Market Directory* are other publications that include specific information about various companies and associations.

Government Publications

Information of many kinds, especially statistical information, is collected and published by the federal government. Some of the sources already described, including PAIS, serve as guides to government publications.

United States Government Publications: Monthly Catalog lists publications issued by all branches of the federal government. This catalog serves as a guide to government publications in the same way that the public catalog (card catalog) serves as a guide to other publications.

Other sources that serve as guides to locating government publications are *American Statistics Index* (Congressional Service); *Guide to U.S. Government Publications* by John L. Androit; *Statistical Services of the United States Government* (U.S. Bureau of the Budget); and *Statistics Sources*, published by Gale Research Company, which also includes sources of statistics other than government publications.

Sources mentioned in the preceding paragraph serve as *guides* to statistical information, not compilations of statistical information. Other government publications serve as direct sources of statistical information, particularly data gathered by the Bureau of the Census. One of the best known is *Statistical Abstract of the United States*, which is issued annually. Supplements to the *Statistical Abstract* include the *County and City Data Book, Historical Statistics of the United States*, and the *Congressional District Data Book*.

Other information provided by the Bureau of the Census is derived from the periodic censuses that have been taken by the United States government. The first Census of Population was taken in 1790, and it has been repeated at ten-year intervals since that time. The Bureau of the Census also conducts special censuses other than at the ten-year intervals and publishes the data collected. These include censuses of housing, agriculture, manufacturers, transportation, mineral industries, governments, retail trade, wholesale trade, and selected services.

Some governmental periodicals are issued monthly. These include *Survey of Current Business*, which provides data on income, expenditures, production, prices, and many other economic elements; the *Federal Reserve Bulletin*, which emphasizes financial data; *Monthly Labor Review*, with data on employment, wages, consumer price indexes, and other similar areas; and *Business Conditions Digest*, an aid to forecasters and business analysts.

Many other government periodicals include various other types of information. Regularly released statistical information is also available from state and local governments.

Miscellaneous Reference Sources

"A Survey of Consumer Buying Power" is published annually by *Sales Management* magazine. This survey reports estimates of figures on population, income, sales, and buying power of cities, counties, and standard metropolitan statistical areas. The *Editor and Publisher Market Guide* provides similar statistics.

Doctoral dissertations can be located through *American Doctoral Dissertations*, 1955/56 to present, and *Dissertation Abstracts International*, 1938 to present. *American Doctoral Dissertations* intends to provide a complete listing of all doctoral dissertations accepted by American and Canadian universities. Abstracts of the dissertations describe the dissertations and provide an overview of each, in addition to providing information on how to obtain a copy of the dissertation. Both of these guides are published by Xerox University Microfilms, Ann Arbor, Michigan.

Another guide to business and economic research is *Index of Publications of Bureaus of Business and Economic Research*, 1957 to present, which is published by the Associated University Bureaus of Business and Economic Research.

Commercial Computerized Databases

Databases now provide valuable information for various research purposes. Many of the printed sources mentioned previously in this chapter also are available as databases to be accessed by computers, including microcomputers. These databases, along with other computer functions and capabilities, are discussed in Chapter 13. The following list is shown here because databases provide an important source of secondary information, with additional advantages of speed and ease of access.

The list of databases is far from complete, but it provides an illustration of the many and various kinds of information that are available as commercial computerized databases.

BCN (Business Computer Network, P.O. Box 36, 1000 College View Drive, Riverton, Wyoming 82510.)

BCN is a subscription service that provides access to a large number of different databases. The user is saved the time and trouble of signing up for each individual system. Among the databases that can be accessed through BCN are the following:

- BRS (Bibliographical Retrieval Service): Contains 70 separate databases covering education, engineering, medicine, behavioral sciences, and business-related subjects.
- DIALOG: Contains over 300 databases covering corporations, engineering and technology, law, medicine, agriculture, education, and physical sciences.
- INFOMAGIC: Contains statistical information relating to securities, economics, banking, finance, aviation, and energy.

- SDC (System Development Corporation): Contains 80 databases of bibliographic information on energy, chemistry, environmental concerns, law, patents, and political science.
- Securities Data Company: Contains reports on bonds, common and preferred stocks, and future issues.

COMPUSERVE (Computer Information Service, 5000 Arlington Centre Blvd., P.O. Box 20212, Columbus, Ohio 43220)

This service contains a wide variety of features for all users. There are on-line editions of some newspapers, a database (Business Information Wire) surveying 111 daily Canadian newspapers, CIS Business Wire—containing 40–50 news releases from major companies—and Standard & Poor's General Information File—containing data on 3000 major publicly-held companies.

ITT DIALCOM (1109 Spring St., Silver Spring, Maryland 20910)

ITT DIALCOM is primarily an electronic mail system for sending and receiving letters, memorandums, and other documents. However, users can also access databases, including:
- UPI News: Contains news wire information and other governmental and broadcast information.
- BNA: Contains databases on business accounting and tax news and the text of the *Security and Exchange Commission News Digest*.
  Other features to this service include access to a phone message system, an on-line text processor, and the *Official Airline Guide*.

NEWSNET (945 Haverford Rd., Bryn Mawr, Pennsylvania 19010)

NEWSNET involves a business-oriented newsletter covering a variety of fields like advertising, gas and oil, government, and technology. It can be searched and read on-line.

DOW JONES NEWS/RETRIEVAL (P.O. Box 300, Princeton, New Jersey 08540)

This is a collection of databases that covers securities and economic news. Users can access current news, current stock prices, historical stock performance, corporate earnings estimations, economic surveys, and excerpts from the *Wall Street Journal* and *Wall Street Week*, among others. Also available on-line is the *Academic American Encyclopedia*.

THE SOURCE (1616 Anderson Rd., McLean, Virginia 22102)

THE SOURCE contains a large number of personal, recreational, and business databases, as well as other computer functions. It is a menu-driven system by which the user can progressively narrow the search for desired information. Some of the relevant databases include Comodity News Service, on-line abstracts from *Forbes, Futurist, Venture, Harvard Business Review*, and others.

This survey has not exhausted all of the thousands of databases available. It should illustrate that there is a wealth of information on almost any conceivable topic waiting to be accessed. A useful source for more information about accessing and using commercial databases is Alfred Glossbrenner's *The Complete Handbook of Personal Computer Communication* (New York: St. Martin's Press), 1983.

A LIBRARY SEARCH PROCEDURE

Suppose that you are authorized to complete the research and to prepare the report for the question presented in Chapter 7, "Should Countrywide Insurance Company provide career apparel for women employees?" Subcategories for this problem are given in Chapter 7, with details for the scope of the problem.

You realize that you cannot depend upon library research alone if the study is to be beneficial for a special purpose and for the particular company for which the research is planned. The researcher obtained the opinions of workers, who would wear the career apparel, by the use of interviews and a questionnaire. She obtained further information by studying professional and sales literature of companies that could supply the apparel and by talking with sales representatives.

Before she took these steps, however, she looked at library sources. Why? No book or magazine article will completely answer her question. She looked at library sources first—as you should do in a project of this type—in order to determine the experience of other companies with career apparel and to learn, if possible, decisions other persons had made in answer to the following questions.

Has this policy been conducive to better employee morale? Have employees objected to this policy or refused to wear the apparel? Does the employing company ordinarily furnish this clothing without charge, or at a reduced charge, or is the employee expected to pay the entire cost? Do policies differ from organization to organization?

Because employees now pay for their clothes, is it reasonable that they should pay at least part of the cost? Can apparel be planned so that the appearance of each employee can be varied from day to day by the use of a change of blouse or accessories? How can each employee be prevented from being identical in appearance to every other employee? Can apparel be purchased that will be flattering to workers of all ages and sizes?

The steps that follow are not necessarily in the order that you should take them. Much could depend upon the arrangement of your particular library, the availability of other libraries in your city, and information given with library sources that lead to additional reference sources.

You realize that it is unlikely that a book will be written on career apparel and that your most likely source of information is in magazines, especially business journals. You are not completely sure, however, that there are no books on career apparel; as you know, books are written on many thousands of subjects. You look in the card catalog and find nothing. You realize, though, that such a book may be in print but not available at this particular library.

A specialized business library, part of the public library system, is located in the downtown area of your city. The main city library contains thousands of books, and many are shelved in the several branches. Several other college and business libraries are within easy driving distance.

You decide to look in *Books in Print* or the *Cumulative Book Index* to determine whether a book has been written about career apparel. You look in one or both of these indexes and find nothing, as you expected. Now what? You consider that your problem is a business area that is a facet of office management, personnel management, and general business management.

You look in *Books in Print* or the *Cumulative Book Index* to find the name of the most recent books in these areas. Then you check the card catalog and find that your library owns these books. You write down the call number. (Some researchers use a pocket tape recorder for call numbers.) If you have access to shelved books, that is, if your library has open stacks, you may find not only the books that you have noted but others on the same or similar subjects, shelved in the same general location. By checking the indexes of these books you find references to your particular subject.

Your next step is to go to the *Business Periodicals Index* to find articles that apply. You check the *Public Affairs Information Service* to find any other relevant articles. You check local newspaper indexes and the *New York Times Index* and the *Wall Street Journal Index* as guides to newspaper articles.

Because you wish to be completely thorough in your approach, you also look in the *Reader's Guide to Periodical Literature*, although you realize that your subject is a specialized business one and not likely to be reported in magazines of general interest. Some business articles, however, do appear in general magazines that are not listed in the *Business Periodicals Index*. Then you ask the reference librarian to suggest additional sources that you may have overlooked.

You read all of the material you find, even though very little may go into the final report. You will have a better overview of the problem after a general reading in the field, even though none of the material seems to describe your own particular problem. Your report, however, will be more convincing if you include a section on how career apparel has worked for other companies.

EVALUATING LIBRARY MATERIALS

Evaluating secondary sources, as well as primary ones, is one of the most important but most difficult phases of the report process.

Evaluation of data is discussed in more detail in Chapter 10, where emphasis is upon the analysis of data you have previously collected. Some evaluation must be done, however, as you proceed with library research. If you do not evaluate during the collection process, you will gather much information that is irrelevant or redundant, perhaps some that is misleading.

Wide research is probably the most dependable method of determining that information gathered through library research is valid and reliable. If, for example, you rely only upon one or a few sources, you do not have complete assurance that you have not by chance picked writers who, for one reason or another, give incomplete or inaccurate information.

Be careful to use only recent sources, except for general, mostly unchanging principles, or for historical research. If you believe that the information that you are seeking fits into the category for which you can use standard, older works (sometimes referred to as classics), be sure to compare these sources with later ones to make certain that the included information is still current.

Books, magazine articles, or any other form of written or spoken communication may be reliable or unreliable, truthful or untruthful. The quality of secondary data depends, to a great extent, upon the author and the publisher, although incorrect information can and does come from the best-known authorities and publishing houses. Reference librarians can be most helpful in your search for data, as well as in giving advice about the probable accuracy of various sources.

Observing the date, edition, and publisher of a book is helpful, but far from being completely descriptive. Learning the identity of the author, as far as his or her position or experience relates to the subject of the book, helps somewhat in judging approach and reliability.

Book reviews, which are usually published within a year after the book appears, aid in overall evaluation of the publication. They also provide information about areas of content. Reviewers often disagree; as in every other instance, the researcher must take final responsibility for judging the value of secondary information.

Book Review Digest is a general index that locates and gives excerpts from book reviews found in popular American, Canadian, and British periodicals.

Business Periodicals Index, beginning with 1972, locates book reviews found in English language periodicals in accounting, banking, communications, and various other business subjects. To locate reviews in the annual volumes from 1972 to 1974, look under the heading "Book Reviews—Single Books." Beginning in 1975, a separate listing of book reviews is found at the back of each volume.

Technical Book Review Index, beginning in 1941, locates and gives excerpts from book reviews published in journals in all fields of science and technology. Other indexes help to locate book reviews of publications in various fields; these indexes include *Education Index*, *New York Times Book Review*, and *Social Science Index*.

GATHERING AND RECORDING NOTES

If you know exactly the information you are looking for, such as a figure on housing or income as reported by the Bureau of the Census, note-taking consists only of writing down the desired information and the complete bibliographical reference, including page numbers. A similar situation exists when you set out to find what one well-known person has written in a particular book or journal article about a particular topic.

Most library research is more complicated and comprehensive than that described above, even if the major portion of your data will come from primary sources. If much or all of the data will come from secondary sources, as can occur in many kinds of business and professional reports, the research procedure requires planning and organization in order to be effective and efficient. Notes must be classified in some usable, accurate, and time-saving arrangement before they are analyzed and presented in final report form.

Perhaps you think that you need no further instruction in the simple matter of taking notes. Nevertheless, time spent in organization during the library search process can save much more time in the final organizing, evaluating, and writing processes.

First, decide which information is to be recorded. This decision will be guided by the specific purpose of your research project. As discussed in Chapter 7, a specifically worded, exactly limited statement of purpose serves as a guide to all steps of the research and reporting procedure.

The statement of purpose may be separated into categories, also illustrated in Chapter 7. The outline of the overall report may be based on such a subdivided statement of purpose. Although the overall organization of the final report may differ from the tentative plan, preparing a tentative outline helps in the data-gathering process by preventing the collection of irrelevant or repetitive information.

Another question is how to record passages from published material. Should it be recorded verbatim, paraphrased, or outlined? Verbatim passages must be clearly distinguished as such. Although you think you will remember exact quotes, when compiling and presenting information it is only too easy to show such passages as paraphrased wording or to omit credit when you consider information to be general knowledge.

A well-known system of gathering and recording information utilizes note cards. Photocopying pages from sources to be used decreases the amount of material to be copied on note cards. This method is especially advantageous if much material is to be quoted verbatim.

Note cards showing the source of information, arranged according to the method shown in the style manual you are using as a guide, are an aid when typewriting the final copy. Small cards (3- by 5-inch) are large enough for this purpose. Larger cards are more convenient for recording excerpts from library sources. The smaller cards that contain bibliographical references can be numbered, with the corresponding number shown on the larger card or cards that contain data taken from the particular reference source. Or, instead of a numbering system, a short form of the reference can be used; for example, "Brown, p. 17." Make sure that page numbers are recorded for all information, whether or not the passage is to be exactly quoted.

These information cards should also be keyed to the portion of the report, or the chapter of the book or other work, to which the passage most specifically applies. Such a system aids in sorting the data and in planning the final organization of the report.

Do not look for authors to support your point of view, and do *not ignore those who disagree with the majority of other writers.* You as a researcher have set out to find the truth, as much as you can possibly do so. At times it is "neater" to include only the authorities who build your case, but to do so is far from being objective.

SUMMARY

Methods of obtaining information include primary and secondary research. The word *secondary* means that the information has already been gathered and recorded by someone else. Much secondary data can be obtained from published sources, but some sources are unpublished. Secondary information can also be found by a search of organizational records. Primary research has *not* been found and recorded by someone else.

Library research should usually be the starting point in the data-gathering process, even if most of the data is to come from primary sources. The competent researcher is familiar with basic reference sources and can find needed information.

Previously prepared bibliographies and basic guides to reference materials should be consulted early in the research process.

Business services publications provide valuable information of many kinds. These publications are available in most large libraries.

The *Business Periodicals Index* is a basic guide to articles that have appeared in specialized business magazines. The *Reader's Guide to Periodical Literature* indexes general-interest magazines. Various other indexes serve as guides to other specialized groups of periodicals.

U.S. government publications, particularly those released by the Bureau of the Census, are valuable sources of statistical information.

Library materials must be evaluated for current usefulness, appropriateness for the particular purpose, reliability, and objectivity. Book reviews, which can be located through various guides and indexes, help somewhat in judging the value of books.

An orderly system of extracting and recording notes helps in all future steps of the report-writing process and increases accuracy, efficiency, and objectivity.

QUESTIONS AND PROBLEMS

1. Prepare a tentative bibliography of at least five recent sources that seem to apply to the problem for which you prepared a report plan. Use the form shown in Chapter 12

2. Prepare an annotated bibliography (see Chapter 12) of five or more recent journal articles on (a) the topic of communication as applied to one of these fields; and (b) recent developments in these fields:

   - accounting
   - business education
   - management of a small business
   - personnel management
   - marketing
   - office management
   - your major field of study, if not listed above
   - word processing
   - computers
   - robots

3. Prepare a list of periodicals that apply especially to your major field of study.

4. Does your school library classify books according to the Dewey decimal system, the Library of Congress system, or both? How does the public library system in your city or town classify books? Write a short memorandum report to your instructor in which you describe the methods of classification in these libraries.

5. Use *Moody's Manuals* or Standard and Poor's *Corporation Records* to find information about a large national corporation. Write a short memorandum to your instructor in which you describe the kinds of information available in the reference source.

6. Examine a recent copy of the *Statistical Abstract*. Determine three topics (from the many) that are included in this reference source. Write a short memo to your instructor listing these topics and including one short bit of information about each, as given in the *Statistical Abstract*. Also specify the library and the location within the library where this reference source is kept.

7. Complete the secondary research of the report you proposed in the report plan assigned in Chapter 7. Write a progress report to your instructor, summarizing your secondary research efforts, problems, and work yet left to do. Ask for your instructor's suggestions.

   See Problems in Appendix B that are based primarily on secondary research, particularly Cases 44, 45, 46, 47, 48, 49, and 50.

Collecting Information Through Primary Research

9

The term *primary* research, as distinguished from *secondary*, includes collection of data by all methods except reading the words of other writers. Usual methods are through observation, experimentation, and surveys of various kinds.

OBSERVATION

Observation, as the term describes a method of research, means the examination of phenomena under real, presently existing conditions. Observation under controlled or manipulated conditions is referred to as *experimentation*. Observation includes both casual and informal observation and planned, carefully recorded and tabulated instances of observed actions or occurrences. The term may also be used to describe a search through company records. Many accounting reports and auditing reports are based on an examination and analysis of financial records. Hence, the method of data collection is observation, although such reports are not usually described as such.

In the research proposed in the report plan illustrated in Chapter 7, the researcher observed present work activities of secretaries at Countrywide Insurance as one of several methods of research used in the study. In another report done for Countrywide Insurance Company, the researcher who studied the advisability of career apparel used casual observation of the present dress of the women employees. The researcher could possibly have used a planned, structured form of observation.

For example, detailed, daily records of the dress of all employees could be used to determine something of their choice of color and style as well as to consider whether career apparel was needed to improve the overall appearance of the employees. This subject would have been a sensitive one if the study had been kept secret from the people being studied. The information to be gained would probably not have been worth the risk of discovery with its subsequent mistrust. If the employees had been informed of the study while it was being done, no doubt their appearance would not have been typical of their usual dress.

The results of information obtained through observation, like that obtained in any other way, can be trustworthy or not, depending upon the care and judgment of the researcher as well as upon many other contributing factors. Comprehensive, carefully planned observational research is more likely to provide dependable results than is the casual and informal notice of conditions and occurrences, although this form of observation should not be overlooked. As in all other forms of research, accurate and complete records should be kept as data are collected. Then the data must be carefully and accurately organized, analyzed, and interpreted.

183
CHAPTER 9
COLLECTING
INFORMATION
THROUGH PRIMARY
RESEARCH

Uses of Observation as a Method of Research

Observation consists of more than "watching." It also includes listening and reading. In addition, the term *unobtrusive measures* is used to refer to indirect methods of observational research, as suggested in the book *Unobtrusive Measures: Nonreactive Research in the Social Sciences.*[1] An example of such research is noting the frequency of replacement of vinyl tile in front of various museum exhibits in order to measure their popularity. Another example is studying the wear and tear of pages of library books in order to measure their use. Another type of such research is analyzing contents of garbage cans and trash barrels in order to estimate such factors as choice of magazines and amount of liquor consumption.

Analyses of nonverbal behavior, as illustrated by C. William Emory, include study of body movements of workers assembling a product, exchanged glances during a discussion, and eyeblink rates as indicators of interest in advertising messages.[2] Such research also includes noticing pupils of the eyes, which expand to indicate interest or acceptance and contract to indicate dislike or displeasure.

1. E. J. Webb, D. T. Campbell, R. D. Schwartz, and L. Sechrest, *Unobtrusive Measure: Nonreactive Research in the Social Sciences* (Chicago: Rand McNally, 1966).
2. C. William Emory, *Business Research Methods* (Homewood, Ill.: Richard D. Irwin, 1976), p. 289.

An analysis of linguistic behavior includes counting the *ah's, oh's, you know's,* and other interrupting or annoying sounds or words that often accompany speech. Extra-linguistic behavior includes other speech characteristics, such as pitch of voice; interaction, such as a tendency to dominate a conversation; speaking rate; and vocabulary and pronunciation peculiarities. The observation of spatial relationships includes aspects such as the study of the arrangement of furniture, crowding in shops or offices, and the personal space maintained between sales representatives and customers.

Advantages and Disadvantages of Observation as a Method of Research

Observation is the only method of obtaining some kinds of information; for example, the study of records, mechanical processes, or actions of animals or young children. Data obtained from the study of group processes are more accurate when observed and recorded by an objective and perceptive researcher than when reported by members of the group itself, as individuals are likely to report group actions based on their own perceptions of the event and upon varying personal relationships. Research through observation, provided that the method is wisely used, is more likely to provide accurate data than personal, mail, or telephone surveys, although information obtained is of a different kind. Observation measures only overt acts; it cannot determine reasons for these acts.

Disadvantages of observation as a method of research are that it is often complicated, time consuming, and expensive. In order to make sure that observed incidents are not isolated events, the researcher must use extreme care in selecting times and sites for research.

For example, suppose a manufacturer of inexpensive toys, displayed on racks in supermarkets, wants to know which family member is most likely to choose the toys—mother, father, or child. Such knowledge could influence advertising, packaging, location of racks, placement on racks, and other decisions. Additional information that could be helpful is the number and kinds of toys chosen. The researcher must consider the time of day, week, month, and year for the study. If, for example, one researcher observed toy racks late at night, results might be quite different from those of another researcher who observed the racks on Saturday afternoons. One more consideration that might affect the results is the location in the city of each supermarket.

Another disadvantage of observation is that the *observer* may influence behavior, especially if the persons being observed are aware of the procedure. Observed behavior, when subjects are aware that they are being studied, is likely to be different from their typical behavior, as illustrated by the well-known Hawthorne effect.[3]

185

CHAPTER 9
COLLECTING
INFORMATION
THROUGH PRIMARY
RESEARCH

EXPERIMENTATION

Experimentation, scientifically done, is reliable and accurate—more so than any other research method. But even experimentation is subject to error. In addition, many business problems are not of the type that lend themselves to the experimental type of research.

In business, as in other areas, the purpose of experimental research is to determine the effect of change under a given set of conditions. The conditions must be carefully constructed so that only one variable is tested at a time. For example, an experiment to determine the effect of career apparel upon employee morale would be difficult to conduct in a completely scientific manner because of the element of human behavior.

Suppose that you want to test the effectiveness of two different sales letters. One is mailed to homeowners in one state, and one is mailed to the homeowners in another state. Depending upon the product, the observed difference in effectiveness of the letters could have a great deal more to do with the choice of states than with the wording of the letter. If you try to sell wind-turned attic ventilators through a letter sent to homeowners in Maine and through another letter sent to homeowners in Alabama, you are adding variables to the one you set out to test—the effectiveness of the differing letters.

If you sell more ventilators to those people in Alabama, you may consider the warmer climate to be a factor—but then you realize that people in Maine really should buy more because they are not so likely to have central air conditioners—and then you consider that people in Alabama need ventilators in order to decrease the cost of electricity. With all these unanswered questions, you cannot be sure that differences in the letter had any effect.

---

3. The Hawthorne effect was discovered as the result of an experiment that was intended to measure the effect of lighting conditions on the output of factory workers. Regardless of what changes were made in lighting, factory output increased. The experimental results seem to illustrate that the increase occurred not because of the lighting changes, but because employees worked harder, knowing they were the object of concerned observation. This study illustrates an important principle of management: *Employees want somebody to pay attention to them.*

This illustration is perhaps a rather extreme example of uncontrolled experimentation. Competent researchers would not attempt an experiment without attempting to control all contributing factors except the one being tested. But, except in scientific laboratories, it is often difficult to control all factors entirely.

The law of the single variable must be followed in every experimental situation: *Vary only one circumstance at a time, and maintain all other circumstances completely unchanged.*

Determine Experimental Design

As with all other forms of research, an experimental study must be carefully planned. Experimentation includes the control and manipulation of the research setting, conditions, and processes in order to obtain the desired information.

Before-After Design Using a Control Group. An experimental research study often involves two or more groups, one of which is the control group. Both groups are measured according to predetermined, specific criteria at the beginning of the experiment; that is, the variable being tested is measured in both groups. Then researchers inject an experimental factor into the experimental group, but not into the control group, and both groups are measured to determine any change that has taken place.

An example of a simple experiment using a control group could be one conducted by a national chain of inns. Suppose, for example, that reservation clerks have not been suggesting to departing guests that they make reservations in another inn in the chain for the following night, although computer reservations are available. In the experiment, inns are randomly assigned to either the experimental group or the control group. Clerks in the experimental group are instructed always to offer to make reservations in another inn, with suggestions to be given in similar ways by all clerks. If reservations greatly increase in the experimental group but not in the control group, a reasonable assumption is that routine suggestions according to a specified procedure have increased subsequent reservations.

Perhaps in this particular situation such an assumption could be made without research, but many experiments are conducted to "prove" less obvious conclusions. In addition, clerks are more likely to be convinced to follow the suggested procedure after learning of the experiment. Another consideration is that routine suggestions may *not* increase reservations, an indication that something is wrong with the procedure or, perhaps, the whole idea.

187
CHAPTER 9
COLLECTING
INFORMATION
THROUGH PRIMARY
RESEARCH

Before-After Design with No Control Group.   An experiment can be conducted without a control group, although such a method is less accurate because there is more likelihood that factors other than the variable being tested have influenced results. In this type of experiment, the chain of inns would simply determine the number of subsequent reservations for a preceding month or other time period, begin the procedure of suggestions from the clerk, and determine the number of subsequent reservations in the following month or comparable time period. By doing so, however, no consideration is given to other factors that may have influenced the outcome. For example, perhaps guests are more susceptible to suggestion in a sunny June than in a dreary March.

Computer Simulation.   A computer can be used to create a simulated environment in which variables are manipulated and analyzed. A researcher can test many more variables than would be feasible in actual research situations. The disadvantage of this method of "research" is that it *is* simulation, not a real-life situation. As techniques improve, research projects now thought unlikely or impossible are likely to be completed by the use of computers. (Computers are used in various other problems of research, as in counting, organizing, comparing, analyzing, and interpreting data.)

Make Sure That an Experiment Is Suitable for Your Particular Research

Although experimental research is highly regarded as the most reliable method of scientific research, it is not suitable for the solution of many problems in business and other social sciences. It is an orderly method of testing, limited to the effects of a single variable on a given set of conditions. If conditions cannot be controlled, results of a research study cannot be accepted as conclusive.

EVALUATION OF SURVEYS USED AS A METHOD OF RESEARCH

Surveys are widely used in obtaining information. They are conducted through personal and telephone interviews and through the use of questionnaires, often sent through the mails.

The survey is open to criticism because it depends completely on verbal responses, and words are inexact. (All other methods of research also have weaknesses.) The respondent, when filling out a questionnaire or talking with a researcher in a personal interview or on the telephone, is likely to provide untrue, incomplete, or inaccurate and misleading information. Even if respondents wish to provide complete and accurate answers, they often do not do so because of inaccurate memories, lack of knowledge and detailed information, tendency to give the expected response, and any number of other reasons.

Influences of all kinds enter into results of interviews and questionnaires, as into all other areas of oral and written communication. People who answer an interviewer's questions are affected by their perceptions of the interviewer, of the situation, and of themselves. Their mood of the moment influences their responses and whether a questionnaire sent through the mail is returned.

Regardless of the interviewer, questionnaire, or topic being investigated, respondents tend to exaggerate incomes, education, social status, and other favorable aspects of their experiences. They tend to minimize unfavorable aspects. These inaccuracies occur even when there is absolutely no possibility that their questionnaires can be identified.

Another weakness of the survey method is that questionnaire design, extremely important in achieving accurate information, is often approached casually and haphazardly. A poor questionnaire or poorly structured interview is almost certain to result in incomplete or incorrect data. Questionnaire construction requires much thought and time. Ideally, a questionnaire is tested with a small group before it is used on a large scale.

Questionnaires and interviews are so widely used, often with poorly designed survey instruments, that respondents do not consider their answers important or do not answer at all. Another factor is that the researcher has no way of being sure that respondents who return questionnaires are representative of the entire population being surveyed. For example, if a member of Congress asks whether or not to introduce a bill, respondents are most likely to be those who will benefit from the proposed law or those who have some special reason for not wanting it. Many people without special interests, who are more likely to make a wise decision, do not take the time to return questionnaires.

If you survey alumni of a school and ask questions about jobs and salaries, those who feel successful are much more likely to return questionnaires, even if their names are not used, than those who feel otherwise. The researcher who attempts to obtain the mean or median salary of such a group would report an average salary higher than the typical salary of all class members.

Even with its many weaknesses and disadvantages, the survey is the only practical way to obtain many kinds of information. It is difficult to determine what people think, know, or believe without asking them. We cannot know their likes and dislikes, their desires, or their intended actions. We cannot gain the benefit of their recommendations without asking for them. In addition, events that have already occurred evidently cannot be observed. They must be described by others in written or spoken words.

Much business research is of necessity done by the use of surveys. Although researchers know that such information will be less than perfectly accurate, a survey wisely planned and conducted can supply information sufficient for effective and efficient management decisions.

189
CHAPTER 9
COLLECTING
INFORMATION
THROUGH PRIMARY
RESEARCH

OBTAINING A REPRESENTATIVE SAMPLE

Unless all members of the entire group are to be surveyed, the assumption must be that those who have been picked to be the respondents are representative of the entire group. Reliability can result only from a representative sample. In research terms, *reliability* is understood to be the assurance that the data are truthful.

To arrive at this truthfulness, surveys must be scientifically administered. In addition, the survey instrument must be *valid*. This word, in research terminology, means that the research instrument measures what it is intended to measure. For example, you cannot find the weight of an object by using a yardstick, nor can you find its length by using a bathroom scale, because a yardstick is not a valid instrument for measuring weight and a scale is not a valid instrument for measuring length. The yardstick is not *reliable* even for measuring length if it expands or shrinks, nor is the scale reliable for measuring weight if it gives varying readings each time an unchanging object is weighed.

An example of data that are not reliable, even though you used a yardstick, are measurements to determine the average height of a group of employees. If you measure three woman and find that their average height is 61 inches, this conclusion seems to indicate that by chance you have chosen a nonrepresentative sample of the total group. (The total group to be studied is known as the population.) What has gone wrong here is that too few employees have been chosen. If the total number of women employees in this organization is 100, certainly you should sample more than three.

If you had measured the height of 25 or 30 women, the obtained average would ordinarily have been fairly close to the average that you would have obtained if you had measured all 100, provided you had used a method of random sampling. However, your average would not be correct, if, for example, you had measured the twenty players on the company basketball teams and had included them in the sample.

When beginning the sampling procedure, the researcher must consider the persons who are to be surveyed, the number, and how to be reasonably assured that those surveyed are representative of the whole group.

A general law of sampling is that a sufficiently large number of items (or opinions, etc.) taken at random from a large group will have the characteristics of the larger group. If the group is small, each item should be examined or each person should be asked for an opinion.

A researcher seeking to improve the sound equipment at Theater Memphis asked for the opinion of all persons who work or have worked with this equipment. In another study about career apparel, each employee was asked for her opinion. Because of the time and expense required for a large-scale survey, however, we cannot economically question each person in a large group. We must limit our questioning to a number that we believe will give reliable results and that will not be extravagant in the use of time and money. Anyway, according to experts in statistics, a well-chosen and adequately large sample is likely to be as reliable as examining the entire group.

Random Sampling

Random sampling is defined as the sampling method by which every item in the population has an equal chance of being chosen. In order to ensure that every individual has the same opportunity to be chosen, the researcher must have a complete list of all items (persons, etc.) in the population.

The old "putting names in a barrel" is a true random sample if you can be sure that the names are thoroughly mixed and that no element other than chance enters into the selection. Remember that random sampling, as it is used in statistics, does not mean *hit or miss* as the word *random* does when used in other instances.

Randomness is most often achieved by the use of a table of random numbers. These tables ordinarily consist of many groups of five-digit numbers. Random numbers can be employed by an systematic method since each of the digits has been selected at random, most likely by a computer. To use these tables, the researcher matches the numbers with previously numbered names or items, taken from a list of the complete group.

Stratified Random Sampling

191

CHAPTER 9
COLLECTING
INFORMATION
THROUGH PRIMARY
RESEARCH

Stratified random sampling is done by conducting a random sample of subgroups within the universe. To sample the opinions of students in your university, you can use subgroups of classes (freshmen, sophomore, etc.), sex, major fields of interest, age, or many other divisions.

Usually the desired number in each division should be the same as the portion of the universe that the group comprises. For example, if you try to find data that apply to the entire student body, and in your school there are twice as many freshmen as there are seniors, include in your sample twice as many freshmen as you do seniors.

Quota Sampling

Quota sampling is similar to stratified random sampling in that sampling is done from subgroups of the entire population. The sample, however, is based on a quota, not on a random selection. For example, if within a student body the freshman class consists of 4,000, the sophomore class of 3,000, the junior class of 2,000, and the senior class of 1,000, the number of students questioned, from a total sample of 100, might be 40, 30, 20, and 10, respectively.

Although this method of sampling is easier to administer, in many cases, results are less likely to be truly representative than in stratified random sampling. As in all sampling, the likelihood of reliability increases as the sample size increases. If quota sampling is used, an attempt should be made to obtain samples from all groups within the subgroups. For example, if you were attempting to obtain a quota of 100 from your senior class of 1,000, results would not be representative if you limited the number in your sample to engineering students.

Systematic Sampling

Systematic sampling is the technique of taking selections at definite and unchanging intervals from a list of the members of the population. If you have a list of all the students in your college, you would do systematic sampling by taking, for example, each fifteenth name on the list.

Although this method is not strictly random sampling, ordinarily the effect will be the same if the sample size is large enough. To ensure an even greater degree of randomness, the researcher could take the first number entirely by chance and proceed through the list using the same number.

Various other sampling methods are described in textbooks and handbooks in statistics. If you have not studied statistics, you should read further into the field of sampling theory before undertaking a research project which makes use of this method of investigation.

Determining Sample Size

Ordinarily, 25 to 30 percent of a large group, based on numbers alone, should provide representative data. At times you will not be able to sample this many because of the time and expense involved. In this case you will need to use some method of determining adequate sample size. A simple method is to split the sample into two or more parts and to compare the results from the various parts. A similarity of results from these parts of the total sample indicates that overall results are likely to be acceptable.

Formulas can be used for checking the adequacy of sample size. These formulas can be applied when you have enough returns to estimate the apparent division of answers. These formulas are given in books on statistics and in books devoted entirely to research.

CONSTRUCTING THE QUESTIONNAIRE

When you plan a questionnaire, your goals are to secure a satisfactory rate of return and complete, objective answers. Another consideration is the ease and accuracy with which results can be tabulated and analyzed.

With the questionnaire, include a convincing explanatory letter, which is usually on a separate sheet but sometimes shown at the top of the printed questionnaire. The most effective way to convince readers to respond is to show them benefits to themselves. Even if there is no immediate benefit, many people will cooperate if you carefully and convincingly explain the purpose of the study and why you need their opinions. To increase returns, do everything possible to make response easy; for example, keep the questionnaire as short as possible, ask for check marks instead of long written replies, and enclose a stamped, addressed envelope.

Write and Arrange Questions Carefully

The construction of the questionnaire, including its physical appearance, will influence the percentage of returns and the value of the answers. Specific principles of questionnaire construction are listed below. In addition, principles of communication you have studied throughout this course are most important as you plan the survey instruments and the cover letter. Clearness, conciseness, the you-attitude, and all the other attributes of effective communication apply to obtaining business information through the use of questionnaires.

193

CHAPTER 9
COLLECTING
INFORMATION
THROUGH PRIMARY
RESEARCH

1. Make the questions easy to understand and concerned with one topic only. Avoid ambiguous wording. For example, the question "Why did you buy your last car?" could lead to the response that the respondent liked the color, the price, or the design. Another respondent might answer that he bought the car because he had wrecked his older one, or because his wife wouldn't let him buy a motorcycle. Avoid broad, relative terms such as *often, a long time*, and *seldom*, unless these terms are specifically defined.
2. Make the questionnaire easy to answer. Providing blanks to be checked facilitates response as well as the researcher's tabulation of the answers.
3. Provide for all likely answers. Although some questions can be answered by a *yes* or a *no*, many are somewhere in between. Provide for categories such as *I don't know*, or *no opinion*, *disagree*, or *strongly disagree*. Allowing for shadings of opinions is much more descriptive and accurate than mere *agree* or *disagree* questions.
4. Ask only for information that can be easily remembered.
5. Keep the questionnaire as short as possible by asking only for needed information.
6. Avoid questions that touch on pride or personal bias, or those that give the effect of prying. Such areas include age, income, morals, and personal habits. A question about education may have a prying effect with persons of limited educational background. Information about age, income status, or education may be necessary in order to accomplish the particular purpose of the report. Even if you need this information, however, you will ordinarily not need the exact age, the exact amount of income, or the exact number of years the person has been in school.

   To encourage response, as well as to facilitate evaluation of the answers, provide ranges from which the respondent may choose to show age and income. For example, you can show age brackets *under 21, 20 to 25*, and set up income brackets in the same way. Age and income brackets can be an important consideration in marketing research when planning products to manufacture or outlets for distribution.

7. Arrange questions in a logical order.
8. If the questionnaire is mailed, enclose a stamped and addressed envelope.
9. Avoid leading questions—those that by their wording suggest an answer.
10. Provide for additional comments, if any, by the respondent by the use of open-ended questions in which comments can be included in the respondent's own words. Although these questions are more difficult to tabulate than answers that are shown by check mark, these comments may be more helpful than all the other answers. In addition, they may encourage respondents to speak freely.

Figure 9-1 is an illustration of a questionnaire sent to furniture manufacturers. In this survey all furniture manufacturers in a particular geographic region were questioned.

The questionnaire itself begins with a short transmittal message. A cover letter on company letterhead, signed by an official of the company, was included with the questionnaire. Such a method is not necessary with all questionnaires. The researcher directed his cover letter to the president or other executive within each organization, some of whom he knew personally. Because the researcher knew that the cover letter might not be passed on to the respondent completing the questionnaire, a note of explanation was included on the first page of the questionnaire itself.

The questionnaire shown in Figure 9-1 illustrates an effective way of handling an approach that is often confusing to respondents, as illustrated in Question 4. The researcher wanted certain bits of information from manufacturers who do not sell scrap materials to employees, based on the assumption that such materials are sold elsewhere. By instructing respondents who answer *Yes* to Question 4 to proceed to page 2, and those who answer *No* to proceed to page 3, confusion is reduced or eliminated.

Arrange Questions in an Appropriate Sequence

The sequence of questions is believed to influence cooperation, interest, and final results. Use special care with opening questions. As in other forms of communication, opening statements are particularly emphatic. If personal questions even slightly threatening to the ego must be included in the survey instrument, they should not be asked first. And, as in instructional material, questions should

Will you help us obtain needed information?

Your answer to the following questions will help us to determine whether to authorize the sale of scrap materials to employees.

This questionnaire is being sent to eighty-six furniture manufacturing companies. Do you want a summary of the findings of this study? _____ Yes _____ No

Will you please return the completed questionnaire so that we will receive it by November 19? We plan to start compiling the data at that time. A stamped, addressed envelope is enclosed.

We shall greatly appreciate your assistance.

1. What is the size of your company measured by number of employees?
   _____ 1-50 _____ 51-200 _____ 201-500 _____ Over 500

2. Does your company sell new raw materials to employees?
   _____ Yes _____ No

3. If your answer is yes, how are raw materials priced?
   _____ Retail   _____ Cost
   _____ Cost Plus   _____ Percent

   _____ Other. Please explain. _____

   _____

4. Does your company sell scrap to employees?
   _____ Yes _____ No
   IF ANSWER IS YES, GO TO PAGE 2.
   IF ANSWER IS NO, GO TO PAGE 3.

Figure 9-1. *Questionnaire combined with cover letter.*

5. Why do you sell scrap to employees?
    _____ Sale of scrap to employees generates goodwill with employees.
    _____ Sale of scrap to employees generates more return than sales to others.
    _____ There is union pressure or contract to sell scrap to employees.
    _____ Other. Explain. _____

    _____

6. What is the average dollar amount of each sale of scrap to employees?
    To $5 $5.01 to $25 $25.01 to $50   Over $50

    _____   _____   _____   _____

Figure 9-1 continued

11. Why do you not sell scrap to employees?

    _____ Sale of scrap to employees may increase scrap production.

    _____ Sale of scrap to employees generates less return than sales to others.

    _____ Other. Explain _____

_____

12. What is the average dollar amount of each sale of scrap other than to employees?

$0	$.01 to $5	$5.01 to $25	$25.01 to $50	Over $50
__	_____	_____	_____	_____

Figure 9-1 continued

move from the simple to the complex. (As much as possible, keep all questions simple.)

Early questions should build reader interest and provide motivation for completing the questionnaire. In some survey situations, questions should proceed from the general to the specific.

Consider the Use of Scaling Techniques

Rating scales measure intensity of feeling; for example, like–dislike, approve–disapprove–indifferent, strongly oppose–oppose–no opinion–favor–strongly favor. Scales are of different lengths. Three-, four-, and five-point scales are widely used. Some scales are even longer.

An example of a five-point scale is given below:

What is your opinion of the following statement?

"If men are drafted, women should also be drafted."

strongly disagree	disagree	no opinion	agree	strongly agree
-2	-1	0	$+1$	$+2$

The five-point scale shown above could be extended to a seven-point scale by inserting another category. For example, the *agree* could be broken into *slightly agree* and *moderately agree*. Such an addition, however, would add little to usable results, perhaps confuse the respondent, and complicate tabulation.

The scale illustrated here is a simple one compared to numerous others that are more complicated and sophisticated. These simpler ones are easier to use and often more practical for most research. If you spend a great deal of time with surveys, however, you should become familiar with the various types of scaling techniques that are beyond the scope of this book. Some of the many reference sources on research methodology are listed in the bibliography of this book.

INTERVIEWING IN PERSON AND BY TELEPHONE

When surveys are conducted through face-to-face or telephone interviews, a form of questionnaire should be drawn up as a guide to the interviewer. Questions should be presented to all respondents in a uniform way, and, as in written questionnaires, wording should be objective and specific. Care should be taken to avoid leading questions or statements, or those that seem to pry. Include necessary information about why you are questioning the reader and how the answers will be used. If you can find a reasonable reader benefit, subtly point it out. And, as in other request letters, a statement of when the completed questionnaire is needed will help to prevent procrastination and a delayed or forgotten return.

Personal interviewing must be limited to a relatively small geographical area unless cost is of no consideration, an unlikely occurrence. Telephone interviewing, although it has other disadvantages, is less expensive and time consuming. All types of interviewing must be carefully planned and conducted, and responses must be recorded carefully and completely.

199

CHAPTER 9
COLLECTING
INFORMATION
THROUGH PRIMARY
RESEARCH

Personal Interviews

As compared with questionnaires sent through the mail, personal interviewing provides some of the advantages of oral communication over written communication: immediate feedback, messages sent through the various means of nonverbal communication, and the ability of the communicator to explain further when the respondent doesn't understand the question. Human errors enter into the interview process, however, through all the many ways that communication goes astray. In addition, the respondent may consider the questions an invasion of privacy. The reaction of the respondent to the interviewer is reflected in the information being supplied. Also, because the interviewer interprets responses, these interpretations may be less than completely exact.

Interviews, especially when they are given to many respondents, are ordinarily limited to specific, factual data that the respondent is likely to remember. All interviews should be given according to the same plan of procedure. Questions should be asked in the same sequence and in exactly the same words, explanations should be given in the same way, and the other details of all the interviews should be the same. Because of the varying reactions of the persons being interviewed, procedures cannot be exactly planned in advance, but an effort should be made for all interviewers to proceed in the same way.

In addition to interviews limited to factual information, *depth* interviews are unstructured and informal conversations. These interviews must be done by competent, highly skilled researchers. Psychologists often use this type of approach.

Telephone Interviews

Interviewing by telephone is quicker and less expensive than personal interviews. Random sampling can be used in selecting respondents to be called, provided the population is limited to individuals with listed telephone numbers. Because of the number of people with no available numbers and because some persons whose numbers are listed are never reached, the selection is not truly random.

Many people object to answering questions during telephone interviewing. The telephone is frequently used for sales promotion, often after remarks such as "If you can answer this question . . ." Because of this approach, listeners are often in no mood to respond to serious efforts to obtain information. Some people consider all telephone calls, except for reasons that are of some benefit to themselves, as an intrusion on their time and an invasion of their privacy. Because of these attitudes, they refuse to cooperate, or, if they do so, are likely to give inaccurate or incomplete answers.

Telephone interviewing, in spite of its weaknesses, may be desirable in many instances. If so, the interviewer should use the same care and courtesy as in personal interviews. As in all surveys, explanation of the purpose and benefits of the survey will help to obtain respondent cooperation.

SUMMARY

Methods of primary research are observation, experimentation, and surveys. Surveys employ the use of mail questionnaires and formal and information interviews; some interviews are conducted by the use of questionnaires or a pre-planned series of questions asked by the researcher. Surveys are conducted by telephone and person-to-person.

Although observation as a method of research is often complicated, time consuming, and expensive, it is the only method of obtaining some kinds of information.

Experimentation, scientifically and objectively done, is reliable and accurate, but even experimentation is subject to human error.

Surveys are widely used in research of many kinds. Their frequent use results in a disadvantage because many respondents are tired of completing questionnaires or do not believe that they are important.

Reliability in sampling can result only with a representative sample. A general rule of sampling is that a sufficiently large number of items or opinions taken at random from a large group will have the characteristics of the entire group.

Random sampling is defined as a sampling method by which every item in the population has an equal chance of being chosen. Stratified random sampling is done by conducting a random sampling of subgroups within the population.

Questionnaires must be constructed with care in order to encourage response, to obtain the needed information, and to facilitate tabulation of results.

All methods of research are subject to the many kinds of human error that result in miscommunication.

201
CHAPTER 9
COLLECTING
INFORMATION
THROUGH PRIMARY
RESEARCH

QUESTIONS AND PROBLEMS

1. Explain the difference between observation and experimentation as methods of research.

2. Describe the difference between the before-after design using a control group and the before-after design with no control group.

3. Can you think of a question that should be answered in your employing organization or in your school or university? Which method or methods of research should be used in finding the answer to this question? Explain.

4. Explain how the following questions (not from the same questionnaire) violate the principles of effective questionnaire construction.

   a. Don't you feel that you earn more interest at United Bank?
   b. Do you bathe daily?
   c. How much do you earn each month?
   d. How much have your grocery bills increased since 1976?
   e. How do you manage when your weekly check won't cover your expenses?
   f. Do you approve of Bill Number 213 now being considered in the Senate? Yes_____ No_____
   g. Do you leave work early? Always_____ Occasionally_____ Sometimes_____ Never_____

5. Find a questionnaire that was sent through the mail or administered during an interview. Analyze this questionnaire according to the ten suggestions included in the section of this chapter entitled "Write and Arrange Questions Carefully." As your instructor directs, present your analysis in a memorandum addressed to your instructor, or be prepared to show the question-

naire to the class and to comment on its construction. (An opaque projector is an aid to showing the questionnaire to the entire class.)

6. Prepare a questionnaire to use in the research project for which you prepared a report plan (Chapter 7). If an opaque projector is available for your use, show your questionnaire to the class. Ask for comments and suggestions for improvement. You may also wish to provide copies and ask students to complete the questionnaire.

7. Write a cover letter to accompany the questionnaire prepared in answer to Question 6.

8. Prepare a questionnaire to use in solving one of the research problems suggested in Chapter 7 or for a similar problem. Assume the type of respondents and any other necessary or helpful details. Show your questionnaire to the class (or ask students to fill it out) and ask for suggestions for improvement.

Interpreting and Organizing the Data

10

203

After the data have been collected, they must be evaluated and organized for presentation in the most appropriate form. A systematic method of collecting and recording information greatly simplifies the remaining steps of the research process.

These processes of evaluating and organizing, as well as preceding and following steps in research and report writing, do not fall into discrete divisions. We do not abruptly begin evaluating material only after the collection process is completed. Ideally, data are evaluated and organized as much as possible as they are collected. We must use judgment in the collection process or we will find that we have gathered great quantities of material, much of it meaningless or irrelevant.

At some point we must stop formally adding to the collection of data and begin the finishing steps of the research process. If additional information or opinions come to light, however, we cannot afford to ignore them merely to end the search, although at times we may be tempted to do so.

DETERMINING THE MEANING OF DATA

In report preparation and presentation, we must be extremely careful to be completely and thoroughly objective. Objectivity from the standpoint of phrasing and word choice is discussed in Chapter 5. But true objectivity consists of far more than nonemotional writing: it is an attitude that must be kept constantly in mind throughout the entire report process. Objectivity, or the lack of it, influences the complete and nonbiased search for information and the organizing, evaluating, and reporting portions of the overall project.

Because we are human, predetermined beliefs or desires tend to affect everything we do, including research and reporting duties. With awareness of this natural tendency, however, we can work toward honest and objective interpretations.

CAUSES OF ERROR IN INTERPRETATION

In order to interpret data correctly and impartially and to evaluate it for accuracy, the researcher must keep in mind the several ways in which communication errors can occur. These errors of evaluation and interpretation are similar to those that occur in the overall process of communication.

Varying Perceptions

A major source of miscommunication of all kinds is differing perceptions in the minds of the sender and receiver of a message. This barrier to communication occurs in research and report writing in various ways. Researchers tend to discount secondary and primary sources that disagree with their outlook about the subject. In turn, readers of reports are influenced by their attitudes and previously formed opinions (their perception) to the extent that they do not understand or believe reported results.

Our emotions affect the perception of words and situations and thus the ensuing words and actions. Even if we could be in perfect control of all emotions, perception would be limited because we cannot perfectly see, hear, taste, feel, or smell. As you look out your window, you cannot see and your mind cannot recognize all the minute details of what is before your eyes. You cannot listen to several conversations at the same time, although all are within hearing distance. You do not see everything that happens in a football game, a play, or an automobile accident.

Your perception and remembrance of a happening or a situation will differ from that of other people around you. This difference has been illustrated many times by varying descriptions of an accident, an individual involved in a crime, or even of a television program. We have all seen pictures that can be interpreted two completely different ways depending upon how we perceive them.

We always perceive a portion of reality, not the whole. Our

perceptions differ because of individual experiences. In addition, we generalize and assume that the whole truth is the part of the situation we recognize and understand.

Another cause of inaccurate perception is that we tend to see what we expect to see, or what we want to see. Research studies in education have indicated that teachers tend to perceive students as they expect them to be, based on information shown by school records of intelligence test scores and behavior patterns. Because the teacher expects certain children to be slow, or to have problems with the expected classroom behavior, they are treated as such; and they will often live up to the teacher's expectations, even if their school records are incorrect.

Perception influences understanding and interpretation. Being subject to all the fallacies of human intelligence, the researcher often foresees results before beginning a research study, although these anticipated findings may be incorrect. Although no researcher is absolutely and completely objective, by being forewarned of the likelihood of incorrect interpretation, we are likely to be less biased and more impartial.

Misinterpretation Through Inferences and Value Judgments

Facts are verifiable by direct observation. An inference is an assumption, or "an educated guess," based on known facts. A value judgment is a subjective evaluation based on an individual's particular way of looking at the world.

One illustration of facts, inferences, and value judgments, attributed to Irving Lee when he was a professor at Northwestern University, is based on the statement, "There are seeds in this apple." Is this statement a factual one, or is it an inference? Or perhaps a statement of judgment? You will be making a logical assumption, or inference, when you say that there are seeds in the apple until you cut the apple open and see the seeds. Your value judgment about the apple could be one or all of these: "This is a good apple." "This apple is sour." "I don't like apples." "This apple is pretty." "This is an inferior apple."

For a discussion of inferences and value judgments (longer than can be included in this textbook), see Chapter 3, "The Language of Reports," in *Language in Thought and Action*, by S. I. Hayakawa. Hayakawa uses the term "reports" instead of the word "facts." He states:

> Reports adhere to the following rules: first, they are *capable of verification*; second, they *exclude*, as far as possible, *inferences and judgments*.

An inference, as we shall use the term, is *a statement about the unknown made on the basis of the known.*

By judgments, we shall mean *all expressions of the writer's approval or disapproval of the occurrences, persons, or objects he is describing.*[1]

Now let's apply Hayakawa's definitions to illustrations of our own. Suppose you say, "A magnolia tree is in bloom in Overton Park—I saw it on the way to work." Is this a report or an inference? If you are not sure that it is a magnolia tree, it is an inference. Suppose you say, "I saw a tree covered with white blossoms, as I drove by Overton Park on my way to work." Perhaps the tree is really a magnolia; inferences can be correct as well as incorrect. Suppose you say, "The blossoms have a sickening sweet smell." This statement is a value judgment.

Inferences are based upon matters that seem to be correct, based upon what one has observed. For example, a person who has never seen a magnolia tree looks at a tree blooming in Overton Park in Memphis and reaches the conclusion that it is a magnolia tree based upon these known facts: Overton Park is in Memphis, Tennessee, but only a few miles from the state of Mississippi. Mississippi is known as the Magnolia State. One variety of magnolia has white blossoms and blooms in late spring and early summer. It is now May; the tree has white blossoms. The assumption that the observed tree is a magnolia is a reasonable inference, but it may be absolutely incorrect. Several other kinds of trees having white blossoms bloom in Memphis and in Mississippi in spring and early summer.

Suppose that you are tailgating and run into the back of a truck ahead of you. This occurrence, unfortunately, is a fact; when you tell others about it, it is a report—as long as you do not embellish it. The driver stops and comes toward you. His face is red, he is frowning, and his fists are clenched. You infer that he is angry, but you can't really be sure—maybe he looks like that all the time! You say (to yourself), "Truckers are nasty, mean people." This is a value judgment.

We cannot live or work without making inferences. Value judgments also will continue to be part of our lives—if we have a system of values, to say nothing of attitudes and opinions of our own. We should not try to eliminate inferences and value judgments, only to recognize them in our own minds and in the communication of others. We cannot limit our conversation to our actual observed experiences; we must make inferences in order to survive. Inferences

1. S. I. Hayakawa, *Language in Thought and Action* (New York: Harcourt, Brace & World, 1939), pp. 38, 41, 42.

and value judgments, however, are a source of human miscommunication because we confuse them. We interpret facts in the light of our limited experiences or nonobjective mind and arrive at inferences that are far from accurate. Then we accept these inferences as facts and communicate them as if they were facts.

Report conclusions and recommendations are often, if not usually, based on inferences. They must be. But the inferences must be based on facts.

Because evaluation and interpretation are mental processes, the ability to evaluate and interpret is closely related to mental capacity. This ability is improved by knowledge gained through experience and by specific and accurate information about the problem being studied. Most of all, critical ability is strengthened by the recognition that we are likely to think and act on the basis of what we believe and feel—that is, upon our emotions, instead of upon verifiable facts or upon reasonable inferences based upon verifiable and observable facts.

A basic cause of error is that of twisting the facts to obtain definite and specific conclusions, especially preconceived ones. Although we should not hedge with an abundance of indefinite terms such as *it seems*, *possibly*, and *perhaps* when conclusions or recommendations are based on inferences, these inferences should be clearly understood.

Most decisions of all kinds must be based at least partly upon inferences. And, being human, we will continue to make decisions based only on value judgments—as perhaps we should. The greatest danger lies in letting our value judgments, which can easily become prejudice and bias, close our minds to the truth, or at least to the search for truth. The gag saying "Don't bother me with facts; my mind is already made up" is a wise commentary, unfortunately, on the usual problem-solving approach.

In summary, errors in communication occur because our attitudes, opinions, and emotions influence our interpretation of events, as well as the interpretation of words and other symbols. Poor communication also occurs because of our lack of ability to handle words sanely and skillfully. Many of these errors are basically due to faulty perception.

Failure to Discriminate

We tend to interpret two events as if they were identical or to think in terms of stereotypes. The job we are now doing is not exactly the same as the one we did last year or even last week. Our co-workers are not the same as those we worked with in another organization.

The employees we supervise are different from one another and will no doubt require different types of instruction and motivation. An application letter sent to one corporation should not be exactly like one sent to a differing organization. You are not the same person that you were ten years ago, last year, or even last week. The report you submit cannot tell everything you know about the subject; how can you be sure that you have chosen wisely the material to abstract?

We tend to see similarities instead of differences. We may communicate and react in terms of categories, generalizations, and stereotypes, when we should be looking for uniqueness. Although we do and should see similarities and use them for generalizing, categorizing, and arriving at conclusions, we should keep in mind that events are not truly identical and that events have unlimited characteristics.

The statement that an event has unlimited characteristics could be restated as "The statement is never the whole story." Can you tell everything about anything? Could you describe yesterday in complete detail, including all the elements of your environment? Could you completely describe the past hour or the past minute? Could you tell all there is to know about the pencil you hold in your hand or the view from your window?

We fail to discriminate when we do not choose the most fitting things to communicate about a particular event or situation, or when we do not adequately judge the most important points of the communication of others. The missing elements are perhaps the most important ones.

From a practical standpoint, we must classify and generalize, for to do otherwise would result only in chaos. We should realize, however, that all classifications will not be completely and perfectly accurate in every respect.

This lack of complete certainty even under the best of conditions is no justification for accepting hasty conclusions. That this lack of perfect classification and judgment is inevitable is only the more reason that we use extreme care in our limited observation so as to present the "true facts" as much as is humanly possible.

We fail to discriminate in our judgment of events as we analyze research findings, as well as in other situations. We tend to think in stereotypes and make false analogies, although in order to reach conclusions of any kind we must generalize. We should avoid making hurried and incomplete generalizations based on insufficient evidence.

For example, a researcher studying the question of career apparel found an article in a business periodical in which the author wrote that the career apparel had been enthusiastically accepted by an organization in New York. If this researcher had assumed that because of this acceptance the apparel was sure to be welcome in her own company, this assumption would not necessarily be correct. The researcher would have failed to discriminate between conditions from one organization to the next as well as from one part of the country to another. If she had justified the cost savings from the fact that the employees invest in a credit union, hence they must have a desire to spend little money on clothing, then the comparison would be even more unconvincing.

Interpreting events as to cause-and-effect relationships may lead to erroneous interpretation. The observed effect may not be a result of a previous event; it may be that another event occurred previously and, by chance, the observed effect followed. Or, as often happens, a result can be attributable to more than one cause, perhaps to many.

Trying to Validate a Point of View

A true report does not present evidence to support a particular point of view, but presents all relevant and obtainable evidence on both sides of a question and interprets the meaning of these findings. Although some so-called reports are planned to present "a case" for a decision or an emotional appeal to action, this kind of writing is not a real report as discussed here.

As you arrange information into report form, remember that most courses of action have disadvantages as well as advantages. Your work will be unconvincing if it lists only advantages—unless you have encountered a rare situation in which disadvantages are so minor that they are not worth mentioning.

Believing That Definite Conclusions Are Essential

You cannot expect to reach definite conclusions at the end of all research studies. (If you *never* come to reasonable conclusions, perhaps you will be reassigned to other work.)

It is far better to say "we still don't know . . ." than to guess at conclusions. In some instances, explanations are necessary, and sometimes the reader may be told that two or more courses of action are likely to be beneficial—or that maybe it does not make any difference, after all.

Cause-Effect Confusion

When one event precedes another in time, the first is assumed to be the cause of the second. Because a rooster crows each morning before sunrise, perhaps he thinks that his crowing causes the sun to rise. After you have had a rather nasty day, you read your horoscope in the newspaper, and find that you were supposed to have a nasty day, and assume that your destiny was already fixed. (If you had read your horoscope in the morning, your bad day could have resulted from a self-fulfilling prophecy.) You walk under a ladder and, on that morning, miss your bus. The superstition itself probably resulted from just such an occurrence, but walking under the ladder did not cause you to miss the bus unless you took a long time in doing it. Yet causes and effects are presented in reports in just this way.

We cannot always determine whether a noted cause brings about an observed effect. Such a question might be the topic of another research study.

Arguing in Circles

An example of arguing in circles is:

> *Fortune teller to client*: "You'll be famous if you live long enough."
> *Client*: "What will I be famous for?"
> *Fortune teller*: "For having lived so long."[2]

In this type of reasoning, what is stated as a conclusion is only a restatement of the original assumption.

Monroe C. Beardsley, in the book *Thinking Straight*, uses this illustration.

> I am sure that none of our really responsible citizens are opposed to the City Council's plan to build a gigantic new municipal sports stadium over the Pennsylvania railroad tracks. Obviously the health of our citizens is a prime consideration, which any responsible citizen supports, and sports mean health. If we attract a major franchise, it will also bring money to the city. I realize that some will question my argument, and cite the names of various people who have expressed disagreement with the City Council's position, but that does not refute my claim. For if they are opposed to so excellent a plan, then by the same token they must be lacking in responsibility.[3]

Beardsley comments on this passage:

> One way of exposing the circularity is to take the first statement, "no

2. Stuart Chase, *Guides to Straight Thinking* (New York: Harper and Row, 1956), pp. 37–38.
3. Monroe C. Beardsley, *Thinking Straight*, 3rd ed. (Englewood Cliffs, N.J.: Prentice-Hall, 1966), p. 86.

responsible citizens are opposed to the plan," as the conclusion. This is supported by a rather shaky syllogism, but let that pass. The speaker seems to be aware that further support would not be amiss, and so he tries a second approach: suppose, he says, that someone is cited as opposed to the plan; since they are opposed, it follows that they are not responsible. . . .

The word "really" in the very first sentence should put us on guard. Not that it is always a sign that a question is being begged, but when a writer or speaker qualifies a general statement with "essentially," or "genuinely," or "truly," or "at heart," there is a strong possibility that something odd is taking place.[4]

Circular arguments, like many of the arguments used in reports, as well as tenets we live by, just don't make sense.

Self-Evident Truths

If the truths were self-evident, you wouldn't need to write a report. Arguing through a self-evident truth is similar to arguing in circles except that the writer or speaker doesn't bother even to reach the conclusion that was originally the assumption. Arguing through self-evident truths is taking for granted that there is no disagreement or using intimidation to keep people from disagreeing (it doesn't work), as in "All thinking people agree . . ."

Other phrases that indicate the use of self-evident truths are these:

> It is common knowledge . . .
> As everybody knows . . .
> You can't deny that . . .
> It goes without saying . . .
> Any child knows . . .
> As known to every schoolboy . . .
> As every intelligent person knows . . .

Black-or-White Thinking

We tend to try to fit all answers into definite categories of black or white, yes or no, right or wrong. Such arrangements simplify thought processes (or dispense with them entirely), but they are not

---

4. Beardsley, pp. 86–87.

always accurate. Not all situations or ideas can be neatly categorized into such opposing divisions. Some areas must remain in varying shades of gray.

Basing Conclusions on Insufficient Data

Basing conclusions on insufficient evidence is an example of over-generalization. Although we will never be able to find absolutely complete information about anything, the cliché "jumping to conclusions" applies to errors in judgment and communication of all kinds.

Basing Conclusions on Noncomparable Data

If the present salaries of World War II veterans should be compared to those of Viet Nam veterans, the conclusion would be meaningless if it is based on the belief that veterans of a "real" war or a "patriotic" war are more dependable and able to earn a higher salary. Various factors have been left out of consideration. For example, World War II veterans are far older; they have had more time to reach their peak earning power. Or, if the same comparison is made later, it would be meaningless to state that Viet Nam veterans are increasing their earning power and World War II veterans are now earning less. The reason for the declining "average" salaries of the World War II veterans is that many have retired.

Basing Decisions on Personalities Instead of on Facts

Even nationally known "authorities" in a field can be wrong, although they are more likely to be correct than people outside the field. Communication error that results from an unquestioning belief in the opinions of other people, especially of well-known people, is described as "wise men can't be wrong." (Wise men and women know that they *can* be wrong.)

Although we should respect authoritative opinions, we should prefer facts if they are available. (We still have the problem of determining exactly what are the facts.) Another guide to valid reasoning is this: "If ten thousand persons say a foolish thing, it is still a foolish thing." If an opinion poll had been taken a number of centuries ago as to whether or not the world is round, overwhelming votes for flatness would have been considered conclusive. At that time, the idea that the world could be other than flat was contrary to ordinary common sense. (It is sad to accept the fact that common sense is sometimes misleading.)

Another self-evident truth and an example of basing conclusions on opinions is this: "Fifty million Frenchmen can't be wrong." They can, as can fifty million Americans. If we are conducting a survey, however, of ten thousand or fifty million respondents, their opinions must be carefully recorded, analyzed, and reported. If the purpose of the research is to report opinions, that purpose has been accomplished even if those opinions are wrong. (You are not required to agree with the opinions.)

CONCLUSIONS, BASED ON FINDINGS; RECOMMENDATIONS, BASED ON CONCLUSIONS

The statement that *conclusions are based on findings* may seem obvious to you, but the principle is often violated. If you make recommendations "off-the-top-of-your-head," why should you gather and interpret data?

Valid conclusions are based on complete and relevant data interpreted objectively in the light of the problem to be solved. Recommendations, or "what to do about it," are based on conclusions about what the data mean.

Ordinarily, the conclusions and recommendation section is the last section of a formal, analytical report arranged in the inductive order, as described in Chapter 3, or the conclusions and recommendations may be presented in two separate sections. In some long and comprehensive reports, each major section is treated as a separate report in that the writer arrives at conclusions based on findings presented in each section. In this arrangement, the effect is of several short reports combined into one. This arrangement is especially appropriate when a major research study is completed by several researchers, as often happens, but it can also be used in a long report prepared by one person. The entire report concludes with a summarizing section.

To repeat and emphasize: *Report evidence, interpret this evidence, and make recommendations. Be sure your conclusions, usually in a report section with recommendations, are based on clearly stated evidence.*

INTERPRETING WITH STATISTICS

Simple statistical terms include the following:

- *Mean*. The arithmetic average obtained by totaling the figures and dividing by the number of cases.

- *Median*. The midpoint, or middle value, in a series of values arranged in the order of magnitude.
- *Mode*. The most frequently occurring value. (The mean, median, and mode are all measures of central tendency.)
- *Range*. The spread between the lowest and the highest values in a series.
- *Standard deviation*. A measure of dispersion in a frequency distribution—a measure of the spread of the normal distribution.

This book cannot cover the study of statistics in a great deal of detail. A basic knowledge of statistics, however, is essential to the analysis of research findings and to their interpretation.

For an interesting and enlightening discussion of how figures can mislead, either intentionally or otherwise, read the book that has now become a classic in its field, *How to Lie with Statistics*, by Darrell Huff.[5] He illustrates how the term *average* can mean almost anything to nothing, depending on how it is used. In other words, the *mean* may be meaningless.

For example, a statement can be literally true that the average income of a college graduating class of a particular year is $97,000 a year, but it is very unlikely that this figure is the typical income. A few extremely high figures distort the mean. Suppose that the graduating class consisted of only ten members. Each of nine of these persons is now earning about $15,000 annually, and the tenth one earns $835,000—thus the arithmetic mean is $97,000. But if the figure is used to mean that each of the members is a potential customer for a yacht, you have misinterpreted the data.

ORGANIZING THE DATA

Organization of the data, like evaluation, should not be left for a certain time period in the research and reporting process. Throughout the study, organization should be kept in mind as you decide what to present where. In addition, the tentative table of contents or outline prepared at the beginning of the study helps the final process of arranging ideas and prevents the investigation from going astray. During your final process of putting the report into written form, you are likely to see needed changes in the preliminary plan. After the first draft of the manuscript, you are likely to make further changes.

5. Darrell Huff, *How to Lie with Statistics* (New York: W. W. Norton & Co., 1954).

A well-known method of organizing material is the card method. Write on separate cards or slips of paper the headings of the report that seem to describe major divisions. Include those shown on the tentative table of contents, as well as additional ones that now occur to you. Be careful not to express the same idea in different words.

After you have noted on the cards the possible divisions, arrange them in the order that seems to be natural, whether or not this sequence agrees with the original outline. As you study and sort the cards, you often find a new arrangement that will best express your ideas.

This method of organization also helps you to see weaknesses and omissions in the presentation, as well as redundancy. A logical sequence of topics of the complete report is essential whether the plan of arrangement is to be the direct (deductive) or indirect (inductive) order, as discussed in Chapter 2. If you are using the traditional and formal report arrangement arranged in the inductive order, you already know you will begin with the introduction, whatever you choose to call it, follow with findings and analyses, and end with conclusions and recommendations, as discussed in Chapters 2 and 7.

Even though you already have this arrangement in mind, you must decide upon the arrangement of topics in the middle section of the report, as well as the arrangement of information in the introductory and concluding sections. The contents of the various preliminary and supplementary portions of the formal report, such as the synopsis, offer few problems in organization. You can safely leave their exact planning until the report itself is completed.

The organization process, when planning reports to be arranged in the direct order, requires the same careful attention to an orderly sequence of ideas. In the direct order, as you remember, you place recommendations at the beginning of the report, as well as any necessary explanatory conclusions, and follow with supporting information.

Choose Appropriate Report Divisions

When the report consists of comparisons, consider the use of the criteria of the comparisons as major divisions instead of the items to be compared. For example, if you are examining three possible locations according to cost of land, labor availability, and access to market, these criteria, instead of the locations, are likely to make for a more easily comprehensible format.

You may find instances in which, for one reason or another,

such reports are best arranged by possible locations, not by the criteria for these choices. Like other problems in communication, use your own judgment based on an individual approach.

The choice of divisions of a report is extremely important to the logical progression of thought and to readability. Spend all the time necessary to achieve the best possible arrangement.

Word Headings Carefully

Each heading describes the contents of the subdivisions that come under it. "A," "B," "C," and "D" headings combine to equal the heading above them. Phrase headings carefully, not only from the standpoint of readability and clarity but also to check the flow of thought. Even when the actual text of a report is arranged in a logical sequence, inexact headings are confusing and misleading.

A discussion of headings is presented in Chapter 4, where emphasis is given to the format of various methods of arranging headings. Perhaps you will wish to reread this particular section as you prepare a longer report than those discussed earlier. Because the precise use of headings is helpful in reports of all lengths and levels of formality, they were discussed early in the text along with the discussion of short, informal reports.

Headings in the text of the report must agree exactly with headings shown in the table of contents.

SUMMARY

In the evaluation of data, as well as in report presentation, we must do everything possible to be completely and thoroughly objective. We must use unbiased evaluation and interpretation in order to present findings in a matter-of-fact way and to show how these findings lead to the stated conclusions and recommendations.

Errors in data interpretation are the same as those that occur in all forms of communication, including inaccurate perception, confusing facts with inferences and value judgments, hasty generalizations, and basing decisions on predetermined beliefs.

Statistical measures are useful in the interpretation of data, although statistics can be used in confusing and misleading ways.

The report writer should carefully consider the organization of the report into appropriate divisions. Headings should describe the material that comes under them. Headings in the text of the report should agree exactly with those in the table of contents.

QUESTIONS AND PROBLEMS

1. More than one overall plan of organization is possible and acceptable for most reports. As discussed in this chapter, a study of three possible sites for a new factory could be presented with major report divisions about each site, or by the arrangement, often preferable, of major criteria by which the sites are judged. As you consider the following report situations, because of limited information you have no way of knowing the best possible arrangement. By assuming reasonable details, however, you can list major categories into which findings could be organized. Describe these categories in the form of major headings of the report.

   a. You have interviewed a representative group of citizens about their opinions of the overall quality of your city government.
   b. You have obtained personnel managers' opinions about the preparation of effective employment resumes.
   c. You have interviewed office managers about the importance of attractively arranged and typewritten business letters and how these letters can be prepared.
   d. You have compared two possible employers in order to determine where you want to apply for a job.
   e. You compare two competing brands of equipment with which you are familiar.
   f. You report on the fringe benefits offered by your employing organization or another organization with which you are familiar.
   g. You question recent graduates of the educational institution that you attended in order to find their opinions of improvements that should be made in the educational program. Assume that this study is limited to students in your major field.
   h. You try to determine how a small real estate company can increase profits.

2. As you did in problem 1, above, determine major report divisions of problems listed in question 1, Chapter 7.

3. If you prepared a tentative table of contents for a major report, as directed in problem 4, Chapter 7, recheck your table of contents at this time. Do you now see ways in which its organization can be improved? Make necessary changes. Also recheck the wording of your headings according to instructions in this chapter and in Chapter 4.

4. You learn that the average family income of your home town, which has a population of 1,500, is $42,000. You know that many of the residents are eligible for food stamps. If you accept both

these descriptions as being correct, explain the apparent discrepancy.

5. Discuss possible errors in interpretation in the following situations:

   a. A researcher finds that engineering graduates of a particular university start at higher salaries than liberal arts graduates and concludes that the engineering school is more efficient than liberal arts departments.

   b. A textbook is described as being superior to a book of poetry because of a far greater number of sales.

   c. A study shows that the writing ability of the average college student is inferior to the writing ability of the average college student of 1915.

   d. A senator reports that the majority of letters he has received supports his bill to increase the salary of postal workers.

   e. You survey alumni of your university to find their present earnings. You receive a 30 percent response to your questionnaire. You find the mean and median earnings of the respondents and report that graduates of your university far exceed the national average of college graduates in earning ability.

   f. A newly appointed woman executive does a miserable job and is replaced. You conclude that women cannot bear the stress of executive responsibility.

   g. A university liberalizes its drop policy so that students can now drop a course at any time before final examinations. The grade-point average increases. You reason that because students now have a less stressful semester, they are able to relax and make better grades.

   h. Magazines sometimes use mailing lists of other magazines to solicit subscriptions. *True Confessions* purchased a mailing list from *Atlantic*. No subscriptions were sold. Sales personnel concluded that direct mail doesn't work.

   i. You learn that more freshmen than seniors drop out of college. You conclude that freshman courses are more difficult than senior courses.

   j. You find that early-stage collection letters bring in more payments, on the average, than late-stage letters. You reason that people who have already received three or four collection letters are tired of them and that you should wait at least three months before sending any letters at all. (Besides, it would save a lot of trouble.)

   k. You report that a statement is unquestionably true because Dr. Brown, who is an M.D. and a Ph.D., agrees with you.

l. You conclude that the cost of a proposed office building is outrageous; it is smaller than the old building, constructed in 1960, and costs four times as much.

m. A newspaper reports that younger married women who have full-time employment are more affluent than older married women who are employed full time. The evidence is that 45 percent of women within the age bracket of 25–39 have household help, while only 20 percent of the women within the age bracket of 40–55 have household help.

n. The newspaper surveys a group of husbands and wives who do not have household help. All husbands and wives are employed full time outside the home. Wives report an average work week of 70 hours, including household duties. Husbands report an average work week of 50 hours. The researcher concludes that men are not able to devote as much time as their wives to housework because of the responsibilities of their career; this assumption is supported by the fact that the men earn approximately 40 percent more, on the average, than the amount earned by their wives.

Interpreting with Graphic Aids

11

Graphic aids are used in both written and oral reports to emphasize important factors and to show trends and relationships. The terms *chart* and *graph* often are used interchangeably. In this chapter, *chart* refers to any form of graphic illustration other than a table.

PURPOSES AND ADVANTAGES OF GRAPHIC AIDS

Graphic aids, if wisely planned and attractively presented, bring out relationships that could be easily overlooked by the reader. A well-planned chart can present and analyze important points that would require many pages to explain and discuss. In addition, attractive graphic aids increase readability of a report merely from the stand-point of format and appearance. As discussed in previous chapters, mechanical aids to readability—white space, listings, subheadings, tables of content, and fairly short paragraphs—help the reader to understand important meanings and to obtain a summary of the overall report, even when it is read hastily. Well-planned graphic aids accomplish the same purposes.

Some reports consist mostly of tables, charts, and other graphic aids, with supporting text to explain and comment on the graphics. These simplified reports may be useful for information material prepared for the general public. They also serve as executive summaries for readers who do not want or need supporting details. For business reports prepared to serve as a basis for decision making, a complete form is preferred, with supporting evidence to justify conclusions and recommendations. In some situations, the same report may be prepared in summary form and in complete form.

Tables present numerical data in tabular form. Charts are used to show relationships, trends, and approximate values.

Tables, not charts, should be chosen for the presentation of numerous figures, particularly if the reader is interested in exact amounts. *Approximations, trends*, and *relationships are best shown on a chart of some kind* A chart can be considered a pictorial representation of data.

Some kinds of information should be shown in more than one way in the same report. For example, the reader may need exact numbers shown in a table in addition to approximate figures used to show trends on accompanying charts. A detailed table can serve as the basis for many charts, which are used to illustrate, interpret, and emphasize various aspects of information shown in the table.

PLACEMENT OF GRAPHIC AIDS

Ordinarily, a chart, table, or other graphic aid should be placed within the text of a report as near as possible to the portion of text that it is used to illustrate or explain. If the graphic is not closely related to the material being discussed, it should be placed in an appendix. Tables and charts, like other supplementary material, should also be placed in an appendix if they cannot be considered as an essential part of the report itself.

Extremely long tables or other kinds of material should be placed as appendices even if they cannot be considered supplemental. The reader is referred to these appendices as relevant material is discussed.

The most desirable placement of graphic aids is sometimes difficult to achieve either in typewritten or printed material. At times a table is too long to fit on the page where it is discussed. Dividing the table would be worse than placing it on a following page. If you are using both sides of the paper, as in a printed book, an illustration can often be placed on a page facing the page on which it is discussed. In addition, sometimes the size of a chart or other illustration can be reduced photographically so that it will fit on a page, but it should remain easily readable. This process, however, could consume more time than the ideal placement would be worth.

Long tables placed in appendices may have short summary tables placed in the text of the report. These short summary tables are known as *spot* or *spotlight* tables. Other short tables, not based on a longer one, can also be placed in this way. They are woven into the discussion, as illustrated below:

```
Sales in August, 1983 ....................... $117,267

Sales in August, 1984 .......................  121,219

Sales in August, 1985 .......................  192,719
```

This simple arrangement, like a listing of other kinds of information or questions, adds emphasis and aids immediate comprehension of the displayed data. This table is in effect part of the discussion. Tables as short and simple as the one shown need not be labeled and numbered unless the omission would result in confusion or inconsistency with other illustrations throughout the report.

All graphic aids, although often longer and more formal than the preceding table, should be part of the discussion in that they directly relate to the point being discussed. Anything that stops the reader's flow of thought, such as an unrelated illustration or inconvenient placement, is distracting and undesirable.

At times the discussion of a chart or other graphic aid may extend through several pages. When this occurs, the illustration should be near the beginning of the discussion.

DISCUSSION OF GRAPHIC AIDS WITHIN TEXT OF REPORT

Introduce a graphic aid before presenting it, and, preferably, follow it with a few lines of discussion. It is important to remember that the complete report should be related through discussion, with illustrations used to emphasize and interpret. Minor details may be shown in illustrations without related discussion.

In introductory remarks to the graphic aid, point out highlights of the information it shows. By identifying items of major importance, as shown on the table or chart, you are able to refer subordinately to the illustration:

```
The greatest increase in sales occurred in District
I (72 percent) and the smallest in District 7 (17
percent), as shown in Table III.
```

Although the table should be referred to, do not build introductory sentences around the fact that certain tables or charts follow, and that the reader should look at them. Instead, emphasize important elements of information that are shown in following tables or graphs, which are referred to subordinately.

IDENTIFICATION OF GRAPHIC AIDS WITHIN TEXT OF REPORT

Use identifying titles and numbers on all illustrations throughout the report with the exception of minor tables or listings that can be considered a part of the text itself, as discussed previously.

Labeling and Numbering

Traditionally, tables are not grouped with other forms of illustrations but are numbered separately throughout the report with Roman numerals: Table I, Table II, and so on. Charts are shown with Arabic numerals: Chart 1, Chart 2, and so on. This traditional method of numbering is being replaced by some writers and organizations with the word *Figure*, which may be used to refer to all kinds of illustrations, and with consecutive numbering throughout. Another variation is to use the word *Table* for tables, numbered consecutively throughout the report with Roman numerals, and to use the word *Figure*, numbered consecutively throughout the report with Arabic numerals, for all illustrations except tables.

Writing Appropriate Titles

Like subheadings in a report and titles of all works, titles of tables and other graphic aids should concisely but accurately describe the data presented in the illustration. Titles of tables are usually placed above the table, shown in larger type than material in the table itself. In typewritten work, use solid capitals with no underscore. Titles of charts or figures are usually placed at the bottom of the illustration, shown in regular type. Titles of charts and other illustrations can also be placed at the top.

Citing the Source

If tables, charts, or other illustrations are prepared by the report writer, they are considered primary. This fact may be shown thus: *Source: Primary*. It is also acceptable, and more usual, merely to omit the source note for primary data. Credit must be given for material taken from another source; for example, "Source: *U. S. News and World Report*, May 15, 1981, p. 34." These source notes are usually placed one double space below a chart or table, but at times they may be placed underneath the title.

FORMAT OF TABLES

Tables are necessary for the presentation of exact, detailed information. They often serve as a basis for additional graphic aids, often in the form of charts of various kinds used to illustrate specific groups of figures shown as part of the total data displayed in the table.

The format of a simple table is shown in Figure 11-1.

Figure 11-2 shows an example of a ruled table.

TABLE I

AVERAGE ANNUAL PAY (ANNUAL PAYROLL DIVIDED BY
AVERAGE EMPLOYMENT) OF SELECTED STATES
1978

State	Average Annual Pay
Alaska	$20,487
California	12,891
Florida	10,613
Massachusetts	11,711
New York	13,427
Texas	11,911

Source: U.S. Department of Labor

Figure 11-1. *Illustration of content and format of simple table.*

Table 25

Employment Responsibilities of Total Group of 565
Certified Professional Secretaries for Editing
and Revising Writing of Other Persons

Frequency	Number	Percent
Regularly or Often	391	69.2
Occasionally	128	22.7
Never	46	8.1

Source: Primary

Figure 11-2. *Short ruled table.*

FORMAT OF CHARTS

A basic consideration in the construction of charts of all kinds is that they be kept simple. Charts that are complexly designed in an attempt to convey many kinds of information are counterproductive because they are harder to understand than carefully chosen words. Several simple charts that clearly show limited quantities of data are preferable to one complicated, hard-to-read illustration.

The types of charts (graphs) most frequently used are the *bar*, *line*, and *pie*, with numerous variations of the bar and line. Vertical bar charts are also referred to as *column charts*, or *column graphs*, and pie charts are also referred to as *circle*, or *segment*, charts or graphs. In addition, types of charts can be combined; for example, a line chart is often imposed on a vertical bar chart, as shown later in this chapter in Figure 11-13.

Simple Bar Charts

Simple bar charts, both horizontal and vertical, compare quantities. The length or height of the bars indicates quantity. All bars should be the same width. As discussed later in the chapter, varying the width of the bars results in distortion of data, at least to the hasty or casual observer. Spaces between the bars should also be equal. (A vertical bar graph with no spaces between the columns is referred to as a *histogram*). A horizontal bar chart is shown in Figure 11-3.

The quantitative axis should begin at zero unless to do so would make the chart too large. "Cutting off the bottom" is an error that sometimes occurs in chart making. When the amounts to be shown are relatively large in value, you may find it necessary to break the scale somewhere between zero and the lowest value. This

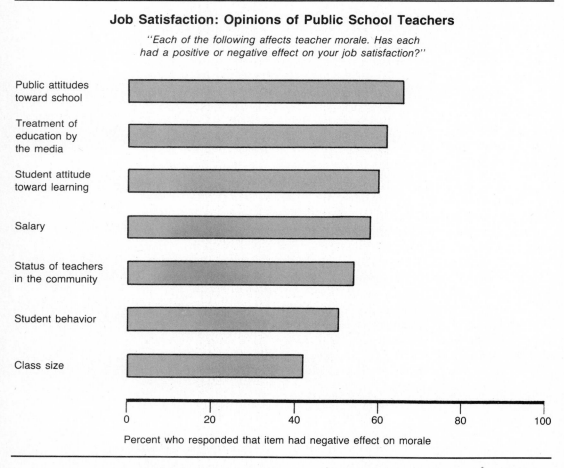

Figure 11-3. Horizontal Bar Chart. (Source: U. S. Department of Education)

break should be indicated to the reader by broken lines between zero and the first value shown.

A bar chart with vertical columns is shown in Figure 11-4. This chart is also referred to as a column chart.

Bilateral Bar Charts

A bilateral bar chart shows increases and decreases from a central point of reference. Bilateral bar charts are especially useful to show changes in percentages, but they may also be used for any series of data that contains negative quantities. Figure 11-5 shows the percentage loss in salary for full-time teachers in higher education.

Bilateral bar charts may be designed with horizontal bars as well as vertical bars, as illustrated in Figure 11-6. A variation shown on this chart is the 40 percent decrease in total education majors, shown in the large column with lighter shading placed under the individual horizontal bars.

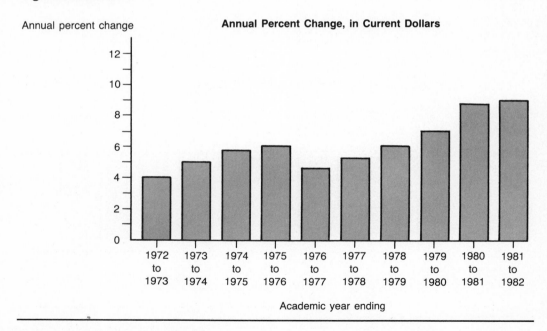

Annual Percent Change in Average Salaries of Full-Time Instructional Faculty in Higher Education

Figure 11-4. Vertical bar chart. (Source: U. S. Department of Education)

Multiple Bar and Subdivided Bar Charts

Variations of the simple bar chart, in addition to bilateral bar charts, include multiple bars and subdivided bars, with variations and combinations of each. A subdivided bar chart is shown in Figure 11-7.

A multiple bar chart is shown in Figure 11-8.

Charts of all kinds, but particularly bar charts, can be varied in numerous ways. Your main purpose in designing charts chould be to choose the arrangement that will vividly, yet simply, compare the relationships you wish to emphasize.

A variation of a horizontal bar chart is shown in Figure 11-9. This design is similar to the usual bilateral bar chart in that bars extend right or left from a central point of reference. The values shown, however, are not truly plus or minus values, but "Professional, managerial, and nonretail sales" and "Other."

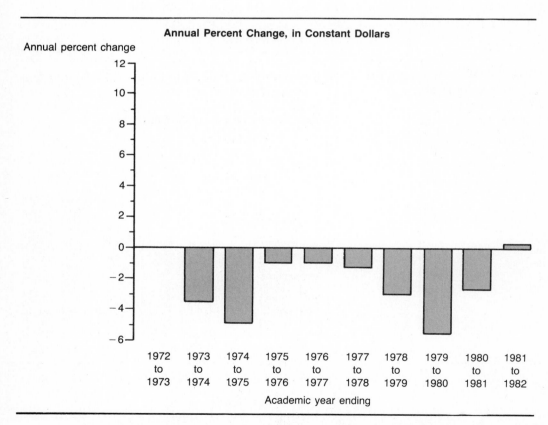

Figure 11-5. Bilateral Bar Chart, Vertical Columns. (Source: U. S. Department of Education)

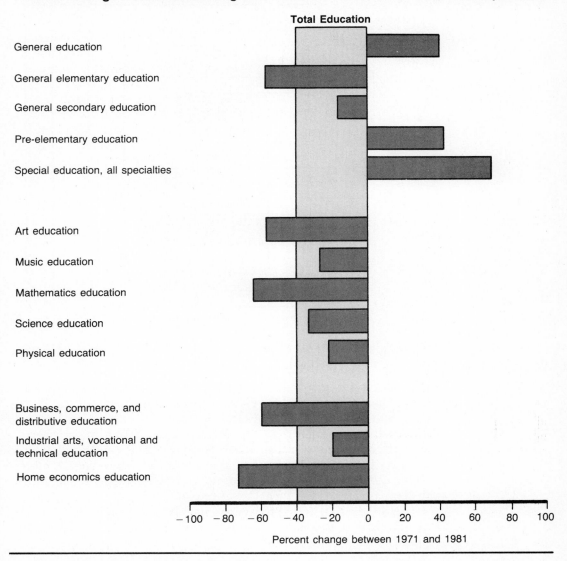

Percent Change in Bachelor's Degrees Conferred in Selected Education Specialties

Total Education

General education

General elementary education

General secondary education

Pre-elementary education

Special education, all specialties

Art education

Music education

Mathematics education

Science education

Physical education

Business, commerce, and distributive education

Industrial arts, vocational and technical education

Home economics education

−100 −80 −60 −40 −20 0 20 40 60 80 100

Percent change between 1971 and 1981

Figure 11-6. *Bilateral bar chart, horizontal bars. (Source: U. S. Depart-ment of Education)*

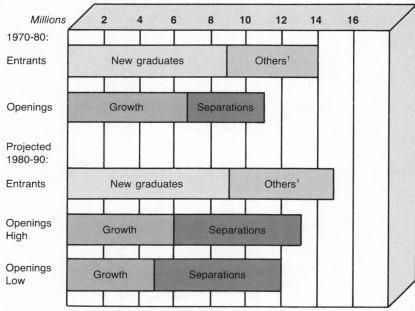

As During the 1970's, College Graduates Entering the Labor Force During the 1980's Are Expected to Exceed Openings by as Much as 3 Million

Figure 11-7. *Subdivided bar chart. (Source: Bureau of Labor Statistics)*

Another kind of bar chart is the subdivided 100-percent bar. These charts may consist of either vertical or horizontal bars. They differ from ordinary bar charts in that all bars are the same length, with each bar representing 100 percent. These 100-percent bar charts serve the same purpose as pie charts (discussed later in this chapter) because they show divisions of the whole. Yet they are far more useful than pie charts when a number of 100-percent items are to be compared, as seven years are compared in Figure 11-10.

A subdivided 100-percent bar chart is shown in Figure 11-11.

A chart that consists of groups of subdivided bars is shown in Figure 11-12.

Range Charts

A range chart shows minimum and maximum values, as illustrated in Figure 11-13. This particular line chart also includes minus val-

ues, showing that employment in agriculture is expected to decrease
during the 1980s.

Line Charts

A line chart is used to show changes over a period of time, as illustrated in Figure 11-14. This figure is described as a multiple line
chart because it has more than one line; the four lines show increases
from 1963 through 1982.

A variation of the usual multiple line chart is shown in Figure
11-15.

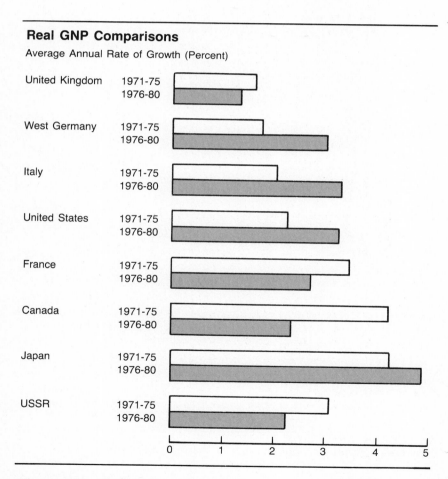

*Figure 11-8. Multiple bar chart. (Source: U. S. Central Intelligence
Agency)*

Proportion of Employed Graduates in Professional, Managerial, and Nonretail Sales Occupations[1] by Major Field of Study (1977 Graduates in 1978)

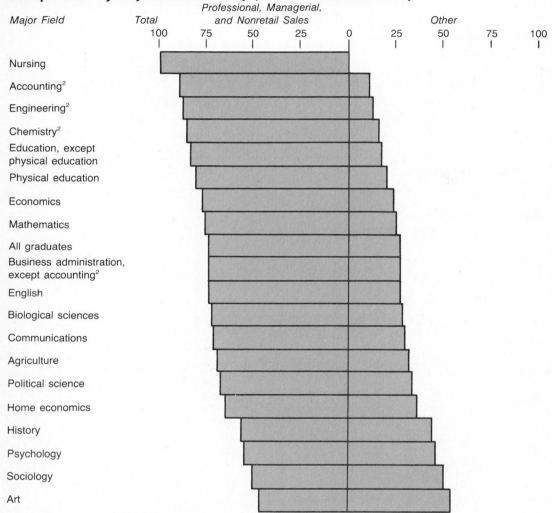

[1] Occupations generally requiring a degree for entry.
[2] About a third of those in the "other" group were in jobs which appear to be trainee positions for recent college graduates.

Figure 11-9. *Variation of horizontal bar chart. (Source: Occupational Outlook Quarterly, Summer, 1982, page 18.)*

State and Local Government Taxes—Percent Distribution, by Type: 1960 to 1980

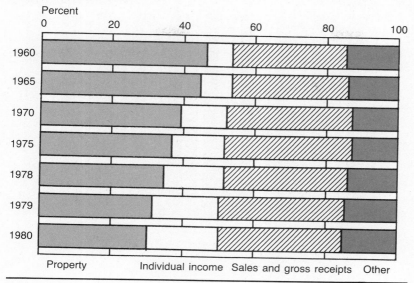

Figure 11-10. *100-percent bar chart. (Source: U. S. Bureau of the Census)*

Index line charts, as illustrated in Figure 11-16, begin at some selected point of reference; in this instance, the year 1960.

In addition to the several variations of the line chart illustrated in this chapter, line charts may be combined with other charts, modified by special illustrations to become a pictorial chart, or presented in various other ways. For example, a line chart can be superimposed over the tops of vertical bars.

Work for simplicity. Regardless of the originality of the graphic aid, it is ineffective if overly complex.

A cumulative line chart also is referred to as a component-part line chart or as a belt chart. As shown in Figure 11-17, the top line represents the total. Color or crosshatching distinguishes the component parts.

Pie Charts

A pie chart, also described as a circle chart (or pie graph or circle graph) shows the component parts of a whole. Examples of two pie charts are shown in Figure 11-18. As in these illustrations, segments

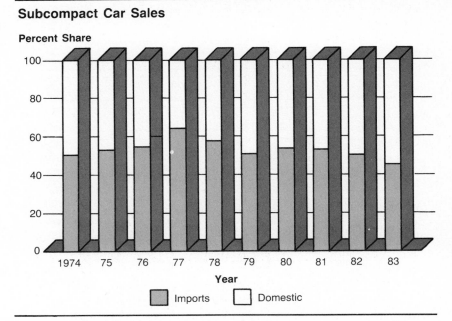

Figure 11-11. *Subdivided 100-percent bar chart. (Source: Bureau of Industrial Economics, U. S. Department of Commerce)*

of the circle should be individually labeled, either within the segments or outside the circle. Exact amounts or percentages also should be shown. Figures in the segments of circles shown in Figure 11-18 represent millions of acres. More often, segments of pie charts are marked with percentages, not numbers.

Combination Charts, Pictograms, Maps, Drawings, Flow Charts, and Other Graphc Aids

As mentioned previously, charts can be combined in various ways. The illustrations shown in Figure 11-19, however, cannot be described as a true combination chart; they are two types of charts shown together. The second pie chart varies from the arrangement often recommended—that the largest segment start at the top, or the twelve o'clock position.

The illustrations of dollar signs in Figure 11-20 replace the usual vertical bars in a simple bar chart. The designer followed a principle of accurate construction by making all the illustrations equal in width.

Data in the pictorial chart shown in Figure 11-21 also could have been shown in pie charts or in the more usual 100-percent subdivided bar.

In the pictorial chart shown in Figure 11-22, individual drawings represent units of data. The designer correctly drew each item (hat, truck, and so on) the same size as all the others in the group. To do otherwise would result in distraction and at least momentary misrepresentation.

Population changes in each major section of the United States are shown in percentages displayed on the map, Figure 11-23.

Drawings are frequently used in many reports and other kinds of writing, particularly technical material. The description of how robots move, as illustrated in Figure 11-24, would require many additional words if the drawing were omitted. Drawings are necessary to depict mechanical processes and equipment.

An example of a flow chart is shown in Figure 11-25.

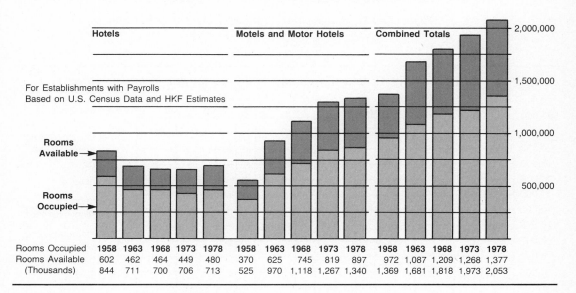

Figure 11-12. *Multiple bar chart with subdivided bars. (Source: Pannell, Kerr Forster)*

Through the 1980s, Changes in Employment Will Vary Widely Among Industries

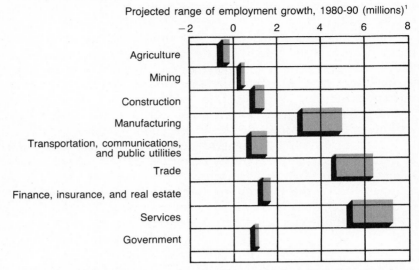

Projected range of employment growth, 1980-90 (millions)[1]

[1] Wage and salary workers, except for agriculture, which includes self-employed and unpaid family workers

Figure 11-13. *Range chart. (Source: Bureau of Labor Statistics)*

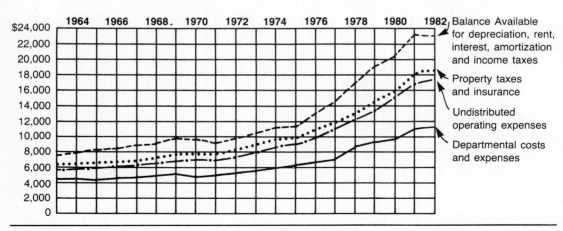

Figure 11-14. *Multiple line chart. (Source: Pannel Kerr Forster)*

Engineers' Annual Salaries Compared With Other Workers'

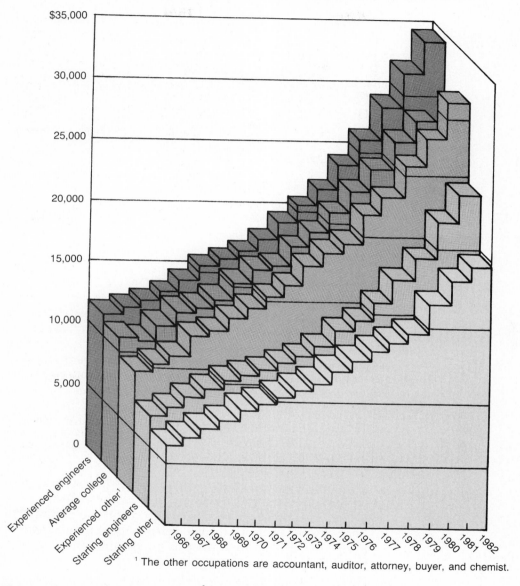

¹ The other occupations are accountant, auditor, attorney, buyer, and chemist.

Figure 11-15. *Multiple line chart.* (*Source: Occupational Outlook Quarterly, Summer, 1983, page 4.*)

Although Farm Output Has Been Increasing, Employment of Farm Workers Has Continued to Decline

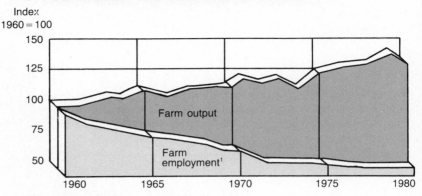

¹ Includes self-employed and unpaid family workers

Figure 11-16. *Index line chart. (Sources: Bureau of Labor Statistics and U. S. Department of Agriculture)*

ACCURATE AND HONEST PRESENTATION OF DATA

The purpose of graphic aids is to show trends and relationships quickly, clearly, and accurately. Poorly constructed graphics do the opposite. Some of the ways these distortions of quantities, trends, and relationships result have already been mentioned as the various types of graphic aids were discussed. In summary, distortions are likely to be due to one or more of the following factors:

1. An inappropriately chosen grid. (A grid is the network of horizontal and vertical lines on which the chart is plotted.)
2. Inappropriate plotting on the grid; for example, not keeping the time schedule uniform.
3. Beginning the quantitative axis somewhere other than zero without making the omission immediately clear to the reader. This omission results in cutting off the bottom of a line or bar chart. Use all such charts with extreme caution. Even when readers are warned by broken lines that the scale has been broken, they are more likely to notice the overall effect of the chart than the broken lines.
   Notice the effect of cutting off the bottom of the vertical bar graph shown in Figure 11-27. If the columns begin at the horizontal line (which has been added to the original

chart), the differences between the amounts shown in the three columns would seem to be drastically increased.

At times, because of lack of space a scale must be broken so that it does not begin at zero. In Figure 11-27, a chart planned to be shown on a projector to illustrate an oral report, the "jog" indicates to the viewer that the entire chart is not shown. If the chart had started at zero and was drawn to scale, it could not have fitted on a transparency in such readable form.

4. Varying more than one dimension in bar charts or pictograms. For example, if you are comparing hog production, use three hogs of identical size to indicate that three million were grown in 1982 as compared to 1972, when one million were grown, shown by one hog of identical size. Do *not* attempt to make one hog three times larger to show the increase in number for 1982. (Unless you need something

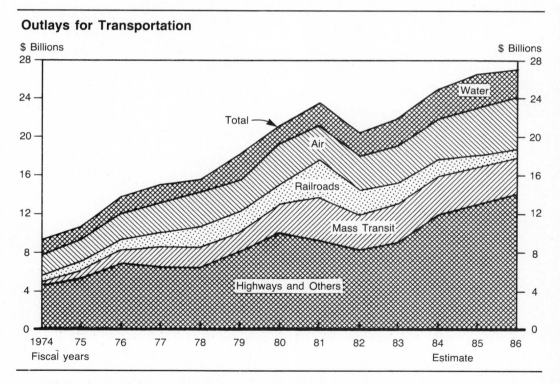

Figure 11-17. *Cumulative line chart. (Source: "The United States Budget in Brief. Fiscal Year 1984," Executive Office of the President, Office of Management and Budget.)*

Land Owned by the Federal Government: 1979

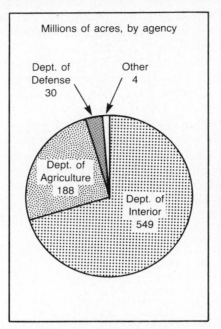
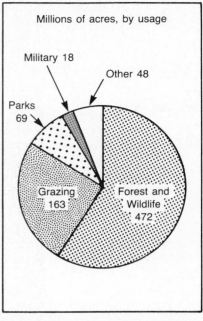

Figure 11-18. *Pie charts. (Source: U. S. Bureau of the Census)*

to do, forget about drawing hogs and use a simple bar graph or table. If your data are no more extensive than the numbers given here, forget about a chart.)

In order to prevent misinterpretation, other than that which can be caused by the design of the graphic aid, observe the following guidelines:

1. Interpret the information shown in the chart to the extent that you are sure your reader will understand its meaning. (The charts shown in this chapter are used to illustrate the different kinds of graphic aids, not to present the information itself. Thus discussion of the information presented on the charts is less than would be required if the charts were used in a business or technical report.)
2. Give credit where credit is due, as when using verbal passages other than your own.

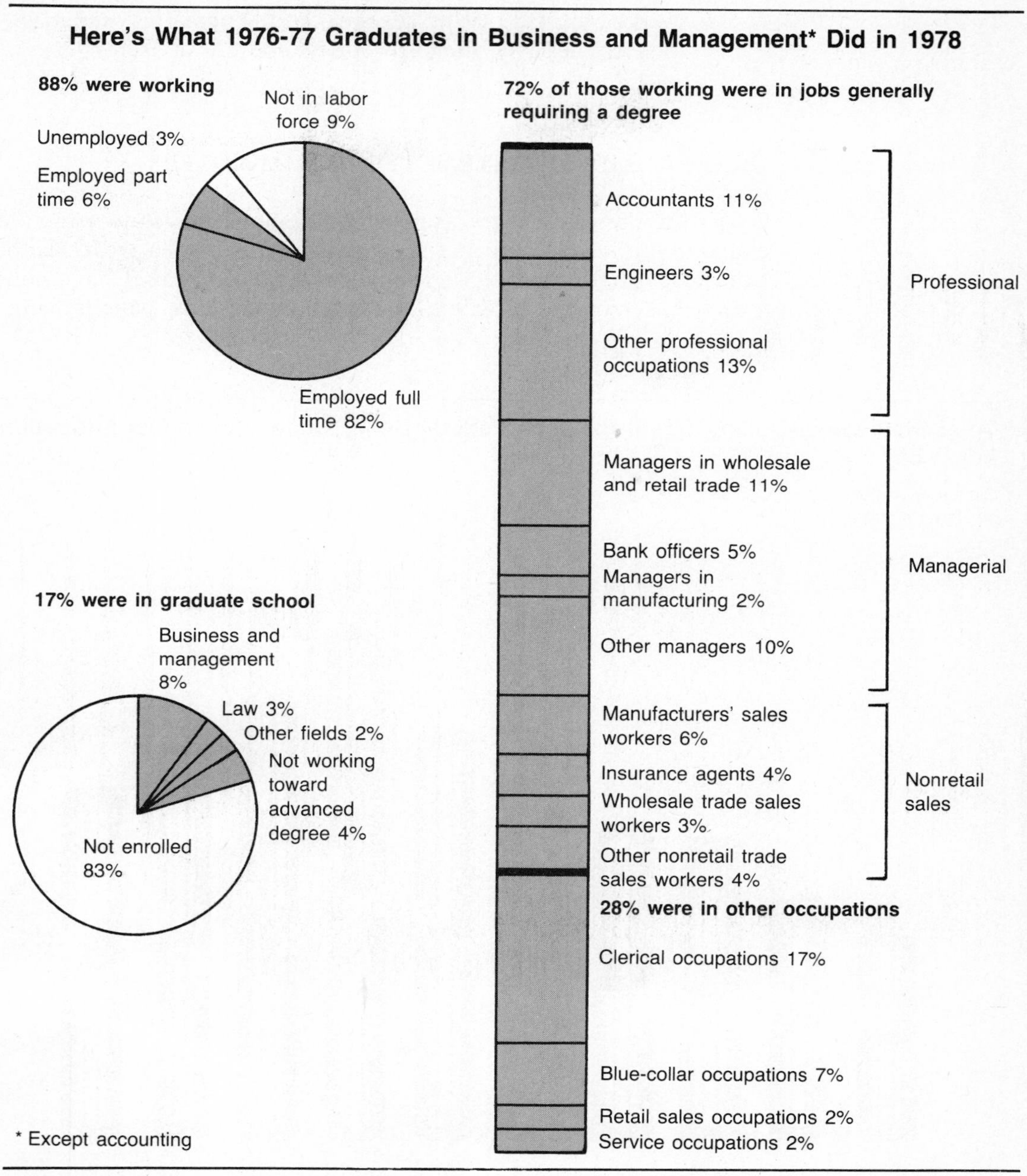

Here's What 1976-77 Graduates in Business and Management* Did in 1978

88% were working

Unemployed 3%

Employed part time 6%

Not in labor force 9%

Employed full time 82%

17% were in graduate school

Business and management 8%

Law 3%
Other fields 2%
Not working toward advanced degree 4%

Not enrolled 83%

72% of those working were in jobs generally requiring a degree

Accountants 11%

Engineers 3%

Other professional occupations 13%

⎫ Professional

Managers in wholesale and retail trade 11%

Bank officers 5%
Managers in manufacturing 2%

Other managers 10%

⎫ Managerial

Manufacturers' sales workers 6%

Insurance agents 4%
Wholesale trade sales workers 3%

Other nonretail trade sales workers 4%

⎫ Nonretail sales

28% were in other occupations

Clerical occupations 17%

Blue-collar occupations 7%

Retail sales occupations 2%
Service occupations 2%

* Except accounting

Figure 11-19. *100-percent bar chart shown with two pie charts. (Source: Occupational Outlook Quarterly, Summer, 1982, page 17.)*

3. Make sure that titles, legends, and explanatory notes adequately describe the purpose and content of each chart.

GRAPHIC AIDS CONSTRUCTED BY COMPUTERS

If you attempted to draw each of the graphic aids shown in this chapter, you would find that such a project requires a great deal of time and artistic ability. A few years ago, you would have constructed any necessary graphic aids by using pens, pencils, com-

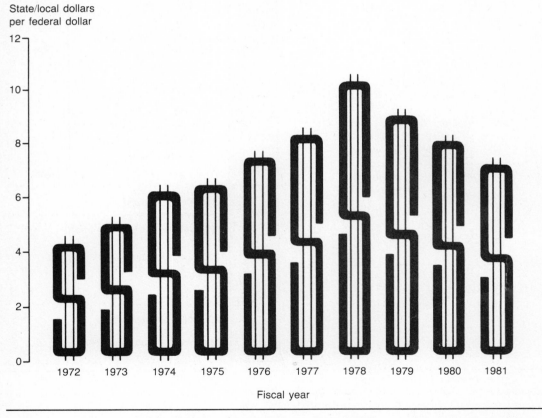

Total State/Local Dollars Spent for Each Federal Dollar Under Vocational Education Act (VEA)

Figure 11-20. Pictorial Bar Chart. (Source: U. S. Department of Education)

passes, protractors, and rulers. For important material, you would perhaps have sent your suggested drawings to a professional artist, within or outside your organization.

Now almost all graphic aids can be quickly and easily constructed by computers, which can convert raw data into tables, charts, and designs of many kinds. Such presentation is possible through the use of mainframe computer terminals or microcomputers. You are likely to have a terminal or a microcomputer at your desk.

If you have the proper equipment and software, you can select the kind of design you wish and, by a simple procedure, instruct the computer to show your selected display on the screen. Then, when

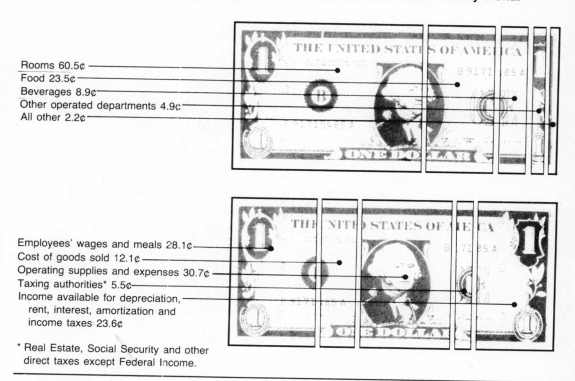

1,000 Hotels and Motels: Source and Disposition of the Industry Dollar

Rooms 60.5¢
Food 23.5¢
Beverages 8.9¢
Other operated departments 4.9¢
All other 2.2¢

Employees' wages and meals 28.1¢
Cost of goods sold 12.1¢
Operating supplies and expenses 30.7¢
Taxing authorities* 5.5¢
Income available for depreciation, rent, interest, amortization and income taxes 23.6¢

* Real Estate, Social Security and other direct taxes except Federal Income.

Figure 11-21. *Pictorial chart showing component parts of a whole. (Source: Prepared by Pannell Kerr Forster)*

Oil and Gas Exploration and Extraction Employ About Half of All Workers in the Mining and Petroleum Industries.

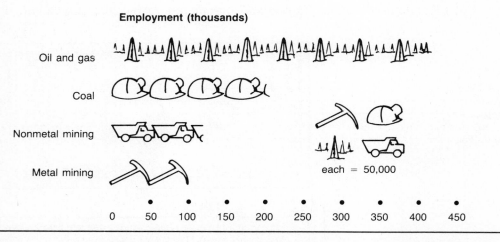

Figure 11-22. *A pictorial chart. (Source: Bureau of Labor Statistics)*

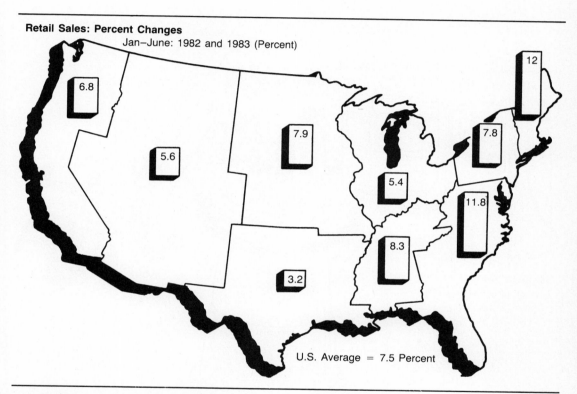

Figure 11-23. Map. (Source: Bureau of the Census)

How Robots Move

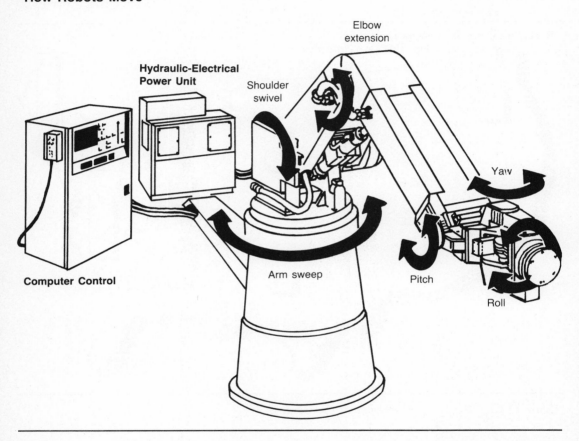

Figure 11-24. *Drawing. (Source: Occupational Outlook Quarterly, Fall, 1982, page 10.)*

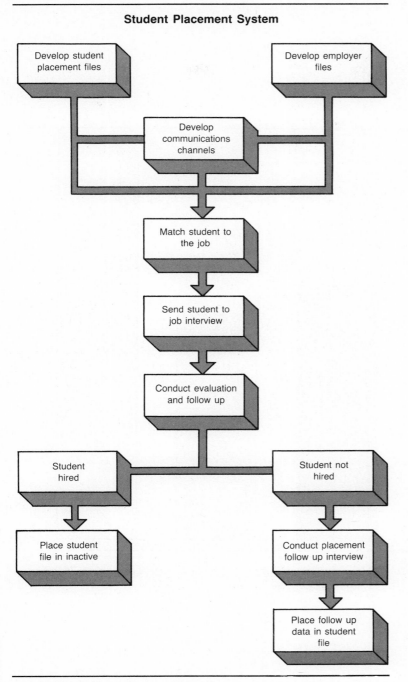

Student Placement System

Develop student placement files

Develop employer files

Develop communications channels

Match student to the job

Send student to job interview

Conduct evaluation and follow up

Student hired

Student not hired

Place student file in inactive

Conduct placement follow up interview

Place follow up data in student file

Figure 11-25. Flow chart. (Source: Occupational Outlook Quarterly, Spring, 1982, page 37)

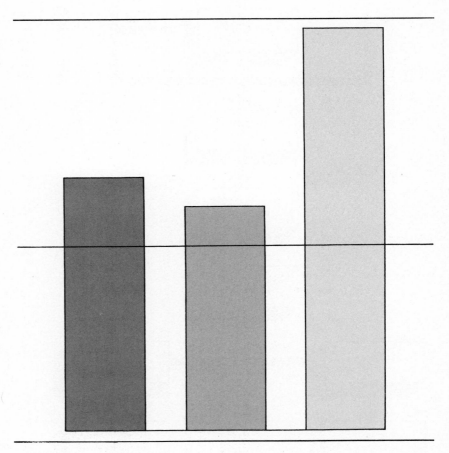

Figure 11-26. *Illustration of how a vertical bar chart can be distorted by starting at some point other than zero.*

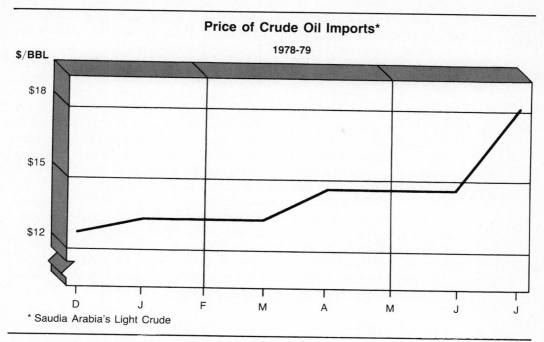

Price of Crude Oil Imports*

1978-79

$/BBL

$18

$15

$12

D   J   F   M   A   M   J   J

* Saudia Arabia's Light Crude

Figure 11-27. *Illustrations of chart with a scale break.*

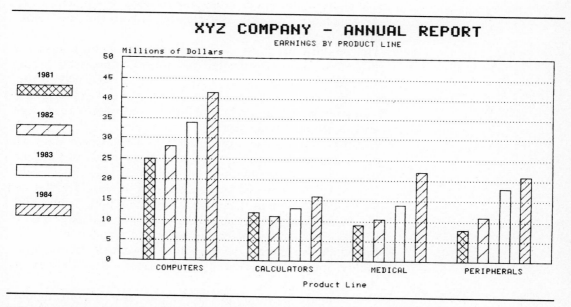

XYZ COMPANY – ANNUAL REPORT

EARNINGS BY PRODUCT LINE

Millions of Dollars

50
45
40
35
30
25
20
15
10
5
0

1981

1982

1983

1984

COMPUTERS   CALCULATORS   MEDICAL   PERIPHERALS

Product Line

Figure 11-28. *Computer drawn line chart. (Source: Memphis State University Office of Financial Planning.)*

your design meets your specifications, it can be printed in various ways. Some equipment will transfer your graphic aids onto color prints, transparencies, and 35 millimeter slides.

Although the actual construction of graphic aids is far easier than it was in past years, you still have the responsibility of choosing the most appropriate chart to display your particular data. In some instances, you will need several different charts in order to present varying aspects of your data. All the principles of graphic presentation discussed in this chapter apply, whether or not they are constructed by a computer. In fact, as construction becomes easier and quicker, you will find that you increase your use of graphic aids. A computer-made graphic is illustrated in Figure 11-28.

As with other improvements and innovations that speed routine work, such as word processing equipment that saves typewriting time, computers do not decrease the importance of your knowledge, judgment, and careful thought. Instead, you will find it even more essential to know the basic underlying principles of communication tasks that now can be handled automatically, once you have made correct choices and given appropriate, exact instructions.

SUMMARY

1. Use charts, tables, and other illustrations as needed to express meaning quickly and clearly, but do not use them merely to impress.
2. Choose the appropriate type of chart, table, or other graphic aid to best convey the desired meaning or comparison. Some information should be shown in more than one way in the same report. For example, the reader may need exact figures instead of trends and relationships; if so, present these figures in tabular form.
3. Ordinarily, a graphic aid should be placed within the text of the report, as near as possible to the portion of the text that it is used to illustrate or explain. If it is not closely related to the material being discussed, it should either be omitted or placed in the appendix of the report. Tables and charts, like other information, belong in the appendix if they can be considered supplementary to the report itself.
4. Introduce the graphic device before presenting it, and, preferably, include a few words of discussion after the device has been presented.
5. Point out the highlights of the graphic aid. By pointing out items of major importance shown by the table or chart, you

are able to refer subordinately to the graphic aid, as in "The greatest increase in sales occurred in District 1 (72%) and the smallest in District 7 (17%), as shown in Table 3."

6. Make sure that graphic aids are constructed so that relationships are not distorted. Use reasonable proportion. Start at zero or show by broken lines that, because of space limitations, it was impractical to start at zero.
7. Carefully label each graphic device. Provide a key (also called a legend) if it will be helpful to the reader.
8. Keep all tables and charts simple. Do not try to show too much information on one chart.

QUESTIONS AND PROBLEMS

1. Which form of graphic illustration would you construct to illustrate the following types of information? Support your decision. For some of the items, several choices could be used.
   a. Record of the earnings per share of The Local Corporation for the past seventeen years.
   b. Comparison of sales of The Local Corporation for three product lines for the past three years.
   c. A comparison of the change in net profit for the twenty restaurants of Bigger Burger, Inc.
   d. Comparison of white collar, blue collar, service, and farm workers in the U. S. labor force for each year ending in five or zero from 1955 to the present.
   e. Breakdown of how the federal government dollar was spent last year.
   f. Mean maximum and minimum temperatures in your city or town for each month of the year.
   g. Average number of days per year with hail, by geographical area of the United States.
   h. Comparison within the Morano Shoe Corporation to show which subsidiary companies account for different percentages of total sales for the product groups.
   i. Comparison of the world's ten largest cities to show population changes for the past ten-year period.
   j. Comparison of the consumer price index to the producer price index over the past twenty years.
   k. Residential buildings permits (single family, multiple family, and total) for Los Angeles County, 1970–1985.

2. Assume reasonable data and construct appropriate graphic aids

to illustrate the comparisons and presentations described in question 1.

3. Bring to class a photocopy of a graphic presentation as shown in a magazine, newspaper, or recent textbook. Be prepared to show this graphic aid on the opaque projector and to comment on the illustration shown. Is the chart the most appropriate one for the particular data and the desired comparison of relationships? Is the chart correctly and accurately made?

4. Present the information requested in problem 3 in a memorandum attached to the illustrated chart or other graphic aid.

5. Write one or more introductory paragraphs to precede Figures 11-3, 11-4, 11-5, 11-6, 11-7, 11-8, 11-9, 11-10, 11-11, 11-12, 11-13, 11-14, 11-15, 11-16, 11-17, 11-18, 11-19 and 11-20. As your instructor directs, write another paragraph to follow each chart.

6. Design a chart to show the data in Figure 11-1 now shown as an example of an unruled table.

Purposes and Methods of Documentation | 12

This chapter discusses the importance and purposes of exact documentation; describes the placement, arrangement, and content of cited material, footnotes, and bibliographies; and lists widely used style manuals. The last section of this chapter summarizes principles of documentation with illustrations from the chapter itself.

PURPOSES OF DOCUMENTATION

When you use material other than your own, whether in the direct words of the author or in paraphrased form, give credit to the originator of the material. Give complete information about the source of the borrowed words. To do otherwise is plagiarism, a form of theft. Penalties are severe.

Information considered to be general knowledge need not be footnoted unless you use the exact words or mode of expression of an individual writer or speaker. For example, if you should state that the computer has brought vast changes to the business world and has influenced our entire society, you need not quote one particular writer or speaker who has made a similar statement.

If you are not completely sure that material you find in secondary sources is considered common knowledge, give credit in the usual way. Even when an item is considered common knowledge, you may choose to footnote in order to add authority to the statement.

MEANING OF THE TERMS "REFERENCE NOTES" AND "BIBLIOGRAPHY"

257
CHAPTER 12
PURPOSES AND
METHODS OF
DOCUMENTATION

Reference notes, which may be arranged in various ways and placed in several positions, quote specific references, including page numbers of written sources. An entry in a bibliography refers to an entire source, such as a book, journal article, personal or telephone interview, or government document. A report or other paper may have footnotes but no bibliography. It is also possible that a bibliography is appropriate when no footnotes are necessary.

Reference Notes

The term *footnote* is derived from the traditional placement of the note at the bottom of a page. References to cited material also can be placed at the end of a manuscript, report, chapter, or book, where they are referred to as *notes* or *endnotes*. Placement also may be within the text of the written work. Regardless of placement, reference notes accomplish the same purpose, that of citing a particular page of a printed source or adding explanatory material.

Bibliographies

The prefix *biblio* is the Greek word that means "book." For this reason, some teachers and researchers prefer not to include non-book sources, such as speeches or personal interviews, under the heading *Bibliography*. Instead, they use *References, Reference Sources, Sources of Data, References Consulted*, or a similar term. In general use, however, and ordinarily acceptable, the term *bibliography* includes interviews, letters, unpublished material, and secondary sources, including those that contributed to the paper without being specifically cited in footnotes. The heading *Works Cited* is more exclusive, including only those works cited specifically in footnotes.

Some confusion of meaning exists between the terms *selected bibliography* and *bibliography*. Campbell and Ballou make these distinctions:

> However, some writers insist that a bibliography should include all the works of an author or all the writings about a given topic; consequently, according to them, a proper heading in a paper or dissertation is *Selected Bibliography, Works Cited*, or something similar.

Current usage and the preceding definition justify using *Bibliography* as a heading if the writer so chooses; the assumption here is that either option is acceptable.[1]

Campbell and Ballou state further:

> You may experience uncertainty about what should or may be included in a bibliography. You should list all sources quoted or referred to in the paper, and you may include useful background references in a selected bibliography, even though they are not cited in the paper. You are not obligated to quote or to list mediocre references; thus, in this sense, most bibliographies are "selected."[2]

Regardless of the title of the reference section usually referred to as a *bibliography*, it must include *all* sources used as documentation and presented in footnotes or endnotes. If sources other than those referred to by footnotes contributed to the content of the report, these sources also must be included in the bibliography.

When determining sources to be included, you should not interpret the word *consulted* to mean all secondary sources you examine in order to determine their usefulness and applicability. For example, you may think that a book listed in the card catalog contains the exact information you are seeking, only to find upon examination that the book is not suitable in any way. Book titles in themselves are often misleading.[3] A thorough examination of the description given in the card catalog, however, will usually indicate the content of the particular book.

USING QUOTED AND PARAPHRASED PASSAGES

As you include information from secondary sources, you may choose to use it *verbatim*; that is, in the exact words of the writer you are quoting. Paraphrased material is expressed in your own words, although you have taken the information from another source.

Passages that you quote verbatim must be clearly distinguished from the rest of the text. Paraphrased passages are not set off, but

1. William Giles Campbell and Stephen Vaughan Ballou, *Form and Style: Theses, Reports, Term Papers*, 5th ed. (Boston: Houghton Mifflin, 1978), p. 77.

2. Campbell and Ballou, p. 79.

3. Wilma Dykeman, who in 1965 published a book entitled *The French Broad*, remarked that the book has sold much better than other books in the *River of America* series. The French Broad is a river in Appalachia.

your footnotes should make clear what portion of the text you are documenting. Footnote numbers follow the cited material.

According to Turabian, ". . . short, direct prose quotations should be incorporated into the text of the paper and enclosed in double quotation marks."[4] Quoted material of no more than three typewritten lines is typed within the text, as illustrated by the immediately preceding sentence. If the quoted material is longer than three typewritten lines, it should be set off from the text by single spacing, as explained in the words of Kate Turabian:

> Longer quotations—two or more sentences which would occupy four or more typewritten lines—should be set off from the text in single spacing and indented in their entirety four spaces from the left marginal line of text, omitting quotation marks at beginning and end. . . . If paragraph indention is necessary, indent another four spaces for the beginning of a paragraph.[5]

The ellipsis is a series of three periods, in addition to a period at the end of a sentence, if necessary, typed with intervening spaces. The ellipsis in the quoted material displayed above indicates that some of the exact words of the original source have been omitted. Because omissions can distort meaning, conventional usage is to insert an ellipsis to indicate that a portion of the original passage is not included. You are further obligated to make sure that omissions, even when so indicated, do not change the writer's overall intent and overall meaning. Omission of a paragraph or more is sometimes shown by a complete line of spaced periods.

Use care and judgment in citing secondary information. When you include a statement or opinion of someone else, you imply that you agree with the cited material unless you state otherwise. The material must be relevant to your overall approach and content. It must carry forward the flow of thought and amplify and strengthen your own discussion.

Barzun and Graff comment on occasions when you may omit footnotes:

> In citing and crediting authors, you must, as in all other phases of research and writing, use judgment. Many obvious quotations need no author's name. For instance, if you are so unadventurous that you find yourself quoting "to be or not to be," leave the author in decent obscurity. If you quote for purely decorative purpose an anecdote that is going the rounds and that you found in your local newspaper, or a

4. Kate L. Turabian, *Student's Guide for Writing College Papers*, 2d ed., rev. (Chicago: University of Chicago Press, 1969), p. 86.

5. Turabian, p. 86.

trifling news item from the same source, no reference is needed to the place and date. . . . Remember, in other words, that quoting is for illustration and citing is for possible verification.[6]

Although you may omit footnotes in instances like those mentioned in the quotation above, be extremely careful not to omit needed documentation. *When in doubt, footnote.*

Even though you give proper credit to the author of the information you include, you are not free to use an unlimited amount of material from one particular source without express permission. For example, an entire chapter from *The Modern Researcher* by Barzun and Graff could not be legally or ethically included in this textbook without permission from the copyright holder. The use of the preceding passage and the following one is permitted under the "Fair Use" provision of the copyright laws. Barzun and Graff state:

> But do you ask for six words? Obviously not. Some publishers allow passages of 250 to 500 words to be quoted without permission having to be asked. This latitude is sometimes stated on the copyright page; look there for the exact wordage granted free. Remember that an aggregate of, say, 300 words quoted by you here and there requires permission as if it were one long passage.[7]

A limit of 250 words is the usual guideline at this time. If you are unsure whether you are exceeding the accepted limit, check with the particular publisher.

PLACEMENT OF FOOTNOTES AND OTHER REFERENCE NOTES

Footnotes may be placed at the bottom of a page, separated from the text by a typewritten line one and one-half inches long, beginning at the left margin. Complete notes are also placed within the text itself, as near as possible to the cited passage. Another method is to place all references at the end of a report or other written work. With this arrangement, the bibliography is often omitted. Reference notes may be placed at the end of chapters in a book or at the end of the book itself.

Placement within the text may be in one of several forms. One arrangement is to separate the footnote from the text by the use of

6. Jacques Barzun and Henry F. Graff, *The Modern Researcher*, 3d ed. (New York: Harcourt Brace Jovanovich, 1977), p. 268.

7. Barzun and Graff, p. 268.

top and bottom lines that extend the full width of the page. Another is to enclose the footnote within parentheses. As with bottom-of-page placement, footnote numbers follow cited material.

A disadvantage of the traditional bottom-of-page arrangement is that it makes manuscripts more difficult to type than when footnotes are placed together on one page at the end of the report. Advantages of bottom-of-page placement are that the reader can more easily see the footnotes than if they are on a later page, especially when the document is recorded on microfilm. They are also not so distracting as when inserted within the text. In addition, an arrangement other than the traditional bottom-of-page placement seems to some readers somewhat less than formal and professional.

Shortened subsequent footnotes, with or without a bibliography, are also used at the bottom of a page, as illustrated by the actual footnotes that accompany this chapter. If you are not sure of the arrangement preferred by your readers, you are wise to use bottom-of-page footnotes in complete form the first time a particular reference is cited, whether or not you include a bibliography. If you are not sure whether to include a bibliography, you are wise to include it.

A great number of footnotes can be distracting regardless of where they are placed, although they must be used when they are necessary for proper credit to the original author. If you find that you are using an excessive number, to the extent that much of your report consists of bits and pieces of others' works, perhaps you are doing too much citing and not enough analysis and interpretation of your own. (An unusual number of footnotes is included in this chapter because the chapter itself is planned to serve as an example of the various uses of footnotes.)

SUGGESTED STYLE MANUALS

If you are requested to use a particular style manual as a guide, or if you are asked to use the format previously chosen for your organization, make sure that you follow the suggested methods exactly. A variation may distract or annoy your reader to the extent that it interferes with the reception of your intended message. In addition, ability and willingness to follow instructions is a necessary part of communication within organizations.

According to Barzun and Graff,[8] if no particular manual is stip-

8. Barzun and Graff, p. 282.

ulated you are wise to choose one of two widely used manuals: *The MLA Handbook*[9] or *A Manual of Style*, University of Chicago Press, commonly referred to as the *Chicago Manual of Style*.[10] A digest of the University of Chicago system has been published by Kate L. Turabian.[11] Another widely used guide is *Form and Style: Theses, Reports, Term Papers*, by Campbell and Ballou, which includes illustrations from other style manuals.[12] Another guide is *Publication Manual of the American Psychological Association*.[13]

FOOTNOTES WITH CORRESPONDING BIBLIOGRAPHIC ENTRIES

The examples of footnotes and bibliographic entries that follow, as well as actual footnotes and bibliographies shown in this textbook, are based on *A Manual of Style*, 13th ed., University of Chicago Press. This manual is the one used by most publishers. It is appropriate for any manuscript unless you are directed to use another arrangement of documentation.

In the following examples, *F* indicates footnote and *B* indicates an entry in a bibliography. Indentations in the finished report are five spaces for footnotes and seven for bibliographies.

For a book with one author:

F   1. Malra Treece, *Communication for Business and the Professions*, 2d ed. (Boston: Allyn and Bacon, 1983), p. 500.

B   Treece, Malra. *Communication for Business and the Professions*. 2d ed. Boston: Allyn and Bacon, 1983.

For a book with two authors:

F   2. William N. Bonner and Jean Voyles, *Communicating in Business: Key to Success* (Houston: Dame Publications, 1980), p. 293.

---

9. *The MLA Handbook for Writers of Research Papers, Theses, and Dissertations.* (New York: Modern Language Association, 1977).

10. *A Manual of Style*, 13 ed. rev. (Chicago: University of Chicago Press, 1982.)

11. Kate L. Turabian, *Student's Guide for Writing College Papers*, 3d ed. (Chicago: University of Chicago Press, 1976).

12. Campbell and Ballou.

13. *Publication Manual of the American Psychological Association*, rev. ed. (Washington, D.C., 1974).

B   Bonner, William N. and Voyles, Jean. *Communicating in Business: Key to Success.* Houston: Dame Publications, 1980.

For a book with three authors:

F   3.   C. W. Wilkinson, Peter B. Clarke, and Dorothy C. M. Wilkinson, *Communicating through Letters and Reports*, 7th ed. (Homewood, Ill.: Richard D. Irwin, 1980), pp. 22–24.

B   Wilkinson, C. W.; Clarke, Peter B.; and Wilkinson, Dorothy C. M. *Communicating through Letters and Reports.* 7th ed. Homewood, Ill.: Richard D. Irwin, 1980.

For a book with more than three authors:

F   4.   Robert J. Kilber et al., *Objectives for Instruction and Evaluation* (Boston: Allyn and Bacon, 1974), p. 153.

B   Kibler, Robert J.: Cegala, Donald J.; Miles, David T.; and Barker, Larry L. *Objectives for Instruction and Evaluation.* Boston: Allyn and Bacon, 1974.

For an edited book or one revised by a person other than the original author:

F   5.   Richard C. Huseman, Cal M. Logue, and Dwight L. Freshley, eds., *Readings in Interpersonal and Organizational Communication*, 3d ed. (Boston: Holbrook Press, 1977), pp. 1–2.

B   Huseman, Richard C.; Logue, Cal M.; and Freshley, Dwight L., eds. *Readings in Interpersonal and Organizational Communication.* Boston: Holbrook Press, 1977.

F   6.   H. W. Fowler, *A Dictionary of Modern English Usage*, 2d ed., rev. Sir Ernest Gowers (Oxford: Oxford University Press, 1965), p. 157.

B   Fowler, H. W. *A Dictionary of Modern English Usage.* 2d ed. Revised by Sir Ernest Gowers. Oxford: Oxford University Press, 1965.

For a book with no author given:

F   7.   *The Chicago Manual of Style*, 13th ed. rev. (Chicago: University of Chicago Press, 1982), pp. 42–44.

B   *The Chicago Manual of Style.* 13th ed. rev. Chicago: University of Chicago Press, 1982.

For a chapter of a collective work:

F   8. Merwyn A. Hayes, "Nonverbal Communication: Expression Without Words," in *Readings in Interpersonal and Organizational Communication*, 3d ed., edited by Richard C. Huseman, Cal M. Logue, and Dwight L. Freshley (Boston: Holbrook Press, 1977), pp. 55–68.

B   Hayes, Merwyn A. "Nonverbal Communication: Expression Without Words." In *Readings in Interpersonal and Organizational Communication*, 3d. ed., edited by Richard C. Huseman, Cal M. Logue, and Dwight L. Freshley, pp. 55–68. Boston: Holbrook Press, 1977.

For a book in a series:

F   9. James A. Smith, *Creative Teaching of the Language Arts in the Elementary School*, Allyn and Bacon Series in Creative Teaching, vol. 2 (Boston, 1967), p. 30.

B   Smith, James A. *Creative Teaching of the Language Arts in the Elementary School*. Allyn and Bacon Series in Creative Teaching, vol. 2. Boston, 1967.

For an unpublished work:

F   10. Myrena Sue Jennings, "A Comparison of Middle Managerial Written Business Communications Practices and Problems and Collegiate Written Business Communications Instruction" (Doctoral dissertation, Georgia State University, 1974), p. 271.

B   Jennings, Myrena Sue. "A Comparison of Middle Managerial Written Business Communications Practices and Problems and Collegiate Written Business Communications Instruction." Doctoral dissertation, Georgia State University, 1974.

For an article in a periodical:

F   11. Robert Gunning, "The Fog Index after Twenty Years," *Journal of Business Communication* 6 (Winter 1968): 3.

B   Gunning, Robert. "The Fog Index after Twenty Years." *Journal of Business Communication* 6 (Winter 1968): 3.

F   12. Fred T. Allen, "Ways to Improve Employee Communication," *Nation's Business* (September 1975), pp. 54–56.

B   Allen, Fred T. "Ways to Improve Employee Communication." *Nation's Business*. September 1975.

F   13. "The Mail," *Atlantic Monthly*, February 1979, pp. 28–32.

B   "The Mail." *Atlantic Monthly*, February 1979, pp. 28–32.

For an article in a well-known reference book:

F   14. *Encyclopaedia Britannica*, 1977, s.v. "Printing."

B   *Encyclopaedia Britannica*. 1977, s.v. "Printing."

F   15. *The Concise Oxford Dictionary of Current English*, 5th ed. s.v. "Communication."

B   *The Concise Oxford Dictionary of Current English*. 5th ed., s.v. "Communication."

For a newspaper article:

F   16. *Boston Globe*, 18 January 1982, p. 1.

B   *Boston Globe*, 18 January 1982, p. 1.

For government publications:

F   17. U.S. Congress, House Committee on Business, *Operating Small Businesses*, 79th Cong., 2d sess., 1946, H. Rep. 1888, p. 63.

B   U.S. Congress, House Committee on Business. *Operating Small Businesses*. 79th Cong., 2d sess., 1946. H. Rep. 1888.

F   18. Social Science Research Council, *Labor Force Definition and Measurement*, Bulletin 56 (Washington, D.C., 1947), pp. 10–11.

B   Social Science Research Council. *Labor Force Definition and Measurement*. Bulletin 56. Washington, D.C., 1947.

F   19. U.S. Department of Commerce, Bureau of the Census, *Twentieth Census of the United States, 1980: Population*, 2: 98.

B   U.S. Department of Commerce. Bureau of the Census. *Twentieth Census of the United States, 1980: Population*, vol. 2.

F   20. U.S. *Constitution*, Art. I, sec. 4.

B   U.S. *Constitution*. Art. I, sec. 4.

For interviews:

F   21. Personal interview with James X. Tennyson, Manager, Conrally Company, Midland, Texas, 19 November 1982.

B   Tennyson, James X., Manager, Conrally Company, Midland, Texas. Personal interview, 19 November 1982.

F   22.   Telephone interview with Mary Key, Supervisor, Raven Corporation, Dayton, Ohio, 19 November 1982.

B   Key, Mary, Supervisor, Raven Corporation, Dayton, Ohio. Telephone interview, 19 November 1982.

For letters or memorandums:

F   23.   Letter from Marjorie Jacobs, President, X-View, Incorporated, to Richard Rayner, 19 November 1982.

B   Jacobs, Marjorie, President, X-View, Incorporated. Letter to Richard Rayner, 19 November 1982.

Footnote and bibliography formats of materials not illustrated in the list above, such as leaflets, brochures, manuals, speeches, minutes of meetings, or radio or television programs, should be arranged similarly to one of the examples shown. A titled brochure or leaflet with no author given is arranged similarly to a magazine article with no author given. A speech is presented similarly to an interview or a letter.

If you cannot find examples or instructions for primary or secondary data that you wish to document, simply give all necessary information in a logical, readable order, as much as possible like the arrangement of other footnotes or bibliographic entries. It is better to give too much information than too little. If expected information is not available—for example, date of a publication—show in footnotes and bibliographic entries that the data was omitted in the source you are quoting.

SHORTENED FOOTNOTES AT BOTTOM OF PAGE

Shortened forms of footnotes are used for subsequent references. A simplified footnote consisting of the author's name, with page numbers, is usually preferable to the older, hard-to-remember Latin forms, although at times the term *Ibid.* may save unnecessary repetition of long titles, such as government publications with no author shown. Use of standard reference forms, including *Ibid.*, is explained below. Unless you see a real need to use Latin abbreviations, however, prefer the simpler, modern arrangement.

For example, in a subsequent reference to a book by Edward

T. Hall, you may use this footnote:

> Hall, p. 217.

If you refer in the same paper to two or more works by the same author, the title must be included in all footnotes:

> Hall, *The Silent Language*, p. 217.

If you use materials written, for example, by both Jane Hall and Edward T. Hall, complete names must be included in all footnotes. Assume that you use two books by Edward T. Hall and one by Jane Hall. The shortest form of the footnote would be as follows:

> Edward T. Hall, *The Silent Language*, p. 217.

Latin abbreviations have long been used as subsequent footnote references. The most commonly used ones are these:

Ibid. (ibidem). This term means "in the same place." It is used to refer to the immediately preceding footnote: Ibid., p. 12.

Op. cit. (opere citato). This term means "in the work cited." It refers to a previous footnote, but not the one directly preceding: Brown, op. cit., p. 14.

Loc. cit. (loco citato). This term means "in the place cited." It refers to a preceding entry but not the one directly preceding. This abbreviation is used only when the page number for the second reference is the same as the first.

The following series of footnotes illustrates the use of *ibid., op. cit.,* and *loc. cit.*

1. Joanna Brown, *Reflections* (Boston: Allyn and Bacon, 1981), p. 8.

2. Ibid, p. 142. [Brown's work, but another page]

3. Ruth Kemp, ''Tomorrow,'' *Reader's Digest*, March 1982, p. 14.

4. Brown, op. cit., p. 147. [Brown's book, different page]

5. Kemp, loc. cit. [same article, same page as footnote 3]

If your report or other written work includes a bibliography, the footnote form, including the first time a reference is cited, may be shortened. It is also correct, and often considered preferable in formal reports, to show complete information in the first footnote reference to a work, even when a bibliography is included. To do so is essential if no bibliography is included.

With a bibliography, shortened footnotes, even when used only once or for the first time, include only the author's surname, title of publication, and page number. If no author is given, the title and page number suffice, as shown in the third example below:

Hall, *The Silent Language*, p. 44. [book]

Swenson, "Relative Importance of Business Communication Skills for the Next Ten Years," p. 16. [article in periodical]

Essays on Research in the Social Sciences, p. 5. [no author or editor given]

These shortened bottom-of-page footnote forms are permissible because complete information is shown in the bibliography.

REFERENCE CITATIONS IN TEXT OF REPORT

Shortened footnotes may be inserted into the text of a report that includes a bibliography. For example, reference to page 22 of a book by Brown could be shown in this way: (Brown, 22.) If more than one work is listed by one or more writers named Brown, adequate information must be given in each note to enable the reader to find immediately the cited source. Another method is to number the references in the bibliography; thus, if a work by Brown is the second one listed in a bibliography, the reference would be: (2, p. 220) or (2:220). Shortened footnotes consisting of author's name, title of publication, and page number can be inserted into the text, within parentheses or between lines that set the reference off from the text.

A widely used method of reference citations within the text is referred to as the APA style.[14] Because this arrangement is easy to type and also convenient to the reader, it is often the choice for articles and reports of various kinds, including business writing. The citation is woven into the text in such a way as to be part of the text and avoid unnecessary distraction. For example:

Caraway (1981) analyzed the relationships of cost-of-living raises to . . .

14. *Publication Manual of the American Psychological Association*, p. 58.

The preceding reference is to a complete study. When quoting a particular page or pages, appropriate citations are still made in the text rather than in a footnote at the bottom of the page or at the end of the paper. Occasionally you may refer to a chapter, rather than to a page, as when discussing ideas or topics presented throughout the chapter. For the most part, however, page numbers are necessary, as when using footnotes. For example:

```
In a study of the cost-of-living raises (Caraway,
1981, p. 20) . . .
```

In choosing the format and placement of footnotes, consideration for the reader should be the determining factor.

BIBLIOGRAPHIES

The bibliography is considered as a supplement to a formal report. It may come before or after appendices, depending upon the material included as appendices. Page numbering is often simplified by placing the bibliography first. The Arabic numerals used in the report proper continue in sequence throughout all supplementary parts.

Example of a Bibliography from a Business Report

A suggested form for a bibliography suitable for business reports is shown in Figure 12-1, which is headed by the term *References*. Some writers prefer *Bibliography*; others do not wish to describe as a bibliography a list that contains material other than written work, such as interviews. Either usage is correct if one definition of bibliography, "a list of references," is accepted.

The Annotated Bibliography

An annotated bibliography briefly describes each listed reference, as in these examples:

```
Gunning, Robert. New Guides to More Effective
Writing in Business and Industry. Boston: Industrial
Education Institute, 1964.
```

REFERENCES

Adams, Linda. Office Manager, Countrywide Insurance, Jackson, Iowa. Personal interview, 7 August 1984.

Barber, Richard D. "Merging Optical Character Recognition Equipment into a Word Processing Environment." Paper presented at the International Word Processing Association Spring Symposium, February 1979, Los Angeles, California.

Green, K. "How to Maintain Your Word Processing Print Quality." The Office LXXXVII (June 1978), 106–108.

Hansen, John R. "Meeting the User's Needs." Infosystems XXIV (October 1977), 51–54.

McCabe, Helen M. and Popham, Estelle L. Word Processing. New York: Harcourt Brace Jovanovich, 1977.

Meyers, Edward. "Meeting of Many Minds." Datamation XXIV (April 1978), 184–185.

Wohl, A. D. "Shopping for Equipment: Today's Bustling Up Market Offers Over 100 Makes and Models." Management World VII (May 1978), 9–10.

Word Processing Glossary. Willow Grove, Pa.: International Word Processing Association, 1978.

Yancey, Hall S., Sales Representative, Words Incorporated, Jackson, Iowa. Telephone interview, 12 July 1984.

Figure 12-1.   Example of a reference format.

Gunning, best known for the development of a readability formula, offers help to the business and technical writer toward the clear expression of ideas. The theme is that clear expression is based upon exact thinking and understanding.

Dohan, Mary Helen. *Our Own Words*. New York: Alfred A. Knopf, 1974.

The story of the making of the American language, from its Anglo–Saxon roots and its beginnings among the earliest settlers and pioneers, through its development during periods of immigration and social change. The book includes an introduction by Alistair Cooke.

271
CHAPTER 12
PURPOSES AND
METHODS OF
DOCUMENTATION

SUMMARY

When a writer uses material first written or spoken by someone else, credit must be given to the originator of the material.

Documentation is usually in the form of reference notes and bibliographies, which differ slightly according to the style manual being used as a guide.

Reference notes are of two kinds, *source* or *content* (or discussion). Source references only cite. Content references explain, comment, or supplement.

Footnotes are placed at the bottom of the page on which the cited material appears. Notes also may be placed at the end of a written work or within the text itself.

Reference notes may be used without a bibliography. Occasionally a report may correctly include a bibliography but no reference notes. If both are used, all sources cited in notes must also be included in the bibliography. A bibliography may include sources not cited through reference notes if these sources contributed to the report.

Shortened forms of footnotes or other reference notes are used for subsequent references. Shortened forms may be used for all footnotes when a bibliography is included. Most business and professional writers prefer simplified shortened footnotes instead of Latin abbreviations.

Bottom-of-page footnotes included in this chapter (apart from those shown as illustrations within the text) are used for these purposes: to give proper credit; to explain or comment; to strengthen discussion by citing authoritative writers and reference books; and to serve as examples of the various ways in which footnotes are used. In other words, the fourteen footnotes used in this chapter each illustrate the rules and usages discussed. Review these footnotes according to the principles and usages they illustrate:

Footnote 1. First footnote, book by two authors.
Footnote 2. A shortened form used as subsequent footnote.
Footnote 3. Content (discussion) footnote. Such comments would be irrelevant if inserted into the text. (Some people will think that such comments are irrelevant, regardless of where they are placed.)

Footnote 4. Short, direct quotation of no more than three lines incorporated into the text.

Footnote 5. Quoted material of more than three lines, single spaced and set off from the text.

Footnote 6. Same as Footnote 5 except that quoted passage is indented to indicate the beginning of a paragraph.

Footnote 7. Same as Footnote 5 except that it does not include an ellipsis.

Footnotes 8, 9, 10, 11. This passage presents an unusual situation in that material paraphrased from Barzun and Graff includes mention of three style manuals, which also must be footnoted. Footnote 8 is placed after the authors' names instead of at the end of the sentence. Because the edition of Turabian's book is not the edition previously cited, a complete reference is needed here instead of a shortened reference.

Footnote 12. This reference was first given in Footnotes 1 and 2. In this instance, reference is to the complete book. In addition, the full form of the footnote could have been used here, as in Footnote 11.

Footnote 13. This reference contains no mention of the author or title; none is given on the Manual.

Footnote 14. Subsequent reference.

QUESTIONS AND PROBLEMS

1. Construct a bibliography that lists the textbooks you are using this semester, including this one; three journal articles in your major field of study; and three journal articles on the subject of communication in management.

2. Construct footnotes for references shown in the bibliography prepared for question 1. Include specific page numbers for passages that you assume you are including verbatim or in paraphrased form.

3. Construct a bibliography based on the bottom-of-page footnotes used in this chapter.

4. Construct an annotated bibliography of the textbooks you are using this semester.

5. Write a memorandum to your assistant, Harvey Coleman, who prepares reports based on secondary data. Summarize the two ways in which quoted material may be placed within the text of

a report. Harvey has been using quotation marks regardless of the length of quoted passages.

6. Explain the form and use of an ellipsis.

7. Discuss this statement: Writers in business and the professions should spend their time more profitably than in exact construction of bibliographies and footnotes, to say nothing of worrying about *ibid's, op. cit's,* and *loc. cit's.*

8. Interview a reference librarian in your college or university. Ask for his or her recommendations for a style manual. Also ask for opinions about bottom-of-page footnotes versus end-of-manuscript notes. Report your findings in the form of a short manuscript. (See Chapter 3.) Remember that the interview itself is a source of information that must be documented.

Using Computers in Preparing Reports

13

Michael L. Kamil
University of Illinois at Chicago

This chapter includes some basic concepts of computing and a discussion of hardware and software that can be used to prepare reports. The glossary at the end of the chapter lists key terms related to computer operations.

Computers can access data on which reports are based. They can process and organize data and prepare tables and graphic illustrations. In addition, computers can be used as word processors in the writing and editing stages of report preparation. Word processing allows a writer to write, edit, revise, and otherwise manipulate the text *before* it is printed as a final copy. Finally, reports can be transmitted quickly and efficiently over long distances by computers.

OVERVIEW OF COMPUTERS

Computers have revolutionized many scientific, numerical, and manufacturing processes in a relatively short period of time. In 1950, there were no more than thirty electronic computers in existence. By 1976, approximately 400,000 were in use.[1] Many microcomputer manufacturers today number their yearly output in the hundreds of thousands. Office automation is one result of the vast number of computers now available.

Computers are electronic devices that can execute instructions

1. Daniel L. Slotnick and Joan L. Slotnick, *Computers: Their Structure, Use, and Influence* (Englewood Cliffs, N.J.: Prentice-Hall, 1979).

automatically, without human intervention. They can store, manipulate and transmit information by representing the data electronically. A computer can perform complex and repetitive calculations rapidly. However, the computer needs to be instructed to do tasks in a precise manner. These instructions are called *programs*, or *software*. Software is distinguished from *hardware*, which consists of all of the electronic and other physical components of the computer.

Mainframe Computers Versus Microcomputers

Computers are often classified by their size, cost, and capabilities. Three categories are *mainframe computers, minicomputers*, and *microcomputers*.

Mainframe computers are valuable because of their speed and capacity. They can hold in memory very large programs and tremendous amounts of data. They also can process data at rates that reach millions of instructions per second. Because of their speed and capacity, many users can be connected to the same computer through remote terminals. The computer rapidly switches from one user to another.

Microcomputers have the advantage of being inexpensive (usually under $10,000) and relatively easy to learn to operate. They are slower than mainframe computers and have less capacity in memory. The fastest microcomputers today are just beginning to reach speed levels of a million instructions per second. However, the use of microcomputers does guarantee that if one machine fails (out of several), the others are unaffected. Finally, microcomputers are less expensive than mainframes, both in initial costs and operating expenses.

Minicomputers fall somewhere between mainframes and microcomputers on all criteria. Technology has made most of the distinctions less clear than they once were. For example, add-on circuit boards for the IBM PC microcomputer allow it to run mainframe (IBM 360) software.

Parts of a Computer

A computer consists of a *central processing unit* (CPU), memory storage, an input device, an output device, and other optional peripherals. These are illustrated in the diagram in Figure 13-2.

The central processor is the "brain" of the machine in which decisions are made about handling information. Before a program can be run, it must be loaded into the memory of the computer. The larger the program, the more memory that is required.

Memory is measured in K bytes or thousands of bytes. Each K is technically 2^{10}, or 1024 bytes. Each byte represents a single computer word, which is in turn made up of bits. Each byte is usually made up of 8 bits, although this number may vary, depending on the computer. Microcomputers usually have from 48K bytes upwards of memory, representing a real total of 49,152 bytes of memory (48 × 1024).

Memory is usually divided into two general types: *RAM*, or random access memory, and *ROM*, or read-only memory. RAM memory is volatile—it can be changed at will. The computer can write into RAM as well as read its contents. ROM cannot be changed by the user; it is memory in which important instructions are stored.

Figure 13-1a. *Mainframe computer.*

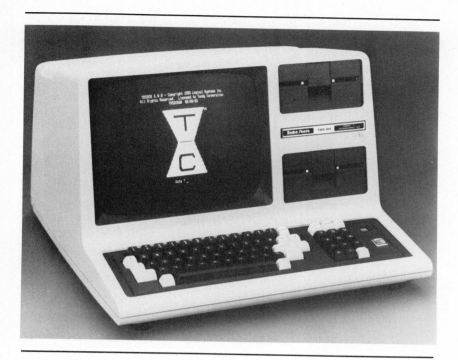

Figure 13-1b. Microcomputer.

For example, instructions that tell the computer what to do when the power is first turned on are often stored in ROM. Many computers also have programming languages or frequently used programs stored permanently in ROM.

Input devices usually consist of keyboards, disk drives, tape drives, or other peripherals. *Peripherals* are devices that are separated from the CPU but controlled by it through interfaces. An *interface* allows different devices to communicate with one another by translating the signals into an understandable code. *Output devices* are peripherals that receive information from the computer. Some common output devices are monitors, printers, disk drives, and tape drives.

Disk and tape drives are both input and output devices because computers can write or "save" programs to these units as well as read or "run" them. Programs can be developed by the individual user or they can be purchased commercially.

One critically important output device for a computer is a printer. While a video monitor can display between 4 and 66 lines of information on a screen at one time, a printer can make copies of much more text—so long as the supply of paper holds out. Printers for microcomputers are of two general types, dot matrix and daisy wheel. *Dot matrix printers* make impressions by striking a ribbon with a "matrix" of pins. This produces characters that appear to be composed of dots. *Daisy wheel printers* produce characters by striking the ribbon with an impression of the character, much like an electric typewriter. For high quality printing, often referred to as "letter quality," daisy wheel printers are preferred. Mainframe computers are often attached to high-speed printers that produce high quality printing by inkjets, from which ink is sprayed directly on the paper.

Finally, computers can be linked together, or to other devices, by using modems. *Modems* are electronic devices that translate computer codes into signals to be transmitted across phone lines or other directly-wired connections. Microcomputers can communicate with other microcomputers or with larger, mainframe computers, since almost all computers use the same set of eight character codes for representing letters, numbers, punctuation, and other common computer control functions. These codes are desig-

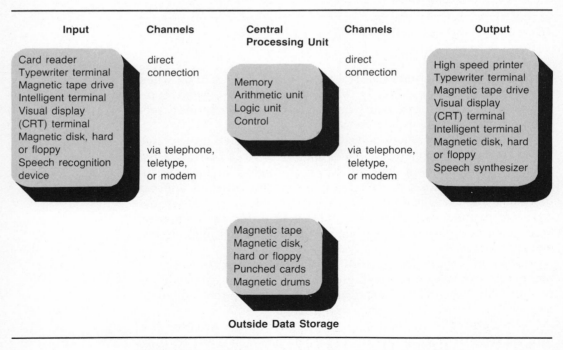

Input	Channels	Central Processing Unit	Channels	Output
Card reader Typewriter terminal Magnetic tape drive Intelligent terminal Visual display (CRT) terminal Magnetic disk, hard or floppy Speech recognition device	direct connection	Memory Arithmetic unit Logic unit Control	direct connection	High speed printer Typewriter terminal Magnetic tape drive Visual display (CRT) terminal Intelligent terminal Magnetic disk, hard or floppy Speech synthesizer
	via telephone, teletype, or modem		via telephone, teletype, or modem	

Magnetic tape
Magnetic disk, hard or floppy
Punched cards
Magnetic drums

Outside Data Storage

Figure 13-2. *Hardware components of a computer system.*

nated by the term ASCII, which stands for American Standard Code for Information Interchange.

This introduction to computers and computing has been very brief. More information on these topics can be found in *The Complete Handbook of Personal Computer Communications*,[2] and many other recent books. A special discussion of electronic office technology can be found in Chapter 2 of *Successful Business Communication*, 2d ed., by Malra Treece.[3]

OBTAINING AND ORGANIZING INFORMATION WITH COMPUTERS

Computers allow information to be gathered from distant sources, provided the information is contained in what is known as a database. A *database* is an organized collection of related information. Computerized databases can be "searched" for relevant information by using key words specified by the user. The computer analyzes each entry in the database and determines whether it contains any of the keywords. If a key word is present in the database entry, the computer prints out the information in that part of the database or saves it for further manipulation or for later printing.

The information in a database can be thought of as a series of records. A *record* is a particular set of related pieces of information. Each record is, in turn, composed of *fields*. To illustrate this, suppose a particular database contains a collection of information about manufacturing firms. A relatively simple database might contain many records. Each record would contain information about an individual corporation. Each field would contain a different piece of information related to that specific corporation. In each record, the same field would contain a similar piece of information about a different manufacturer. For example, the first field might be the name of the company. A second field might be the street address, while the third might be the city, and the fourth and fifth could be the state and zip code. A sixth field might contain a code representing the manufacturing specialty. Other fields could contain information such as the number of employees or annual gross sales of the product. This use of fields is illustrated in Figure 13-3.

Each field usually has information that can be searched by the

2. Albert Glossbrenner, *The Complete Handbook of Personal Computer Communications* (New York: St. Martin's Press, 1983).

3. Malra Treece, *Successful Business Communication*, 2d ed. (Boston: Allyn and Bacon, 1984.)

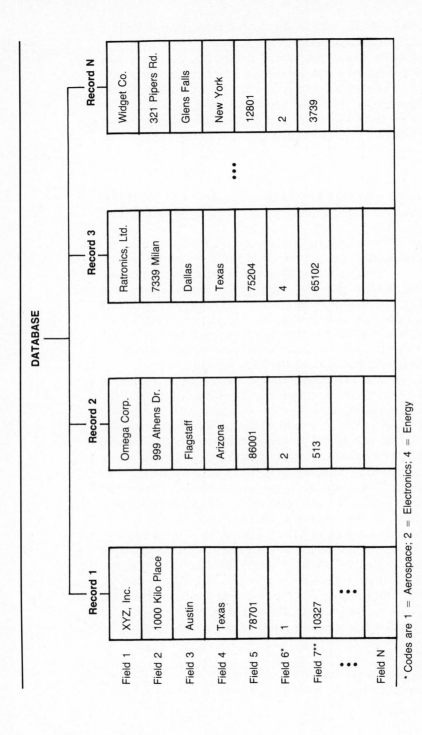

Figure 13-3. *Schematic representation of a hypothetical database.*

key words specified by the user. For example, in order for the computer to display or print the specialty of Corporation XYZ, the key word might simply be the name XYZ. The computer could be instructed to print out field 6 for every entry that had XYZ in field 1.

The greatest advantage of database searches is that key words can be combined with logical operations. For example, a computer could search the hypothetical database for all corporations in Texas with gross sales of more than $10,000,000. This example illustrates why a field should contain only one piece of information. If the city and state were in the same field, the researcher would not be able to ask about manufacturers in a given state without specifying the city as well. The separation of information in fields allows the database to be searched efficiently and quickly with maximum flexibility.

Commercial Databases

A *commercial database* is organized, collected, and updated by professionals in a given area. Subscribers usually are allowed to access a database for fees based on the amount of time actually spent in accessing it. These fees range from $5 an hour to $500 or more. Often an initial subscription fee is charged to set up an account and to provide a password for the user. Passwords are necessary for accurate billing and to prevent the unauthorized use of an account.

Self-generated databases can range from simple to fairly complex ones. Microcomputers can handle small to moderate sized databases, but the largest databases require the speed and capacity of mainframe computers. Speed is important because the search of a large database takes a great deal of time, overall, even though each individual record can be handled rapidly. Advantages of self-generated databases are their relatively low cost and the fact that they can be tailored to meet the specific needs of the user.

With a modem and the appropriate software, a microcomputer can function as a terminal to access remote databases. The range of information available from these on-line databases is extremely comprehensive. Database services include weather reports, sports scores, movie reviews, and shopping by catalog. For a growing number of these services, special software for microcomputers allows a user to download the information from the database to the microcomputer. Then the data can be used at a later time in other applications or as input for other programs.

A partial list of commercial databases is included in Chapter 8, "Gathering Information from Secondary Sources."

Self-Generated Databases

Database software packages are available for almost every micro-computer. One of the most common of these database programs is called *dBase II*. Others include *pfs*, *Rbase*, *Profile Plus*, and *Knowl-edgeman*, and there are many more. Software packages for both mainframes and microcomputers also allow a user to create data-bases for individual situations.

The performance of a database system is judged by the speed of searching and sorting records, the number of entries that can be searched, the amount of information that can be stored in a record, and the ease of entering records and changing information. Many of these capabilities depend on the amount of RAM memory available in the computer and the speed and type of CPU. Thus, some com-puters are better suited than others for database functions.

Many database programs allow users to construct their own report formats; a user can specify how the data are to be searched, summarized, and printed. Some software imposes limits on these choices. Often the program can be set up so that data can be entered in response to prompts such as these: Name of Corporation? Street Address? State? Zip Code? The computer moves the cursor to the next field after the information is entered from the keyboard. Some-one with little or no computer experience can then enter data or update records. Many of these functions are handled by menus, from which a user selects the number of the actions for the computer to perform.

Using Database Information

The information in a database can be accessed and used like infor-mation from any conventional source. An additional advantage is that information from these databases often can be downloaded into another, smaller computer. It can then be used as input for manip-ulation by other programs. One major use for data obtained in this manner is as input to electronic spreadsheets, which are discussed later. The information from a database also can be incorporated di-rectly into word-processed documents, which also are discussed later.

MANIPULATING INFORMATION

Computers are at their best when they are called on to manipulate, calculate, transform, or process numbers. Data processing is therefore a major function of computers. Data processing is largely a matter of performing calculations with numbers. Computers are most useful when necessary calculations are complex, numerous, or highly repetitive. Determining trends, performing statistical tests, and summarizing many disparate pieces of raw data are among the tasks of data processing.

Microcomputers have introduced the concept of distributed data processing. When mainframe computers are used for data processing, all users are dependent on a single machine. Microcomputers allow each user to do data processing when and where it is desired. The emphasis on making microcomputers easy to use has reinforced the distributed data processing concept.

Spreadsheets

One of the most impressive developments for microcomputers in business contexts has been the introduction of the electronic spreadsheet. Conventional spreadsheets can be used to summarize data, make projections, or to prepare data for complex calculations. Electronic spreadsheets can be used for all of those functions, only with greater ease and convenience. In addition, they can be used to create tables and, in some cases, figures or graphs representing the data. Spreadsheets can produce derived data to be used in other programs or applications. Entries in a spreadsheet can be changed or edited at will, with the results on the entire spreadsheet available almost immediately.

The first of these spreadsheets was *Visicalc*. Since its introduction there have been many improvements and enhancements in other programs. More recent spreadsheet programs include *Supercalc, Multiplan, Perfect Calc*, and *Calcstar*.

How a Spreadsheet Works

In an electronic spreadsheet, each cell is defined by the intersection of a row and a column. Earlier and less complex spreadsheets are often limited to 254 or fewer rows and 64 or fewer columns, for a total of about 16,000 cells. Newer and more complex spreadsheets can have numbers of rows and columns limited only by the available memory.

Each cell can contain data, formulas, text for headings, labels, and so on. Each cell can be formatted to display the contents in decimal, integer, or dollar and cents formats. Most electronic spreadsheets also have built-in functions to perform complex calculations, such as taking the average of a range of scores or finding the maximum or minimum score in a row or column of numbers. Some spreadsheets have financial functions like Net Present Value. Spreadsheets can be used to make different decisions (or calculations) depending on the logical "truth value" of the contents of a cell. For example, one function might be to indicate that a discount rate would apply *only* if the contents of a cell were greater than a fixed amount. The spreadsheet would automatically apply the discount when the amount in the cell was greater than the specified number.

A *template* is the underlying skeleton of a spreadsheet. It contains all headings and formulas necessary to combine data from the entries. A template contains no raw data. Thus a template can be used to solve similar problems, repeatedly, with different data. Once the data are entered in the sheet, the entire sheet can be stored for use at a later time. For example, summaries of sales by regions could be entered on a monthly basis. Rather than create a different spreadsheet each time, the same template could be used, with new data entered in the appropriate cells. Filled spreadsheets can be stored for later reference.

Figure 13-4 was generated as a report on the activity of a stock portfolio. It was printed from data contained in a *Visicalc* spreadsheet. The entire spreadsheet was not produced. The columns labelled STG, STL, LTL, and LTG represent short- and long-term gains and losses. The spreadsheet automatically computes the gains and losses and assigns them to the appropriate column. Note that the dates had to be entered in an odd form to be used in calculations. Newer spreadsheets have specialized functions for handling date calculations.

Stock	No. Shrs	Pur. Date	Cost	Sale Date	Proceeds	Net	STG	STL	LTG	LTL
ABC	100	1.181983	1914.75	6.091983	2251.73	336.98	336.98	0	0	0
DEF	100	10.151982	2526.01	2.011983	2092.28	-433.73	0	-433.73	0	0
GHI	100	11.301981	3068.98	4.221983	2006.43	-1062.55	0	0	0	-1062.55
KLM	100	9.221982	2131.24	7.261983	1920.57	-210.67	0	-210.67	0	0
NOP	200	10.201982	2250.42	11.091983	2320.28	69.86	0	0	69.86	0
XYZ	100	6.171983	3070.71	12.221983	2024.52	-1046.19	0	-1046.19	0	0
Totals						-2346.3	336.98	-1690.59	69.86	-1062.55

Figure 13-4. *Hypothetical stock report generated by Visicalc.*

Generally, data for entries in a spreadsheet come from conventional sources and are keyed in manually. Data also can be retrieved from commercial or self-generated databases. Special software is available for microcomputers to allow a user to download information from commercial databases in forms that will automatically load into a spreadsheet template of the appropriate type. Many self-generated database programs allow the user to prepare a file of data to be loaded into a spreadsheet. Direct loading of information is particularly useful when the data in the database change frequently. For example, stock prices can be downloaded into programs that will track the progress of the issues over periods of time.

Integrated Spreadsheets

Many spreadsheets have more sophisticated features than the original *Visicalc*. For example, columns can be made different widths, and they can be sorted to appear in different orders. A very useful feature is the ability of a spreadsheet to have *windows*. On the computer screen, a window allows the user to examine different portions of the entire spreadsheet and manipulate the data in each. The original program had the capability of displaying two windows; newer, more sophisticated versions can display many more.

Another feature of some software programs is the ability to access different files to be used in the same spreadsheet. Thus, for example, a user might want to produce a profile of results from past years. The program would access the results of other spreadsheets for information to be used in the current one.

As with database programs, the presence or absence of various features depends on several things. First, the type of machine is important. While most computers have some sort of spreadsheet available, those with more complex CPUs can handle more sophisticated spreadsheet programs. Second, a critical variable is the amount of memory. Memory limits the amount of data and the number of cells that can be included in a spreadsheet file. Finally, the ability of a computer to produce graphics will determine, to an extent, the sophistication of the programs that can be used.

Some of the newer spreadsheets are combined in a single software package with a database system incorporated in the program. Some packages allow the user to create graphics automatically from the results of the spreadsheet. Thus a user can create a database and then use the database to provide data for the spreadsheet. The popular *Lotus 1-2-3* program is designed to perform database, spreadsheet, and graphic functions from the same file. *Lotus 1-2-3* also has the ability to do minimal word processing. Newer programs will include expanded word processing capabilities and far greater graphics features.

WORD PROCESSING

Word processing involves using the computer to store, format, and print written text. Unlike a typewritten document, a word-processed form of the material does not have to be produced or printed until it is in its final, complete, and edited form. Changes can be made quickly and easily with the computer adjusting the text to incorporate the changes.

In their electronic form, word-processed documents can be

Figure 13-5. *A typical word processing installation.*

transmitted rapidly between computers. In addition, several writers can work on different parts of the same report simultaneously. When all the parts are completed, they can be merged into a single document to produce the final report, with all the pages correctly numbered and in the appropriate sequences.

When one or more reports contain the same language, a word processor eliminates the need to re-type the sections that remain the same. Similarly, letters that are to be sent to a number of persons can be generated by entering the names and addresses of the recipients in a separate file. The word processor (or, more correctly, the file-merging portion of it) automatically inserts the name and address of each person in the appropriate location in the letter.

Components of a Word Processor

A fully functioning word processor must consist of a computer, a keyboard, a video display, a storage device (usually a disk drive), and a printer. Figure 13-5 illustrates a common word processing set-up. Any computer can act as a word processor so long as it has the appropriate software package. Dedicated word processors are simply single-purpose computers that do word processing only.

Word processing software has two functions. First, it must have a method of allowing the user to enter text. Second, it must be able to tell the computer (technically, the CPU) how to format the text on the printed pages. This instruction is accomplished by having the text-formatting program interpret commands inserted into the text file. The computer can tell when the writer wants to have a paragraph begin or how wide the margins are to be. Figure 13-6a shows an example of a table prepared on a word processor. Figure 13-6b shows what the computer file looked like before it was printed. This example comes from a mainframe word-processing package called *Script*, running on an IBM system.

Secretary	Average Time	Shortest Time	Longest Time
Fink	23	14	32
Saliba	21	12	37
Thompson	16	10	19
AVERAGE	20	12	29 1/3

Figure 13-6a. *Minutes spent in step 4 or manually prepared returns based on ten returns prepared by each secretary.*

```
.im paper
.co no;.ss
.ce on
Table 4
.up;minutes spent in step 4 of manually prepared returns
Based on Ten Returns Prepared by Each Secretary
.ce off
.sk
.tb 24c +24c +24c
.us;Secretary@Average Time@Shortest Time@Longest Time
Fink@23@14@32
Saliba@21@12@37
.us;⌐Thompson@⌐__16__⌐@⌐__10__⌐@⌐__19__
AVERAGE@20@12@29 1/3
```

Figure 13-6b. *Listing of computer file to produce figure 13-4a.*

For microcomputers, word processing is possible if the appropriate software is available and a printer is attached. Some of the more common word processing programs are *Wordstar*, which has versions available for many computers; *Word*, primarily for IBM and IBM-compatible microcomputers; *Scripsit* for Radio Shack computers; and *EasyWriter* and *EasyWriter II*, available for several different machines. Programs like *Bank Street Writer* allow microcomputer users to begin producing word-processed documents almost immediately. However, not all of these programs will allow the user to perform all the functions of a word processor. For example, the spelling-check feature is not available in some packages, and some do not allow the integration of other files into the word-processed document. Usually, the features in a word processor are related to the price of the package and the underlying capabilities of the computer for which the program was written.

Editing with a Word Processor

Once the text has been entered in a file, a word processor can be used to edit the text. Simple editing functions include inserting words, deleting words, changing words or parts of words, inserting or deleting blocks of text, changing line lengths or margins, and moving segments of the text to different locations. The computer automatically adjusts the length of lines and positions on pages to account for differences caused by changes made in the file.

Word processors can perform even more sophisticated functions, depending on the computer and the program. A common function is to *justify* the text, so that both the left and right margins are even. Justification is accomplished by inserting spaces between words or between letters. Proportional justification is accomplished by printing different letters in different widths, a function that is available with some software and some printers. All of these functions can be created by entering, at most, a few commands into the text file.

Once the text has been keyed into a file, the computer can be used to check the text file for spelling and for simple grammatical errors. The computer also can do hyphenation, although some exceptions may have to be entered by hand, even when the program is designed to be "automatic."

Another useful feature is that most word processing programs will allow a user to make wholesale changes in the text. For example, suppose someone had written a report that consistently used the phrase "annual dividend" instead of "quarterly dividend." A few commands will replace *all* instances of the former with the latter. At the same time, the program will adjust the text to account for differences in length of the two items.

Depending on the type of printer attached to a word processor, type styles can be changed within the text. The word processor can, again depending on the type of printer, underline, print in italics or double width, and arrange material in many other styles. For some

```
This is typed so the computer prints  each character twice.
```

```
This is printed in italics.
```

```
The printer has been instructed to emphasize this line.
```

```
This line is in double width type.
```

```
This line is in compressed characters.
```

Figure 13-7a. *Samples of type styles for a dot matrix printer.*

printers, a user can design type fonts in any desired style. Figure 13-7a shows some examples of type styles produced on a common dot matrix printer. Figure 13-7b shows an example of printed output from a common daisy wheel printer.

Integrating Information into Reports

In addition to typing, editing, and printing text, word processors have one other powerful feature. Files that have been produced by other computer programs can be inserted in the middle (or any other part) of the word-processed file. Thus computations on a set of data can be inserted directly into the body of the report without being type-written into the report file. If a database or spreadsheet has produced a table, that table can be inserted directly into the report at the appropriate point. Graphic illustrations also can be inserted. The computer (with appropriate software and printer) can insert bar charts, graphs, pie charts, and other illustrations in the text at the appropriate point. In short, anything that can be placed in a computer file can be entered into the body of the report.

Two important limitations, however, are that the word processing program must be sophisticated enough to allow these features and the files must be compatible. Not every word processing package allows the insertion of other files into the text. In addition, some files, particularly those written on different computers, cannot be used in particular word processing programs. The problem with files is that they may be in different formats or they may not be readable by the program being used. Another limitation can be with

---

```
This line is in a single style.   Other fonts can be used if the wheel is changed.
As many fonts are available as there are type styles for a normal electric
typewriter with interchangeable elements.

This was typed in artisan

This was typed in prestige elite

This was typed in letter gothic

This was typed in courier 10

This was typed in light italic
```

Figure 13-7b.   *Sample of type fonts from a daisy wheel printer.*

the hardware. For example, some printers cannot produce graphics. The user must be certain that the printer is appropriate for the task at hand.

For many business applications, it is necessary or desirable to use all of the functions of the computer in preparing reports. Integrated software allows the user to perform all of the functions from the same program without having to worry about problems such as file incompatibility.

Recent microcomputer programs do spreadsheet functions, combine them with databases, access many different sets of data, produce graphics, and do word processing—all from the same program. The compatibility problem is eliminated, and users are required to learn only a single set of commands and operations. Production of reports is easier and more efficient. Some representative examples of this sort of software are *Symphony*, *Framework*, and *Desq*. Others like *Context MBA* and *Lotus 1-2-3* are integrated but have fewer different functions. The final advantage of this type of package is that it allows the user to see the results prior to having them printed.

ELECTRONIC MAIL

Once a report is in final edited form in a word-processed file, it can be printed or transmitted directly to the recipients by electronic mail systems. The only requirements are that the sender and the receiver have appropriate computer terminals or other data communication equipment. In addition, commercial services may be used to transmit a document electronically, produce a hard copy (printed version), and deliver it in person.

Some of the commercial computer mail services include *MCI Mail*, *Western Union EasyLink*, and *ITT's DIALCOM*. The United States Postal Service provides an electronic mail service to selected cities. *The Source* and *Compuserve* also have facilities for exchanging messages or other mail. Charges are incurred based on the type of service (e.g., hardcopy or electronic version) and length of the message.

In some instances, a computer file can be transmitted directly to a printer or other reproduction machine. One or more copies can then be produced at the receiving end. In still other cases, the transmitted file can simply be stored on disk, at the receiving end. Advantages of this last option are obvious. The receiver can make alterations and return a copy to the original sender. In short, the report never has to be physically produced to have the receiver examine it. (It should be noted, however, that printed copies often are easier to read and edit than versions produced on video terminals.)

The future of electronic transmission of written material looks extremely promising. Even now, there are optical readers—devices that can translate printed pages directly into computer code. Thus even documents that were not produced with a word processor may be electronically transmitted. In the future, electronic documents will have the capacity to have either voice or text comments accompany the body of the document. That is, each reader will be able to do revisions, make comments, or ask questions about specific portions of a report, either by typing or speaking, or both.

SUMMARY

Computers can create, access, and retrieve information from databases. Databases can be those created at a local site or they can be centralized, commercial subscription services.

Computers also can manipulate data in many different ways. Electronic spreadsheets like *Visicalc* perform complex functions and are useful in manipulating and preparing data, generating tables, and summarizing or forecasting business trends.

Word processing is, perhaps, the most common function of computers in preparing reports. Word processing allows text to be revised, edited, and electronically transmitted in computer form. Word processors also allow for the preparation of customized reports, letters, or other documents by eliminating the need for retyping the text each time a new, but similar, document is to be produced.

Integrated software allows a user to perform most, or all, of the computer functions from a single program.

The future holds the promise of greater productivity through increased use of the present technology as well as the development of new technology.

GLOSSARY OF COMPUTER TERMS

ASCII codes

A set of standard codes for representing the 128 characters used for text, numbers, and computer control functions. The acronym comes from American Standard Code for Information Interchange.

Basic	The most common language for microcomputers. Basic is easy to learn and use. The acronym comes from: *B*eginners *A*ll-purpose *S*ymbolic *I*nstruction *C*ode.
Baud rate	A measure of the rate at which *bits* of computer information can be transmitted. As an example, 300 baud represents a transmission rate of 300 bits per second.
Bit	The smallest unit that can be represented by computers. Bit is short for *bi*nary dig*it*. A bit is always represented as a 1 or 0.
Boot	To load and activate the operating system of the computer; short for bootstrap program.
Byte	A group of bits (0s and 1s) used to represent a character. Commonly, bytes are composed of 8 bits.
COBOL	A computer language for business applications. It is relatively easy to use. The name comes from *C*omputer *B*usiness *O*riented *L*anguage.
Computer languages	Software that makes it possible to instruct the computer to carry out specific actions.
CP/M	A common disk operating system used by many microcomputers. The microcomputers that use this system have a CPU called a Z-80.
CPU	The "brain" of the computer. The CPU controls what the computer does by executing commands and instructions. The acronym comes from *C*entral *P*rocessing *U*nit.
CRT	A video display or monitor for a computer. CRT stands for Cathode Ray Tube, although this is mostly an outdated usage. (See also VDT.)
Daisy wheel printer	A printer that prints like a typewriter, in which the elements have the characters arranged on a circular disk. The print quality is very good, usually referred to as letter-quality.
Database	An organized collection of information that can be accessed and manipulated by a computer.

Data processing	Using a computer to manipulate data, usually numerical. Data processing includes doing statistical analyses or summarizing large amounts of data.
Dedicated word processor	A single purpose computer that can only do word processing. (See also word processing.)
DOS	The generic name for computer systems that operate with disk drives.
Dot matrix printer	A printer that prints by impacting wires or rods against a ribbon in patterns to produce character images. These are usually less expensive than other types of printers.
Download	To transfer information from a larger computer to a smaller one. Uploading is the reverse process—transferring the information from a smaller to a larger computer.
Floppy disk	A storage device that uses floppy diskettes— thin, circular, plastic sheets covered with magnetic oxide. Information is stored on diskettes much as it is on recording tape, except that access is easier. Common sizes are 8″, 5¼ ″, and 3½″.
Formatter	Software that instructs the computer to print out the text in specific manners and styles.
Fortran	A computer language used for data processing and scientific and engineering applications. Fortran is an acronym for *For*mula *Tran*slator.
Hard disk	A storage device in which the information is stored on rigid surfaces that are coated with magnetic oxide. Hard drives have larger capacities and can access stored information faster and more reliably than floppy disk drives. These are sometimes called winchester disk drives.
Hardware	The physical parts of the computer, including the keyboard, CRT or VDT, printer, disk drives, and other peripherals.
Interface	A circuit board or other device that translates signals from one piece of hardware to another. Interfaces allow all of the periphals to "understand" each other.

K	When combined with byte, K represents 1024 (2^{10}). Thus, 64K bytes actually represents 65,536 bytes rather than 64,000.
Local Area Network (LAN)	A method of connecting computers in a limited area. This allows computers to communicate with each other and users to share information directly. Two LANs are Ethernet and Decnet.
Menu	A software device that presents the user with choices that can be easily selected. A user asks the computer to perform complex functions by choosing a number or a letter representing that choice. Menus are one way to make software user-friendly.
Modem	A device for translating computer language into a form that can be transmitted over telephone lines, as well as the reverse. Modem comes from *mod*ulator—*dem*odulator.
Mouse	An electro-mechanical peripheral that can be used instead of a keyboard for many computer control functions. A mouse can be used for selecting from a menu, for doing graphics, and for many other functions.
MS/DOS	A common disk operating system used by IBM-compatible microcomputers. It is very similar to PC Dos, the IBM system.
Operating Systems	Software that manages the internal functions of the computer, routing information and instructions to the appropriate devices (disk drives, printers, VDTs, etc.).
Pascal	A popular computer language that is easily transported from one computer to another. It is named for the philosopher, Blaise Pascal.
Port	A connection to the computer through which peripherals can be attached.
RAM	The memory from which or to which computer information can be read or written by the CPU. RAM is usually volatile; that is, its contents disappear when the power is removed. RAM stands for *random access memory*.
ROM	This is memory which can only be read. The CPU cannot write information to ROM

	memory. ROM is an acronym for *read only memory*.
RS-232 standard	A standard method of interfacing computers and data communications equipment. This standard helps to ensure that different manufacturers will produce compatible equipment.
Software	The programs that tell the CPU what instructions to carry out. *Integrated software* is software that carries out several different sorts of functions in a single program.
Terminal	A device for communicating with a computer. Terminals display output. They consist of keyboards and either a CRT or a VDT. Some terminals produce printed output. (See also CRT and VDT.)
Time-sharing	An arrangement in which many users can use the same computer by interacting with it from terminals. The computer switches rapidly between users.
Upload	To transfer information from a small computer to a larger one. (See also download.)
User-friendly	A term applied to computers and software when specialized computer knowledge is not required for effective operation.
VDT	A video display or monitor for a computer. It stands for video display terminal. (See also CRT).
Voice input/voice output	Voice input is a method for communicating with a computer by which the user can speak commands rather than using a keyboard. Voice output involves having the computer "speak" rather than print information on paper or a VDT. Speech output is usually *synthesized*, or produced by rules, rather than as recordings.
Word processing	Using a computer to write, edit, and otherwise manipulate text materials.

Formal Analytical Reports | 14

299

The basic principles of report writing apply to all kinds of reports, whether they are of minor, limited nature or extensive in coverage.

The researcher must understand the problem and be able to state it exactly. The next steps are to find the necessary information, evaluate and interpret this information, and organize it in the most readable and appropriate form. This procedure remains the same although the finished report may be presented in one of several forms: the complete, formal arrangement, a more informal report arrangement in that some or all of the preliminary and supplementary parts are omitted, a letter, or a memorandum.

A complete formal report, by its very nature, requires more time, effort, and instruction than shorter, more informal arrangements. You are likely to present reports in this formal arrangement much less frequently than in the shorter and more informal formats. By learning how to prepare a complete formal report, however, you will also be learning to prepare shorter ones, or those with differing formats.

Your ability to do an outstanding job on an extensive report project, which would likely be presented in a rather formal arrangement, could be an aid to the advancement of your business career. Even more important are your increased confidence and sense of accomplishment.

THE REPORT PACKAGE

Complete formal reports are comprised of three major divisions: preliminaries, the report body (or report proper), and supplementary parts. These three major divisions make up the *report package.*

The following list of report parts is not intended to be used for all formal reports, regardless of length. *Few reports will need all of these preliminaries,* and preliminary parts not shown in this list are desirable for some reports.

The preliminary and supplementary parts preceded by a check are the ones that are most often used. The others may be included or omitted depending upon the particular report situation. An index is likely to be omitted from all kinds of business reports. A well-made table of contents makes an index unnecessary and even undesirable, except in book-length manuscripts. In addition, an index is most difficult to construct, and an incomplete one is worse than none at all.

Preliminaries:

√   Cover
     Title fly
√   Title page
     Letter of authorization
     Letter of acceptance
√   Letter of transmittal
√   Table of contents
     List of charts and tables
√   Synopsis

Body of the report:
    Introduction
    Text of the report, usually divided into several major sections
    Conclusions and recommendations, which are usually combined into one section

Supplements:
√   Appendix (or appendices)
√   Bibliography
√   Index
    (The bibliography may precede other supplements.)

PRELIMINARY REPORT PARTS

The following paragraphs describe the usual preliminary report parts. The illustrations shown are not intended to illustrate a sequence of preliminary parts from the same report. Instead, they are taken from various reports. In addition to the illustrations in this section, other examples of preliminaries are included later when discussing the remaining portions of a formal report.

The Cover

The *cover* is used to protect and to hold the report together, as well as to add to its attractive appearance. A cover also shows that you are careful enough about your report to present it in a neat manner. Don't force your reader to open the cover to find the title and author; this information should appear on the cover itself or through a cut-out section.

The Title Fly

The *title fly* is a full page. It shows only the title. This page serves no useful purpose and may be omitted unless the particular handbook you are following tells you to include it.

The Title Page

The *title page* includes the title of the report, the complete identification of the report writer and the person to whom the report is submitted, and the date.

Work for a concise but descriptive title. Although some titles are unnecessarily wordy, short ones are likely to be vague, nondescriptive, and overly broad, promising more than the report includes.

A specific title indicates the nature, purpose, and limits of the research. The title is the major heading of the entire written work. Like all other headings, it must describe the contents that come under it. The title should rule out what does *not* come under it, at least to the extent that a reader could reasonably expect to find such information.

If you have stated the purpose in a concise, appropriate form, you should have no difficulty writing a suitable title. In some instances, the statement of purpose may be an appropriate title, which, unlike the title, may be worded to show the results of the investigation. For example, a problem statement worded in this way:

```
"Should Dillard Enterprises Move to Commerce
Square?"
```

may be stated in a title in this way:

```
"Why Dillard Enterprises Should Move to Commerce
Square."
```

This title could also correctly remain in question form. An example of a title page is shown in Figure 14-1.

To repeat and emphasize: *Make sure that the title is stated specifically.* The same considerations that apply to a specific problem statement, as discussed in Chapter 7, apply to the final title of the report.

The Letter of Authorization

The *letter of authorization,* as the name indicates, is written by the person who authorizes the report. It may not be a letter at all but a memorandum. In addition, some authorizations are given orally.

When you receive a written authorization, either a letter or a memorandum, include it in the finished report. This authorization serves as a reminder that the report was prepared and presented according to specific instructions. If the report is to be read by persons other than the authorizer, the letter or memorandum of authorization adds dignity and importance to the work, especially if the report is authorized by a person in a responsible position in the organization.

The Letter of Acceptance

The *letter of acceptance* is written by the researcher near the beginning of the report process as an acknowledgment of the letter of authorization. It makes clear that the report writer understands the problem and any specific instructions given orally or in the written authorization. Like the letter of authorization and the letter of transmittal, this message may also be in memorandum form. The letter arrangement has the advantage of being slightly more personal, yet more formal, as this important situation merits.

The Letter of Transmittal

The *letter of transmittal,* as the name indicates, transmits the finished report. It may be used for helpful and informative comments about the research process, particularly those that do not seem to fit into the report itself. It should include some reference to the authorization and to the purpose of the study.

Other information that may be included in the letter or memorandum of transmittal are suggestions for follow-up studies or other

WHAT IMPROVEMENTS SHOULD BE MADE IN THE PHYSICAL
ASPECTS OF THE GOLD BOND DISTRICT OFFICE
TO IMPROVE EFFICIENCY AND MORALE?

Prepared for

Richard Lunner, District Manager
Gold Bond Building Products

by

Sue Richardson
Office Manager

July 5, 198–

Figure 14-1. *Example of title page.*

side issues of the problem. It may mention special limitations or difficulties encountered in the research or in the report-writing process, as well as the highlights or other details of the research process. Do not include in the letter of transmittal a synopsis or statement that sums up the findings and recommendations if you also prepare a separate synopsis.

If there is no need for a separate synopsis, the transmittal letter will serve both purposes. Often the synopsis included in a letter of transmittal can be adequately presented in a paragraph or two. The letter of transmittal and synopsis should not be combined if doing so will make the letter longer than one page.

An example of a letter of transmittal that does not include a synopsis is shown in Figure 14-2.

The Table of Contents

The *table of contents* is the report outline, or the tentative table of contents, in its final revised form, with the addition of page numbers.

A table of contents is helpful in many reports that would not be described as formal from the standpoint of arrangement or format. If a table of contents is well made, it serves as a summary of the entire written work and shows the flow of thought from beginning to end. It indicates the topics covered in the report, the sequence of those topics, and the relative importance of the divisions and subdivisions. It also gives the page number where each of the topics can be found. It is helpful to readers who are especially interested in particular sections of the report, or those who wish to reread particular sections.

As mentioned in previous chapters, it is essential that all headings and subheadings of the table of contents agree exactly with the headings and subheadings in the report itself.

Outline symbols may be used before the various captions of the table of contents. The relative importance of various headings is shown by choice of type and by placement. The reader should be able to see immediately the level of each heading and its relationship to all other headings. Major headings should stand out clearly from lesser ones, and subheadings of lesser weights should be clearly placed under each main heading. Avoid a complicated breakdown of subheadings. In most business reports, two or three levels adequately describe the contents.

The page is headed with the caption *Contents* or *Table of Contents*. An illustration of a table of contents is given in Figure 14-3.

April 13, 198–

Mr. Yancey Rowland, President
Rowland's of South City, Inc.
4515 Poplar Avenue, Suite 330
South City, Florida 33505

Dear Mr. Rowland:

The accompanying report contains projected figures and actual test
results of the Salesmaster sales program as it would be used in your
stores.

The material was compiled in order to determine whether the program
would be an effective sales tool as an addition to your current and
future point–of–purchase marketing efforts.

The program is presented on the basis of additional gross profits
versus the cost of ownership and operation of the machines.

Additional factors such as customizing of the cabinets to match store
interior colors, logo applications, and financial arrangements are
mentioned briefly. I would be very happy to discuss these with you at
any time.

Sincerely,

Stuart Levine

Stuart Levine
Sales Manager

Figure 14-2.   *Illustration of letter of transmittal.*

TABLE OF CONTENTS

Figure 14-3. *Example of table of contents.*

Lists of Charts and Graphs

A list of charts and graphs may be headed: *Table of Illustrations, List of Illustrations, Table of Charts and Illustrations,* or *Table of Figures.* The report may also include separate lists, as a *List of Tables* and a *List of Charts.* This report part should be headed by the most descriptive term for the illustrations used. It can be a continuation of the overall table of contents or shown on a separate page.

The Synopsis

A *synopsis* is a much condensed review of the entire report, including the introduction and the conclusions and recommendations. In order to stress results, the synopsis is often arranged in the direct order even if the report itself is presented in the indirect order. Usually two-thirds to three-fourths of the synopsis should be devoted to the final results. The remaining portion of the synopsis contains a very brief statement of the purpose, scope, methods, and, perhaps, the background and need for the study.

Many synopses that accompany reports arranged in the inductive order are similarly arranged. The synopsis must be brief, no more than one-tenth of the length of the entire report. For a very long report, the proportional length of the synopsis is even shorter. At its longest, the synopsis should fill no more than two typewritten pages, single spaced. Some company and government officials insist that all synopses, regardless of the length of the entire report, be limited to one page.

You may be able to write an acceptable synopsis of the report by condensing each major division of the report into one paragraph. Thus a report consisting of an introduction (Part I), four sections of findings (Parts II, III, IV, and V), and the conclusions and recommendations (Part VI) could be condensed into a six-paragraph synopsis.

If the direct order is used for a synopsis, the first paragraph sums up the conclusions and recommendations section of the report. The second paragraph sums up the introductory section, and the four remaining paragraphs summarize the four middle sections of the report (Parts VI, I, II, III, IV, V).

Neither of the preceding arrangements is necessary, but a synopsis should truly sum up the entire report. *Because emphasis is on results, more space is often given to conclusions and recommendations.*

The use of the synopsis, in effect, presents the report package in the direct order, although the report proper (beginning with the introduction and continuing through the conclusions and recommendations) is arranged in the indirect order. Because giving the "answer" before the presentation of reasons can be a psychological disadvantage, some report writers prefer to omit the synopsis unless it is an expected and traditional part of the formal report as used in the employing organization. Usually the synopsis should be included, even in reports with disappointing recommendations, because it is likely to be an expected part and, even more importantly, because it is an effective aid to readability. (This question is also discussed in Chapter 2 with the explanation of the direct and indirect order.)

The synopsis is sometimes reproduced and distributed to people who do not read the entire report, or it may be printed in professional journals or company publications. A written synopsis is also useful as the basis for a condensed oral presentation.

Illustrations of synopses are shown in Figures 14-4 and 14-5.

Terminology differs for the part usually described as a synopsis; for example, *epitome*, *précis*, or *abstract*. The term *abstract* is often used to describe a very short summary of a dissertation or scientific study.

One variation of a synopsis is described as an *executive summary*, which tends to be longer than the usual synopsis. This term is used to describe a customary part of all reports prepared in some organizations. An example is shown with other portions of the report written by a researcher with Federal Express and illustrated in Figure 14-9.

Other Preliminary Parts

A preliminary part not shown in the list at the beginning of this chapter, which may be desirable for some reports, is an acknowledgments section. Acknowledgments may also be included in the letter of transmittal unless they are so numerous that the letter would be longer than one page.

Another preliminary part that is useful in some reports is a list of definitions of specialized terms used in the report itself. Definitions may also be placed in the introduction, if the list is fairly short—for example, no more than half the page. Another choice of placement is in the supplementary section of a report, where it is usually described as a *glossary*.

SYNOPSIS

The purpose of this report is to determine the profitability of using Salesmaster Moving Message sales display machines in all nineteen stores of the Rowland's South City chain.

Information was obtained from manufacturer's sales representatives; from literature distributed by the manufacturer; from reports of results obtained by other users, as published in trade magazines and described in interviews; and, most important, from results of actual tests in restaurants similar to Rowland's in South City.

This report concentrates on the direct point–of–purchase usage of the machine; that is, the advertising of featured items or special prices that change from day to day. Other uses of the Salesmaster include goodwill and civic messages, supplemental advertising for national or regional advertising campaigns, and local promotions.

The machines have been tested in several different restaurants, including five Krystal stores in Atlanta and two Rowland's in Blytheville, Arkansas. Results have been extremely favorable when the machine is in a restaurant with a high traffic volume, such as Rowland's. In Blytheville, a tape advertising sundaes, shown on a Salesmaster for four weeks, increased sales of sundaes by 67 percent.

Results from these tests provide a basis for the estimate that installation of the Salesmaster program in all nineteen stores should result in annual additional gross profits of more than $60,000 a year. Results from the actual testing program in Blytheville support this estimate, which is also supported by the reports of other users.

The program, if utilized in all nineteen stores, would cost $12,973 for equipment, plus an annual cost of $3,268 for the 115–character message tapes. The machines are guaranteed by the manufacturer for three years. The anticipated return for the second and succeeding years should remain fairly constant.

Salesmaster Moving Message sales display machines should be installed in all nineteen stores of the Rowland's South City chain.

Figure 14-4. *Example of a synopsis.*

SYNOPSIS

The cost of general purpose computer systems should be
distributed to the users. Even though the users may be diverse and
many and the problems in assigning costs complex, users of a service
should be charged for that service.

This recommendation is based on a review of current literature
on costing practices of general purpose computer systems and on past
personal experience as a user of general purpose computer systems.

The major costs of a general purpose computer are hardware,
software, machine maintenance, and personnel expense. These costs
may be large and out of the control of the users.

Accepted cost accounting practices require that direct cost in
the production of a good or service be shown as a part of the total
cost of that good or service. Alternative suggestions such as
establishing a computer operation cost outside the good or service or
allocating these costs to overhead are not acceptable treatment of
the cost of services rendered. Therefore, the distribution of
computer cost should be made to users even though it is not, in
practice, satisfactory to all users.

iv

Figure 14-5. *Example of a synopsis.*

Pagination of Preliminary Report Parts

Preliminary pages (everything up to the first page of the report itself, which is the first page of the introduction) are numbered with lower case Roman numerals, if they are numbered at all. These Roman numerals are centered about one inch from the bottom of the page. Preliminary pages are counted beginning with the title page.

The title page is not numbered. The letter of transmittal and table of contents may be numbered or correctly left unnumbered. The synopsis is usually numbered, although it and all other preliminary pages may be left unnumbered unless to do so disagrees with the particular handbook you are using as a guide.

Thus, if a report contains a title page, a letter of transmittal, a one-page table of contents, and a one-page synopsis, these pages are counted in the numbering process as *i*, *ii*, *iii*, and *iv*.

Arabic numerals are used for the rest of the report, beginning with the first page of the introduction.

THE BODY OF THE REPORT

The body of the report, or the "report proper," begins with the introduction and continues through the conclusions and recommendations—if the report is arranged in the indirect (inductive) order. In a report arranged in the direct order, which is less likely to have preliminary parts, the report body begins with the gist of the message, which is ordinarily the recommendations section.

The Introduction

To review and summarize, the introduction may include these sections:

1. Authorization. (Not necessary if you use a letter of authorization.)
2. Purpose. (Essential.)
3. Scope. (Essential if it is not obvious from the title and statement of purpose. Scope may be combined with limitations.) tations.)
4. Limitations. (Use only as needed—and with caution. Limitations often appear as excuses for a poor report.)
5. Historical background. (Also described as background, background conditions, history, or in other terms.) This section

should be included in the introduction only if it can be kept brief. In some reports this information deserves a complete division, often as Part II of the report body.

6. Sources and methods of collecting data. (Essential.) In a few long reports for which detailed and complicated methods of collection or analysis are used, these methods can be reported in Part II of the body of the report.

An example of an introduction is shown in Figure 14-6. This information is based on the tentative report plan shown in Chapter 7 as Figure 7-1.

The Text

The *text* of a report is used to mean the divisions of the report that come after the introduction and before the conclusions and recommendations section. This is not a completely descriptive term, for in a sense the entire report is the text. These middle sections are also referred to as the "findings" portion of the report. (Terminology as it concerns different sections of reports differs slightly according to the handbook or textbook you are using as a guide.)

The text of the report presents the data you have gathered and upon which you base conclusions and recommendations. *For the most part, this is the only kind of information you should present in the text of the report.* Leave your interpretations and recommendations for the concluding section or sections. For clarity and completeness, however, you will at times need to state an analysis of the meaning of some of your findings as they are presented. In addition, each section of a very long report can be treated as a separate report, with findings stated in each major section, followed by conclusions and recommendations that pertain only to those particular findings. Such an arrangement is illustrated in the report prepared by an electrical engineer employed by Energy Management Consultants, Inc., of which portions are illustrated in Figure 14-8.

Conclusions and Recommendations

Conclusions and recommendations are based upon the findings presented in the middle section of the report. *Do not bring new information into these concluding sections.* Conclusions and recommendations may be presented in two sections or, occasionally, shown as two separate parts of the report. In the conclusions you present an analysis of what the findings, presented in the earlier sections of the report, mean to you.

PURPOSE, SOURCES, AND METHODS
OF RESEARCH

Purpose

The purpose of this report is to explore the possibilities of
word processing and administrative support operations for the
Chickasaw Branch of Countrywide Insurance Company and to determine
the feasibility of converting to a word processing system. The study
is necessary because of rapidly increasing costs in administrative
operations, as well as an increased volume of typewriting and related
printing.

Scope and Limitations

This study deals primarily with the potential for a word
processing system to cut secretarial administrative costs by
increasing the productivity of each secretary because of
specialization. Not included in this research is a complete analysis
of the most desirable equipment, as presently owned equipment will be
adequate at the beginning of the operation and possibly for some time
to come. Another aspect of the problem not considered is the exact
nature of the training to be provided to secretaries and executives.
Also excluded is consideration of the increase or decrease in morale
because of the conversion to word processing.

Sources and Methods of Collecting Data

Secondary sources provided information about the use of data
processing systems by other firms. Interviews with management and
the secretarial staff of the Chickasaw Branch were conducted to learn
the general functions now being performed and the percentage of time
being spent in each function. The work was broken down into two major
categories: typewriting and administrative functions. IBM sales
representatives provided consultations as to the advisability of
establishing a word processing center. Professional consultation is
not readily available on word processing needs except from vendors of
equipment.

Figure 14-6.   *Introduction of a formal report.*

314

Even though these are your conclusions, if you are writing the report in the impersonal tone, do not switch here and include the use of *I*. You can present your conclusions and recommendations without the use of *I*, as illustrated in some of the examples shown in this chapter. Avoid using the term *the writer*. Since you have collected and analyzed the data, obviously the conclusions are yours unless you state otherwise. Be as objective and impartial as possible in presenting the conclusions and recommendations.

To repeat and emphasize: Conclusions and recommendations are made upon the basis of the findings presented in the earlier sections of the report. If you use the conclusions and recommendations section or sections merely as a means of expressing your unsupported beliefs and ideas, then you had no reason to collect and analyze the data upon which these conclusions and recommendations were not based.

SUPPLEMENTARY REPORT PARTS

The *appendix* section is used for supplementary material. (Both "appendixes" and the Latin "appendices" are now correctly used as the plural form of appendix.)

If a questionnaire has been used to gather information, a complete copy of the questionnaire must be included as an appendix; otherwise the reader cannot judge the validity of the reported information. The covering letter, or letters, that accompanied the questionnaire should also be included as an appendix. Sometimes statistical formulas or computations are appended, as are computer printouts. Extensive tables, large maps, diagrams, or other long materials are placed in the appendix section if they are too bulky for inclusion in the report itself.

The main consideration as to whether materials should go in the report itself or in the appendix section is whether the material relates directly to the text of the report or can be considered as additional and supplementary.

The *bibliography* lists secondary sources used in gathering data and in writing the report. A list of interviews or similar materials may also be included with the secondary sources; to be strictly correct, however, do not include interviews under the heading *bibliography*. *Reference sources* is a descriptive term that includes both secondary and primary research. Illustrations of bibliographies are shown in Figure 12-1, Figure 14-7, and Figure 14-8.

An *index* is unnecessary in almost all business reports; it is used only for very long, extensive ones.

AN ENERGY CONSERVATION STUDY
FOR THE FIRST BAPTIST CHURCH
MEMPHIS, TENNESSEE

Prepared for

Mr. Henry Love, Administrator
First Baptist Church
2200 East Parkway North, Memphis, Tennessee 38112

Prepared by

David R. Weigel, Electrical Engineer
EMC, Inc.
5909 Shelby Oaks Drive, Memphis, Tennessee 38134

March 31, 198–

Figure 14-7. *Portions of a long, formal report. (***Note:** *This figure was shown in a shorter format in Figure 3-8.) (Source: David R. Wiegel, electrical engineer.)*

316

March 31, 198–

Mr. Henry Love
Administrator
First Baptist Church
200 East Parkway North
Memphis, Tennessee 38112

Dear Mr. Love:

This report is the result of the energy conservation survey which you requested of TVA approximately five months ago. We at EMC, Inc. were contracted by TVA to perform the survey.

To help you and your staff decide how to go about reducing your utility bills and save energy, we made a thorough inspection of your facilities and their blueprints in order to identify areas in which energy is being used needlessly. Recommendations for correction of substandard situations are presented with calculations of expected energy savings.

The energy use standards which were used for comparison were those found available through the American Society of Heating, Refrigeration, and Air Conditioning Engineers and the Illumination Engineering Society. Calculation of projected energy savings was performed using methods found in publications of these organizations.

I am very glad to see your interest in energy conservation, and I enjoyed working with the people in your organization. I sincerely hope that our work will prove beneficial to you. Should you need any assistance in interpreting any of our analyses, please give us a call.

Sincerely yours,

David R. Weigel

David R. Weigel
Electrical Engineer

Figure 14-7 continued

CONTENTS

iii

Figure 14-7 continued

318

INCENTIVES FOR IMMEDIATE IMPLEMENTATION OF RECOMMENDATIONS

iv

Figure 14-7 continued

319

SYNOPSIS

   Through the implementation of 11 recommended energy
conservation measures, 13 percent of annual energy consumption and
21 percent of annual dollar expenditures can be eliminated at the
First Baptist Church. Total initial expenditure for the
implementation is approximately $62,350, and estimated first-year
savings at current fuel and electric prices is nearly $9,500. As a
package, the 11 measures will yield a rate of return of 21 percent, a
net present value of nearly $80,000, and a simple payback period of
6.6 years. Economic assumptions made are a 7 percent long-term
inflation rate, a 20-year study life, and a 10 percent cost of
capital.

   Retrofit opportunities in the space conditioning area include
installation of inserts into the firetubes of the boilers at a cost
of $800 with a projected first-year savings of $514. Insulating hot
water piping that passes through unconditioned spaces would reduce
heat loss and save about $106 annually at a cost of only $95. Chiller
controls and a time clock/operating schedule would show a reduction
in bills of $697 per year; these can be implemented for about $2,500.
Demand costs can be reduced by $4,288 through the installation and
operation of a peak-shaving generator, which can be put on line for
$37,650.

   More than $1,000 worth of first-year costs can be avoided by
changing the type of fluorescent lamps presently used to more energy
efficient ones, at a very slight premium per lamp. Replacement of
incandescent lighting in halls, lobbies, athletic facilities, and
the building perimeter with more efficient luminaires will also show
substantial savings. The halls and lobbies should be fitted with
fluorescent fixtures, and the athletic facilities and decorative
outdoor fixtures should be changed to metal halide. These four
changes (indoor halls, outdoor, gymnasium, handball court) can be
accomplished for around $16,640, and will enable a first-year cost
avoidance of $2,215.

v

Figure 14-7 continued

The only architectural structures identified as needful of conservation measures are exterior doors and casement windows. A sum of $4,648 should cover all necessary weatherstripping, with calculated annual savings of $535.

These recommended conservation measures are based on a thorough inspection of buildings and grounds. Present conditions were compared to current standards for space conditioning and illumination as set by the American Society of Heating, Refrigeration, and Air Conditioning Engineers (ASHRAE) and the Illumination Engineering Society (IES).

First Baptist Church should put these recommendations in effect immediately in order to conserve energy and to decrease expenditures.

vi

Figure 14-7 continued

INTRODUCTION

Purpose

The purpose of this report is the identification of energy–using systems within the First Baptist Church, analysis of their efficiency as compared to current standards, and recommendations for improvement in the area of energy conservation. Because of the recent realization that the supply of fossil fuels is being rapidly depleted, prices of these fuels are rapidly escalating. Thus, energy–saving measures requiring large dollar amounts of investment can be justified. In essence, a package of recommendations economically attractive to the Church is presented in the interest of conserving energy.

The Tennessee Valley Authority (TVA) also has an interest in this study. TVA would like to spend money now to conserve electric energy and reduce the demand on the power grid, rather than spend it ten years from now to construct a new nuclear generating plant. TVA is charged by the Congress in its charter with providing electricity to the residents of the Tennessee Valley at the lowest possible cost.[1]

Hence, ratepayers' money spent today will defray future costs, which are subject to inflation. As a means to this end, TVA contracts with architectural/engineering firms such as EMC, Incorporated, to identify energy conservation opportunities within existing buildings. This service is provided free of charge to the ratepayer. Funds are also made available to the client by TVA at very attractive interest rates for the implementation of identified measures.

---

[1]Gordon R. Clapp, <u>The TVA: An Approach to the Development of a Region</u> (Chicago: University of Chicago Press, 1955), p. 171.

1

Figure 14-7 continued

322

In summary, the purpose of this report is twofold. Financial benefits will be realized by the First Baptist Chuch. Customers of TVA will benefit by furthering the overall goal of providing energy for future generations.

Scope and Limitations

Primary research will cover the energy consumption of the facilities for the most recent twelve months, and the architecture, lighting, and space conditioning systems as they exist and operate at present. These items are necessary for the proper breakdown of energy consumption by systems.

For each profiled system, a great number of possible changes in operation, maintenance, and equipment are available. Time, engineering judgment, and aesthetic considerations will limit the quantity of energy conservation opportunities to be studied in depth. Examples of areas to be discounted in this manner are solar air conditioning and photovoltaic arrays, neither of which is economically feasible nor technically fully developed.

Some opportunities to conserve energy and avoid energy costs are presented that do not lend themselves to rigorous engineering calculations. These are discussed in terms of general recommendations, as opposed to evaluated recommendations.

Evaluated recommendations are studied as to estimated annual energy and cost savings, based upon projected conditions. An estimate of implementation cost and abbreviated economic analysis are presented for each, as opposed to a thorough life cycle cost analysis.

Figure 14-7 continued

Methods and Sources of Data

Types and sizes of equipment and lights have been obtained from the blueprints of the facilities. These data were verified by walking through the buildings. Also noted during this audit were equipment condition, thermostat settings, space temperatures, and levels of illumination. Operation and maintenance procedures were discussed with the building engineer in order to obtain schedules of equipment use and occupancy. Information on past energy consumption was provided by the Memphis Light, Gas and Water Division in the form of the most recent twelve months' utility bills.

Current standards for space conditioning and illumination of the American Society of Heating, Refrigeration, and Air Conditioning Engineers (ASHRAE) and the Illumination Engineering Society (IES) are used for comparison to existing conditions so that substandard areas can be identified and investigated.

The necessary data for recommendations on retrofitting new equipment were provided by manufacturers' catalogs and salesmen. Cost estimates were obtained through catalogs and/or local contracting firms.

Plan of Presentation

Material is presented in five major sections: space conditioning, lighting and architecture, economic analysis, a summary, and a discussion of incentives for implementation of recommendations. Within each of the first two major sections are specific categories, composed of a discussion of present conditions and an analysis of potential energy conservation measures. Space conditioning breaks down into heating, air conditioning, and water heating and ventilation, while the lighting and architecture section is divided into lighting, building architecture, and solar retrofit evaluation.

Figure 14-7 continued

The economic analysis presented contains two sub-sections, the first dealing with identified recommendations individually and the second covering the recommendations as a whole. The summary serves to tie together the previous sections, with a list of energy conservation opportunities ranked in order of simple payback period. Finally, the section concerned with incentives for implementation contains a discussion of reasons for avoiding delay in acting upon the recommendations.

Sample calculations for the identified energy-saving measures are presented in the appendices at the end of the report. Formulae depicted are consistent with ASHRAE and IES standards for energy consumption projection.

Figure 14-7 continued

ENERGY CONSERVATION IN SPACE
AND WATER CONDITIONING

Space Heating

Space heating for the facilities is provided by a central system
consisting of two natural gas–fired low–pressure steam boilers.
These boilers are of the firetube type, meaning that hot gas is
passed through tubes which are immersed in water, heating the water
to provide steam. Operation is a base–peak schedule, with one boiler
providing primary heat, and the second providing booster heat on
extremely cold days. Manual night shutdown is also practiced, except
on very cold nights when a danger of system freezing exists.

The steam produced by these boilers serves radiators and
convectors directly and is converted to 180–degree hot water by a
heat exchanger. The hot water is pumped to individual fan–coil type
single–zone air handling units which make up the balance of the space
heating system.

In addition, one of the two boilers has an auxiliary fuel oil burner
for standby operation in the event of a natural gas curtailment.
Regardless of the natural gas situation, fuel oil is burned for
heating during one month out of each heating season in order to purge
the burner and fuel lines of moisture and sludge and to top off the
fuel tank with fresh oil.

Identification of Inefficiencies

Operation of the heating system is already designed around the
conservation of energy. Thermostat settings of 65 degrees, with
manual night shutdown and the base–peak boiler firing arrangement
cannot realistically be improved upon. Although automatic boiler
controls are available which would free maintenance personnel for
other tasks, the reduction in maintenance cost would be far too small
to justify the high initial cost of an automated system.

5

Figure 14-7 continued

In the area of actual equipment efficiency, only three problem areas can be identified. Condition of equipment in general is good; filters, heating coils, and burners are clean; and fans, belts, and motors are properly aligned and lubricated. However, the boilers and the hot water circulating system both show room for improvement.

Flue gas analysis of the boilers indicates a problem that is inherent in forced-draft firetube heating arrangements. Due primarily to high gas velocities, a great deal of hot gas passes directly down the center of the firetubes and out the stack, having never had a chance to release its heat to the water by coming into contact with the outer surface. Analysis of a flue gas sample indicates approximately 5 percent carbon dioxide, 8 percent oxygen, and a net stack temperature of 400 degrees. Combustion efficiency, based on these figures, is 73 percent.[1] This indicates that 27 percent of the heat generated by burning fuel is being lost through the stack. Experience has shown that efficiencies of 80 to 85 percent are attainable through proper boiler design.

In the hot water side of the heating system, two problems can be identified. The first is quite obvious upon inspection: the main circulating pump is leaking at the shaft seal, allowing heated water to be discarded down the equipment room drain. The second problem is a lack of insulation on the hot water piping. As this pipe passes through unconditioned equipment rooms and attic spaces, parasitic heat loss from the water occurs, detracting from the overall system efficiency.

Recommendations

The leaking pump should be repaired. This repair amounts to re-packing the shaft seal and can be accomplished by maintenance personnel. No calculation of energy savings is presented for this

---

[1]Packaged Firetube Section of the American Boiler Manufacturers Association, Engineering Manual (Newark: ABMA, 1971), p. 82.

Figure 14-7 continued

recommendation, as the cost is minimal and the wastefulness of the situation is obvious.

To improve the efficiency of the boilers, inserts should be installed in the firetubes so that the gas flow will be slower and more turbulent, allowing a more thorough transfer of heat to the water. According to a local contractor, this installation will cost approximately $800. Manufacturers of these inserts claim a minimum of 6 percent reduction in fuel consumption,[2] and in this case, approximately 1,000 ccf of natural gas and 400 gallons of fuel oil will be saved annually (see Appendix A for calculations). Thus, a minimum of $500 in annual fuel costs (at current prices) can be expected from this installation.

To reduce heat loss through uninsulated hot water piping in unconditioned spaces, one inch of fiberglass wrap pipe insulation should be added to the pipe. Pipe that carries 180—degree hot water through these spaces amounts to 45 feet of 1½ inch line. Calculations presented in Appendix A show that the energy—equivalent heat of 560 ccf of natural gas is being lost annually through the pipe walls. The addition of the insulation will reduce this to about 77 ccf. The net reduction at current prices, therefore, is nearly $92 per year. At $1.50 per linear foot of insulation (according to a local insulation contractor), implementation of this recommendation should cost no more than $68.

---

[2]American Boiler Manufacturers Association, Packaged Firetube Boiler Engineering Manual (Newark: ABMA, 1971), p. 65.

Figure 14-7 continued

BIBLIOGRAPHY

American Boiler Manufacturers Association. Packaged Firetube Boiler
    Engineering Manual. Newark: ABMA, 1971.
ASHRAE Handbook & Product Directory — 1977 Fundamentals. New York:
    ASHRAE, 1977.
Clapp, Gordon R. The TVA: An Approach to the Development of a Region.
    Chicago: University of Chicago Press, 1955.
Dubin, Fred S. and Chalmers, G. Long, Jr. Energy Conservation
    Standards for Building Design, Construction, and
    Operation. New York: McGraw-Hill, 1978.
Griffin, C. W. Energy Conservation in Buildings: Techniques for
    Economical Design. Washington, D.C.: The Construction
    Specifications Institute, Inc., 1974.
Tennessee Energy Authority. The Tennessee Energy Authority Audit
    Training Manual. April, 1979.

Figure 14-7 continued

ANALYSIS OF FEDERAL EXPRESS
AIRPORT REQUIREMENTS

DETROIT, MICHIGAN

Figure 14-8. *Portions of report prepared by an airport engineer.*

ANALYSIS OF FEDERAL EXPRESS
AIRPORT REQUIREMENTS

DETROIT, MICHIGAN

Prepared for

James Weaver

Manager, Airport Planning

Prepared by

David Bourland

Airport Engineer, Airport Planning

Properties Department
Federal Express Corporation

March 24, 198—

Figure 14-8 continued

March 24, 198–

Mr. James Weaver
Manager, Airport Planning
Federal Express Corporation
Box 727
Memphis, TN 38194

Dear Jim:

As you requested, I have examined the airports within the Detroit, Michigan metropolitan area in order to determine the best airfield facility for the company's short and long range aircraft operations. The attached report is the culmination of my analysis.

This report evaluates three airports in the Detroit area and subsequently evaluates two alternative parcels of property for a Federal Express facility. The report includes preliminary designs of the potential development of the properties plus cost estimates. The Executive Summary condenses the information in the form that you requested.

If this project is accepted for further development, I will be pleased to assist you during the design and construction phases.

Sincerely yours,

David W. Bourland

David W. Bourland
Airport Engineer

Figure 14-8 continued

TABLE OF CONTENTS

iv

Figure 14-8 continued

LIST OF FIGURES

LIST OF TABLES

v

Figure 14-8 continued

EXECUTIVE SUMMARY

Situation

Federal Express is currently serving Detroit, Michigan, with one 727 aircraft through the Detroit Metropolitan Airport. The aircraft parking site is on an abandoned runway and is subject to a one-year lease which expires on August 31, 1980. The Wayne County Road Commission will not allow FEC to continue using this site and consequently will not renew the lease. There is no other developed ramp area on the airport for Federal Express to lease either from the airport or from other airlines. Federal Express must act immediately to construct its own ramp area at Detroit Metropolitan Airport or obtain satisfactory facilities at another airport in the Detroit area.

Mission

The immediate objective is to acquire an airport facility that will handle the FEC aircraft operations at the expiration of the current lease. These operations include the regularly scheduled 727 flight from Memphis, a Saturday 727 charter flight, and two Falcons or supplementals that serve the two cities of Battle Creek/Kalamazoo and Saginaw/Bay City. In addition, passenger charter flights are scheduled to begin in Detroit in January, 1980. The FEC facility will handle the conversion of the aircraft and store the associated equipment. All passengers will be boarded at the terminal building.

With adequate room for expansion, long-term FEC requirements may be met. These requirements include an increase in the number and/or size of aircraft operating in Detroit. A city station may be located on the site to replace the existing Romulus station at the expiration of the station's lease in September, 1982.

Execution

The best alternative for Federal Express is a long-term lease on a 350,000 square foot parcel at Detroit Metropolitan Airport with the

Figure 14-8 continued

intent of ultimately constructing 300,000 square feet of aircraft pavement, a twenty-truck city station, and a 9,600 square foot ground support equipment storage building. This facility will accommodate two 727's and eight Falcons/supplementals at an estimated total cost of $2,118,000.

The construction of this project may be divided into two phases to reduce the initial capital outlay of the company. The first phase will be constructed in fiscal year 1981 and will satisfy the short term FEC airfield requirements at an estimated cost of $1,484,000. With the construction of the city station during the airport fiscal year 1983, the remainder of the site may be developed as proposed.

It is recommended that the Board of Directors of Federal Express Corporation approve a fifteen-year lease with the Wayne County Road Commission for the proposed site plus the proposed construction program at a cost of $1,484,000 in fiscal year 1981 and $634,000 in fiscal year 1983.

<u>Administration</u>
The Properties Department will be responsible for the overall administration of the project. Facilities Planning will coordinate the general and specific requirements of all Federal Express departments with the consulting engineer who is retained to produce the construction drawings. The Regional Properties Administrator will work with the consulting engineer to supervise construction. A completion date of November 16, 1980, has been set in accordance with the schedule shown in Figure 6 of this report. Since the completion date is approximately two months past the expiration date of the current lease, the airport authority has agreed to allow Federal Express to continue using the present parking site until construction is completed.

Figure 14-8 continued

Control

Three significant progress points for this project are:

1. The completion of the design and the construction documents with FEC approval.
2. The receipt of bids and the award of construction contract.
3. The completion of the construction.

Facilities Planning and the Regional Properties Administrator will maintain a close contact with the consulting engineer and the contractor to provide proper control and coordination. These departments will also review any requests for partial payment with respect to the progress of the project. The Accounts Payable Department will review all payment requests for conformity with the terms of the contract.

Figure 14-8 continued

ILLUSTRATIONS OF REPORTS

An Energy Conservation Study

The report shown in Figure 14-7 (some portions are omitted) is an actual one prepared by an electrical engineer employed by Energy Management Consultants. It is used here with the permission of the writer, his employing organization, Tennessee Valley Authority, and First Baptist Church, Memphis, Tennessee.

Sections of the report shown here include all preliminary parts: title page, letter of transmittal, table of contents, and synopsis. Also included are the complete introduction, the discussion of space heating under the second main division of the report, "Energy Conservation in Space and Water Conditioning," and the bibliography.

Notice on the table of contents that in this particular report recommendations are included after the discussion of "Space Heating," "Air Conditioning," "Lighting," and "Architecture." This long report was divided into discrete categories, with presentation of recommendations immediately after the related discussion, resulting in an appropriate, easily read arrangement.

Bottom-of-page footnotes are used with this report, which is followed by a bibliography. Compare this method of footnoting with the method of documentation used in Figure 4-2, Chapter 4, and in Figure 14-9.

NOTE: This report is a variation of the report illustrated in Figure 3-8, Chapter 3, shown here in a more formal version. The purpose is to show how the same report can be prepared in different forms, depending upon the situation and the preference of the readers.

Analysis of Federal Express Airport Requirements, Detroit, Michigan

Figure 14-8 (only the beginning portions are shown) is an actual report prepared by an airport engineer at Federal Express, Memphis, Tennessee. It is used with permission of the writer and Federal Express.

Parts of the report shown in this chapter are the title fly, title page, letter of transmittal, table of contents, list of figures, list of tables, and executive summary.

Feasibility Study for Retail Bookstore

The following feasibility study (analytical report) answers the question of whether a retail bookstore should be opened in the Kirby-

SHOULD A RETAIL BOOKSTORE BE ESTABLISHED
IN THE KIRBY–KESWICK COMMUNITY?

Prepared for

Mrs. Helen Rockwell, Owner
Rockwell Bookstore
397 Grove Park
Memphis, TN 38117

by

Blair Diamond, Consultant
Diamond Research Associates
1917 Catbird Court
Memphis, TN 38119

December 14, 1984

Figure 14-9. *Feasibility study.*

DIAMOND RESEARCH ASSOCIATES
1917 Catbird Court
Memphis, TN 38119

Telephone: 901 685-5624

December 14, 1984

Mrs. Helen Rockwell, Owner
Rockwell Bookstore
397 Grove Park
Memphis, TN 38117

Dear Mrs. Rockwell:

Here is your report on the feasibility of establishing a retail
bookstore in the Kirby—Keswick community.

As you requested, I concentrated on in-depth data concerning both the
industry and the community. According to your instructions, I have
carefully documented all data except that derived from my personal
observations, which are described as such. The report is arranged in
a format that should be acceptable to the bankers from whom you
planned to request a loan.

Comparisons emphasize the similarities and differences between the
Kirby—Keswick community and the Laurel—Meade community, where your
presently owned store is located. Although the neighborhoods are
similar in many respects, their differences could affect the success
of your proposed bookstore.

The information included here should enable you to make a wise
decision. Please telephone me when I can help further.

Sincerely,

Blair Diamond

Blair Diamond, Consultant

dw

Figure 14-9 continued

CONTENTS

iii

Figure 14-9 continued

341

SYNOPSIS

The Kirby—Keswick community should not be considered a feasible
location for a bookstore under current conditions.

Information about the community and the bookstore industry was
obtained from published sources, including latest U.S. Census data;
from personal observation and analysis; and from people experienced
in the retail book industry. These sources were also used to obtain
information about the Laurel—Meade neighborhood, the locale of the
bookstore now owned by Mrs. Rockwell, in order to predict the
probable success of the proposed bookstore in Kirby—Keswick.

Overall, the Kirby—Keswick community is less desirable for a
retail bookstore than the Laurel—Meade community. It is a younger
neighborhood, with fewer persons of retirement age or near
retirement age and far more children under age 15. Although it has
somewhat more college—age individuals, it is a great distance from
all Memphis colleges and in a rather isolated residential area,
although an affluent one. Because of location and age of residents,
Laurel—Meade is better able to attract both college—age and older
customers, the two groups that are assumed to buy the greatest number
of books. In addition, the present Rockwell store is in the
Laurelwood shopping center, a larger center than Ridgeway, the
proposed location of the second store.
Although the Kirby—Keswick community has no other bookstores within

Figure 14-9 *continued*

its boundaries, at least eight other bookstores, including large chain outlets in shopping malls, exist within a five-mile radius. In addition, paperback books are sold throughout Kirby-Keswick and the entire city in grocery stores, drugstores, and other outlets.

The retail book industry as a whole, although improved since 1982, is still weak. Competition continues to intensify, especially for paperbacks, which increase in number as hardbacks decrease.

A new bookstore in the Kirby-Keswick area would face extraordinary challenges.

v

Figure 14-9 continued

SHOULD A RETAIL BOOKSTORE BE ESTABLISHED

IN THE KIRBY–KESWICK NEIGHBORHOOD?

Overview

Before time and money are invested in establishing a business, predictions based on objective evidence should indicate that the venture will be successful. Although no prediction is conclusive, decisions can be wisely made only on the basis of accurate and complete information.

Authorization, Purpose, and Scope

This report was authorized by Helen Rockwell, owner of Rockwell Bookstore at 397 Grove Park, Memphis, Tennessee, on November 1, 1984. She is considering establishing a bookstore near her home in the Kirby–Keswick community in East Memphis, in addition to her present store.

The purpose of this report is to determine whether the Kirby–Keswick neighborhood is a feasible location for a new bookstore and whether such a store should be established at the present time.

Excluded from this study are the questions of whether Mrs. Rockwell should open an additional bookstore in some other area of the city or expand the one on Grove Park.

1

Figure 14-9 *continued*

<u>Sources and Limitations</u>

Information about the community and bookstore industry was obtained from published sources, including latest (1980) Census data; from personal and telephone interviews with people experienced in the book industry; and from personal observations and analysis. These sources were also used to obtain information about the Laurel–Meade community, the location of the bookstore now owned by Mrs. Rockwell, in order to predict the probable success of the proposed store in Kirby–Keswick. (These sources are documented by use of a simplified system; for example, the citation (4:51) refers to Item 4 in the bibliography, page 51.)

A major source of published data used in this research study is a new release of the Bureau of the Census described as the Neighborhood Statistics Program (NSP) report, which classifies information according to neighborhoods within cities. For the first time, data are available by neighborhoods rather than by census tracts, which often contain parts of several neighborhoods. (Census tract information is still available, but it is not used in this report.) The NSP report was released in January, 1984 (5), based on 1980 data. (A limitation of census reports is that they are several years old before they are available for use.)

Officials of Memphis and Shelby County asked all established neighborhood groups, about 150, to participate in the statistical program. Areas without established associations with clearly defined

Figure 14-9 continued

boundaries were eliminated from the statistical program. All areas continue to be included in census tract data (3:Al).

Regardless of government classifications, no particular boundaries would specifically apply to customers of any retail store, a fact that is discussed later in relation to bookstores.

Feasibility of the Kirby–Keswick Community

The Kirby–Keswick community of Memphis, Tennessee, reported by the Bureau of the Census as Neighborhood 40 (5) lies between and slightly to the south of the heart of East Memphis and Germantown (3:Al). It is a fairly new development, with most of the houses and commercial buildings constructed since 1965. It is bounded by Southern Avenue on the north, Ridgeway and Quince on the east and south, and Kirby Road on the west.

The total population reported by the 1980 Census was 3,258, with 1,034 households.

Based on personal observation, the Kirby–Keswick community is heavily populated by mobile executive families. Homes are sold, the owners move on, and other highly paid families move in.

The community is in a rather isolated position from major thoroughfares except that its northern boundary is fairly close to Poplar Avenue. The neighborhood is quiet and well kept, almost exclusively residential except for Ridgeway Shopping Center at its

Figure 14-9 continued

outmost boundaries. Except for groceries and incidentals, it is safe to assume that residents do most of their shopping outside their own neighborhood, possibly in the shops in Germantown and other areas of East Memphis.

Age of Residents

Age groups influence book sales. A great number of avid readers in the United States are within two age groups, according to managers and owners of Memphis bookstores (7, 9, 11). These two groups are people of college age, or near college age, and retired individuals, or those nearing retirement age.

The Kirby-Keswick community does not have a high percentage of individuals in either of the two age groups that are assumed to buy the most books, although the college-age group may increase during the next few years. If the families now remain there or are replaced by families of similar age, the number of students in the college age group is expected to increase proportionately with the national trend, as shown in Chart 1. Because the residents are mobile, however, families may be replaced with even younger families; they are unlikely to be replaced with older families.

Figure 14-9 continued

Chart 1
U.S. School and College Age Population (In Millions)

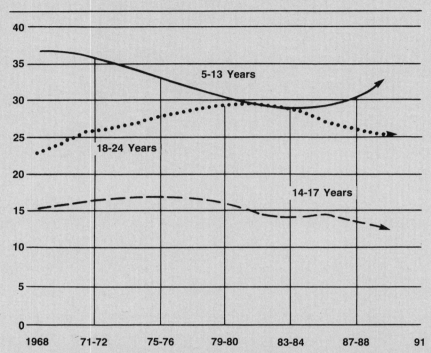

Source: U.S. Department of Education National Center for Educational Statistics

As shown in Chart 1, the number of college–age individuals is expected to remain about the same until about 1987, when the number will begin to increase. Although this expected increase may make a

Figure 14-9 *continued*

348

slight difference to book sales overall, it would be unlikely to have a major effect on the Kirby–Keswick area because of its location, as will be discussed later.

The median age of the neighborhood is 35.2 (5:4). Further analysis of certain age groups is given in Table 1, which shows that older residents (age groups 55 to 64 and 65 or older) total only 309, or 9.4 percent of the total population. The 779 children under 15 make up 23.9 percent of the total population.

Table 1

CERTAIN AGE GROUPS IN THE KIRBY–KESWICK COMMUNITY, 1980

Age	Number	Percent of Total Population
Under 5	125	3.8
5 – 9	246	7.6
10 – 14	408	12.5
15 – 19	369	11.3
20 – 24	175	5.3
55 – 64	171	5.2
65 and over	138	4.2

Source: Bureau of the Census

Economic and Educational Factors

As reported by the 1980 Census, the mean annual household income in

Figure 14-9 continued

the Kirby—Keswick neighborhood was $40,217; the median household

income was $31,897 (5:36). This mean income is the fifth highest of

all reported Memphis neighborhoods (5, 3:A1). In addition, Kirby—

Keswick is adjacent to the Greentrees community, which has a mean

annual household income of $51,971 (5:36).

Of the 1594 employed persons age 16 and over, 636, or 39.9

percent, are employed in professional and managerial positions; 632,

or 41 percent, are in technical, sales, and administrative support

positions (5:28).

As could be expected, residents are well educated; 95.1 percent

of the adults age 25 and over have completed high school, and 47.4

percent have completed four or more years of college. School

enrollment for persons 5 through 18 is virtually 100 percent (5:40).

Other Variables

Although no other bookstores are now in the Kirby—Keswick area,

a number of stores, including large chain outlets, are already well

established in nearby communities. Eight bookstores exist within a

five—mile radius, with three in the Mall of Memphis and one in

Hickory Ridge Mall. In addition, books, particularly paperbacks, are

sold in drugstores, grocery stores, and numerous other outlets in

Kirby—Keswick and nearby areas.

Another disadvantage is that the Kirby—Keswick community is

located at least eight miles from all Memphis colleges. Regardless of

Figure 14-9 *continued*

the number of students in the community itself, many students are likely to buy books from their college store or from another outlet near their school. Because of the residential nature of the community, it is not on a direct route to any Memphis college, except for students living in the community itself.

Although Mrs. Rockwell has never stocked textbooks as such, related books and material used by college students constitute a considerable portion of the sales of the present Rockwell store, according to Jason Harrison, Assistant Manager (8). Mary Donnelly, owner of a bookstore near the campus of Shelby State Community College, agrees that sales of such books and materials are important to overall bookstore sales (7).

Concerning the question of a possible site, a desirable store in the Ridgeway Shopping Center, at the corner of Quince and Ridgeway, offers ample space and a reasonable price. The store, now vacant, will be redecorated to meet the specifications of the renter.

Financial Strength of the Retail Book Industry

Bookstores, as a group, have not prospered during recent years, as described in Publishers' Weekly:

The 1981 American Booksellers Association financial profile of its membership, specifically the independent bookseller segment, shows a

Figure 14-9 continued

decline of net profits for book retailers over the past four years. . . .

This most recent survey (based mainly on 1980 statistical data) matches the major findings of ABA's earlier financial survey, based on fiscal year 1976, conducted in 1977. (4:15)

Sales of hardcover trade books for adults — fiction or non-fiction sold in bookstores — totalled almost 10 percent less in 1982 than in 1981, as discussed below.

Demand for such books is becoming increasingly price sensitive, a recognition of the public's unwillingness to pay $13 to $20 for hardcover works whenever the possibility exists that such titles may appear later in less expensive paperbound format. (6:7–8)

According to a report in Standard and Poor's Industry Survey, 1983, textbook sales increased steadily, although not dramatically, from 1966 through 1980, the last year for which data were available. (Textbooks sales are discussed here because of their relationship to other books sold to college students.) The amount of dollar sales increased from about 700 million dollars in 1966 to about 1,800 million in 1980. Much of this increase, however, can be attributed to inflation. In addition, increased dollar sales do not guarantee increased profits (2:C74).

Conditions in the book industry have improved since 1982. According to the U. S. Industrial Outlook, 1984:

A return to consumer confidence led the way for more book sales in 1983, with both individual and institutions increasing their purchases. After adjusting for inflation, sales were up 1.4 percent from 1982. . . . The

Figure 14-9 continued

number of retail outlets increased, relecting in part the industry's belief that the general public was ready to buy more books. (2:7—8)

The U. S. Industrial Outlook, 1984, also reports thus:

Book publishing in the United States is undergoing a number of changes. Priced considerably below hardbound, paperbound books now occupy more than 75 percent of the display space of most bookstores. (2:8)

A further prediction from the same source is for a 2.1 percent increase in book sales from 1983 to 1984. (2:8). Another prediction, stated in the U.S. News and World Report, June 18, 1984, is this: "The Commerce Department predicts that books sales will increase almost 10 percent this year to 9.2 billion dollars" (1:64). (This figure is evidently an updated prediction, as the U.S. Industrial Outlook is also a publication of the Department of Commerce.)

As these preceding statements indicate, the retail book industry is improving. It is important to remember, however, that percentages of increase are based on years when sales were much lower than in previous years, indicating that the book industry has not yet fully recovered.

Figure 14-9 continued

<u>Comparison of the Kirby–Keswick Community
with the Laurel–Meade Community</u>

Similarities or differences between Kirby–Keswick and the
Laurel–Meade community, the location of the present Rockwell
bookstore, could affect the success of the proposed store.

The Laurel–Meade neighborhood is comparable in educational
backgrounds, occupations, and income. The residents are older, with
a median age of 54.8 (5:5). The number of college–age individuals is
fewer. The number of people of retirement age, or near retirement
age, is much greater (5:5).

Age groups in the two communities differ, as shown in Table 2,
along with comparisons of certain other factors.

Table 2

COMPARISON OF CERTAIN FACTORS OF KIRBY–KESWICK
AND LAUREL–MEADE NEIGHBORHOODS

<u>Characteristics</u>	<u>Laurel–Meade</u>	<u>Kirby–Keswick</u>
Total population	1,756	3,258
Households	817	1,034
Mean size of household	2.5	3.15
Mean household income	$46,347	$40,217
Median household income	$26,184	$31,897
College graduates	641	939
Median age	54.8	35.2
Residents 65 or over	532 (30.2%)	138 (4.2%)
Residents 60–64	162 (9.2%)	135 (4.1%)
Residents 15–24	200 (11.3%)	544 (16.7%)

Source: Bureau of the Census

Figure 14-9   continued

The Laurel—Meade community has an unusually large percentage of older persons, who are assumed to be good customers of book stores. In addition, although not shown on the table, the rather small Laurel—Meade neighborhood is surrounded by other communities that are similar in age, income, and occupations (5).

Another important difference is that Mrs. Rockwell's presently owned store is in the Laurelwood Shopping Center in Laurel—Meade. This center is much larger than the Ridgeway center, the proposed location of the additional store. In addition, the present Rockwell store is approximately one mile from Memphis State University and one block from Poplar Avenue, a heavily traveled thoroughfare for students and many other residents of Memphis and outlying areas.

<u>Recommendations</u>

The Kirby—Keswick community should not be considered a feasible location for the establishment of a retail bookstore at this time. This recommendation is based on the following factors:

1. The Kirby—Keswick community, although affluent and well—educated, contains a relatively low percentage of individuals in the age groups that are assumed to buy the most books.

Figure 14-9 continued

2. The Kirby—Keswick community is a rather isolated residential area, relatively far from all Memphis colleges and most major thoroughfares.

3. The retail book history as a whole, although improved since 1982, is still weak. Competition continues to intensify, especially for paperbound books, which increase as hardbounds decrease.

4. Residents of Kirby—Keswick already have access to numerous book outlets within a few miles of their homes, although no bookstores exist in the neighborhood itself.

5. Overall, the Kirby—Keswick community presents fewer opportunities for success than Laurel—Meade, the location of the present Rockwell store.

Figure 14-9 continued

REFERENCES

Published Sources

1. "Book Publishers Turn to a Happier Chapter." U.S. News and World Report, June 18, 1984, p. 64.

2. "Book Publishing." Standard and Poor's Industry Survey, January 1983, p. C74.

3. "Neighborly Memphians Put into Statistical Focus." The Commercial Appeal. January 30, 1984, Section AI, pp. 4–5.

4. "New ABA Financial Study Shows Bookstore Profitability Down Again After Four Years." Publishers' Weekly, January 29, 1982, pp. 51–54.

5. U.S. Department of Commerce, Bureau of the Census, Twentieth Census of the United States, 1980: Neighborhood Statistics Program, Memphis and Shelby County Office of Planning and Development.

6. U.S. Department of Commerce, Bureau of Industrial Economics, U.S. Industrial Outlook, 1984, pp. 7–7, 7–8.

Interviews

7. Donnelly, Mary, Owner, Midtown Bookstore, 918 Union Avenue, Memphis, Tennessee 38111. Personal interview, November 21, 1984.

8. Harrison, Jason, Assistant Manager, Rockwell Bookstore, 397 Grove Park, Memphis, Tennessee 38117. Personal interviews November 2, 5, and 10, 1984.

9. Johnson, Matthew, Manager, Books and Such, 2211 Winchester, Memphis, Tennessee 38118. Telephone interview, December 2, 1984.

10. Rockwell, Helen, Owner, Rockwell Bookstore, 397 Grove Park, Memphis, Tennessee 38118. Personal interviews November 10, 14, 22, and 24, 1984.

11. Rogers, Ruby, Owner, Books and Books Shop, 1911 Poplar Avenue, Memphis, Tennessee 38111. Personal interview, November 29, 1984.

Figure 14-9 continued

Keswick community, Memphis. Much of the data are based on information from the Census Bureau.

Data collected in the 1980 Census were first available in libraries in early 1984, at least in the Memphis area. Census information, although detailed and often invaluable, is at the best somewhat out of date.

Compare the method of documentation used for this report with the method shown for Figure 14-7, which includes bottom-of-page footnotes.

SUMMARY

Complete formal reports are comprised of preliminary parts, the report body (or text), and supplementary parts. The complete report, consisting of preliminaries, the report body, and supplementary parts, is known as the report package.

Even when reports are correctly described as complete, formal reports, their content and arrangement often differ, as illustrated by the three reports shown in Chapter 14. Many other variations also occur; for example, recommendations and conclusions may be given first (although not so often as in informal reports), and various other preliminary parts may be used.

The executive summary illustrated in Figure 14-8 seems to be increasing in use. It is longer than the synopsis illustrated in Figures 14-7 and 14-9.

As with all report-writing situations, the writer must use judgment and discretion in choosing the most appropriate format and arrangement for complete formal reports.

CASES

No cases are included at the end of this chapter because of the great number included in Appendix B. These cases are planned to accompany Chapter 14 and preceding chapters that pertain to analytical reports, but some also apply to informational reports. The cases in Appendix B are based on principles discussed throughout this textbook.

Oral Reporting to Groups $\Big|$ 15

In this chapter, the term *oral reporting* is used in its broadest sense to include oral presentations of many kinds. Much of public speaking in general is some form of oral reporting, planned especially to inform or to convince.

DEFINING AN ORAL REPORT

The word *report*, like *oral reporting,* is also a broad term. It applies to and includes much of business and professional communication. Remember the definition given in Chapter 1, "A report is a written *or oral* message planned to convey information or to present a solution to a problem." Another definition, stated by C. William Emory, applies to both written and oral reports: "What is a report? It is a statement of results, events, conditions, progress or interpretation of information in communication; if written, it provides a record."[1]

Although reports are thought to be basically the imparting of information, other purposes of communication, including persuasion and conviction, enter into various kinds of speaking for business and the professions. And there is no reason that oral reports should not entertain, also using this word in a broad sense.

The three often stated purposes of communication—to inform,

1. C. William Emory, *Business Research Methods* (Homewood, Ill.: Richard D. Irwin, 1976), p. 416.

to persuade, to entertain—cannot be separated. Although the reporting of factual information differs from an after-dinner speech planned primarily for entertainment, all elements of communication are interrelated and do not exist as separate entities. All communication, even that which seems to be only routine and factual, is influenced by the individual emotions of the sender and receiver of the message. The intellect does not function separately from the emotions or without regard to physiological conditions.

All intentional communication is persuasive in the sense that the speaker or writer wants the reader or listener to understand the message and to accept and be influenced by the message. David K. Berlo states: "In short, we communicate to influence—to affect with intent."[2]

The third purpose of communication, entertainment, is not necessarily excluded from the presentation of most business and professional reports, although in some instances a light approach is completely out of place, as in serious or somber situations. In most other oral presentations, a light, humorous touch is to be preferred to an overly serious one so long as all remarks are related to the general subject matter.

The three purposes of human communication according to Lee Thayer apply to all forms of reports. These purposes are:

1. To affect one's own or another's knowledge of or thinking about something in some way—by attempting to alter a present conception, to add to it, to establish a new conception, etc.
2. To affect one's own or another's attitudes or orientation toward himself, others, or some aspect of his (or one's own) environment in some way; or
3. To affect or influence one's own or another's behavior in some way.[3]

An oral or written report can accomplish all three of Thayer's stated purposes. A report planned for the purpose of gathering information from which to make a decision (1) affects the reader's or listener's knowledge of the situation; (2) affects the reader's or listener's attitudes or orientation from the standpoint of how the information shown in the report relates to sales, location, personnel, publicity, or any other aspect of the organization; and (3) motivates

2. David K. Berlo, *The Process of Communication* (New York: Holt, Rinehart & Winston, 1960), p. 12.

3. Lee Thayer, *Communication and Communication Systems* (Homewood, Ill.: Richard D. Irwin, 1968), p. 145.

the reader or listener to take the steps necessary to implement recommendations given in the report.

In simple terms, successful communication has occurred when:

1. The message received is approximately the same as the one that is sent;
2. The message obtains a favorable response, although this response is not always apparent, and what is considered favorable differs according to the sender, the receiver, the message, and the environment;
3. The sender and the receiver of the message maintain favorable relationships.

Notice that in this discussion about the purposes of communication, emphasis is upon the receiver of the message. When sending written or oral messages, keep the receiver constantly in mind. This is a restatement of the you-attitude.

Some oral presentations are referred to as *briefings.* A briefing involves the presentation of long, complex bodies of information in a condensed oral summary. These briefings may be given for the purpose of presenting recommendations to an audience for approval or disapproval or may be merely informational. Some briefings and other oral reports are based on previously written reports; others are presented only in oral form.

You as the speaker, or the "briefer," should be considered the most knowledgeable person on the subject, at least insofar as you are presenting the results of your own research. You should exhibit confidence, yet remain open to the suggestions, questions, and criticisms of other people.

The audience at a briefing is likely to consist of executives, department heads, professional people, or others whose time is valuable. The speaker is obligated to present information in a concise, well-organized way. Briefings may be as short as fifteen or twenty minutes, plus additional time for questions and discussion. Some briefings run for more than an hour, or, conceivably, for a much longer time. You as a speaker should plan your talk with extreme care so as to present the desired material in the allotted time period.

COMPARING ORAL REPORTS WITH WRITTEN REPORTS

The principles of effective communication through written reports discussed in preceding chapters also apply, for the most part, to effective oral reporting. Precise use of language, clarity, empathy, knowledge of subject matter, appropriate emphasis and organization—all these qualities are necessary for the successful transmission of a message in either written or oral form.

Both written and oral reports must be preceded by careful and thorough research and an objective analysis of data. As in other forms of communication, a speaker must consider the probable reactions of the audience to ideas and suggested recommendations.

The principles of effective writing, as well as of competent research, apply to effective oral reporting, although there are certain differences that must be taken into consideration. The speaker need not worry about spelling, paragraphing, punctuation, and typewritten arrangements. Neither is the speaker benefited by these factors, which, when effectively used, are aids to immediate understanding of the written message.

The same principles that apply to objective interpretation and presentation of data in written reports apply when making an oral presentation. Emphasis must be on data, and what the data seem to indicate, not upon the writer or speaker. Evidence is more important and convincing than the writer's or speaker's beliefs and desires.

Like written reports, oral reports can be presented in the direct or the indirect order. A report arranged in the indirect (inductive) order begins with the introduction, followed by a discussion of findings, and ends with conclusions and recommendations. In the direct (deductive) order of arrangement, recommendations are presented first, followed by supporting details. When presented in the direct order, however, an oral report should have a specific, emphatic ending, often in the form of a short summary.

A written report may become the basis for an oral report. The synopsis can be distributed before the oral presentation for the purpose of informing listeners of the overall picture. This procedure is not advisable, however, if the audience can be expected to have adverse reactions before the research and circumstances are thoroughly explained. In addition, distributing a synopsis or any other written material immediately before an oral presentation distracts listeners' attention from the spoken message.

Many people find oral reporting much easier than preparing written reports. For others, facing an audience is terrifying. The best way to build confidence in yourself, as well as to make your report convincing and informative, is to know your subject thoroughly and to take the attitude that your purpose is to inform and to convince—and perhaps to entertain—but not to impress.

If you are completely familiar with all aspects of the problem, even though you don't know all the answers, and if you sincerely want to pass this knowledge on to your listeners, you are likely to express your ideas clearly and convincingly.

An advantage of oral communication over written communication is that you have instant feedback. Another advantage is that your facial expressions, tone of voice, and gestures help to make your words clear, convincing, and effective.

Graphic illustrations are used in oral reports as in written reports. They can be used effectively or, as in written reports, they can be misleading, distracting, or unnecessary. The principles of graphic illustration discussed in Chapter 11 apply to reports of all kinds. An additional consideration when using illustrations in an oral presentation is that every member of the audience must be able to see the illustration, easily and completely. As in written reports, the illustration should not be expected to convey the most important elements of the presentation, but to supplement the information presented in words.

Another important difference between written and oral reporting is the extreme importance of nonverbal communication in oral messages of all kinds.

DETERMINING THE PURPOSE AND CONTENT OF AN ORAL REPORT

A *statement of purpose,* as the term is considered in planning an oral report, is used in two ways.

First, make sure that your audience understands exactly, early in the presentation, why you did the research study on which the report is based. If this purpose is not made clear immediately, your message will be even less understandable than a similarly organized written report would be because the reader has the opportunity to turn through pages in order to find explanatory information that should have been given earlier. Your listening audience does not have this opportunity.

The second way in which the *statement of purpose* should be considered early in the planning stages of an oral presentation is this: In addition to making sure that your audience understands the purpose of your research study, consider the purpose of your presentation to the audience. In other words, exactly why are you speaking to the group? What do you want to accomplish? What are some likely barriers to the accomplishment of your particular goal?

Often the purpose is to provide information, in condensed form, so that listeners will know basically what you have found in a research study. Perhaps you have the further purpose of convincing your audience to accept your recommendations. Even if this is the case and you have decided beforehand that your purpose is to bring the audience to your way of thinking, you should not interpret this approach as being manipulative. You do not convince by giving only one side of a story; to do so is perhaps the surest way to convince your listeners that you are less than open in your approach and that you cannot be believed or trusted. As in a sales letter or oral sales message, you convince by giving specific reasons, supported by evidence, why your recommended course of action is the most beneficial one to your listeners and to the organization as a whole.

Write a Statement of Your Exact Purpose in Specific Words

As when you are beginning a research project, you should state the purpose of your oral report in specific written words. This purpose should include the desired response from your audience.

This statement of purpose describes what you want to accomplish by your oral presentation. For example, you may wish to evoke one or more of these responses from your audience:

1. The acceptance of a recommended course of action;
2. A realization that your organization is contributing to the welfare of the community;
3. A feeling of pride in the organization and of self-confidence in their own abilities.

Write Your Central Idea in Specific Words

The central idea is the gist of what you want to *say*. The central idea, as described above, is what you want to *accomplish*. Both the purpose of your oral report and the central idea are related to the purpose of a previously prepared written report—if the oral presentation is based on the written report. The purpose of your oral report, however, is not the same as that of the previously completed research study.

If you cannot state the purpose and the central idea in specific words, you are not yet ready to proceed with the planning of the oral report.

ESTIMATING LISTENERS' REACTIONS

As with all communication, predicting the probable responses of your listeners will enable you to express your ideas more persuasively and diplomatically. If your listeners will be pleased with your findings and eager to follow your suggestions and recommendations, your report will be far easier and more enjoyable than if opposite reactions are expected.

Understand Your Listeners as Individuals

James W. Holm, in his book on oral communication, describes audience analysis in this way:

> . . . .What present desires or hopes may you be able to help fulfill? What do they lack at the moment? What problems, difficulties, fears, or discouragements exist that can be related to your message? The answers to some of these questions will provide you with the key which opens the way to their attention, their interest, and their motives.
>
> In addition to these things, you must also try to assess the possible attitudes of your auditors. What attitudes toward you as a person will they likely possess? Will they be hostile toward or suspicious of you? Will their attitude be positive and friendly, disposing them to an open mind? Or will they more likely be neutral or passive in attitude? And what attitudes may govern their reception of your subject? Are they concerned with it, indifferent to it, or averse to hearing about it? Further, what of their attitudes toward your purpose? Will their predisposition to respond be negative, positive, or neutral? Each listener will have a complex of attitudes toward you, your subject, and your purpose. With these you must deal to attain success.[4]

Estimate the knowledge and background of your listeners according to the subject of the report. Everything you say will be influenced by the past experiences of the audience, especially as these experiences pertain to the content and approach of the report.

Understand the Audience as a Group

Consider your audience as a group, as well as a collection of individuals who make up that group. What characteristics do the listeners have in common? Do the members of your audience think of themselves as part of the group, subject to group values, goals,

---

4. James N. Holm, *Productive Speaking for Business and the Professions* (Boston: Allyn and Bacon, 1967), p. 336. Used with permission of the author.

and standards of behavior? Do the members of the group have a common motive or goal? Do they like and accept one another?

Some groups contain individuals whom other members recognize, sometimes unconsciously or informally, as leaders. If you can identify these leaders, perhaps you should direct a portion of your message directly to them, although this approach must be used with extreme caution and should not be noticeable to the rest of the audience.

Understand the Occasion and the Environment

Communication of all kinds is affected by the environment in which it occurs. You as a speaker can do much to control that environment or to adapt the presentation according to the setting and the situation. The acceptance of your remarks, of your ideas, and of yourself will be influenced by the setting in which they are presented. As you plan your report or other oral presentation, make sure that you have the answer to these questions:

1. Why is the meeting being held? Is it a regularly scheduled meeting or one called for a special purpose?
2. What is the relationship of your report to the presentation of other speakers?
3. What is the sequence of oral presentations?
4. How will listeners be affected by the time your report is presented?
5. How much time do you have available for your presentation, and can you expect to have your listeners' undivided attention for this period of time?
6. Where is the meeting to be held?
7. Is the room small or large, and will listeners be crowded together or scattered over a too-large area?
8. Will you need and have available a public-address system?
9. Is a speaker's stand available?
10. Is equipment available for the use of transparencies or other graphic aids?
11. Will there be enough light for you to read your notes without hesitation?
12. Will the room be heated or cooled to a comfortable temperature?
13. Will the room be free from outside noises?
14. Will your listeners be comfortable in all other respects?
15. Is the room of a size and arrangement that all members of

the audience can hear your words and see you? Can you see all members of the audience?

If possible, examine the room and equipment well in advance of your talk. If it is not possible to do so, at least arrive early on the day of your presentation and consider the relation of the environment to your talk. An early examination of the setting may result in a modification of your planned presentation. For example, if you have planned to use transparencies and find that they cannot be easily seen by every person in the room, you are wise to omit them altogether or to enlarge them.

Even the most thorough preparation and planning cannot prevent all distractions or disturbing elements. Although you should do everything possible to arrange for the environment most conducive to the acceptance of your talk, an outstanding, interesting, convincing presentation will do much to atone for unfavorable aspects of the setting in which the talk is given. The most pleasant room and conditions will not compensate for a mediocre presentation.

PLANNING AND PREPARING AN ORAL REPORT

As you proceed with the preparation of an oral report, keep in mind your specifically stated purpose and central idea.

Analyze Your Subject to Decide What to Include

Expressing your central idea in a few words enables you to see the subject in its entirety and to understand the relationship of each part of the report to the central idea. Only when you look at your topic in this way can you decide upon the best way to present your topic so as to achieve the desired results.

If a report is to be given for the purpose of helping your listeners make a decision, consider carefully the issues involved. Does the recommended action provide a solution to an existing problem? What benefits will accrue from your suggested solution? Are your recommendations practical and realistic? Is the topic a controversial one about which you are not likely to obtain agreement? Will your recommendation, although beneficial overall, result in undesirable side effects? Most important of all, does your report supply sufficient evidence, provided by objective and reliable methods of research, to convince your listeners of its credibility?

Decide upon the essential information and explanation to be included, then decide how to present it in the available time. Always work for simplicity. Be interesting and clear. At times you must also be convincing. A multitude of details is not simple, interesting, clear, or convincing.

Write an Outline of Key Ideas in the Order of Presentation

After you have stated specifically the purpose you hope to accomplish through your oral report and your central idea, estimated your listeners' reactions, considered the occasion and the environment, and analyzed the subject in terms of what must be included, you are ready to prepare an outline of how you will express and expand upon the central idea. This planning process is similar to preparing a tentative table of contents for a written report.

The outline is the skeleton of your entire speech; it contains your main ideas in the sequence you will present them. Other helpful, interesting, or perhaps amusing details will be added as you progress in the planning of your talk.

Even though you are giving an oral presentation based on a previously prepared written report, do not assume that your oral report should follow the same outline. For one reason, you are not likely to have enough time to discuss each subdivision in the same order and detail as in a complete written report. In addition, you may need to include some information not in the report itself. And, from the standpoint of emphasis and interest, you may wish to spend more time on conclusions and recommended actions than on detailed findings, as you often should do when preparing a written synopsis.

Consider Time Limitations

It is absolutely essential to plan oral presentations in order to ensure that the desired material is given in the allotted time. The best way to plan your time exactly is to practice your speech with the aid of a tape recorder. Even this timing will not be exact, except in the case of a speech that you read word for word, because of unintentional departures from the planned sequence of topics and unforeseen interruptions.

Oral presentations should not be read unless your speech is to be recorded or published in your exact spoken words. In such a situation, do everything possible to avoid possible misinterpretation. In most business and professional presentations, reading the report is much less desirable than the more casual and usual method of "telling" or "talking" the report.

Even without the use of a tape recorder, you can estimate time fairly well by estimating the number of words in a planned talk. Although speaking rates vary somewhat, the average rate is 110 to 150 words a minute. If you do not have interruptions because of questions or periods of presenting graphic aids, your average speaking rate can be used to determine how many words you can speak in, for example, a 25-minute period.

You should work to make the report or other oral communication no longer than it needs to be to convey the desired information and to achieve the desired results. As with written communication, however, too much concern with brevity often results in lack of understanding, acceptance, and conviction.

Even more important than length is quality, although from the standpoint of courtesy and consideration speakers should stay within their specified time periods. It is extremely inconsiderate to run on into the time allotted for a following speaker. You are also being inconsiderate of your audience when you are unnecessarily slow and repetitious. Such an approach is not likely to build favorable listener response.

SPEAKING TO GROUPS

Of course you can speak to groups! You can do it well. To build confidence, do not concentrate on the term *public speaking* but think in terms of talking with your listeners.

Consider your talk as planned conversation with a group of friends. Do not think of yourself as a performer but as a communicator. You are conversing with the audience, not acting a part. As in all effective communication, consider the interests of your audience and present your material in a positive, listener-oriented approach.

Holm expresses the you-attitude as it pertains to public speaking in the following paragraphs.

YOUR LISTENERS HAVE RIGHTS; YOU HAVE OBLIGATIONS

You noted earlier that business and professional people attending conventions look forward to definite benefits from their experience. We also observed that listeners to a good will speech resent a speaker who uses their time to sell something instead of giving them the new ideas and information they were expecting. A crew of workers expects its foreman to have something to say when he calls them together, and many salesmen would be less apathetic about the weekly sales meeting if they could look forward to a productive investment of their time. All listeners, as a matter of fact, invest valuable time in a speaker. For this investment they have a right to expect certain returns. It is your obligation as a speaker to make sure the listener receives useful goods. Your obligation is four-fold.

Listeners Have a Right to a Message Worth the Time and Effort Invested in Listening

If you talk to thirty people for twenty minutes, the audience has collectively given you 10 hours of time. And while the value of no speech can be measured purely in dollars and cents, we can reach an approximation of value by supposing that this time represents a full eight-hour day, with two hours of overtime. Multiply this time by the hourly income of your average listener, and you will arrive at a figure which stands for their minimum investment. In addition, many may have traveled a distance to hear you, may have altered the day's schedule at some inconvenience, or otherwise made arrangements to be present. It is your obligation to see that what they hear from you is worthwhile.

Furthermore, these are people with business and professional problems. They may hope to learn something which will help them make a difficult decision, they may want technical or engineering information, they may need encouragement or hope, or they may simply be wishing for new insights into time-worn topics. At any rate, they look to you with an anticipation you cannot disappoint. Even a sales message must be presented for the benefit of the listener, for if a salesman cannot benefit his customers he should shut up shop. The listener is eager for an idea that will make a difference in his affairs.

Beyond these considerations is the fact that you or your company have something at stake in your talk. Your reputation may be increased or diminished. Future business may depend on the address. The efficiency of production, the safety of a group of workers, the cooperation of other organizations, the success of a new policy, or some other outcome may hinge on your ability to present a worthy message clearly and effectively.

All this means that your first obligation is to have a message for your listeners. You must give them some new ideas or must present a fresh approach to old ideas, for they will have a right to complain if they hear the same old message in the same old words. The audience, as a general rule, is eager to learn from *you*; it is not interested in the second-hand material you have appropriated from somebody else. This is not to say you shouldn't do research on your subject—you should. But the research should be to develop and to round out your own thinking, since the integrity of your message depends on its being essentially your own. This is the only way public address attains its best, and the only way you can give your listeners what they have a right to expect.

Listeners Have a Right to an Orderly
Presentation of Material

Even an important message can become almost repulsive to an audience if it is not presented in a clear and easy-to-follow way. When the listener is forced to submit to a confused jumble of words and ideas, when he would like to understand the speaker but is frustrated by hearing a hodge-podge of unassorted thoughts which do not merge into a clean-cut development of theme, the speaker has failed to meet his second basic obligation.

Your listeners have a right to expect that you will have taken the time and effort to plan what you have to say so they can follow you without trouble. They have a right to expect that you will be able to give them a complete message within the time limits which have been set for your talk, or within a reasonable length of time if no limit has been set. Your obligation, then, consists in so arranging your material, in so planning the order or sequence of your remarks, that your audience will be able to think with you without effort, from a specific conversational opening to an ending which wraps up the speech with satisfaction and completeness. And you are obliged to make certain that you do not overstep the bounds of courtesy and common sense by talking longer than you should.

Listeners Have a Right to Direct
Communication, Sparked with Enthusiasm

Your listeners are not at all unreasonable to insist that you talk *with* them. They have a right to sense that you seek mental and emotional rapport and that you do so because you have a high desire to communicate something of importance. . . . You may want notes at times, and rarely a manuscript, but under no conditions will your audience become a part of the communicative process with you if you are not free from all encumbrance and able to converse with directness.

Furthermore, your audience expects, and you have an obligation, to talk with verve, enthusiasm, and physical animation. This does not mean that you must be a table-thumping rabble-rouser, but that you must be alive with the excitement of your message and the opportunity to do something for the audience. . . .

Listeners Have a Right to Material Which
Is Specific and Factual and Therefore
Interesting

Unless your audience is captive, it will walk out on you if you insist on talking in generalities and abstractions. And if it is captive, it may sit before you but won't listen. It will go to sleep—and audiences can easily sleep with eyes wide open! You will have to pin your ideas down with illustrations, examples, instances, facts, and figures. You will have to express your thinking in specific words—in words which sparkle because they have meaning in the everyday life of the listener.

A quip on a five-cent card reads, "Your argument is sound. All sound." Unless you want the audience to make remarks like this about your speech, you must substitute facts for sound. You cannot interest or impress business and professional audiences with noise and fireworks, but you can do so with specific materials which show that you know what you're talking about and which make sense to the listener. This is your obligation.

If you can give your audiences these four things which they have a right to expect, they will appreciate you as a speaker, and you can reasonably anticipate success in achieving the results you are after. A solid message, clear arrangement of material, enthusiastic delivery, and specific content are the minimum satisfactory requirements. This is not to say that you should not aspire for greater virtues as a speaker, but that you cannot get by with less. The minimum requirements are based on the rights of the listeners.[5]

Talk with People and Look at Them

You are talking with *people*, not with a vague, collective *thing*. Although it is true that individuals within a group may react to your talk, and to you, in relation to the reactions of other members of the group, you are communicating with *individuals*, with people like yourself.

When you talk with people, look at them. In a pause just before you begin speaking, look out over the room and see somebody— then look at other people. Let your eyes meet theirs, briefly. Make sure that you include members of the audience at far edges of the group. This action is a form of greeting, perhaps even more important than your spoken words of greeting. In addition, the pause prepares your audience for your opening remarks by getting their attention. Otherwise, if you rush too quickly into your spoken greeting, some of your words will be lost to some of your listeners. By your glances, you invite your audience to enter into a conversation with you.

The audience's part of the conversation, when you are speaking without verbal responses from your listeners, is communicated through facial expressions, nods or frowns, posture, and actions. As

5. Holm, pp. 320–323.

will be discussed further in regard to nonverbal communication, your listeners provide vivid, instant feedback without saying a word.

An opening pause (do not extend it too long) relaxes you because it takes your mind away from yourself, the speaker, so that you can concentrate on your audience. When you think of your audience instead of yourself, your stage fright will decrease.

After you have prepared your listeners and yourself, start talking with them. Speak rather slowly at first until your listeners have had time to become accustomed to your voice. Every person has unique voice qualities and speaking characteristics. After a few sentences, speak at your natural rate, making sure that each word is distinct. (If you have not listened to your recorded voice, preferably as rehearsal of the particular talk you are preparing, you are not yet ready to give that talk.)

As in the initial eye contact with your audience, continue to include your listeners in all parts of the room. Avoid directing your attention to one part of the room or to only a few individuals. Do not look very long at any one person.

Make sure that everyone in the room can hear you. If you are not sure, ask. If necessary, adjust the public address system or project your voice.

Speak conversationally with a relaxed voice. If you shout or strain, or assume the pose and gestures of an orator, you are not being conversational.

As mentioned earlier, the use of a tape recorder is of immense help toward improving your tone of voice, gaining a conversational approach, as well as being a check on pronunciation, logic, appropriate use of emphasis, conciseness, timing, and all other qualities of effective speech. A tape recorder is almost as essential as a pen or typewriter in preparing yourself to give an outstanding oral presentation. Video equipment that records both sight and sound is even better, but more expensive and less convenient to use.

Understand the Importance of Nonverbal Communication

Nonverbal communication occurs constantly, whether we are speaking to groups or engaging in conversation. It is impossible not to communicate with other people around us, even when we do not speak.

Nonverbal communication includes gestures and other bodily movements, facial expressions, posture, clothing and overall appearance, use of time and space, and various other methods of expressing meaning. We communicate by tone of voice, rate of speech, the "oh's" and "ah's" that we insert into speech, pauses, hesitations, and silence. We communicate through what we omit from our spoken words.

Like all other forms of communication, nonverbal messages should be sincere. Planned gestures and body movements usually appear to be just that—faked. They are also silly. Gestures should be used naturally, reinforcing the meaning being expressed through words. Too much hand movement is distracting and annoying.

Videotape equipment is helpful in determining whether your gestures and other forms of nonverbal communication are appropriate and effective. If such equipment is not available, ask friends to evaluate your speech from all aspects, with special attention given to the use of gestures, posture, and overall movement. It may be dangerous to try to "spice up" your talk by adding gestures, even if you are now using none. In case you are using too many hand movements, however, make an effort to avoid these distracting movements.

Following the advice given in preceding sections of this chapter will take care of many problems of nonverbal communication. For example, if you are sincere, enthusiastic, and knowledgeable, with a well-planned presentation, your sincerity, enthusiasm, knowledge, ability, and consideration of your audience will be apparent to your listeners. You will exhibit confidence and develop belief and trust by the overall excellence of your presentation.

Enthusiasm is contagious. If you are not enthusiastic about your subject, you cannot expect your listeners to be.

You communicate more through your nonverbal messages than with words. Authorities in the field estimate that about 70 percent of the communication that occurs in oral messages is through combined methods of nonverbal communication. Much of nonverbal communication is unplanned; thus, it is a sincere form of communication. Your nonverbal messages are influenced by your feelings about your listeners, your subject, and yourself. Nevertheless, some nonverbal communication is unlike your real feelings. For example, if you frown because you are nervous or afraid you will not be understood or accepted, the frown may be mistaken for dislike of your listeners. Even if the frown is correctly interpreted, it results in a negative impression and is a form of distraction.

Suggestions for effective nonverbal communication are these:

1. Sincerely like your audience.
2. Know your subject thoroughly in order to appear confident.
3. Be well dressed, but not overdressed.
4. Look your listeners in the eye (but not too long at any one person) and talk with them.

5. Avoid excessive, meaningless gestures and nervous movements.
6. Keep calm.
7. Remain objective. Do not let your anger show, no matter what the provocation.
8. Speak clearly and pleasantly. Make sure that you can be easily heard throughout the room. But don't shout.
9. Make sure that you have an excellent command of language usage. (Yes, it's a little late to start if you must give a speech next week and still are not sure whether it's *for my wife and I* or *for my wife and me*. But do what you can, including study of Appendix C.) This suggestion may seem to apply to verbal communication, but not to nonverbal messages. Actually, it applies to both. Obvious and repeated errors (we all slip now and then) tell your audience far more about you than you could put into words. Recording your talk and listening to yourself on tape serves as a check for lack of clarity, slurred pronunciation, and tone of voice, as well as occasional grammatical variations.
10. Relax. You can't if you're unsure of yourself. That's why the nine preceding suggestions are important.

Also use your knowledge of nonverbal communication to analyze the feedback you receive from your audience. Nothing is more satisfying to a speaker than to notice a look of intense interest on the faces of the listening audience. After a few speaking engagements you will soon learn to recognize sincere interest and approval. Even if your listeners are only pretending to be interested in your remarks, you can soon recognize simulated approval and agreement. If your listeners are sitting straight in their chairs and looking you in the eyes steadily and directly, beware. This is a pose of faked attention. Watch for listeners leaning toward you. If you are sure that they are having no difficulty in hearing, this action is a sign of sincere attention.

Notice such telltale signs of boredom as fidgeting, random glances around the room, and looking at watches. (If they are pretending to be interested in your remarks, they wll not look at their watches. At least you will know that frequent checkers of time are honestly telling you to move on.)

You can tell by facial expressions, to a great extent, whether or not your audience agrees with you. You can tell when they do not understand or when they are disappointed or annoyed. You can always tell when your audience is pleasantly surprised that you are doing such a good job.

Build Self-Confidence

Remember that you will naturally feel somewhat nervous before you are to make an important oral presentation, or maybe an unimportant one, if you are inexperienced in public speaking. Some speakers of long experience state that they continue to have stage fright before they actually begin speaking but that it disappears as they address the audience. Some people believe that this stage fright is beneficial as long as it is not so severe as to be paralyzing. They say that when they are not nervous at all they know that they are too complacent—and that they will not give an enthusiastic presentation.

Nevertheless, your nervousness should not be so extreme as to result in shaking hands or a trembling voice, which are embarrassing not only to yourself but to your listeners. As a word of comfort, though, most of the terror you feel will not be apparent to the audience. A slight touch of shyness is more appealing, to some people, than the opposite approach of being extremely confident and overly aggressive. On the other hand, being ill at ease indicates that you are more interested in making a good impression than in bringing a message to your audience or in talking with them.

Some techniques that may help to build confidence are these:

1. Try not to be afraid in advance. Worrying or being afraid won't change anything, but only make matters worse. Use the time you would spend in being afraid in preparing your talk.
2. Be completely and thoroughly prepared. After all that preparation, you'll be an expert on the subject. And why should an expert be nervous?
3. Unless you are positive that your listeners are actually hostile, an unlikely situation, assume that they are friendly and supportive. This assumption is likely to be correct whether they are friends, acquaintances, or strangers.
4. The audience is made up of *people*. Don't think of your audience as a mass of faces. Speak to your audience as you would to one friend or a small group of friends.
5. Look at people and notice their reactions. As you see your audience accept and respond to your words and actions, your confidence will increase.
6. You are likely to make a few mistakes. So do all the other experts.
7. After the presentation, when you are complimented, say "Thank you," "I'm glad you liked it," or something else

that indicates you also think you did a good job. Don't say "Oh, that was terrible" or "I was absolutely scared to death."

Consider the Use of Graphic Aids and Other Illustrations

Graphic aids, such as charts displayed on transparencies, can add to the clarity and interest of an oral presentation. They can also weaken the oral presentation and detract from the spoken words. Use illustrations only if they are needed to supplement your talk. Do not assume that your most important goal is to comment on the information presented in the graphic aids, but that the illustrated material supplements your spoken words.

Graphic illustrations such as bar or line charts express relationships much more quickly and accurately than spoken words. The same advantages that graphics bring to written reports apply to oral reports; in many instances, these aids are even more necessary.

The opaque projector is the simplest and easiest way to project any written or pictorial material. No reproduction of the copy is necessary, as the material to be shown is inserted into the projector and enlarged on the screen. If there is sufficient distance between the projector and the screen, and if the screen is large enough, the copy can be made large enough to be easily seen by all persons in most rooms.

A disadvantage of the opaque projector is that the room must be dark. More light can be used with an overhead projector, but the use of this equipment requires that a transparency be made from the original copy. Many photocopy machines can make a transparency from the original copy in a few minutes.

Duplicated handouts also serve as a form of visual aid. Some speakers believe, though, that the use of such material distracts from the immediate proceedings. Avoid distributing several pages at one time, some of which do not apply to what is being discussed at the moment. Members of the audience, instead of looking at the speaker or participating in discussion, may spend their time reading the handouts.

Graphic aids and other illustrations, wisely planned and used, are helpful in presenting an interesting, informative oral report. To be effective, however, they require the same careful planning and organization as the remainder of the report.

Be careful not to "lose" yourself in the illustrations being presented to the extent that you lose your audience. You are communicating to your listeners through the *use* of graphic aids. Talk with the audience, not to the illustrations. The illustrations are not telling the story; you are.

In addition to distractions previously discussed, various other actions and mannerisms hinder the understanding and acceptance of your intended message. Although you cannot eliminate all distractions, careful planning will do much to prevent them.

Avoid the annoying, time-consuming practice of shuffling sheets of paper that contain your notes, particularly if you are using a public-address system. The sound may be greatly amplified.

Also avoid moving the microphone unless it is necessary to achieve a desired volume of sound. Many speakers move the microphone unnecessarily, resulting in distracting noise.

Prefer note cards, approximately 5 by 8 inches, to sheets of paper. They are easier to handle without shuffling and noise. You can turn them less obviously. Put the cards into a notebook designed especially for the size cards you are using.

Make sure that your notes are large enough for you to see as the notebook lies on the speaker's stand so that you will not be forced to lower your head or hold the notebook in your hands. If you have thoroughly prepared yourself for the presentation, you will have no need for constant use of your notes, but having them available will add to your poise and confidence. Do not write your notes in great detail; they will be harder to refer to and will require more cards and thus more turning of the cards than if only major ideas are listed. Do not take the risk, however, of omitting important information from your talk because you do not have it in your notes.

Another distraction is frequent glances at your watch or at a clock in the room. Although you must keep close track of time, you should do it inconspicuously. A solution that you may find helpful is to tape a wristwatch with an easy-to-read dial to the inside cover of the notebook containing your note cards, opposite the cards. If you are standing, with the notebook placed on a speaker's stand, you can look at the watch so unobtrusively that your viewers will never guess it is there.

In addition to taking your listeners' attention away from your spoken words, distracting actions and mannerisms indicate lack of confidence. They result in a rather negative approach, not a cheerful, positive one.

SUMMARY

Principles of effective communication through written reports also apply to effective oral reporting.

Determining the purpose of an oral report is essential early in the planning stages. The statement of purpose, as for a written report, should be expressed in a few specific words. The central idea should also be put into specific words. The purpose of an oral report is what you wish to accomplish. The central idea is the core of the message.

Predicting the probable response of your listeners will enable you to communicate more persuasively and diplomatically. The environment, as well as the speaker and other members of a group, influences listener response.

Careful planning of all phases of an oral presentation is necessary for success. This planning should include an analysis of which items of information must be included, how to present necessary information in a specified time, the sequence of presentation, and control of the environment.

QUESTIONS AND PROBLEMS

1. Give an oral report to the class based on a written report you have prepared earlier in the course. Adhere strictly to your allotted time as assigned by your instructor or as agreed upon by you and your classmates. If appropriate and practical, use audiovisual aids to illustrate and emphasize. Allow time for questions from your audience.

2. Prepare an outline of a speech on a subject with which you are thoroughly familiar. Prepare your report and present it to the class.

3. Prepare a short talk to be presented to your classmates. Plan the time according to your instructor's specifications as to the amount of time available. Choose some subject that is related to communication but preferably one that is not discussed in this book. For example, discuss the use of graphic aids in oral presentations, perhaps limiting your talk to the use of one particular kind of graphic aid. Other possible suggestions include recent developments in technology that speed the process of transcription; the choice of a voice-writing machine; differences between language usage in Great Britain and America; regional differences in pronunciation or word usage.

   All these topics are broad enough for long presentations. If you attempt to cover them in a short talk, you will of necessity be giving a broad overview. Perhaps you can limit your topic to some particular aspect of these subjects; for example, a few examples of extraordinary word usage in the Ozarks or from any other section of the country that you know well. In addition to these suggested topics in communications, you can think of many more.

4. Tape-record a speaker on television or on the radio. Evaluate the performance according to principles presented in this chapter.

5. Members of the class are to form into four- to six-person groups. Assume that the members make up a panel on a convention program. Each group is to select a topic similar to the one described in problem 3. One member of the panel is to act as both chairperson and master of ceremonies. On the day of the class presentation, each member is to be allowed a specified time, according to the total time available, in which to present a report on one aspect of the overall subject. The chairperson is to introduce the panel members to the class before they make their presentations. After all presentations have been made, allow time for questions from the audience, which may be directed to any member of the panel.

6. Use one or more of the many topics suggested in Cases 49 and 50, Appendix B, as the basis for an oral report.

Communicating about Employment

PART V

Planning the Search for Career Employment

16

Chapters 16 and 17 are planned to help you communicate effectively in order to secure employment. Chapter 16 emphasizes the research phase of the job-seeking process and the preparation of the resume. Chapter 17 presents a consideration of the application letter and other letters about employment, plus a discussion of the employment interview.

An outstanding letter of application, with a well-organized, attractive, and convincing resume, can make the difference as to whether you find the kind of employment you are seeking. Although no written presentation will get a job for you, it can provide an opportunity for an interview, at which time you continue the process of convincing the interviewer that you are the best possible choice for the position.

The most important factor in the search for employment is that you are qualified for the job for which you apply. The most creative, attractive, and appropriate letter and resume will not substitute for having something valuable to sell, just as a cleverly worded sales letter must be written about a good product if it is to be truly effective on a continuing basis.

METHODS OF OBTAINING EMPLOYMENT

Consider the various ways in which employment is obtained. Some of these methods are more effective than others, depending upon the applicant's background and goals and upon job requirements and hiring policies of the potential employer. You should decide upon the approach that seems to be best for your particular situation, but you should also use all other appropriate methods.

Regardless of your outstanding qualifications or of a favorable job market, you should take the initiative in your job search instead of waiting for an employer to offer a position or even to advertise one. Taking the initiative has several advantages. You become aware of differing opportunities and are able to compare prospective employers and employment opportunities. You are more likely to find a better job when you actively seek one, instead of waiting for one to come your way, because you learn about more openings. You are better able to consider your particular strengths in relation to the needs of differing employing organizations.

Another obvious advantage is that your initiative in looking for a job tells the employer a great deal about you, including the fact that you have enough energy and ambition to plan and conduct a thorough, organized campaign to place yourself. The quality of your work after being hired, with resulting opportunities for advancement to a higher position, is likely to be similar to your efforts in finding and obtaining the job.

In addition, as you survey employing organizations, you will no doubt find one or more in which you are especially interested. Your special interest in a particular organization, which will be apparent in your written application and interview, is a definite positive factor from the standpoint of the employer. An applicant who very much wants a job with a particular organization has a definite advantage over one equally qualified who just wants a job—anywhere.

SOLICITED APPLICATION LETTERS AND RESUMES

A solicited letter of application, with or without an accompanying resume, is written in reply to advertisements, announcements, or other requests for applicants. Ordinarily, you should prefer the two-part application (letter and resume) for applications of all kinds.

You may find advertisements in your local newspaper for the kind of work you are seeking. Another place to find announcements of openings in a specialized field is professional journals, although these openings may require moving to another part of the country. Many advertisements, particularly for executives and engineers, appear in *The Wall Street Journal*.

Writing a solicited application letter differs little from writing a solicited sales letter. You must convince the reader that the product you are selling—yourself—is the one that should be selected. As in all sales messages, the reader is convinced by specific evidence, not by a high-pressure approach.

The opening section and all remaining sections of the application letter and data sheet should be built around a central selling point. The central theme, based upon the central selling point, tells how your most important qualification, or perhaps a group of related qualifications, can benefit the particular employing organization. Emphasize the strength or strengths you believe will be most applicable to the particular position, but include other positive factors as well. The employer looks at your entire background, personality, ability, attitude, and, especially, potential value to the organization.

UNSOLICITED APPLICATION LETTERS AND RESUMES

Unsolicited applications can be considered a form of direct-mail advertising, similar to messages planned for direct-mail campaigns to sell a product or service.

Prepare a mailing list of organizations for which you would like to work. This mailing list should consist of the names of the organizations and the names, titles, and addresses of people responsible for receiving and reviewing applications. Try to find the name of the person who will be responsible for hiring you instead of sending your application to the personnel department. This person is likely to be a department head or the manager of the office or division where you would be employed.

Make absolutely certain that the individual's name is spelled correctly and that the title is correct. Preparing your mailing list will require a great deal of research in order to select the organizations and individuals to receive your application.

Some books and consultants on the job-seeking process advocate sending out several hundred letters and data sheets. If you attempt such a broad-scale mailing, you lose any hope of tailoring your approach to individual companies, to say nothing of the great amount of time and expense involved. You are better advised to be more selective in your choice of organizations.

Remember, however, that you are not likely to receive favorable replies from all the applications you mail. Depending upon current employment conditions in your area of specialization and upon your background and qualifications, you may receive a request for an interview or for further information from only a small percentage of your total list.

The two-part application consisting of a letter and resume

should ordinarily be sent as a unit. Some applicants, however, send only a prospecting letter and offer to send a complete resume upon request. If you decide to use only the letter, include enough convincing, specific details to make the reader want to know more about you. An example of a letter that combines the functions of an application letter and resume is illustrated in Figure 16-7. All the other data sheets shown in this chapter are intended to be sent with the application letters illustrated in Chapter 17.

Each letter you send should be individually typewritten. To do otherwise is to suggest that the letter is only one of many, that you are looking only for a job, any job, that you are not especially interested in the organization to which the letter is addressed. Letters that are prepared by the use of automatic typewriters, of which there are several kinds, retain their individually typewritten appearance.

Resumes are often printed or reproduced by some process, such as photocopying, that results in attractive copies difficult to distinguish from typewritten material. Resumes, whether individually typewritten or reproduced, should be on bond paper identical to that used for the accompanying letter.

As a practical matter, if you send out many unsolicited applications the resume should be duplicated in some way. If you are applying to organizations that are similar in nature and supposed needs, a resume can be made to "fit" all of them, although not so exactly as one especially written for each organization.

PLACEMENT SERVICES

The college placement office, for graduating college seniors, is often the best means of securing career employment. The services of these offices are available also to alumni and to students who are dropping out of the college for one reason or another.

Placement offices, in addition to arranging interviews with company representatives, usually maintain a library of brochures and literature about employing organizations, including various government agencies. The number of employing organizations that hire through college placement offices changes from year to year, depending upon the economic situation and upon other varying factors.

If you find employment through a college placement office, you may not use an application letter or resumé as they are discussed in this chapter. You will almost certainly make a written application of some kind, however, even if it consists only of filling in the standard application form of the particular organization. In addition, you will probably write follow-up letters and a thank-you letter after the interview.

Some organizations ask the applicant to prepare a letter of application and a data sheet, similar to those discussed here, after the applicant has been interviewed. This instruction may be given to test the communication ability of the applicant or perhaps in order to determine whether there is a sincere interest in the job. Usually, however, the purpose of an application letter and a resume is to obtain an interview.

Private and government employment agencies place thousands of persons each year. Government agencies are free. Placement fees are paid to privately owned employment agencies, either by the individual who is hired or by the employing organization, or the fee may be divided between the employer and the employee. Although these fees to private agencies seem high, if you can find a better job through an agency than you could find on your own, your actual value received exceeds the cost. You are wise, however, to check with your local Better Business Bureau before signing a contract with an employment agency.

Jobs are also obtained through the simple process of going to personnel offices and placing applications or by making telephone calls. Although these methods may constitute a satisfactory approach to some kinds of jobs, including those that college students find as part-time work as they complete their schooling, they are not usually the best approach to full-time career employment.

An unsolicited two-part application, based upon research into the company to which the application is sent, shows more care and preparation and more actual interest in the organization. In addition, it can be read when time is available for it to be given complete attention. A telephone call may come at an inopportune time and result in a hasty "no."

ANALYZING YOUR QUALIFICATIONS

When planning a sales campaign, one of the first steps is to make a product analysis. You look at the product, test it, and compare it with competing brands. Then you decide upon your central theme, or the most important selling feature, also called the central selling point.

As you plan a job-seeking campaign, you make this analysis about yourself. You analyze the "product," compare it with competing ones, and note how the product fits the market for which you are preparing your application. Although this analysis is for your use only, it will be far more beneficial and complete if it is in written form.

You will have several features to stress, but the main theme of your presentation will depend upon the kind of work for which you are applying, as well as upon the type of organization. Because the emphasis will differ according to these factors, an individually tailored application letter, as well as an individually planned resume, is more likely to be effective than using the same two-part application for organizations with varying needs.

Because you will not always be sure of these varying needs, you will not always be exactly correct in your choice of the central selling point. Usually the central selling feature will be either your education or your experience. For most persons completing a college degree, especially young college graduates with limited experience, the central selling point is some facet of the educational background, ordinarily the major field.

After people have been out of school for several years, experience is likely to become the most important selling feature if it is similar to the kind of work for which they are making application. People with diversified experience should stress successful experience in a job similar to the one being sought.

In certain instances, extracurricular work or an avocation will be the most convincing central theme. For example, a football star may be hired as a sporting goods salesman. In this case, the football experience is of more value than is the student's major in, for example, journalism. If the student is applying for a job as a newspaper reporter, the academic major should be stressed to the extent that the application is built around it. The football experience should be mentioned but given only limited coverage.

As when selling a product, do not stress the central selling point to the extent that other selling features are omitted or overly subordinated. You cannot be completely sure that you are choosing the most logical central selling point. In addition, you are likely to be hired on the basis of total qualifications, consisting of education, experience, personality, attitude toward work, and the ability to grow and develop in usefulness to the employing organization.

As you analyze yourself, you will no doubt find that you have weak and strong points. As you present yourself to the prospective employers, stress strong points and subordinate or leave unmentioned those factors that you consider to be weaknesses. *Never misrepresent in any way.* The positive approach, as in other communications situations, "accentuates the positive and eliminates the negative." What you consider to be a weakness can often be presented in positive terms. For example, instead of saying, "I have no experience except for part-time work in a grocery," say

```
My four years' experience as a checker and office
employee with A&P Grocery Company were valuable in
that they gave me experience in working harmoniously
with other employees and in courteously serving the
customers. I worked an average of twenty-five hours
a week during the entire four years of attending
college, yet maintained a grade point average of
3.2, a score that qualified me each semester for the
Dean's list.
```

Other examples of points to emphasize and subordinate will be given later in this chapter as you learn to prepare the application letter and resume.

Education

If you are completing college, your education to be considered in your self-analysis consists especially of work leading toward a degree. Other educational preparation consists of high school subjects, technical or business courses, and other specialized schooling, as well as educational experiences obtained in military service. Consider courses that apply to the job you are seeking, including those within your major field and any others that especially relate.

Consider also your scholastic standing overall and in your major field. Whether or not you mention your scholastic standing depends upon what it is. According to the principle of the positive approach, you are not obligated to emphasize a negative aspect. If you have an average only equal to that necessary to obtain a degree or very slightly above, emphasize the degree and leave unmentioned the actual grade point average.

The degree is a real accomplishment even if other persons have surpassed you in A's and B's. But if you are asked for your exact standing, be truthful. By being truthful, according to an old adage, you are not forced to remember what you said. Some organizations immediately disqualify any applicant who is discovered to have misrepresented even the slightest bit of information.

You may wish to give your grade point average only in your major field, not the overall average, as the standing in your major field is likely to be higher. This performance in your major field should be of most concern to the employer. In some instances you should mention research projects or papers that are particularly relevant. After you have completed graduate work, mention of a thesis or dissertation is considered an essential part of your educational preparation.

Remember to include specific skills and abilities developed in your educational program, such as ability to work with computers or various office machines, especially if you are likely to use these machines in your future work. If you have used these machines in previous employment, the mention of this ability should be listed in the section on experience. If you have not actually used them in employment but have had training in their use, mention your ability in the educational section of your data sheet.

As you complete the analysis of your educational preparation, you will probably find that it should be your central selling feature. From a standpoint of emphasis, as you have already learned, a description of your education in terms of how it will benefit the reader should be described in more detail than other factors. Also from the standpoint of emphasis, educational preparation should be presented before other less important factors.

Work Experience

Work experience is ordinarily one of the two most important factors of career preparation, although a few college students complete degrees with no work experience whatsoever. If you have no work experience, educational preparation must be stressed to an even greater extent. You should also show how participation in professional and social organizations has provided experience in leadership positions and in working with other persons.

Some applicants have the idea that only related work experience should be mentioned in the application letter or on the data sheet. This approach is unwise. Work experience of any kind, as long as it is legal and honorable, is better than no experience at all. Any job, even the most menial, indicates that you have the energy and initiative to seek and hold a job.

Remember to include work experience acquired in military service. In many instances this will be your most important and relevant experience, or even the central theme of your entire application.

As you continue with your self-analysis, remember to make a note of accomplishments, such as exceeding a sales quota, earning a promotion, or receiving certificates of recognition for unusual achievement. Begin to think of the best ways to present these successes to show how you can benefit the prospective employer. You also have the problem of presenting these successful experiences without appearing egotistical.

Activities, Achievements, and Personal Characteristics

In this portion of your analysis, list extracurricular activities in high school and college; social and professional organizations, including membership and offices held; and any other meaningful activity or accomplishment. Include honors, awards, publications, and other recognitions. (Scholastic awards are usually presented in connection with your other educational achievements.) Foreign language abilities, hobbies, personal business ventures, and many other facets of your total experience may have a bearing upon your ability to fit into the particular organization to which you are applying.

Check yourself in these and similar areas:

Ability and willingness to assume responsibility
Ability to adapt to changing situations
Ability to communicate in oral and written form
Ability to work with other persons
Leadership
Judgment
Self-confidence and poise
Appearance
Sense of humor
Neatness

Ability to make decisions
Ability to persevere
Ability to think logically and creatively
Courtesy and diplomacy
Emotional and physical health
Maturity
Dependability
Promptness
Ambition and enthusiasm

Most important, ask yourself if the field of work being considered is in line with your real interest and ability. What do you want from your career?

To prevent the resume from becoming extremely long, as well as from the standpoint of presenting only necessary and relevant information, use discretion as you present this type of somewhat supplementary information.

As you remember from the study of emphasis, when you attempt to emphasize a great many things you succeed in emphasizing nothing. On the other hand, you are not presenting the best possible picture of yourself if you omit favorable data that may show your ability to be a good employee.

After you have made a complete and objective self-analysis, you should have a realistic approach to the job-seeking process. You still have the task of choosing the best method of presenting qualifications and determining which factors to stress and which to subordinate. In order to answer these questions, you need to know something of your prospective employer.

ANALYZING THE EMPLOYMENT MARKET

The market analysis is the next step in the job-seeking process. You must know your employer and the job requirements in order to show how your qualifications meet the employer's needs. Although many items of information cannot be obtained until the interview, or perhaps not until you actually begin work or have worked for a considerable time, much information will be available if you diligently look for it.

First of all, what information will you need? You will need enough information to indicate that an organization is one that will offer you sufficient opportunity, provided you are hired, to justify your accepting this employment. Although this statement may seem obvious, it is the most important answer you are seeking. As you make this investigation, you will also gain enough information to help you intelligently plan your presentation to the specific organization.

You should not take the attitude that you must accept a job that offers little opportunity for growth or for the kind of work you prefer. You may be forced to accept an offer that is less than ideal, but at least you should aim high. On the other hand, remember that you are not stuck forever in any job. Although frequent changes do not look good on your record, many if not most persons change jobs several times during their lifetime.

Although you may not stay with your first full-time job, it should be chosen with care. In one way or another, it will affect your entire career. In addition, the employing organization will spend time and money in hiring and training you—perhaps a great deal of time and money. If you do not enter into the employment contract with the sincere desire to succeed and to remain with the organization, you are not being completely fair to the employer or to yourself.

Another purpose of research into potential employing organizations is to obtain information about how to sell yourself intelligently. If you can determine your possible duties, you can choose the particular qualification or qualifications to emphasize.

Another advantage (as well as an obvious necessity) of doing research into the job market is to know which organizations have openings for persons like yourself. You can assume that many large organizations will periodically employ persons with widely used specializations, such as engineering, accounting, or sales. For positions such as these, unsolicited letters of application are appropriate and useful. You can, in fact, use unsolicited letters for all possible openings, but you will be less sure of receiving a favorable reply.

Even if an unplanned "hit-or-miss" approach seems to succeed, it is still far from being the best method. You are not able in this way to fit your qualifications to the particular employer. You are also likely not to find the organizations for which you would most like to work.

Where will you find all this information? Printed sources will provide some of the information you seek. Annual reports of the firms in which you are interested include far more information than the financial statement. They also tell something of the product or services, as well as the location of the home office and branch offices. They may give information about management policies.

The *College Placement Annual* is especially applicable to persons graduating from college. A copy of this book is often available through your college placement office. Employing organizations are listed alphabetically and also by occupational specialities and geographic locations. Other information includes brief notations as to the kinds of openings, the educational background of the applicants being sought, and the proper person in the organization whom you should contact.

Moody's Manuals of Investments, although intended primarily to provide information to potential investors, also provides information essential to the potential employee. Information included in these manuals consists of a summary of the history of each organization, method of operation, location, products or services, and the financial structure. These books are available in most libraries.

Standard and Poor's Manuals are also planned primarily for investors. They contain information similar to that contained in *Moody's Manuals*. Another publication of this corporation is *Poor's Register of Directors and Executives, United States and Canada*. This directory may be useful in finding the name and title of the person to whom you should send your application for employment.

You may be able to find a specialized guide to employing organizations, with a listing of their management personnel, for your own particular city. Check with your college or public library. Such a guide will contain information about local companies that are not included in national reference books, as well as information about branch offices of national companies. This kind of guide will be your most likely source of exact names and titles of people to whom you wish to address your applications. In addition, if you wish to send applications to organizations in cities other than your own, you may find similar guides to these cities in your local library.

The Business Periodicals Index, the *Wall Street Journal Index*, and other indexes are useful in locating magazine articles that have been written about particular business organizations in which you are interested.

Many government and professional organizations issue publications of their own planned to describe employment opportunities and the necessary qualifications for employees. Much of this literature is available through college placement offices and public and school libraries. You can also learn about job openings from professional journals in your field.

Perhaps the best way of all to learn about prospective employers is to ask other persons who are employed in these organizations doing work similar to the kind you would be doing. As in any other survey, however, the more people you ask, within limits, the more valid your data are likely to be.

ADVANTAGES OF THE TWO-PART APPLICATION

A two-part application enables you to use the letter to present highlights of the detailed information included on the resume. These factors are stated in light of what your qualifications will do for the reader. As in other sales messages, the letter is more coherent and emphatic when it is built around a central theme.

Prepare the resume, then choose from it important elements to be included in the letter. The letter can be considered as an interpretation of your most important qualifications of all those shown on the resume in terms of reader interest—much as you present important elements of a product as you write a sales letter to be sent with leaflets and brochures. Both of these parts of the two-part application are prepared after you have made a detailed analysis of your qualifications and researched the companies in which you are interested.

YOUR RESUME—A REPORT ON YOURSELF

The resume (also described as a data sheet) can be the deciding factor in getting the interviewer's attention. It can also continue the sales presentation throughout the interview and the negotiation process.

A well-prepared resume should be a truly superior expression of your talents and background. It should be a credit to your creativity and ability to put ideas into convincing words. The most effective resumes sell ability, talent, and potential, as well as education and past experience.

You should not understate your qualifications, but you also must not misrepresent in any way. Two or three hundred applicants may also want the job for which you are applying; now is no time to be modest.

A resume, like the letter that accompanies it, should be striking in appearance. It should be absolutely perfect in typewritten form and arrangement. Use good paper, a good typewriter, and a typewriter ribbon that gives a clear copy. Special paper, such as a heavy bond in a light cream or buff color, may make your application stand out from all the rest. A perfectly typewritten copy, however, with correct punctuation and exact wording and spelling, will be superior to many others, even if it is on plain white paper of good quality. Why anyone would send out unattractive and incorrect applications is difficult to understand, considering the importance of the message. Make sure that you do not leave in such obvious errors as strikeovers, misspelled words, messy erasures, and uneven margins.

Every resume should contain certain basic parts, although the format may and should vary according to the aspect to be emphasized. Each should contain the employment objective (this may be included in the heading); education and work experience. You may or may not wish to include a list of references and a personal data section.

The Heading

The heading should include your name, address, and telephone number. Sometimes these items of information, used alone, make up the entire heading without some kind of descriptive title such as *Resume, Data Sheet, Vita,* or *Qualifications of.* Your objective may be included in the heading instead of being listed in the first section of the data sheet; for example, *Sherry Clara Aldridge's Qualifications for Accounting Work with Arthur Andersen and Company.* Another method of showing the objective in the heading is to follow your name with a description of your occupation, provided you are applying for similar work; for example *Joe Lee Cole, Industrial Psychologist.*

To list "accounting work" in the heading or in the section of the data sheet entitled *Objective* is too vague and general if you are aware of a particular opening that can be described in more specific terms. Avoid being overly specific when you are not exactly sure of the kind of work available to you; on the other hand, don't be so general that you say nothing at all. "I'll do anything, and I can do everything" is not usually a good approach when seeking career employment—although being a generalist is often more advantageous than being able to work only in a narrow specialization. You are likely to have much competition. Don't eliminate possible opportunities by a too specific description of the job you seek.

Perhaps you should give two addresses and telephone numbers in the heading of the data sheet, especially if you expect to change your address soon. Students often give their school address and their home or permanent address.

Employment Objective

If you do not state the employment objective in the heading of the resume, it should be stated in the first section of the report. Although the objective is sometimes or often omitted, the data sheet is much less readable without it. The reader must look through other sections, or at the accompanying letter, in order to determine your employment goals. This factor alone could result in your application being discarded when many other more complete and readable data sheets are on the reader's desk.

As a truly qualified candidate, you will be able, with training and experience, to handle a variety of responsibilities related to your educational background and past experience. Even if you begin in a specialized area, you must be able to assume additional duties if you are to be truly valuable to the employing organization, to say nothing of reaching a higher level of responsibility for your own benefit. In addition, few organizations want an applicant who will be content to remain in an entry-level position. Thus your objective may indicate, without appearing presumptuous or obvious, that you are looking for employment with opportunities for growth. For example:

```
Objective:  Beginning accounting and auditing work
            with eventual managerial
            responsibilities.
```

Even if the heading of your resume refers to your employment objective, you may also include an employment objective section as long as you avoid exact repetition. Such an arrangement emphasizes the objective.

The Introductory Summary

The objective may be included in a section of the resume referred to as an *introductory summary, summary, overview,* or a similar term. The summary includes an abstract of the overall capabilities of the applicant. Such a summary is especially beneficial in a long resume, one of several pages, but it may be used in one of regular length.

An introductory summary serves the same function as the *synopsis* or *executive summary* of a report. The most important and relevant elements are given first, in a very much condensed form, followed by supporting details. As with a synopsis of a report, the reader knows immediately what the entire resume is about and the outstanding qualifications of the applicant. A resume long enough to benefit from the use of an introductory summary is more likely to be one of a person with considerable work experience, not a person with little experience who is about to finish college, although such a summary is an aid to readability in any resume.

The introductory summary may be used in addition to, and immediately following, the objective section. Often the two sections should be combined to make the data sheet concise.

Education

An important section of most data sheets is entitled *Education, Professional Training and Education, Professional Education, Academic Experiences,* or some similar designation. Choose the most appropriate, simple heading that best describes the educational experiences that come under it. The section on education should often come after the objective section, or after the summary if included. Place the section you want to emphasize first. If you are a young graduate with little work experience, education is probably your central selling point, as mentioned previously in this chapter. If you have extensive work experience, even though you are just now completing college, related work experience is likely to be more important than your degree. After you have been out of school a few years, work experience is almost sure to be the major qualification for work in the same field, although education remains important. Sometimes you will not be sure which is more important. In any event, give sufficient emphasis to both experience and education to convince the reader of your qualifications.

Use care in the wording of the education section of the data sheet. Ordinarily, if you mean education say *Education,* not *Mind-*

Expanding Experiences Encountered at the Renowned University of the Intellectual. When you word headings, use the same simple, direct, straightforward, specific approach that is best for all business and professional communication. You need not and should not work for a "cute" or "clever" approach. If you are qualified for the opening, say so in simple, concrete language.

The content of the section on educational experiences, whatever you call it, is discussed earlier in this chapter under "Analyzing Your Qualifications."

To repeat and emphasize: give specific, concrete details (which are of necessity incomplete), interpreted in the light of how these particular educational experiences have prepared you for the job for which you are applying.

Work Experience

This heading, like that for education, is entitled in various ways. Although you are not limited to *Work Experience, Present and Past Employment,* or any other exact phrases, the reader should know immediately that you are describing your past employment, including any self-employment, in terms of how this employment relates to the job you seek.

Much of the content of the employment section of a data sheet is discussed earlier in this chapter under "Analyzing Your Qualifications." As mentioned earlier, this section should often precede education, especially when you consider your experience more valuable for a particular application than your education.

Your present or most recent experience is ordinarily the experience that is most relevant to your application. In the usual course of events, the most recent experience is the most relevant. In addition, from the standpoint of a potential employer, what you are doing now is of far more concern than what you did five years ago.

At times, however, a period of employment other than your present or most recent becomes the period you should emphasize or even build your entire application around. For example, if you worked for seven years in sales, decided to try teaching, then gave up teaching to apply for another sales job, you should stress your sales experience even though it is not the most recent.

The traditional method of arranging periods of work experience on the data sheet is in *reverse chronological order.* (Another resume arrangement, described as the *functional,* is discussed and illustrated later.)

Ordinarily your present job is considered to be the most important, the second most recent next in importance, and so on. If you are using the reverse chronological arrangement, be consistent even when you consider your present job to be one that does not deserve major emphasis, as in the illustration of teaching and sales work. In such a situation, emphasize by giving more details about your sales experience. In addition, you may be able to interpret your teaching experience in the light of how it applies to sales work.

Continuing with this hypothetical application for employment, teaching experience could be the most important factor of your overall experience and the major field to be emphasized. For example, if you have been a high school teacher and are now applying for a job with a publisher that distributes high school textbooks, your teaching experience is likely to be far more valuable than previous experience in selling real estate. If you are now applying for a job that is related to real estate, you should stress your experience in real estate, whether or not it is the most recent.

All these considerations of how to present your qualifications, and determining which qualifications are most relevant, are examples of the *you-attitude* in action. Present your qualifications from the standpoint of how the employer will benefit from hiring you. To do so, emphasize your experiences that seem to be the most advantageous to the successful handling of the job.

When using reverse chronological order, account for all periods of time since you began work. Or, if you have many years of experience, account for the past ten years if you prefer. When you have had many short-time or part-time jobs, it is not essential to give exact dates of employment, with names and addresses of all employing organizations. You can summarize some work experience: "1981–1982, part-time jobs at service stations, grocery stores, and drugstores while attending college full time."

A *functional* resume groups items around four to seven key job functions. This arrangement is particularly appropriate for a "job-hopper" whose frequent changes would receive unwanted emphasis if presented in reverse chronological order. The functional arrangement can be beneficial for other reasons, as it emphasizes important and impressive capabilities and accomplishments, not years of experience.

The functional arrangement can also be used to avoid mention of dates, names, and places that might be considered undesirable in a resume but would be necessary if you used the reverse chronological order, in which you must account for all time periods.

Examples of both chronological and functional resumes are shown in this chapter.

You are free to choose headings to best describe your qualifications, accomplishments, and abilities that do not fit under headings of experience or education. Some examples of often-used sections are *Professional Affiliations, Publications, Activities, Community Work,* and *Interests and Hobbies.* A section described by such a heading as *Personal Data,* which includes age, height, weight, marital status, and other such bits of information, is no longer included in all data sheets. At one time the inclusion was so customary that it was almost mandatory. Now this information is more likely to be omitted.

The question of whether to include age and other personal data with your application is still debatable. Most people who work in placement or personnel departments agree that you are free to omit completely all such information if you choose to do so. On the other hand, there is nothing to prevent you from giving information that you feel will be to your advantage, although you should not imply that you feel you will be hired because of these factors.

Some items of personal data almost always should *not* be mentioned, including race, religion, and political party. Even these kinds of sensitive information, however, may belong on some data sheets. For example, if you wish to be an assistant to a congressman who is a Democrat, you should mention your activities in the Democratic party. (If you worked for his election and don't mention that fact, you don't deserve the job.)

In some instances, experiences in church work, religious organizations on campus, or political organizations may be relevant to a job for which you are applying. Such work may show leadership ability and assumption of responsibility. If you have spent a great deal of time in these activities, perhaps you have few other outside interests to report. You must use your own judgment whether to show these items in your employment application.

References

References are not always listed on a resume. This section, ordinarily the last section, may be replaced by a statement similar to this one: "References will be furnished upon request," or you may omit the section entirely. Whether or not to include specific references is another debatable question. If you are applying to only a few employers and you have been given permission to use as references people whose names may favorably impress the employers,

REBECCA S. ROSENBERG

1472 Tutwiler Avenue   Cincinnati, Ohio 45208   513 272-3625

Objective
To obtain a position in Sales Training/Development in a business
setting, preferably with Electronic Data Systems Corporation, and to
use ability to help others increase sales effectiveness through
positive personal relationships.

Work Experience
October, 1980—Present. Sales representative, Checks, Inc.
    Responsible for establishing and increasing sales through
    direct personal contact at approximately 200 banks in northern
    Kentucky.

    Conducted and aided cross-selling and security training
    programs for bank personnel in more than 30 banks. Now writing
    training programs for all branches of Checks, Inc.

    Perform cost analyses of banks' operating procedures. Develop
    and implement cost-saving programs tailored to meet the
    particular needs of each bank.

    Have maintained healthy growth in sales each quarter, often
    reaching highest sales per quarter in company.

November, 1978—October, 1980. Customer service representative,
Checks, Inc., Cincinnati, Ohio.
    Responsible for phoned-in questions or problems from bank
    customers.

    Promoted and established goodwill through written and telephone
    communications.

Figure 16-1. *Example of resume emphasizing work experience, with secondary emphasis on education. Accompanying letter is shown in Figure 17-1. (Based on resume prepared by Rebecca Russell) (In typewritten form, this resume would fit on two pages.)*

Served as support representative between salespersons and production.

June, 1978–November, 1978. Sales clerk, Gold's Appliances, Cincinnati. Supervisor, Harris Gold. 513 282-3333.

September, 1978–June, 1979. (Part–time) Seating hostess, cocktail hostess, bartender, Steak & Ale Restaurants, Cincinnati. (Supervisor is no longer there; address is unavailable.)

Education

Completing Bachelor of Business Administration degree at University of Cincinnati at end of Spring semester, 1985. Have completed entire college program while attending classes at night and working full time.

Double major in marketing and industrial psychology. Minor in education.

"A's" and "B's" in the following courses related to sales training and development:

Basic Marketing	General Psychology
Sales Fundamentals	Psychology of Personality
Consumer Behavior	Public Speaking
Business Communication	Human Relations in the Organization

"A's" in all six education courses required for minor.

Completed Motivation Sales workshops by Zig Ziglar (1984) and Don Judson (1983).

Completed Dale Carnegie courses in Human Relations and Sales (1982–83.).

Figure 16-1 continued

Other Facts

Born 1958 . . . single . . . excellent health . . . enjoy sailing,
backpacking, jogging, reading, gardening, and the challenge of
helping people learn to increase their sales ability.

References

References will be furnished upon request.

Figure 16-1 continued

```
HARWOOD E. LOGAN
4784 Craigmont Avenue                    Telephone: 801 386-4108
Salt Lake City, Utah 84103
```

OBJECTIVE:	Telecommunications Management

SUMMARY:	Twenty-three years of experience in the operational control and management of communication systems, using a wide variety of transmission means and terminal devices. Retired major, Marine Corps. Bachelor of Business Administration degree, 1985. Speak three languages.

SYSTEMS MANAGEMENT:	Managed operation of European portion of worldwide communication system comprised of data, teletype, and voice networks. Directed corrective action to restore disrupted service. Presented system status briefings to top-level management. Wrote procedures manual for internal functioning of operations center.

CUSTOMER SUPPORT:	Determined requirements, planned, installed, and directed operation of communication systems designed to support the needs of customers. Trained customers in use of systems. Identified, isolated, and resolved system operation problems. Provided advice and information to customers.

Figure 16-2. *Example of functional resume. Application letter shown in Figure 17-2. (Based on resume prepared by Albert E. Harwood) (In typewritten form, this resume would fit on one sheet.)*

407

NETWORK DEVELOPMENT:	Performed administrative duties related to the installation and activation of an automated-switching voice communications network in Europe.
TELEPHONE MANAGEMENT:	Administered plant maintenance and services contract with a Japanese telephone company. Provided telephone services; billed, collected, and accounted for $3,000 a month in revenues. Supervised Japanese employees.
OTHER EXPERIENCE:	Taught electronics. Maintained digital computer and peripheral equipment. Maintained electronic control equipment.
EDUCATION:	Bachelor of Business Administration degree, University of Utah, to be completed in May, 1985. Bachelor of Liberal Arts, 1962. Electronics and engineering courses throughout military service.
REFERENCES:	References will be furnished upon request.

Figure 16-2 continued

CAROLYN HARRISON

Address: 6235 Rolling Water, Houston, TX 77069   Telephone: 274-6306

EMPLOYMENT OBJECTIVE

Merchandising trainee, preferably in Fashions, Lone Star Department
Store, Houston, with opportunity for promotion to buyer.

PROFESSIONAL EDUCATION

Bachelor of Business Administration degree with major in marketing,
concentrating in retailing and marketing management, from
University of Houston, June 1985. Related courses in Department
of Home Economics.

B average in the following courses related to merchandising:

Marketing Management   Retail Merchandising
Marketing Promotions   Credit and Collections
Fashion Merchandising   Advertising Fundamentals
Retail Store Management   Advertising Design

WORK EXPERIENCE

Sales clerk for The Dandi Lion, 1481 Gold, Houston. Small specialized
dress shop. Sold merchandise in all departments. Designed shop
windows. Wrote some advertising copy. Modeled in fashion shows.
Summer and part-time during school year, 1984-85. Full time,
June, 1985-present.

Office clerk and receptionist, Crump London Underwriters, Houston,
Summer, 1983.

Figure 16-3. *Resume prepared by young graduate with little work experience. Personal data section could apply to position sought as merchandising trainee in fashions. Application letter is shown in Figure 17-3. (This
resume would fit on one typewritten page.)*

<u>Receptionist</u>, L. Henning Mayfield, M. D., 2525 South Voss Road,
    Houston. Summer, 1982.

PERSONAL DATA

Born October 19, 1963, Houston, Texas. Excellent health. Single.
    Enjoy reading, music, tennis, swimming.

REFERENCES

Ms. Ruth Fly, Manager	L. Henning Mayfield,	Ed Ray, Ph.D.
The Dandi Lion	M. D.	Professor
1481 Gold	2525 South Voss Road	Business Building
Houston, TX 77069	Houston, TX 77071	University of Houston
783–2151	694–3231	Houston, TX 77079
		429–1683

Figure 16-3 continued

SHERRY CLARA ALDRIDGE'S QUALIFICATIONS FOR
ACCOUNTING WORK WITH ARTHUR ANDERSEN AND CO.

2305 Scraper Street   Jonesboro, AR 72401   501 258-3514

SUMMARY

Completing Bachelor of Business Administration degree with major in accounting. Graduating summa cum laude, 3.83 on a scale of 4. Completed four-year degree in two years and nine months of uninterrupted study. Valedictorian of high school class of 259. Designed and supervised accounting system of Jonesboro electrician.

EDUCATION

Will receive BBA degree in May convocation, 1985. Major in accounting, minor in finance, Arkansas State University, Jonesboro.

University Courses Especially Valuable as Preparation for
Corporation and Financial Accounting

Principles: accounting theory, financial transactions.
Intermediate and Advanced: corporate accounting records, miscellaneous ratios, partnerships, consignments, insurance, annuities.
Federal Income Tax.
Consolidations.
Corporation Finance.

Auditing: elementary and advanced public and internal auditing with emphasis on internal control.
Systems: problems involved in designing systems for various types of businesses, including processing data by computers.
Business Communication.
Investments.

Figure 16-4. *Data sheet of accounting graduate with outstanding academic record and little experience. Letter is shown in Figure 17-4. (This resume would fit on one typewritten page.)*

411

WORK EXPERIENCE

Summer of 1984 (part-time): Accountant for James M. Johnson, electrician, 1923 Washington Avenue, Jonesboro, Arkansas 72401. Designed and supervised the accounting system.

PERSONAL DATA

Born October 26, 1965, in Jonesboro, Arkansas.
Single. No absence from school or work because of illness in past three years. Enjoy cooking, bowling, running, sewing, writing. Member Poets Roundtable, Arkansas. Girl Scout leader.

REFERENCES

References and further information will be furnished upon request.

Figure 16-4 continued

MONROE J. WALDRON

2745 Elmwood Avenue
Berkeley, CA 94705

415 527-9233

SUMMARY OF
QUALIFICATIONS
AND OBJECTIVES

Aggressive and capable manager with nine years of experience in
manufacturing management. Presently Assistant Packaging
Manager for division of major corporation. B.S. degree in
manufacturing technology. Good promotion history. Looking for
position in manufacturing management where future opportunity
will be based on performance and results. Particularly well
qualified as production department manager.

EXPERIENCE

Assistant Packaging Manager, Conrad Division, Rivley, Inc.
Responsible for packaging drugs and cosmetic products; direct
and control 18 salaried employees and 251 union personnel;
develop, maintain, and coordinate production scheduling for 38
production lines; responsible for maintaining quality control
standards and assuring that products are in compliance with CGMP
and FDA guidelines; enforce applicable OSHA regulations;
represent management in union related activities. March 1981 to
present.

Major accomplishments include:

* Selected by upper management to correct reject problems on
  major product lines.

Figure 16-5. Resume prepared by applicant with three jobs in one company. Emphasis is on accomplishments. Letter is shown in Figure 17-5.
(Based on material by W.J. Hughes)

413

MONROE J. WALDRON, Page 2

* Instituted new sanitation and operating procedures.

* Assumed chairmanship of weekly production committee that
  regularly makes significant contributions to plant
  efficiency.

* Increased production efficiency of seasonal pre-packs,
  resulting in a cost saving of $50,000 annually.

* Trained supervisors in safety program that resulted in
  decrease in accident frequency rate by 51 percent and severity
  rate by 22 percent.

* Decreased absentee rate by 3.5 percent in one-year period.

Compounding Section Supervisor, Conrad Division, Rivley, Inc.
Was responsible for the production of emulsions, suspensions,
creams, ointments, powders, and tablets. Responsibilities
included direction and control of three salaried employees and
fifteen hourly personnel. Responsible for ensuring that
compounding of formulations was in strict accordance with
established procedures and formulas. Developed, maintained, and
coordinated schedule with packaging and inventory control;
advised and assisted in adapting procedures from laboratory to
actual production conditions and requirements. May 1976–March
1981.

Major accomplishments included:

* Installed a product transfer system which resulted in improved
  sanitation of production lines.

* Effectively supervised production area during period of major
  expansion. Assumed total responsibility for hiring and
  training personnel. Specified equipment needs to increase
  production.

Figure 16-5 continued

MONROE J. WALDRON, Page 3

   * Updated majority of manufacturing procedures to bring into
     compliance with CGMP standards.

   Packaging Line Supervisor, Conrad Division, Rivley, Inc. Was
   responsible for production of assigned packaging lines. Trained
   and supervised personnel. June 1973—May 1976.

MILITARY SERVICE

   Progressed from private to captain in twelve years of active
   service with Army National Guard. Completed five phases of
   Command and General Staff School. Commanded company during
   period of major reorganization which required special skills to
   assign, train, and develop officer and enlisted personnel;
   simultaneously reduced company readiness time by 50 percent.
   President of 30th AR Bde Officers' Association.

EDUCATION

   B.S. degree in manufacturing technology, San Francisco State
   University, 1973. Various job related courses, workshops, and
   seminars, including a sixteen—week Management by Objectives
   program for manufacturing management.

Figure 16-5 continued

WILLIAM THOMAS KING'S QUALIFICATIONS
FOR AIRFRAME AND POWERPLANT MECHANIC

Home <u>Address</u>   School <u>Address</u>

3931 Meadow Lane   Memphis Area Vocational—
Olive Branch, MS 38654   Technical School
601 895—2066   Aviation Complex
                                     2752 Winchester Road
                                     Memphis, TN 38116

Available to begin work on July 1, 1985.

<u>Education</u>

Diploma, Airframe and Powerplant License, Memphis Area Vocational—
Technical School, Aviation Complex, 2752 Winchester Road, Memphis TN
38116 (September 1983 — June 1985)

Diploma, Aviation Structural Mechanic H, Hydraulic A, Marine
Aviation Training Support Group—90, Naval Air Technical Training
Center, NAS, Millington, TN 38054 (December 1979 — March 1980)

Diploma, Hillcrest High School, 4184 Graceland Drive, Memphis, TN
38116 (June 1979)

<u>Work</u> <u>Experience</u>

<u>Attendant/Mechanic</u>, Roy's Chevron, 7144 Old Highway 78, Olive
Branch, MS 38654 (Part—time) Supervisor: Roy Collier (January 1985 —
Present)

<u>Aircraft Hydraulic/Pneumatic Mechanic</u>, United States Marines, VMAT—
102, MCAS, Yuma, AZ 85369 Supervisor: GynSgt. H. A. Omach (December
1978 — December 1984) Honorably discharged as E—5 Sergeant. Major

Figure 16-6. *Resume of graduate of technical school. Military experience*
is an important qualification. Accompanying letter is shown in Figure 17-6.

duties included inspecting, repairing, and performing preventive maintenance on the Douglas A–4M/TA–4F hydraulic and pneumatic systems and components and wheel braking assemblies.

Maintained power control packages, used specifications, blueprints, and necessary tools and test equipment. Requisitioned supplies, equipment, and special tools required in missions. Performed and supervised technical training of personnel, maintained records and reports, inspected shop maintenance as a Collateral Duty Inspector for Quality Assurance.

Attendant, Guidry's Texaco, 1315 Winchester Road, Memphis, TN 38116
Supervisor: Joe Guidry (August 1976 – November 1979)

Organizations and Licenses

Aviation Maintenance Foundation, Inc. From 1978 – Present

Airframes License December 4, 1984

Powerplants License to be completed on July 1, 1985

Qualified to Operate the Following Equipment

AHT–63/64 Hydraulic Test Stand
TA/JG–75 Aircraft Tow Tractor
Cornice Brake
Oxyacetylene Welding Equipment
Maintenance Info. Automated

MMG–1a/2MG–2 Electric Power Unit
NAN–1/1a/2/3 Nitrogen Servicing Unit
Microfiche Maintenance/Parts Reader Retrieval System Machine (MIARS)

Own a complete set of hand tools for airframe and powerplant maintenance

Figure 16-6 continued

Personal Data

Date of Birth: July 29, 1961, Memphis, TN
Health: Excellent
Marital Status: Single
Hobbies: Woodworking and RC Airplanes

References

Mr. John Litterer
Machinist
4601 Gwyck
Olive Branch, MS 38654
601 895-3325

Mr. Jack Doty
Instructor
Memphis Area Vocational-
   Technical School
2752 Winchester Road
Memphis, TN 38116
901 354-1955

Sgt. Earl Combes, USMC
Instructor, F-18 Program
860 E. Grangeville
Apartment #68
Handord, CA 93230
209 584-9436

Mr. Roy Collier, Owner
Roy's Chevron
7144 Old Highway 78
Olive Branch, MS 38654
601 895-6676

Figure 16-6 continued

1987 East Mexicali Drive
San Diego, CA 92123
February 22, 1985

Mr. Henry C. Cotton
Personnel Manager
First National Bank
8047 West Loma Boulevard
San Diego, CA 92107

Dear Mr. Cotton:

Three years of banking experience and a college education in
marketing should enable me to be successful as the Trust Department
Officer for whom you advertised in the San Diego Times.

I am now employed full-time in the Trust Department of a San Diego
bank. Past experience in banking includes two and one-half years at
Mercantile Bank in Long Beach, California. This experience would be
helpful to First National, as the Mercantile Bank is similar in size
and organization. In addtion, I spent nine months there in the Trust
Department.

In early 1979 I began work at the Mercantile Bank as a clerical
employee. In May of 1980 I was offered a full-time position as a
supervisor of three other persons. Later that year I moved to my
present position in the Trust Department in a bank in San Diego. (My
employers will recommend me highly, I feel sure, and I will give you
their names at our interview. In the meantime, however, I ask that
you keep this application confidential.)

As I have always worked toward high goals, I will continue my
education after graduation from San Diego State College in May of
this year. While working full-time and going to college at night, I
have also attended four American Institute of Banking seminars in
finance and international investment banking.

Figure 16-7. *Frank B. Scott's letter. Example of a "letter resume"—a letter
that serves the purpose of the usual separate application letter and resume.*

Previous experience includes seven years of sales experience (automotive parts and industrial paper) and four years in the U.S. Navy.

I am 32 years old and single, although I plan to be married in June. My health is excellent.

Will you write me at the address shown above—or telephone me at 458-2514—in order to arrange an interview? I can begin work two weeks after notifying my present employer.

Sincerely,

Frank B. Scott

Frank B. Scott

Figure 16-7 continued

list these names. Some employers still expect references, or the mention of references, as an essential part of all data sheets.

When you are sending out a great many unsolicited applications, you are wise to omit the names of people who will recommend you and offer to send further information later. Although potential employers are unlikely to contact the persons you name until after an employment interview, they could do so. You then run the risk of having the persons who have agreed to recommend you bothered unnecessarily by many inquiries.

If you do include references, always state the individual's full name, title, business organization or occupation, address, and telephone number.

ILLUSTRATIONS OF RESUMES

Illustrations of resumes are shown in Figures 16-1, 16-2, 16-3, 16-4, 16-5, and 16-6. Letters to accompany these data sheets are shown in the next chapter, Figures 17-1, 17-2, 17-3, 17-4, 17-5, and 17-6.

The "letter resume" shown in Figure 16-7 is an illustration of a letter combined with a data sheet. This letter, sent in reply to an advertisement, contains information that should *not* go in a letter of application that is sent with a separate resume, for example, personal data and a chronological listing of positions. On the other hand, the letter does not include some information that would ordinarily be given, such as the name of present employer. Although this letter does not give complete information (evidently Frank Scott did not want to chance at this stage of the job search that his present employer would be informed), the letter contains convincing details. It is a good choice for this individual's particular situation.

SUMMARY

When looking for employees, most organizations consider these factors: related experience, related education, dependability, the ability to cooperate with others, and a willingness to work.

When looking for employment, the use of an unsolicited application letter and resume is an advantage in that you show a special interest in a particular organization, a plus factor in the evaluation process. This approach also shows that you have the initiative and ambition to research employing organizations and to make an intelligent effort to place yourself. Another advantage is that you are more likely to find the kind of work for which you are best suited and that offers the opportunity you are seeking.

In order to plan an effective search for employment, analyze your qualifications and the employment market. After these analyses are completed, the letter and data sheet are planned and written to show how your qualifications meet the needs of the employer.

The application letter is a kind of sales message. The accompanying resume is a report on yourself and is also a form of sales presentation. Like other sales messages, these materials are most effective, as well as concise, when they are built around a central selling theme.

For most young college graduates, education is the most appropriate central selling point. Other factors that may be central selling themes are work experience, and, in special circumstances, extracurricular activities, hobbies, or special interests.

Like other business messages, the two-part application should make the most effective use of the you-attitude and the positive approach.

PROBLEMS

1. Prepare a self-analysis, similar to that discussed in this chapter. Include all aspects of your education, experience, hobbies, personal characteristics, or anything else that will affect your success throughout a career, as well as your success in obtaining employment. Make this study complete. Ordinarily it will be more detailed than your résumé but by making a thorough self-analysis, you will be better able to decide which items to include and which to emphasize on your final data sheet. This analysis is for your own use only, not to be prepared as a classroom assignment, so be complete and objective.

2. From your detailed self-study, make a list of the kinds of employment for which you are qualified and in which you are interested. Approach this study from one of two ways:

   a. Assume that you are near graduation and that you are looking for full-time career employment. This assumption is probably the more valuable one if you expect to graduate within a year or, regardless of your standing in college, if you now have in mind definite career objectives.

   b. Prepare a list of various kinds of work in relation to part-time or summer jobs. If applicable, include only the kind of work in which you are sincerely interested and which offers opportunities for career employment.

3. After you have made your self-analysis and listed the kinds of work that you prefer and for which you are qualified, make a study of employing organizations that seem to offer the opportunities you are seeking. Use the sources described in this chapter and any other appropriate and useful ones. Write a short report, in the format that your instructor directs, of how you proceeded in the investigation. List the three organizations toward which you plan to direct your efforts and the reasons for these choices.

4,5,6. Prepare a résumé from the detailed studies you have made so far. You are to send the letter and a résumé to each of the three organizations that you have chosen. Perhaps you should prepare three different résumés; or, if the organizations are similar, you may be able to use the same résumé for all three.

Completing the Job-Finding Process | 17

After you have analyzed your qualifications and the job market, and after you have completed a resume, you are ready to write the application letter.

This chapter includes discussions and illustrations of application letters, the employment interview, and related letters you may write as you complete the job search. After you begin work, you may write letters to other persons about aspects of employment; such letters are also illustrated here.

THE LETTER OF APPLICATION

As you plan your letter of application, keep in mind the following guides:

1. Use the positive approach. Emphasize strengths and subordinate weaknesses, but do not misrepresent.
2. Use the you-attitude in that you stress what you can do for the reader. Do not use a "hard-sell" method, but state your work experience and educational background in specific and positive terms, especially as they relate to the work for which you are applying.
3. Show that you are definitely interested in the position, but don't sound as if this is your last chance.
4. Do not copy a letter written by some other person—or one from this book or any other book. This warning applies to

426

all material. Such copying, even with changed details and paraphrasing, is almost certain to result in stilted, unnatural writing. In addition, sometimes personnel managers learn to determine exactly the book in which the letter originally appeared.

5. Although you will of necessity use *I*, try not to use the word to excess. Avoid starting several sentences with *I*.

6. Don't ask for sympathy. This is not the you-approach or the positive approach. You will not be hired because your baby needs shoes, but because you can do a good job and earn more for the employer than you are paid. (You *must* earn more, or you are not a profitable investment.) Even if a job should be filled because of sympathy, the applicant begins work at a disadvantage and not on a businesslike basis.

7. Don't be unduly humble, and don't apologize for taking the reader's time. Remember that the employer is not doing you a favor by hiring you. If you are qualified and a hard worker, the employing organization will benefit from the employment.

8. Don't complain about past or present employers. Even if you have real grievances, your discussion of these things almost always sounds as if you are to blame. If you find it necessary to explain why you are leaving, and this explanation is because of a real dissatisfaction that must be stated, at least *do not mention it in the letter or data sheet.* Save this discussion for the interview.

9. Don't boast or sound overly aggressive or presumptuous—although it is just as important not to sound unsure of your abilities. A straightforward, businesslike approach will let you take the middle road between egotism and a doubtful, overly humble tone.

10. Don't lecture or waste time stating the obvious.

11. Don't mention salary, fringe benefits, or working conditions in the application. To do so will emphasize the I-approach, not the you-approach. Such information will be given to you during the interview. If it should not be, ask at that time for information you must have before making a decision.

12. Don't try to be overly clever, at least for most jobs. If you are being considered as an advertising copywriter or for similar work, your application letter and data sheet may be in a more original or unconventional form. Regardless of the position, you have the problem of making your letter stand out from all the others, but you could work so hard

for attention that you receive the wrong kind, even to the extent that your application is eliminated from consideration.

13. Work for original phrasing and eliminate trite, unnecessary stereotyped wording. Avoid such phrases as these: "May I present my qualifications?" "This is my application. . . ." An aptly worded letter will make this fact clear without stating it obviously. As in other communications situations, however, you are wiser to be clear than to be completely concise, if there must be a choice. The reader should recognize that your letter is an application without having to read halfway through it. To leave a letter in this state is much worse than saying "This is my application," "I am an applicant," or "Consider me as an applicant for this position," although you can usually find more original wording.

ILLUSTRATIONS OF LETTERS OF APPLICATION

Examples of application letters are shown in Figures 17-1, 17-2, 17,3, 17-4, 17-5, and 17-6. These letters accompany the data sheets illustrated in Figures 16-1, 16-2, 16-3, 16-4, 16-5, and 17-6.

THE EMPLOYMENT INTERVIEW

When your data sheet and application letter accomplish their purpose, you will be asked to come for an interview. A successful interview is crucial to your obtaining the employment you wish.

Except in unusual circumstances, more than one person is interviewed for a single opening. This necessary and desirable competition requires that you continue the sales presentation throughout the interview, presenting the superiority of your qualifications and potential for service and development.

Preparation for an Interview

Much of your life has been spent in preparation for an interview for employment in which you are interested and for which you are qualified, although you may not have been consciously making this preparation. Your educational background, your avocational interests, your work experience—all these have prepared you for the work for

1472 Tutwiler Avenue
Cincinnati, Ohio 45208
April 22, 1985

Mr. Ray Fleming, Director
Sales Training/Development
Electronic Data Systems Corporation
7171 Forrest Hill Lane
Dallas, TX 75230

Dear Mr. Fleming:

Three years of experience in sales and a degree in marketing should
enable me to contribute to your Sales Training and Development
Department. In addition, I have experience in sales training and a
record of growth in employment responsibilities.

As a sales representative for a bank supplier, Checks, Inc., I
conduct training classes in cross-selling and security for bank
employees. My ability to work with others, as well as to lead, is
established by the success of these programs.

My education has been directed toward sales and training. While
working full time and going to college at night, I have also
completed several Motivation/Sales seminars. To supplement the
requirements in the College of Business Administration at the
University of Cincinnati, I completed courses to fulfill
requirements for a second major in industrial psychology, in
addition to marketing, and a minor in education.

My present employers will substantiate the information in my
application. After I have talked with you and am being seriously
considered for employment, I will ask you to get in touch with
officials at Checks, Inc.

The enclosed data sheet provides further information about my
skills, abilities, and interests. Please contact me at the address
shown above—or telephone me at 513 272-3625—to arrange a time to
discuss my career with your firm.

Sincerely,

Rebecca S. Rosenberg

Rebecca S. Rosenberg

Enclosure

Figure 17-1. *Application letter to accompany data sheet illustrated in*
Figure 16-1. (Based on material by Rebecca Russell)

4784 Craigmont Avenue
Salt Lake City, Utah 84103
March 10, 1985

Mr. Harrison McCullar, President
Modern Communications, Incorporated
4824 West Williams Boulevard
Denver, Colorado 80218

Dear Mr. McCullar:

Congratulations on your amazing success in building Modern
Communications in only ten years. May I help you in the area of
communications management?

My twenty-three years of military experience spent mostly in the
field of communication systems, plus two years of civilian
experience in the same field, should be specific and complete
preparation for leadership in your corporation. In addition, I am
fluent in the French and Japanese languages and am eager to expand
your operations abroad.

I have thoroughly researched your organization—products, people,
progress, and you. Of the many other organizations studied in order
to determine where to build a career, yours seems to be the one that
offers the greatest challenges.

Will you let me know when I can talk with you about your organization
and its future? I can be reached at 801 386-4108 or at the address
shown above.

Sincerely,

Harwood E. Logan

Harwood E. Logan

Enclosure

Figure 17-2. *Letter to accompany functional resume illustrated in Figure
14-2. (Based on material by Albert E. Harwood)*

6235 Rolling Water
Houston, TX 77069
July 3, 1985

Mr. Fred Koch, Personnel Manager
Lone Star Department Store
Houston, TX 77062

Dear Mr. Koch:

Because of my college training in marketing and work experience in retailing, I could do a good job in Lone Star's merchandise training program.

The courses in merchandising listed on the attached data sheet have given me a good background in retailing. This specialized training, along with other knowledge obtained in working for a Bachelor of Business Administration degree, should enable me to adapt to your merchandising procedure.

Working in sales for The Dandi Lion, a small, specialized dress shop, gave me experience in dealing with people. Because it was a small store, I could observe all of the store operations and participate in most of them. I checked the stock, notified the manager when items were needed, planned window and interior displays, and modeled in fashion shows.

I grew up in Houston and am acquainted with Lone Star's layout and its reputation for having an excellent merchandise training program. I would really like to be a part of your organization.

Please telephone me at 274-6306 to arrange a time to discuss my qualifications for work in your merchandise training program.

Sincerely yours,

Carolyn Harrison

Carolyn Harrison

Figure 17-3. *Letter to accompany data sheet illustrated in Figure 16-3.*

2305 Scaper Street
Jonesboro, AR 72401
May 5, 1985

Mr. Doyle J. Smith, Personnel Manager
Arthur Andersen Corporation
8776 Mount Pilot Avenue
Miami, Florida 33155

Dear Mr. Smith:

My thorough education in accounting, plus a willingness to learn,
should enable me to succeed as an accountant with your firm.

A comprehensive program of accounting instruction at Arkansas State
University prepared me to assume responsibility in your organization
and to adjust to changing conditions and procedures. All of my
college work, leading to a Bachelor of Business Administration
degree with cum laude honors, was directly related to the work done
by your organization—as described by Mr. Robert Maxwell, your
Arkansas State University representative.

To increase my usefulness and efficiency, I plan to study for the
Certified Public Accountant Examination and to take it next year.
Even after passing the examination, however, I shall continue to
study and learn—for the benefit of my employer as well as for myself.

Four months as an accounting systems designer and supervisor for
James M. Johnson, an electrician in Jonesboro, forms my foundation of
experience. As systems designer, I developed an accounting system
for an electrical partnership. As supervisor, I was in charge of two
bookkeepers. I also filed all the required tax returns for the
business, quarterly and yearly.

Should you need more information than is shown in this letter and on
the enclosed data sheet, I shall be glad to supply it.

Will you write or telephone me about the possibility of working for
you? Perhaps I could talk with someone in your Memphis office as a
preliminary step. Or, if you wish, I will arrange to come for an
interview in Miami.

I am ready to begin work immediately.

Sincerely,

Sherry Aldridge

Sherry Aldridge

Enclosure

Figure 17-4. *Sherry Aldridge's application letter. Data sheet is shown in Figure 16-4.*

2745 Elmwood Avenue
Berkeley, CA 94705
July 24, 1985

Mr. William J. Hughes
Vice-President, Manufacturing
Snyder-Plover, Inc.
P. O. Box 377
Memphis, TN 3810

Dear Mr. Hughes:

For the position in manufacturing management advertised in the <u>Wall Street Journal</u>, I offer twelve years of progressively responsible experience with a drug and cosmetic manufacturer, a company similar in many respects to Snyder-Plover.

Since 1970, when I completed a B.S. degree in manufacturing technology at San Francisco State University, I have devoted my entire career to the Conrad Division of Rivley, Inc. My efforts have resulted in cost savings and increased efficiency from several standpoints, as explained in more detail on the enclosed resume.

The president of Conrad Division and other management personnel will recommend me, but please do not contact them at this time. In addition, I can furnish other business and personal references and any further information you require.

I have done thorough research into the manufacturing division of Snyder-Plover. Some of your problems are of the same type as those I successfully solved for my present employer. I also know that you offer opportunities for increased responsibility based on a record of successful accomplishment. This increased opportunity for growth is the only reason that I would consider leaving my present employer.

Please schedule an interview at your convenience—but will you let it be soon? I have two weeks' vacation beginning November 2. Then, after I am hired, I will give two weeks' notice to my present employer.

You can reach me at my home telephone any evening after six.

Sincerely,

Monroe J. Waldron

Enclosure   Monroe J. Waldron

Figure 17-5. *Letter of application to accompany data sheet shown in Figure 16-5. (Based on material by W. J. Hughes)*

3931 Meadow Lane
Olive Branch, MS 38654
April 30, 1985

Mr. Thurston Drew
Maintenance & Engineering Department
Federal Express Corporation
P.O. Box 727
Memphis, TN 38194

Dear Mr. Drew:

Mr. Jack Doty suggested I contact you about your opening for an
aviation mechanic in your Memphis Maintenance & Engineering
Department. Mr. Doty is an instructor at Memphis Area Vocational-
Technical School, where I will soon complete a 22-month training
program in aviation mechanics.

Military training, as described on the enclosed data sheet, provided
actual experience in performing preventive maintenance inspections
and repairs on aircraft hydraulic and pneumatic systems. While
supervising the training of technical personnel, I coordinated
maintenance records and allocated tools and materials.

In December, 1984, I received an Airframes License. I will receive a
Powerplants License in July of this year. I have the tools necessary
for airframe and powerplant maintenance. I am willing to travel or
relocate and can begin work on July 1.

You can reach me by telephone (601 895-2066) most evenings after
seven. Will you please call to arrange a time when we can talk about
putting my maintenance and repair skills to work for Federal Express?

Sincerely,

William Thomas King

William Thomas King

Enclosure

434

Figure 17-6. *Letter from aviation committee to accompany resume shown in Figure 16-6.*

which you are now applying, as well as for a favorable presentation of your qualifications during the interview.

Research to enable you to decide upon the organizations to which to submit your written application will also enable you to participate in a pleasant and successful employment interview. Your knowledge of the organization, as well as your interest in it, can favorably impress the person or persons with whom you talk. This knowledge will be even more beneficial because it adds to your self-confidence and enables you to ask necessary and intelligent questions.

If you have made a detailed self-analysis, as discussed earlier in relation to beginning a job search, and if you have made a study of the particular organization to which you are applying as well as of related organizations, you have accomplished a major portion of your preparation for a successful interview. Review your self-analysis and a copy of the letter of application and the resume before you go for the interview. Make sure that the details are firmly in your mind. Giving conflicting information will cast doubt upon either your integrity or your memory.

You and the Interviewer

You may wish to take with you to the interview two copies of your data sheet, even if you have previously submitted one to the employing organization. The interviewer is not certain to have a copy, although, ideally, the person with whom you talk has recently reviewed a copy of your letter and resume. In some cases you will go for an interview with organizations to which you have not submitted a data sheet, especially when the interview has been arranged through college placement offices. In such interviews your bringing along two copies of the resume can save a great deal of time that would otherwise be spent in giving information that can be concisely stated in a well-organized resume.

Moreover, your additional effort, interest, and consideration for the interviewer are points in your favor as you are compared with other applicants. Your carefully prepared resume continues your sales approach in an orderly manner that may not be possible in the half-hour or so exchange of information.

The interviewer will ask you, perhaps, to expand upon the information you have shown in written form, which is of necessity presented in condensed wording. You may be asked, for example, to give more details about your work experience.

You may be asked to explain why you left a position or positions, to describe the type of work that you liked best and least, to state what you feel you accomplished on each job, and to express your opinions as to whether your supervisor and co-workers were capable and cooperative. Be careful when commenting on this topic; your interviewer is not really asking about your co-workers and supervisors, but about yourself. But, as in all other situations, do not be untruthful. Remember, though, that your own competence and spirit of helpfulness and dedication will usually result in your finding the same qualities in other persons.

Principles of communication you have studied previously apply to your attitude toward the interviewer and your approach to the interview. You have learned, as in written communication, to enter into all business interpersonal situations on a straightforward basis of equality. Although you may have much to gain or lose according to the outcome of your search for employment, or upon the outcome of a particular interview, the representative of the employing organization also has a purpose essential to the welfare of the organization—that of finding the best person for the job.

If you sincerely believe that you are this person, and can convince the interviewer of this fact without building resentment because of your egotism or an overly aggressive approach, both you and the employing organization will have benefited from the relatively short time spent in talking about your professional future.

Questions to Ask

What questions will you ask? Don't be in a hurry to shower the interviewer with questions, many of which will be answered in the course of the conversation. On the other hand, don't merely sit and wait for information to come your way, and do not answer in monosyllables. Although you should not try to take charge of the interview, seize the opportunity to present yourself in the most favorable light. If you cannot communicate well enough to do so, you may leave the impression—probably an accurate one—that your communication skills will be less than ideal for your career. At some time you are likely to be asked if you have questions, or if you have further questions. Inexperienced applicants have been known to blurt out rather odd questions or statements at this time, such as "Where did you get that tie?" (an actual question) and, from a twenty-one-year-old, "Most of all, I am interested in your retirement plan."

If you have done adequate research into an organization, along with other organizations, you already know something about the company, including its offices and branches, products, and services. You can also find its recent growth and earnings. By reading company brochures, you will know a great deal about training programs and employee benefits.

One area of vital concern will be your opportunities for growth and responsibility. Are you likely to become "locked in" regardless of your hard work and ability? You will also need to know the company policy on promotions, whether higher positions are filled from the outside or whether you will need to count on moving within a few years to an organization that offers greater opportunity.

Most of all, you will want to know whether the work is the kind for which you are especially well prepared. Is it the kind in which you can excel and maintain a sincere interest? Is this an organization in which you can feel that your work matters and of which you can be proud, not only for the benefit of the employing organization but for yourself and your family? If you cannot feel a sincere pride in the organization that you are joining, you as an idealistic person will not be satisfied, regardless of the salary. Conversely, a good income is essential for most persons as a symbol of competence and accomplishment—to say nothing of its being necessary for comfort and security.

Remember that if you are not fitted for the job for which you are being considered, or if it is not a job in which you can be content to spend a portion of your life, the real benefit to be derived from an interview could be the fact that the job is given to someone else.

Your Appearance

Careful attention to your appearance, including neat and appropriate dress, favorably impresses most interviewers and adds to your own self-confidence. A neat business suit or a conservative sport coat, with a dress shirt and tie, is appropriate dress for male applicants. Some interviewers prefer a suit. Care in your appearance shows that you have a sincere interest in both the job and the organization.

Women applicants are appropriately dressed, according to the opinion of most executives, in a conservative dress or a matching or coordinated jacket and skirt. All applicants should choose conservative, attractive, flattering, and appropriate clothing and then forget about their appearance and concentrate on the conversation.

Ending the Interview

You are not likely to be offered a job during the interview, although often you can tell whether or not you are being given favorable consideration. Before you leave, you will need some kind of commitment as to when the interviewer will let you know the decision.

Ordinarily you will not need to inquire about salary, but if the interviewer does not tell you, you will be forced to ask.

The basic principles of communication—the you-attitude, the positive approach, consideration, conciseness, completeness, and courtesy—added to your self-confidence and your attractive appearance, will make your interview successful if you apply for a position for which you are qualified and one in which you are interested.

Remember that communication throughout your interview, like all other communication situations, will be less than perfect and complete. Remember that nonverbal communication, including such things as your arriving and leaving on time, your posture and facial expressions, your dress, and your voice, will tell the interviewer as much or more about you than your words can do.

FOLLOWING THROUGH IN THE EMPLOYMENT SEARCH

Thank-You Letters

Within a day or two after your employment interview, mail a thank-you letter. This letter is a matter of courtesy; you should send it whether or not you feel that you are being favorably considered. The thank-you letter is ordinarily short because you have little to say. It is a form of a goodwill message. Sincerity and a natural, conversational tone are the major requirements (see Figure 17-7).

Many applicants do not send thank-you letters after an interview, perhaps because of a mistaken idea that to do so is presumptuous, or, more likely, because of simple procrastination or lack of effort. That few persons send these letters is a point in your favor that may make you stand out from other applicants. It serves as a reminder as to who you are. After a few days of interviewing, many personnel interviewers are not sure who is who. For this reason a picture on the data sheet can be helpful, although it is not likely to be requested and may even be returned.

At times you will have additional information to convey in the thank-you letter. For example, perhaps you have been asked whether you would move to another city and you have requested time to think it over. If you have made up your mind in the day or two before the thank-you letter should be mailed, your decision may be stated in the letter. Or perhaps you have read the brochures that were provided for you, or you have been asked to submit the names

November 20, 1985

Mr. Henry W. Samuels
Vice President, Yohanak Corporation
Manitowoc, WI 54220

Dear Mr. Samuels:

Thank you for a most pleasant and informative interview.

After your discussion of the opportunities for growth as a sales representative with the Yohanak Corporation, I am even more eager to go to work for you.

I will be glad to supply any more information that you may need in order to make sure that I am the best choice for the job.

Sincerely,

John Clifft

John Clifft

Figure 17-7. *Example of a thank-you letter.*

of persons to recommend you, if these names were not included on the data sheet.

Additional information is not a requirement. Send a thank-you letter even if you have no new information to convey.

Follow-Up Letters

Follow-up letters, in addition to thank-you letters, may be helpful when you have not heard from the employing organization within a reasonable amount of time after the interview. The exact time varies; some college seniors are interviewed near the beginning of their senior year and notified within a month or two of graduation. Usually, the applicant is notified within a few weeks or even within a few days.

Follow-up letters are also used after the submission of the application letter and data sheet if too much time seems to elapse before the applicant is called for an interview.

Follow-up letters, provided they are well written and used at the proper time, accomplish several purposes. They show that you are still interested in the organization and that you are diligent in your efforts to obtain employment. These letters may also report additional information not included in the application letter and data sheet or reported in interviews—for example, the completion of related courses, additional work experience, or special scholastic honors or other accomplishments.

Avoid a demanding or hurt tone, and don't indicate surprise that you have not been asked for an interview. But don't apologize for writing.

Job-Acceptance and Job-Refusal Letters

Job-acceptance letters, like other good-news and routine informational letters, are usually best arranged in the direct order, with the acceptance in the first sentence. Adapt your job-acceptance letter to include any additional information that the employing organization may need or to ask questions of your own.

In job-refusal letters, remember to express appreciation for the employment offer. As in other negative messages, your letter will be more psychologically convincing and acceptable if reasons are given before the refusal.

Do everything you can to keep the goodwill of the reader and of the organization as a whole.

The application letter, although sometimes sent alone, is ordinarily a covering letter for the data sheet. In addition, it is a sales letter that should be built around the most outstanding qualifications of the applicant in relation to the position sought.

The purpose of the application letter and the resume is to obtain an interview. As in other letters requesting action, the request for an interview should be stated specifically, but diplomatically, near the end of the letter.

The tone of the application letter should be straightforward and businesslike; the applicant must show confidence in his or her ability but refrain from appearing egotistical or overly aggressive.

A thank-you letter should be sent after an employment interview. Other letters written in the search for employment are follow-up letters, job-acceptance letters, and job-refusal letters.

Inquiries about prospective employees and replies to these inquiries, like other routine inquiries and requests, are best arranged in the direct order. Job-refusal letters are best arranged in the indirect order.

PROBLEMS

1. Write a letter of application to accompany the resumes you prepared for problems 4, 5, and 6 in Chapter 16. These letters should vary according to the organization to which you are applying.

2. Mail these letters and data sheets. (Make sure that the envelopes you use are of good quality and of standard business length so that the letter can be folded in approximate thirds. The envelopes should match the paper in weight and quality.) Or, if you still have considerable time left before you complete your degree or your occupational preparation, or if there are other reasons that you do not wish to mail your letters and data sheets at this time, complete some or all of the following assignments as your instructor directs.

   If you do mail the application letters and resumes, follow through with your interview or with follow-up letters, thank-you letters, acceptance letters, or whatever is appropriate to complete your job search.

3. Assume that three weeks have elapsed and that you have not heard from the organization that you considered to be your first choice. Write a follow-up letter indicating your continued in-

terest and asking again for an interview. Avoid sounding hurt, doubtful, or demanding.

4. Assume that you have received a letter from the second organization asking you to come to their local office to talk with Mrs. Helen Woolner, the district manager. The time set is 1 P.M. on Wednesday of the following week. (Use exact date.) You are asked to write to Mrs. Woolner to confirm the suggested time. Do so.

5. You received a letter from the third organization on the day after you have mailed your reply to Mrs. Woolner. You are surprised that Mr. Harry B. Hicks and Mr. John Jerry, who are identified only as being from the personnel office, wish to see you at 1:30 P.M. on the same day that you are planning to talk with Mrs. Woolner. Write an appropriate reply. Suggest another time for the interview.

6. You receive a letter from the organization that you had considered to be your first choice. You are told by Ms. Rachel Welsh, Personnel Director, that the organization is not now hiring anyone with your particular background but that she will keep your application on file. Although her letter does not necessitate a response, you decide to write a short letter that will perhaps be placed in your file. Decide what you want to say in this letter. Write it.

7. You go for the scheduled interview with Mrs. Helen Woolner. You are favorably impressed. You believe that you have a good chance to be hired. Write a thank-you letter for the interview. Assume reasonable details.

8. You receive a letter from Mr. Harry B. Hicks in response to your letter written for problem 5. He wishes to talk with you at 10 A.M. on Monday of the following week. You have a final examination scheduled at this hour. You talk to your professor, who refuses to give you the examination at any other time. Because this is the second time you have been unable to come for the interview, you realize that you must convince Mr. Hicks that you are still sincerely interested. (He has not mentioned the date you suggested in your last letter to him, which is now more than two weeks past.) State that you will complete your final examinations on Thursday of the following week, at which time your college work will be finished.

What should you say in this letter? You wish to make it clear that you are still interested in the organization and that you are not giving him the runaround. It has now been six weeks since you mailed your application letter and data sheet. Should you mention that you have already been interviewed by Mrs. Woolner? Should you write or telephone? If you decide to telephone, make detailed notes as to the information and ideas you intend to convey.

9. You receive from Mrs. Woolner a letter offering employment beginning four weeks from next Monday. The salary is about $100 a month less than you expected, and you are to begin work in a district more than 500 miles from your home. You believe that the company offers growth opportunities and, although you do not want to move, you realize that mobility is often necessary in order to avoid limiting opportunities for success.

   What will you say in your reply? Will you want to ask for more time in order to investigate further the possibilities of beginning work with organization number three? Plan or write your letter according to your decision.

10. At last you go for an interview with the third organization on your list and talk with Mr. Harry B. Hicks, Personnel Manager; Mr. John Jerry, District Manager; and Mr. H. D. Blackburn, Assistant Vice-President. You are given a tour of the offices and plant.

    Write an appropriate thank-you note to all three of these persons. The actual choice of the person to whom you should send a thank-you letter will depend upon circumstances, including the consideration of the person who seems to be the one most directly responsible for making the decision. When in doubt, write to each person who spends time with you or who helps you in any way.

11. It is now two weeks later. You receive from Mrs. Woolner a letter stating that she must have your decision immediately. (For this assignment, assume that in problem 9 you ask for more time in which to make your decision.) In the same mail you receive a letter from Mr. Hicks who offers you work in the local office. He has told you that there is a possibility of transfer within a year or two when you are ready for a promotion, but there is also a possibility that you can be promoted and remain in your home city. Your beginning salary is $200 a month greater than that offered by Mrs. Woolner's organization. You decide to accept Mr. Hick's offer. Write the letter of acceptance.

12. Write to Mrs. Woolner. Keep her goodwill.

13. You receive a letter from the organization which was originally your first choice. They ask you to come for an interview and to telephone and arrange a time that will be convenient for both of you. Plan what you will say in the telephone conversation.

Appendices

Dictating Business Messages

You may dictate to a secretary or to a machine. The secretary may be a person who works for you exclusively or one who works as departmental secretary or in a stenographic pool. You may dictate through the use of a voice-writing machine or your telephone to a word-processing center, where your words are recorded to be transcribed by one of many typists.

If the services of a responsible, competent secretary are provided for your use alone, you are indeed fortunate. Many of your communication problems are over. But you are not sure to have a full-time secretary, or even a part-time one, especially in your early years in business—and that's the period when you need help the most.

If you are a good communicator—that is, if you are a good manager—you will communicate well with your secretary or with the other person or persons who transcribe your words. Communicate you must. If you do not know or see the transcriber, it is even more important that your instructions be clear on the tape or belt that is to be transcribed. Here, as in all other communication situations, the basic principles apply: courtesy, consideration, clearness, completeness, and all the rest.

Do not dictate unnecessarily. Many people in business do not delegate as many of their communication responsibilities as they should. Secretaries who are perfectly capable of writing memorandums or other material are not given an opportunity to do so. Even though you have a private secretary, however, you will have some material that only you should write.

Some business persons, especially young ones, lack confidence in their dictating skills and are fearful of what the stenographer will think of their communication ability. If this is your problem, you know the answer: increase your communication ability. The best way to decrease frustration is to improve competence.

The first and most important factor of effective and efficient dictation is to be able to compose effectively and efficiently. If you cannot write a good letter with a pen or a typewriter, you cannot dictate one. Even if you are proficient in composing, you will need to develop skill and confidence in dictating practices and procedures in order to become an expert dictator of effective business messages.

SPECIAL CONSIDERATIONS WHEN DICTATING BUSINESS MESSAGES

1. A secretary or a stenographer will probably be able to take dictation at the rate of 80 to 100 words a minute. An expert rate is 120 to 140 words a minute. In order to get some idea of what this rate means, time yourself for a minute or so as you read aloud from prepared material and count the words you have read. Although your rate will not be the same as that of a shorthand teacher who dictates at a predetermined rate from prepared copy, it is approximately the same. Your average speed in actual dictation will be considerably less, unless you are dictating routine, repetitive material, because you will need time to think. But it is not the average rate that bothers the person taking the dictation; it is the spurts of rapid speech, often followed by hesitations, pauses, or revisions.

Make sure to spell out unusual terms, especially if the secretary is not likely to be familiar with certain specialized words or phrases. Anticipate these terms, if you can, in order to prevent wasted time in the transcription process as the secretary ponders over a sentence or transcribes it incorrectly. Or, if a secretary asks you how to spell or to use such a term (a wise procedure), do not look or act surprised at this lack of knowledge. All employees should be encouraged to ask questions in order to decrease the possibility of error, as well as to encourage an understanding of company terminology and procedures.

2. Some persons are reluctant to express their thought-in-progress to the ears of someone else. As a result, the dictation, and thus the typewritten message, sounds strained and stilted.

3. Some persons want to impress secretaries or other typists transcribing the material and thus tend to dictate too fast or to use unnecessarily long or unusual words.

4. The dictator does not have the advantage of immediate re-

vision, which is easy to do when writing with a pen or a typewriter. Dictation, especially by inexperienced persons, tends to be longer and less concise than material written with a pen or typewriter. Because it is more like "talk language," however, it is likely to sound natural and conversational if the dictator is not making a conscious effort to impress.

5. Errors that would be immediately noted when we are writing, or that would not occur at all, can creep into dictated material. When composing with a pen or typewriter, we look at the sentences as they are being recorded. When dictating, especially if the sentence is long and involved, the wrong form of the verb or pronoun is likely to be used because the dictator has forgotten what was said in the earlier part of the sentence. Part of the transcriber's responsibility is to correct obvious grammatical errors, but the transcriber may also overlook them. The final responsibility is with the dictator.

6. As a general rule, dictated material will require more revision than personally composed material. In most offices, however, time does not permit extensive revision of routine letters and memorandums. These factors point again to the importance of the competence of the dictator as well as to the competence of the person who transcribes the material. Long reports may require a great deal of revision, which is made much easier by the use of word processing equipment.

POINTERS FOR EFFECTIVE DICTATION

1. Before you call the secretary in for a dictation period, or before you turn on the voice-writing machine or equipment, plan the content of each letter or other bit of writing to be dictated. A brief outline of each letter or memorandum may consist of notes about the contents of each paragraph. Less detailed planning will suffice after you have obtained considerable experience in writing and in dictating, but some planning will always be essential.

2. Speak clearly, at a fairly even pace. If you are dictating to a machine, make sure that it is adjusted properly and that you speak directly into the telephone or microphone. Make sure that no distracting noises detract from the clarity of your voice.

3. Give special instructions before you begin dictating the material to be transcribed. For example, specify the number of copies, unless you want only the usual file copy, and the persons to whom the copies are to be sent. If a particular letter is to be transcribed first, say so at the beginning of the dictation, most especially if you are using a machine. Give special mailing instructions.

Perhaps for a long report the first copy should be in the form of a rough draft for you to revise before the final copy is typewritten. If so, give this instruction at the beginning of the dictation or the transcriber is likely to type a copy in mailable form. Making corrections requires more time than typewriting in rough draft form, even when using sophisticated equipment.

4. If you are dictating to a secretary, set aside a certain time of the day for this work. A morning hour is best. The secretary then has the rest of the day to complete the transcription process and return the material for your approval. Do not dictate late in the day and ask that the work be completed before the secretary goes home unless the material is unexpected and urgent.

5. Make sure that a dictionary and other reference materials are available for use by the secretary or other person who transcribes the work.

6. Dictate paragraph endings. If you are an expert writer, you know more about where paragraphs should begin and end than does the transcriber. In addition, as you have learned in preceding chapters, paragraph construction is a part of the composition; you can change emphasis and meaning by rearranging paragraphs.

7. Dictate unusual punctuation. Punctuation is also a part of the composition itself; and, as in the construction of paragraphs, punctuation comprises a portion of the meaning. If you are sure that the transcriber knows the rules for the ordinary and expected use of punctuation, to dictate each comma may indicate that you do not trust the ability of the person transcribing the work.

On the other hand, some persons prefer that all punctuation be dictated. This approach has an advantage in that your meaning as it comes through spoken words is more immediately clear, just as meaning through the written word is made more immediately clear by the use of punctuation. Dictating all punctuation speeds up the transcription process. If you follow this procedure, make sure that you are completely sure of the best punctuation for your work.

8. If you use a machine, always indicate the approximate length of the material to be dictated. This estimate enables the transcriber to set the margins of the report or other communication so that it will be attractively centered on the page.

9. When dictating to a secretary, ask that the material be read back when desirable or necessary. This reading-back process is one of the advantages of having an individual take your message in shorthand instead of using a voice-writing machine.

10. Provide the transcriber with the letter to be answered or any other related materials that will assist in the transcription process.

11. Spell out all proper names if they are not available in the

letter being answered or in related materials. Spell out all unusual terms.

12. Even though errors that occur in the transcription process are not your own, you are responsible for them. You are responsible for all facets of your written communication, including the work of the person who transcribes your words and the person to whom you delegate writing assignments. Check all work carefully and thoroughly, most especially until you are assured that the transcriber or writer is conscientious and accurate. Even if you are confident of your assistant's ability and dedication, your checking of the copy is an extra safeguard.

Undetected errors can be costly and embarrassing. If you feel that a transcript should be redone, ask the person who transcribed it to retype the material, but make sure that your instructions are clear and that your reasons are justified. Time and money are wasted if the dictator of the message requires work to be redone if it is only slightly less than perfect.

Some persons read their finished work and notice that the phrasing, although correct and clear, could be improved from the standpoint of graceful wording—and the letter is redictated or retyped or both. Almost all written work could be improved by rewriting and rewriting again, but in the usual business office there is no time to construct literary masterpieces. The efficient business writer is able to dictate good letters on the first trial, in most instances, although they may not be as good as they could be with endless time.

Under the best of circumstances, however, some letters and other communications must be dictated and transcribed more than once. And, as mentioned earlier, a rough draft of complicated material may save time in the overall process. But excessive duplication of effort is an expensive procedure.

13. Penwritten notes may be added to the typewritten message as long as they are used with judgment and discretion. In some types of letters these additions should be avoided, and some organizations frown upon this practice in any kind of letter. Sometimes penwritten notes are added deliberately, not because of an unintended omission but to add a personal touch. Penwritten notes serve as attention-getters if they are not overused. If they are overused, or used inappropriately, they appear as an inconsiderate shortcut to prevent retyping of the message.

14. When dictating to a machine, play back your voice occasionally. You may be surprised!

Word processing systems are planned for receiving material through dictation. Although handwritten materials often are supplied to keyboard specialists in a word processing center, this procedure takes more time than dictation, especially for the originator of the materials.

Dictation is given over the telephone to recording machines in the word processing center. Dictation also is done through the use of individual desk or portable voice-writing machines, with the cassette sent to the word processing center for transcription.

In organizations where word processing is used, efficient dictation practices are even more important than in other organizations. You may never meet the secretaries who transcribe your words. Thus it is very important that dictation be clear, with all necessary instructions.

SUMMARY

The first and most important factor of efficient dictation is the ability to compose effectively. Even when you are proficient in composition, you may need to develop skill and confidence in dictating practices and procedures.

Revision is often necessary for all kinds of written work. As a general rule, dictated material requires more revision than material that is handwritten or typewritten by the composer of the message.

Your ability to dictate will increase the efficiency with which you work with word processing operators. Word processing systems are designed for receiving material through dictation. In organizations where word processing is used, efficient dictation practices are even more important than they are in other organizations.

Cases | **B**

455

INSTRUCTIONS

In the following cases, except where additional research is required, much of the necessary information is given. You are free to make reasonable assumptions and to add minor details. Retain the overall content and meaning of the problem to be solved and do not change facts and instructions given with each case.

The names of individuals and organizations are fictitious. Addresses given are not actual ones. If real names of individuals or organizations are used, the use is completely coincidental. Some cases are intentionally poorly organized, with sentences and phrases that need improvement, in order to provide practice in organization and phrasing.

Unless you are given specific instructions in the case itself, or with a group of cases, use the format and arrangement you consider best for the particular information and situation. Follow directions given by your instructor. For all cases, more than one format and order of arrangement is acceptable and appropriate. As in all writing, work for simplicity, clarity, and reader interest.

As you have no doubt assumed, far more cases are given here than you could write in one semester, or several semesters. The numerous assignments are included to provide choices for you and for your instructor. In addition, you can benefit by reading all the problems and thinking about appropriate ways to approach the solution of each. Perhaps some of the cases will be used as a basis for class discussion even though you do not prepare written solutions.

456 Certain problems apply to particular educational majors or professional fields. You may be more interested in these problems than in those outside your field. Do not think, however, that you should restrict yourself to these problems. Good reports in all professional fields are far more similar than they are dissimilar. A few problems should be undertaken only by those of you who already know something about the subject matter; for example, one case calls for setting up a system of accounting for a printing firm and presenting the system in layman's language to the owner. An accountant should be able to do a better job with this case than, for example, a sales engineer.

Other short problems follow preceding chapters, especially Chapter 3.

CASES THAT REQUIRE NO FURTHER RESEARCH

Case 1. *Remodeling of Offices**

You are the office manager. Remodeling of offices is scheduled to begin on Monday of next week. This remodeling will require rearrangement of desks and other furniture, sharing of offices, and other changes, some inconvenient, as each work proceeds from one floor of offices to the next. The entire remodeling process is scheduled to last three or four months.

All loose paper and files need to be secured inside the desks before the furniture can be moved. All books on shelves and personal items must be packed and labeled. Packing material will be available in your secretary's office tomorrow. Several of the offices look as if they have never been straightened. The sales representatives always say they are too busy to do housekeeping chores. You believe that this packing will require quite a bit of time, but some people are likely to find things they thought lost forever.

You fear that there could be problems in sharing offices, even temporarily, because of some personality conflicts.

Assume that all details, such as the remodeling time schedule (tentative) and temporary office assignments, are on a separate sheet attached to your written message. Refer to this schedule. You need not prepare it.

Individuals who want to pick the colors of the walls of their remodeled offices should pick the color from the seven choices available; these colors are illustrated in a folder in your secretary's office.

* Problem suggested by Judy G. Cox.

Her name is Mrs. Helen Brown. If they have not made their choice by Friday of next week, their offices will be scheduled to be painted an off-white—really a kind of soft cream. This color is one of the seven colors shown in the folder.

Write a memorandum to the group of employees on the floor that is to be remodeled first. Choose an appropriate arrangement and approach for your memorandum.

Case 2. *A Christmas Bonus*

You are the personnel manager. Write *one* letter to *all* employees based on this information. Make any reasonable assumptions.

1. All employees are to receive a Christmas bonus—although this does not apply to those who have worked for less than six months.
2. The amount of the bonus is two weeks' base pay. No overtime, commissions, or any kind of extra pay will figure into the amount of the Christmas bonus.
3. The bonus will be added to the paycheck of December 11.
4. Some employees have been working extra hard because of the end-of-year rush.
5. All employees will receive a food basket containing a turkey or ham, fruitcake, and other food and gift items.

Assume that this is to be a form letter prepared through the use of automatic typewriting equipment; that is, letters are typewritten automatically, then names and addresses are added.

For the purpose of this assignment, show the inside address and the employee's name in the usual way. (Letters prepared by this method cannot be distinguished from individually typewritten letters.) Use this inside address:

```
Mr. James T. Holloway
1967 Luzon Cove
Oklahoma City, OK 73077
```

Use your choice of the semiblocked, modified block, or full-blocked letter style. Why do you think that one letter, sent to *all* employees, is a better choice than different letters to the two groups?

Case 3. *Testing for Temporary Secretarial Employees**

You are a personnel recruiter for an agency that provides local businesses with temporary employees, particularly secretaries and typists. Your agency recruits, screens, and tests these employees. In fact, they are *your* employees, but you "rent out" their services on a temporary basis and receive a portion of their earnings.

The agency goes by the name of White Gloves, as it has for many years. The temporary employees (more than 99 percent are women) are sometimes referred to as "our ladies." You believe that something should be done about this dated terminology, which also includes wording that is considered sexist by some people, even in your conservative Southern city. Employers have not objected. But the consideration of terms must come after the present report is completed.

Although many employment tests are available, you use only a test of typewriting ability because you fear you will violate various employment laws that you haven't had time to research. You use five-minute timed writings to test the straight-copy typing ability of applicants. In college, where you majored in business education, you were taught that three-minute timed writings adequately measure typewriting ability. You know that three-minute tests would be quicker and less expensive to administer and grade.

You feel that you have been with the agency long enough to submit a suggestion for a change in policy, but you realize that Ed Amos, the division manager, will have to be convinced.

From your college notes and working experience you have the following information:

A doctoral dissertation was written in 1964 by Dale Atwood. He measured the effectiveness of ten-minute timed writings as opposed to five- and three-minute timings. His findings, reached through the use of photo equipment, resulted in the recommendation that three-minute writings are best. Business letters normally fall within a range of 125 to 175 words. In a five-minute writing, with an applicant typing only 45 words a minute, 225 words will be typed.

Some organizations ask for a report on the typing ability of employees that you send to them. You report their speed as shown by the five-minute tests, which tends to be somewhat lower than the results of three-minute tests, according to your own experience and observation, and as reported in textbooks and studies. Thus, your employees appear to be slower typists than if reports were made on the basis of three-minute timings.

You also report the errors made by an applicant during a timed

---

* Problem suggested by Judy G. Cox.

writing. Naturally they make more errors in five minutes than in three minutes. They also tend to make more errors per minute in longer writings than in shorter ones. Employers don't understand this situation, and it puts your firm at a disadvantage as compared to competing firms that use three-minute writings.

Write a report that will convince Mr. Amos to change to three-minute writings. Remember, you convince by facts and objective writing, not by emotional persuasion. At this stage, you have collected the evidence and are convinced that you have the correct answer, but you cannot expect your reader to change his mind just because you tell him to do so.

NOTE: This problem can be expanded by further research, as explained in Case 38.

Case 4.   *The Telephone Call* *

You are a student who visited Europe recently on a study-tour. While in Germany, you placed a long-distance call to the U.S., telling the desk clerk at your hotel, Hotel Köln, to make the call collect. Because of communication barriers in German-English translations, the call was charged to your room at the hotel. Because you did not have the cash to pay the bill, you agreed to leave your address and passport number and mail a check from the States after your return home.

Before departing, you and the manager of the hotel were unable to agree on the amount due. Since the call was not made collect, you were charged a 100 percent surcharge by the hotel, plus local taxes. You considered this charge unfair because the clerk was in error when he put the call through. After a long discussion, the manager of the hotel agreed to drop the hotel charge, reducing the total claim from DM 264.00 to DM 132.00 (or about $74.00). The reduced charges are still much more than a collect call would have cost you. You insisted that you should be charged half of this amount. The manager said that he would look into the matter and let you know.

Now, several months later, you have received a letter and a follow-up bill asking for payment in full of DM 264.00. The hotel management is threatening to contact the American Consulate in Germany if you do not "forward your settlement by return mail."

You check with the telephone company and learn that the call

---

* Jean De Vita provided the basic idea for this problem.

would have cost about $25, or DM 45, if it had been placed as you requested.

Write a letter. Give the facts. Convince your reader to accept a check for $25, which you enclose. The address is: Mr. Karl Schäfer, Hotel Köln, Domstrasse 10–14, Köln, West Germany.

Case 5.   *Sales Ticket Confusion*

You are a management trainee in Miller's, a large department store. Recently Miller's updated the registers in the store. Now there seems to be confusion about the correct sales ticket to be used.

Two types of sales tickets are available for use; the two-part and three-part form. Both types were designed for charge sales. No ticket is necessary for a cash sale except for the cash register receipt.

You have noticed a large increase in the use of the three-part ticket. You know that something is wrong. You report to your supervisor. She asks you to investigate and to present your findings in written form, as she wants the data on record. She also wants your report to use in a management meeting, where she will discuss the subject.

The three-part ticket is to be used when making a charge-send sale. One part is given to the customer, one part is sent to auditing, and the other part is taped to the outside of the package to serve as an address label and speed delivery. The two-part ticket is to be used for a charge-take sale. One part is given to the customer and one is sent to auditing.

Some of the sales clerks have been using the three-part ticket in this way: one part sent to auditing, one part given to the customer, and one part kept in the department to help keep track of sales. The clerks have been writing the customer's name and address on each package, usually, but some packages have been delayed until the customer telephoned to report non-delivery.

A record of the sales of each department is provided on a computer printout.

Some departments have been using the two-part ticket for cash sales. One is given to the customer and another kept in the department as a record of sales, a duplication of effort because the record is shown by the computer printout.

You learn that two-part tickets cost $6.64 per thousand, and three-part tickets cost $10.36 per thousand. During the past month, about 10,000 two-part tickets were used and about 20,000 three-part tickets. You do not know how many should have been used and cannot find out without spending more time than you can afford.

Anyway, the added cost is not the main consideration. The most important thing is to keep everything straight.

1. Write a report to your supervisor explaining the situation.
2. Write a memorandum to all sales clerks. Tell them what to do.

Case 6. *The Dungreen Townhouses: Asking to be a Part-time Manager*

You and your spouse live in one of the townhouses recently purchased by Mr. and Mrs. Melvin Hobbs. You are an employee of the University of Houston, where you work in the Information Systems Department. You attend classes part time and are working on an MBA degree.

You believe that the townhouse is a good value. You felt fortunate to rent it, although it costs more than you can afford. Soon, though, your spouse will complete a bachelor's degree in education and go to work, you hope. But teaching positions are becoming scarce.

You believe that Mr. and Mrs. Hobbs will need help in managing the project. They are both busy professional people. He is a salesman who has recently come into money by writing inspirational books. (You don't like the books, but you don't dislike them to the extent that you will move from his townhouse.) She is a professor at the University of Houston.

You would like to offer your services as part-time manager, although you really don't have a lot of time to spare. You consider offering your services in exchange for the rent, but Bob Hutchinson, the CPA who handles their affairs, says they are tight with the dollar. (You realize that your friend, Bob, shouldn't discuss his clients, that to do so is completely unprofessional. But you are glad to get the information.) You are afraid that if you are paid the full amount of your rent, they might expect too much of you. You have little enough time as it is.

You are young, strong, and healthy, as well as good-looking and a near-genius. It is unfortunate that you don't have any money.

Your father, however, taught you how to work, an ability that will be to your advantage in caring for the townhouses. You know how to repair leaking faucets, mow the lawn, and change light bulbs. You also know how to use a hammer, paint brush, and screwdriver. Your spouse can't tell the paint brush from the screwdriver but can answer the telephone and mow the grass. There are only eight townhouses in the complex, including yours, but there is a large backyard.

Write a letter to Mr. and Mrs. Hobbs. Convince them to reduce your rent in exchange for work that you and your spouse will do in managing the townhouses. How much should you ask? What will you do to earn this amount? How can you convince Mr. and Mrs. Hobbs? (You were a little late with your rent this month, which is the first month they have owned the complex.) Assume necessary details, but do not misrepresent the facts in any way. After all, you hope to keep on living in the luxury townhouses for a long time.

Case 7.   *The Dungreen Townhouses, Continued: Reporting on Monthly Activities*

Assume that you have come to an agreement with Mr. and Mrs. Hobbs based on the successful letter you wrote for the preceding problem. One month has passed. You report on your activities and responsibilities for the month at the *Dungreen Townhouses.* You have been wise enough to keep a day-to-day record. You hadn't thought such a "picky" procedure necessary, but your spouse convinced you to keep detailed records. (You are now convinced that your spouse's talents lie in the area of delegation and supervision.)

Your journal, naturally, is arranged in chronological order, as that's the way all these things happened. It would have been more convenient, of course, if everything that went wrong could have been in one townhouse one day and in another townhouse on another day. Or if complaints from the tenants could be on one subject—or expenditures could have occurred by classifications. (Your spouse says that you're just delaying again. Go on and organize the report so that it will make sense to the Hobbs couple—and they won't have a lot of time to figure out what you mean.)

Mr. and Mrs. Hobbs have authorized you to make minor purchases and charge them to their accounts. You also take care of routine problems in the townhouses. Major purchases, such as the replacement of a refrigerator, are to be left for Mrs. Hobbs's decisions. They will also select tenants if a vacancy occurs, although you may be asked to show an empty townhouse. You and your spouse cut the grass.

Your diary for July has the following events listed:

> *July 6.* Cut the grass. Noticed that shrub at 3398 Dungreen had died. Removed shrub and decided that it should not be replaced until autumn, as it would just probably die again. (They really should be watered.)

July 7. Noticed that board was missing from fence surrounding patio at 3396 Dungreen. Bought materials for $11.20 and charged to the Hobbs account at Tops Building Supply. [Haven't yet had time to replace board.]

July 12. Removed worn trash container from rear lawn. It was no longer being used. To reach the rear yard, drove automobile through the alley at the end of the complex. The bumper ruptured the gas meter at the side of 3402.
Evacuated Miss Lela Morris, the tenant, who was unhappy because she was dressing for an important appointment. She threatened to move, but I don't think she will. (In case she does, I would like to move to her townhouse, as it has thick new carpet throughout.)
Called the gas company. Repairmen soon arrived, replaced the meter, and said they would send a bill sometime later in month. (Don't quite know what to do about the bill.)

July 13. Replaced a light bulb in one of the outside lights of the complex. [Lights are on posts; there are two posts with two lights each.] The bulb cost $1.21, plus tax. Paid for it plus bought four more light bulbs at the same price to keep for future replacements.
Repaired dripping faucet for Lela Morris.

July 14. Randolph Barnes, in 3404 Dungreen, said that he wouldn't pay the rent at the end of the month until something was done about the deplorable condition of his townhouse. Asked him what he meant. He said that the dining room paper needs replacing, that the carpet needs cleaning, that really it should be replaced, and that he has had a dripping faucet for months, but that last night he got tired of it and repaired it himself. He said that nobody owes him anything. Looked at the paper. It does not look sparkling new, but it is in good condition. Told him that the tenant is responsible for cleaning the carpet, although it is always cleaned before a tenant moves in. Then Randolph confessed that he has lost his job and that's why he probably won't be able to pay his rent at the end of the month. [You both cried.]

Told Lela Morris that she is responsible for replacing light bulbs inside her townhouse.

July 15. Randolph said that he is on the trail of another job, better than the one he had.

July 16. Randolph told me that he didn't get the job.

July 19. Spent $17.20 to replace a small light fixture in our townhouse. It was cracked when we moved in.

On July 19 also received a request from a new employee at the University to be put on the waiting list for a townhouse. Agreed to do so, although, as far as I know, there is no waiting list. Her name is Georgia Gale.

July 20. Spouse cut the grass. Another shrub looked wilted so I watered all the shrubs with a hose attached to a faucet on my townhouse, and the water cost will be on my bill. Spouse says forget it. Don't see any way to determine how much of the water bill should be charged to the townhouses.

July 21. It rained a flood.

July 22. Spent $24.30 (cash) for lawn mower repair.

July 23. Learned that I must be out of town on business from August 8 through August 13.

July 24. Lela Morris asked me to clean the wall covering in her kitchen. Told her diplomatically that I don't do walls.

July 25. Saw Josie Canastrarie in the backyard. She lives at 3408. [The large backyard is used by all tenants.] She asked, "What are you doing in our backyard?" She said she was going to call the police. Explained that we live in the complex and are the part-time managers.

Lela Morris asked me to cut the weeds on the little strip of ground between her patio and the fence that surrounds the patio. Told her that

everything behind the patio fence is the
responsibility of the tenant.

July 26. Bought hedge clippers for $37.20 from
Hardy's Hardware. Charged them to the Hobbs account.
Used them to trim a crape myrtle by Lela Morris's
patio, behind the fence. Also need the clippers for
shrubs outside individual patios.

July 31. Harold Blevins, in 3410 Dungreen, said
he would be moving at the end of August. He said
that he would be late with this month's rent.
Randolph Barnes found a good job.

Prepare a written report for Mr. and Mrs. Hobbs. Arrange in a
format that is easy to read. Use headings to show organization. Consider carefully which information should be included and which
should be omitted, and, in some instances, whether or not you
should make recommendations at this time. (This report can be
prepared either as a letter or a memorandum, with or without attachments.)

Case 8. *The Dungreen Townhouses, Continued: Letter to Tenants*

Write a letter to be sent to all tenants. (You have decided to write
one letter and make photocopies.) Introduce yourself and your
spouse. Tell them anything else that you think they need to know,
based on your experiences in July.

Case 9. *The Dungreen Townhouses, Continued: Advice from Spouse*

Assume that you are the spouse of the protagonist of the three preceding problems. You look over the journal for July and consider
that your spouse needs the help of a consultant, you. You offer an
oral conference, but your spouse tells you to put it in the form of a
memorandum.

Case 10. *Writing a Position Paper to Disagree with Management's Current Policy of Accounting*

You have recently joined the staff of a large public organization that
raises money for charity. In your position as director of administra-

tive services you are responsible for purchasing and control of all support staff, including word processing, duplicating services, and maintenance. One of your prime directives from the executive director was to cut the internal operating costs and increase efficiency.

Probably the greatest task ahead of you is the control of inventory and disbursement of supplies to the various departments within the organization. The current process is so complicated that one must requisition a requisition to receive supplies. That policy, you are told, was the brainchild of the director of accounting, who believes in charging each department for every item they use. The accounting clerks must spend a great deal of time each month processing the many forms being used and charging each department.

After taking a look at the process, you have decided that the organization is small enough (only thirty-five employees) that it does not need such an elaborate system. Further, you have determined through analysis that each department uses an average percentage of supplies and duplicating time which has held constant over the last several years. Your analysis shows the following figures for each of the departments:

No. of Department		Supplies	Printing
1	Administration	35%	30%
2	Budgeting	20%	23%
3	Campaign	25%	40%
4	Community Service	20%	7%

You did notice that the charges would vary from month to month, affected mostly by the timing of the campaign to raise funds. Yet, over the past three years, these percentages have been accurate.

You have now decided to write a memorandum to the executive director, Mr. Harry Goodsen, to whom you report. He is a man who requires details, presented in a personal tone. He will usually go along with his subordinates' recommendations if they are supported by a thorough analysis. You propose that the nitpicky accounting system be dropped for a percentage system, a plan that will save many hours of labor for both employees as well as those in accounting.

Case 11. *The Company Store* *

You are an accountant with Paule Manufacturing Company, a division of the conglomerate, Worldwide Corporation. Paule, which

---

* Based on material written by Paula McCurley.

employs 520 people, manufactures sprinkler systems. Other divisions of Worldwide manufacture a wide range of products, including small appliances, candy, barbecue grills, household items, books, cameras, lights, and many more. Several employees have inquired about the possibility of purchasing, at below retail cost, products produced by other divisions of Worldwide.

An inquiry was made to other divisions about purchasing their products. They offered to sell their products to Paule at cost, plus a small percentage margin and freight and handling expenses. Even with these added costs, the price to employees would be less than could be found at discount stores.

Because management officials want to give employees every possible benefit, they opened a company store to sell products at the same price it costs Paule to make or purchase them, with no added charges for selling expense or providing the space for the store. These costs are to be considered additional employee benefits.

A vacant room was converted into the company store, which is open two hours a day, two days a week. Employees come into the store during their coffee breaks or at lunch time. They have the option of paying cash for their purchases or paying through payroll deductions. Repayment through payroll deductions can be spread over one, two, three, or four pay periods.

Employees seem to be delighted with the store. Reaction has been extremely favorable.

It is now the time of year when the annual cost of living increase is announced to employees, along with a statement and breakdown of additional benefits they are receiving. The benefits are quoted on a dollar-per-hour basis. You have been asked to determine how much the company store benefits the employees in the form of a dollar amount per hour, per employee. This determination is necessary in order to determine whether the amount should be included in the annual statement to employees. (For morale purposes, you want to include the amount if it "looks good." If it is extremely small, just let the employees know the store is there—although most of them have already used it.)

Data for cost breakdown are these:

Depreciation of the 15-foot by 20-foot room is to be considered over a period of 15 years, or at the rate of $30 a month.

A one-time expenditure for equipment for the store (sign and lock for door, shelving, telephone, cash register, and showcases) is $700.

Two employees work in the store. One is a middle management employee who earns $12 an hour. Another is a clerical employee who earns $6 an hour. Each works in the store two hours a day, two days a week. In addition, the middle management employee spends approximately eight hours per month placing orders, verifying shipping dates, receiving merchandise, handling returns, and in other miscellaneous duties. In addition to these two employees, you consider that other personnel expenses should be charged to the store, including a receiving department clerk, an account clerk who handles the banking function for the store, and a payroll clerk who handles payroll deductions. You have no way of knowing exactly how much of their time should be charged to the store and decide to estimate these costs at $100 a month.

You know that the regular hourly wage is not all each employee earns, so you add a benefit factor of 25 percent to the personnel costs of the two employees assigned to the store. You decide to leave the miscellaneous cost at $100, an estimate that you believe to be high enough to include added benefits.

The average monthly inventory of the store is $5,000. The cost of money, at the present time, is 14 percent. The average monthly receivable balance of the store is $2,000. (As an accountant, you know you must include interest costs.)

Telephone expense allotted to the store is $5 a month.

Find the hourly benefit to each employee. Report to President Susan Bradley. She has had no part in the store development and may not be familiar with why it was organized, how it works, and how much it costs. She does take responsibility each year for writing the message to the employees, as she wants them to be happy.

Case 12. *The Company Store, Continued: Reminder to Employees** *

Write an item for the company newsletter telling employees about the store. (Regardless of the outcome of the analysis you made for the previous problem, do not mention benefits per dollar amount per employee in this news release.) The editor tells you that he has room for about 200 words, but that if you don't want to use that much space he has a few short jokes he has been wanting to use as fillers.

Case 13. *Should Scrap Materials Be Sold to Employees?*

This problem is based on the results of the questionnaire in Figure 8-2, Chapter 8. Assume that you mailed the questionnaires and re-

---

* Based on material written by Paula McCurley.

ceived usable returns from sixty of the eighty-six manufacturing companies. Results are as follows:

Company Size:
6 companies, fewer than 50 employees
6 companies, 50–200 employees
12 companies, 201–500 employees
36 companies, more than 500 employees

Companies Selling Scrap Material to Employees:
Fewer than 50 employees   Yes 4 No 2
50–200 employees   Yes 2 No 4
201–500 employees   Yes 6 No 6
Over 500 employees   Yes 2 No 34

Average Amount of Each Sale to Employees:
Less than $10   10
$10–$100   4
Over $100   0

Average Amount of Each Sale Other Than to Employees:
Less than $10   6
$10–$100   12
Over $100   42

Opinions on Whether Scrap Production Is or Would Be Increased with the Selling of Scrap Materials:
Yes   42
No   10
No answer   8

Reasons for Not Selling Scrap (most important reason):
Administration too
   burdensome   29
Increases scrap production   11
Less return for scrap   6

Companies Now Selling Scrap That Would Prefer to Stop:
Yes   10
No   4

Draw up tables and charts to present the highlights of your study.

Include these tables and charts in or with a report to Mr. Sam Myatt, president, Myatt Furniture Manufacturing Company. Assume that you are his assistant.

As director of the Transportation Department of Macon Industries, a large corporation with a fleet of 5,000 vehicles, you have been asked to look into what the president feels is an excessive number of accidents involving company vehicles.

From your records you find there were 2,319 accidents during the past 24 months. The causes of 1,725 of these accidents were charged to the employee operating the vehicle. Of these accidents, 401 involved 157 employees who had had two or more accidents in the 24-month period but 53 of these 157 have left the company.

The remaining 104 employees were given a series of tests:

1. Eye test by company doctors to check vision.
2. The standardized Porter Reaction Test.
3. Road test (in a vehicle similar to the one(s) in which the accident(s) had occurred) to determine driver habits, driver attitudes, operating proficiency, and knowledge of vehicular equipment. The road tests were conducted by driver-training experts supplied by the National Safety Council.

The results of these tests, along with other employee information (age, sex, date of initial employment with company, previous job, position or positions held in company, accident record, etc.), were placed in individual employee portfolios.

An examination of the 104 portfolios reveals that of these 104 employee accident repeaters:

98 are in 19–27 age group
63 have eye deficiencies
89 have bad driving habits
94 have fewer than 5 years with the company
all 104 are male
88 are on their first job
21 have very poor reaction time
91 do not have adequate knowledge of equipment
61 have received no formal company training
72 have poor driving attitudes

Write a memorandum-report to the president clearly defining the problem, presenting your data, interpreting the data, and making suitable recommendations.

---

* Used with permission of Dr. Ruth G. Batchelor, Associate Professor Emeritus of Business Communication, New York University.

Case 15. *Hudson Textiles, Inc.* *

Hudson Textiles, Inc., a large manufacturing company with 12 plants throughout the nation and with the head office in New York, will pay a full tuition refund to those New York office employees who have completed one year's service and who are matriculated in a degree-granting institution. Originally designed to combine business experience with formal education for the benefit of the company which pays the bills, the plan is generally regarded as a fringe benefit and as an incentive to ambitious employees to go to college. At the present time, 44 of the 200 eligible employees in the New York office take advantage of this benefit.

A recent survey showed that over the past four years, an average of 75 percent of those obtaining a college degree at company expense quit Hudson within one year and 12 percent quit before attaining a degree. The company is expanding each year and needs college-trained personnel for middle-management positions not only in the New York office, but also in the various plants throughout the country. Thus, Hudson pays college tuition for lost employees, and is forced to hire college-trained personnel from the outside at substantial wages for middle-management positions and to train these employees who have had no company experience. More than three-quarters of the existing middle-management positions are filled with employees having fewer than four years with Hudson.

You have been asked by Mr. Thomas J. Robertson, president of Hudson Textiles, to make some recommendations to ease this situation.

As a beginning, assume you review written exit interviews of lost employees for the past four years and find that 92 percent of 125 ex-employees who received their college degrees at Hudson expense gave as their reason for leaving Hudson the fact that they had received no recognition in the form of promotion after their graduation. Further, 84 percent added that they felt "mere payment" of tuition had not been sufficient reward for their six to eight years of attending evening classes for a degree. Over half of these ex-employees (67) expressed a feeling of bitterness toward Hudson because "outsiders" with college degrees held management positions.

Assume also that you collect data by conducting a series of individual interviews with a sample of 100 employees (44 student-employees, 50 non-student employees eligible for college entrance, and six recent college graduates, at Hudson expense) in the New York office.

---

* Used with permission of Dr. Ruth G. Batchelor, Associate Professor Emeritus of Business Communication, New York University.

Of the 44 student-employees, five frankly state they intend to clear out of Hudson for better jobs as soon as they complete their degrees; ten hint at the same by saying they will "probably" look around after graduating; and the remaining 29 say they have no plans. None indicate any definite plans to stay with Hudson.

Of the six graduates, two were promoted to middle-management positions after receiving their degrees; but only one of these seems happy with his promotion, which included a raise as well as a title. The remaining four are frankly looking around for jobs with other companies. One of these four summed up the feelings of the others when he said: "No one in management or in personnel ever asked me how I was getting along [in college] nor congratulated me when my name was on the Dean's List for five successive semesters. I thought surely when I graduated, Mr. Robertson would write me a letter. If Dean Crosby had not sent me carbons of the letters he sent on six separate occasions to Mr. Robertson regarding the honor I had received, I would have believed no one at Hudson knew I was attending college. . . . Of course, I'm grateful to Hudson for paying my tuition; but I represented Hudson at the university and I can honestly say I was a good representative . . . frankly, I expected a promotion and a raise."

You select the 50 non-student employees out of the total of 156 of those eligible on the basis of their indicated interest in obtaining a college education, although they are not currently participating in Hudson's tuition refund plan. Forty-eight of these 50 expressed their belief that it is company policy to fill middle-management positions from the outside; 27 of these 48 feel the extra work involved in getting a degree would not pay since the degree apparently would not lead to a promotion. Two of these 50 employees are not in the plan because they are momentarily expecting transfer to a western branch. Both express the hope that Hudson will extend the benefit to employees in other cities where colleges offer evening degree programs.

All of the student-employees and the six graduates indicate that there is no periodic review made of their academic progress or achievements, that no recognition is given in the form of raises or promotions based on academic achievement, and that some supervisors are seemingly not aware of the fact that an employee in their charge is attending school. Ten of the 44 student-employees feel that their supervisors are holding them back from promotion because they are attending college. Thirty of the student-employees and only one of the college graduates indicate they think it Hudson's policy to recruit outsiders from middle-management positions.

Write a report to Mr. Robertson, clearly defining the problem and its implications to the company, using the information given to you but presenting it logically and in your own words. Before you present your data, tell how you secured it and why you chose this particular way of collecting data. Why was it necessary to interview the non-student employees? State specifically the questions you asked each group of employees. Present the data clearly, draw your conclusions from the data, and state your recommendation to Mr. Robertson.

Case 16. *Recommending an Accounting System* *

Ms. Ann Lee has decided that her small printing business needs an accounting system. Currently, she has none. As a result, she has no idea whether she is making a profit. (She has other sources of income.) Income tax time is a nightmare. Often customers are not billed. Ms. Lee wants as simple a system as possible. She needs five main categories of information, which are as follows.

1. cash flow—money coming in and going out
2. costs—costs that should be taken into account in quoting a price for a job
3. accounts receivable—bills to be sent and collected
4. accounts payable—bills to be paid (They are not now being paid on time.)
5. inventory—too much cash should not be tied up in inventory, yet there should not be shortages

Items appearing on the asset side of the balance sheet are cash, accounts receivable, inventory (paper plates, and miscellaneous supplies), and fixed assets (press, typewriter, light table and plate maker). Liabilities include trade payables (purchases of supplies and negatives) and a Small Business Administration loan. Revenues are from printing. Costs are paper, plates, negatives, and supplies.

Design a system for Ms. Lee. Remember that she is not an accountant, but she wants sufficient information to handle her own books except at income tax time. Present this system in a simple, informal, easy-to-read report which will serve as instructions for setting up and maintaining the system.

---

* Based on a discussion with Lisa Jones.

This problem is included here for two purposes: to provide data for you to use as a report assignment and to furnish recent information about the preferences of personnel officers in regard to application letters and personal résumés.

Interpret these findings and present your interpretations in a formal analytical report, or in the format designated by your instructor. Assume that you direct your report to Mr. Ronald Wilson, Director of Alumni Placement, your university. Mr. Wilson helps graduating seniors and past graduates find employment. Although much of his responsibility and that of his staff consists of arranging interviews with company representatives who come to the campus, he also encourages students to send unsolicited résumés and application letters. In addition, he and members of his staff conduct workshops and short courses in the job-seeking process.

For the purposes of this assignment, you may assume that you are one of the researchers.

Review Chapters 16 and 17 before beginning this report assignment.

The Procedure. Faculty members at the University of Southwestern Louisiana conducted a survey of the 500 largest corporations in the United States as listed in the *Fortune* directory, 1977. This survey asked the chief personnel officer of those corporations his or her preferences concerning content, appearance, and length of cover letters and résumés. Of the 500 opinionnaires that were mailed out, 175 were returned; a 35 percent response. The respondents were asked to indicate (1) strong agreement, (2) moderate agreement, (3) undecided, (4) moderate disagreement, or (5) strong disagreement, (A) meaning not clear, (B) no response intended, to a series of statements about initial contact by job applicants, cover letters, and résumés. The respondents were then asked to indicate which college courses they believed would be of considerable value to prospective job applicants in preparing letters of application and résumés. Finally, they were asked to indicate the major problems encountered by personnel directors involving application letters and résumés, and the major trends for the future they could foresee in the content of job application letters and résumés.

The responses of the corporate chief personnel officers are as

* Based on a study by Barron Wells, Nelda Spinks, and Janice Hargrave, reported in *Proceedings: 1979 Southwest ABCA Spring Conference*, pp. 89–105. Used with permission.

follows (abbreviations apply to categories above; for example, *SA* means strong agreement):

1. The initial contact with a job applicant should be a personal interview. SA: 8%; MA: 14%; U: 3%; MD: 50%; SD: 21%; MNC: 3%; NRI: 1%.
2. Written information about the applicant is preferred for the initial contact with the job applicant. SA: 55%; MA: 38%; U: 2%; MD: 4%; SD: 0; MNC: 0; NRI: 1%
3. If the initial contact with the job applicant is to be in writing, a résumé *only* is preferred. SA: 10%; MA: 22%; U: 9%; MD: 41%; SD: 17%; MNC: 1%; NRI: 0
4. Both a cover letter and a résumé must be obtained from a job applicant for a personnel director to have all the necessary information. SA: 26%; MA: 35%; U: 7%; MD: 18%; SD: 11%; MNC: 1%; NRI: 1%
5. A letter of recommendation concerning the applicant is enough information for hiring a person. SA: 0; MA: 1%; U: 0; MD: 14%; SD: 85%; MNC: 0; NRI: 1%
6. The cover letter and résumé should be typewritten. SA: 58%; MA: 30%; U: 2%; MD: 8%; SD: 0; MNC: 0; NRI: 1%
7. Handwritten cover letters and résumés are acceptable. SA: 4%; MA: 31%; U: 14%; MD: 23%; SD: 26%; MNC: 0; NRI: 1%
8. Cover letters and résumés may be either handwritten or typewritten; there is no preference. SA: 6%; MA: 21%; U: 6%; MD: 34%; SD: 29%; MNC: 0; NRI: 5%
9. Graphoanalysis is used on handwritten letters and résumés to match the right persons to the right jobs. SA: 1%; MA: 0; U: 2%; MD: 11%; SD: 75%; MNC: 3%; NRI: 9%
10. With the use of graphoanalysis, handwritten letters and résumés can reveal characteristics of the writers. SA: 2%; MA: 5%; U: 16%; MD: 12%; SD: 37%; MNC: 3%; NRI: 25%

Cover Letter. The following rankings were given by the respondents to the statements concerning cover letters, or job-application letters, that accompany résumés.

1. A cover letter *only* reveals all the needed information about a job applicant. SA: 0; MA: 1%; U: 3%; MD: 26%; SD: 67%; MNC: 2%; NRI: 1%
2. Letters of application are welcomed even though there are

no job openings at present. SA: 36%; MA: 53%; U: 3%; MD: 3%; SD: 3%; MNC: 1%; NRI: 0

3. Letters of application should include a reason why the job applicant is interested in *this* job. SA: 35%; MA: 46%; U: 10%; MD: 7%; SD: 1%; MNC: 1%; NRI: 0

4. An attention-getting first sentence will stimulate interest in a particular job applicant's letter of application. SA: 11%; MA: 30%; U: 27%; MD: 7%; SD: 7%; MNC: 1%; NRI: 1%

5. The tone of the letter of application is important. SA: 34%; MA: 56%; U: 4%; MD: 4%; SD: 1%; MNC: 0; NRI: 1%

6. Good grammar and spelling are essential in the letter of application. SA: 80%; MA: 17%; U: 2%; MD: 0; SD: 0; MNC: 0; NRI: 1%

7. A job applicant should state his or her understanding of the requirements of the position in the letter of application. SA: 13%; MA: 40%; U: 19%; MD: 21%; SD: 4%; MNC: 2%; NRI: 1%

8. An application letter should show how the job applicant's education and experience fit the job requirements. SA: 32%; MA: 46%; U: 10%; MD: 10%; SD: 10%; MNC: 0; NRI: 0

9. A potential employee should ask for a personal interview in the letter of application. SA: 20%; MA: 49%; U: 18%; MD: 10%; SD: 3%; MNC: 0; NRI: 0

Resume. The following rankings were given by the respondents to the statements concerning resumes that are sent to prospective employers for the purpose of securing a job or further consideration as a potential employee.

1. A resume of one page is preferred. SA: 29%; MA: 38%; U: 17%; MD: 10%; SD: 1%; MNC: 1%: NRI: 5%

2. Two-page resumes are preferable and cover the person's qualities well. SA: 10%; MA: 26%; U: 23%; MD: 26%; SD: 9%; MNC: 1%; NRI: 6%

3. A three-page resume is the type most preferred. SA: 2%; MA: 2%: U: 11%; MD: 32%; SD: 49%; MNC: 0; NRI: 5%

4. Keeping a resume neat is essential. SA: 71%; MA: 25%; U: 1%; MD: 1%; SD: 2%; MNC: 0; NRI: 1%

5. A photograph included with the cover letter and resume is desirable. SA: 3%; MA: 17%; U: 10%: MD: 25%; SD: 41%; MNC: 1%; NRI: 3%

6. Social aspects concerning the job applicant should be listed in the letter. SA: 3%; MA: 26%; U: 15%; MD: 28%; SD: 14%; MNC: 13%; NRI: 1%

7. Commendations of the job applicant should be listed in

the resume. SA: 10%; MA: 43%; U: 17%; MD: 18%; SD: 9%; MNC: 3%; NRI: 1%

8. One reference is adequate in the resume. SA: 2%; MA: 8%; U: 18%; MD: 41%; SD: 20%; MNC: 1%: NRI: 11%

9. Two references are adequate in the resume. SA: 2%; MA: 23%; U: 19%; MD: 29%; SD: 16%; MNC: 1%; NRI: 11%

10. Three references are adequate in the resume. SA: 7%; MA: 38%; U: 15%; MD: 15%; SD: 15%; MNC: 1%; NRI: 10%

11. More than three references should be included in the resume. SA: 0; MA: 5%: U: 14%; MA: 35%; SD: 34%; MNC: 1%; NRI: 11%

12. The types of persons listed as references in the resume are important. SA: 13%; MA: 41%; U: 9%; MD: 16%; SD: 13%; MNC: 3%; NRI: 4%

13. The prospective employee should bring a copy of the resume to the job interview. SA: 61%; MA: 36%; U: 0; MD: 1%; SD: 1%; MNC: 0; NRI: 0

14. Military service of the applicant should be included in the resume. SA: 42%; MA: 45%; U: 6%; MD: 4%; SD: 0; MNC: 3%: NRI: 1%

15. A complete transcript of college grades should be attached to the resume. SA: 7%; MA: 31%; U: 20%; MD: 32% SD: 11%; MNC: 0; NRI: 0

16. Personal information such as date of birth, phone, address, marital status, dependents, etc., should be included in the resume. SA: 28%; MA: 33%: U: 11%; MD: 7%: SD: 12%; MNC: 3%; NRI: 6%

17. A resume should contain an applicant's physical and health status. SA: 11%; MA: 34%; U: 18%; MD: 20%; SD: 10%; MNC: 1%; NRI: 6%

18. General as well as specific educational qualifications such as major, minors, and degrees should be included in the resume. SA: 54%; MA: 41%; U: 2%; MD: 2%; SD: O; MNC: 1%; NRI: 0

19. Willingness to relocate should be included in the resume. SA: 55%; MA: 36%; U: 4%; MD: 3%; SD: 1%; MNC: 0; NRI: 1%

20. A list of scholarships, awards, and honors should be included in the resume. SA: 39%; MA: 51%; U: 6%; MD: 3%; SD: 1%; MNC: 0; NRI: 0

21. The resume should contain previous work experience concerning jobs held, dates of employment, company addresses, and reasons for leaving. SA: 74%; MA: 24%; U: 1%; MD: 2%; SD: 0; MNC: 0; NRI: 0

22. Special aptitudes should be listed in the resume. SA: 30%;

MA: 50%; U: 12%; MD: 5%; SD: 1%; MNC: 1%; NRI: 1%

23. A list of grades in major or minor subjects in college should be included in the resume. SA: 15%; MA: 26%; U: 18%; MD: 30%; SD: 10%; MNC: 0; NRI: 1%

24. A resume should list the high school attended, class rank, and date of graduation of the job applicant. SA: 13%; MA: 28%; U: 19%; MD: 28%; SD: 10%; MNC: 1%; NRI: 1%

25. The major source of a person's financing while in college should be contained in the resume. SA: 10%; MA: 42%; U: 24%: MD: 14%; SD: 9%: MNC: 1%; NRI: 1%

26. A resume should contain the salary requirements of a job applicant. SA: 20%; MA: 37%; U: 18%: MD: 14%; SD: 10%; MNC: 0; NRI: 1%

27. Social data, such as fraternities, athletics, clubs, and sororities should be listed in the resume. SA: 11%; MA: 37%; U: 26%; MD: 19%; SD: 4%; MNC: 1%; NRI: 2%

28. The traditional order in which information is presented in a resume is desirable. (Personal information, education, experience, references) SA: 23%; MA: 48%; U: 10%; MD: 13%; SD: 3%; MNC: 1%; NRI: 2%

29. An applicant's experience should be listed first in the resume. SA: 7%; MA: 12%; U: 26%; MD: 40%; SD: 5%; MNC: 1%; NRI: 8%

30. The education of the applicant should be listed first in the resume. SA: 7%; MA: 25%; U: 25%; MD: 28%; SD: 4%; MNC: 2%; NRI: 9%

31. The first listing on a resume should be the names of personal references. SA: 1%; MA: 2%; U: 8%; MD: 29%: SD: 52%; MNC: 1%; NRI: 7%

32. The applicant's strongest points (education, work experience, etc.) should be listed first in the resume, without regard to any rule for presentation. SA: 29%; MA: 20%; U: 14%; MD: 23%; SD: 8%; MNC: 1%; NRI: 6%

Case 18.   Choosing a Production Manager

You are vice president of manufacturing of Torgensen Corporation, which manufactures farm equipment. The address of the corporation is 2608 West Thayer Avenue, Fargo, North Dakota 58102.

You have been in charge of hiring a production manager for your organization. The decision has not been made, and you must write to the three finalists for the job, who have been told (wisely or unwisely) that the choice has been narrowed to three. You also plan to write a memorandum to Mr. J. R. Torgensen, president, explaining your choice of applicants. This memorandum will remain in the employment files in case your decision should be questioned. President Torgensen has said that he will abide by your decision.

The three applicants are these:

Applicant A: *Linda Lee Larson,* who has a bachelor's and master's degree in mechanical engineering from Massachusetts Institute of Technology and an MBA from Yale. After receiving her master's degree in engineering, she taught for two years in a technical institute in Pennsylvania, then returned to school to work on an MBA. After completing this degree, she worked with two manufacturing organizations in Pennsylvania, the last five years at the managerial level.

You have checked with her past employers, as she requested. They gave her outstanding recommendations from every standpoint.

Ms. Larson's resume does not include a *Personal Data* section. She grew up in Fargo and wants to return. Three months ago she married Neil Larson, also a native of Fargo. He is president of Larson Farm Equipment Company, a family-owned business that sells farm equipment, including machinery that you manufacture.

At a church social, you heard Neil's mother remark that she was glad that her son had finally married—but whoever thought he would marry an engineer—and that she hoped they would soon start a large family before it is too late.

Ms. Larson's address is 1101 Summit Blvd., Fargo, ND 58102

Applicant B: *Stanley Miller,* now serving as assistant production manager. He has worked for Torgensen Corporation for 27 years. He has served in his present position for the past 12 years. He has done a good job. He is liked and highly respected throughout the organization. You feel sure that he is now doing much of the work of the production manager, who is to retire because of poor health.

Stanley Miller started work with Torgensen Corporation when he was 18 years old, as a production worker. He slowly worked his way up, step by step. He is now 45 years old. Three years ago he completed a degree in manufacturing technology at North Dakota State University. All his college work was completed at night over a period of 11 years. He earned no academic honors. He has raised seven children, five of whom are still in school. His address is 921 13th Avenue, North, Fargo, ND 58102

Applicant C: *Collin Torgensen,* now a sales representative for Larson Farm Equipment Company. He holds a B.A. degree in English from Oberlin College, a bachelor's degree in mechanical engineering from the University of North Dakota, a master's degree in American literature from the University of Iowa, and a master's degree in manufacturing engineering from the University of Colorado. He has worked in his present position for seven months. Previous work includes jobs as a radio announcer, newspaper reporter, high school teacher, and Social Security claims representative. He also spent two years with an oil services firm immediately after receiving his bachelor's degree in engineering. He worked for two years, immediately prior to returning to Fargo and accepting work with Larson Farm Equipment Company, as an engineer with Chrysler Corporation.

All college work was completed with honors. He furnished references from Chrysler and the oil services firm. Both corporations reported that he was well liked and a hard worker.

Collin Torgensen is a nephew of J. R. Torgensen, president of Torgensen Corporation, but Collin's family owns no part of the corporation. His father is a physician in Fargo. Collin is a nationally known poet.

He is twice divorced. He is extremely handsome and has a winning personality. You don't know how old he is, but he completed his first degree (from Oberlin) in 1965. Because of his relationship to J. R. Torgensen, he is well known by many employees, having attended Christmas parties and summer picnics since he was a child. He seems to be well liked by everyone who knows him. His address is 319 Nottingham Lane, Valley City, ND 58072

1. Assume that you have made your choice of one of the three applicants. Write a memorandum to Mr. J. R. Torgensen, giving your choice, with reasons. Remember that you must convince President Torgensen that your choice is a wise one. Also remember that your memorandum is to be kept on file. (Unlike math problems, there's no "correct answer.")
2. Assume that you must write to the two applicants who have *not* been chosen. After each of the interviews, the applicant left you with words to this effect: "I know that two of us will not be hired. But at least you owe us the courtesy of telling us *why*." You are not convinced that you have this obligation, but you know you'll never hear the end of it unless you give convincing reasons—diplomatically.

Write to the two applicants who were not chosen. Also write to the one selected. The modified block arrangement is used throughout your organization.

CASES THAT REQUIRE FURTHER RESEARCH

Case 19.   Your Own Subject, Your Own Report

Follow through with the report you began with your study of Chapter 7, the project for which you prepared a report plan. Present the results of your investigation in a complete formal report as discussed and illustrated in Chapter 14. If you did not prepare a report plan with the study of Chapter 7, at this time present a report plan or a proposal in some other form and submit it to your instructor for approval. Ideally, this problem is an actual one you have encountered in your business or profession. You can solve a real problem and complete a class assignment at the same time.

Case 20.   So Many Problems

With your instructor's approval, prepare one or several short reports based on real problems or questions in your business or profession. This assignment is in addition to or instead of the longer report requested in Case 19.

Case 21.   Recommending Equipment

Assume that your office has need for one of the following items:

- an electric typewriter
- a spirit duplicator
- a photocopier (some models have both duplicating and photocopy features)
- a voice-writing and transcribing machine (or machines) for use in a private office
- an intercommunication system
- a small computer
- word processing equipment
- a similar item of equipment or office furniture

Investigate the brands available and recommend your choice, considering the particular needs of your organization.

Case 22.   Combining Your Efforts

With your instructor's permission and assistance, investigate some problem in your school or community. This research can be planned as a class project with individual class members investigating some phase of the problem and preparing individual reports. The total findings can then be combined for an overall report on the situation. Or the class can be divided into committees with each to assume special responsibilities in regard to researching and reporting a portion of the situation. If your topic has been investigated previously, try to obtain the results of these investigations. Test these results, or use the information to form the basis for further investigation of the problem. Present the results of your study in the form suggested by your instructor.

Case 23.   Career Apparel

This problem is similar to the one referred to in preceding chapters: "Should Countrywide Insurance Company Provide Career Apparel for Women Employees?" Your study at this time should include information applicable to an organization with which you are familiar or one that you can study in the research process in order to determine particular needs in regard to career apparel. Include information based on library research, the opinions of persons to wear the apparel, possible suppliers, and costs.

Case 24.   A Report of Three Cities

Your company is preparing for labor negotiations. The manager of industrial relations wants figures for comparison of living costs in Houston, where the company has headquarters, and with two other cities in which branches are located, Seattle and New York. Find the latest figures published by the U.S. Bureau of Labor Statistics or find the figures in another recent and reputable source. Write a memorandum report to Miss Roberta Hardin, manager of industrial relations. You are her assistant.

Case 25.   Three More Cities

Follow the instructions given in Case 24 but compare your city with two others in which you think you would like to live.

Case 26.   Have-a-Happy-Day Inns of America

You work for Have-a-Happy-Day Inns of America. You have been asked to investigate three companies that are possible considerations for acquisition. (For the purposes of this assignment, choose the three companies or study those suggested by your instructor.) No negotiations have yet been made with any of these companies, and you do not want your research publicized. You cannot go to these companies for information but must confine your investigation to their annual reports and other published sources. Find all the published information you can about these companies. Present a summary of your findings in a report to the president of Have-a-Happy-Day Inns of America. Include possible problems and advantages that are likely to occur with the acquisition of each company.

Modify this problem as your instructor directs. Perhaps you will wish to consider only one company or to prepare the report for your own organization. You have not been asked to make specific recommendations about any of the companies as much further research will be necessary.

Case 27. Determining Employment Opportunities in Your Career Field*

Examine the classified advertising section of five consecutive Sunday editions of your local newspaper. (If you do not live in a large city, examine issues of the Sunday newspaper from a nearby city.) Try to determine employment opportunities for people like yourself.

For example, if you are a beginning accountant, look for openings that you feel capable of filling. The advertisements may include such terms as *junior accountant, entry-level accountant*, or *recent graduate*. If you are an experienced accountant, look for openings at a higher level. Examine advertisements carefully. Some do not have descriptive titles, yet offer employment opportunities in your field.

As other examples, if you are looking for a job as an executive secretary, look for this job description or such terms as *administrative secretary*, or *secretary to top executive*. Be as specific as you can. If you are a mechanical engineer, you need not be concerned with opportunities for chemical engineers. You can perhaps be even more specific and investigate, for example, opportunities for mechanical engineers in manufacturing or in whatever area you are experienced and interested. State exactly the purpose and scope of your research.

Determine from the advertisements answers to these questions: Which qualifications are most often listed? What is the av-

---

* This problem is adapted from one written by Dr. Ed Goodin, Associate Professor of Management, University of Nevada, Las Vegas. Used by permission.

erage salary? How are you asked to apply? Do advertisements indicate opportunities for promotion? Is travel or relocation necessary?

Present the answer to these questions, plus others that you believe to be important, in appropriate report form. Charts or tables will be helpful to present your findings in the most readable style.

Case 28. Market Survey, Clothing

You have read news reports that sales of clothing are down. Is this true? Draw up a questionnaire that you will submit to at least twenty students or, if you prefer, persons who are employed in positions similar to your own. Limit your study to either women's clothing or men's clothing. In addition, interview at least three shop owners, managers, buyers, or others who are in a position to know the answer to your question. Summarize your findings. Use tables and charts as necessary for readability.

Case 29. Market Survey, Other Products

Instead of clothing, study some other product or line or products, as in Case 28, and report your findings. Choose some "nonessential" expenditure, such as sports equipment or dining in restaurants.

Case 30. Investigating Employment Opportunities with Differing Companies

Investigate two organizations for which you would like to work. Study their annual reports, recruiting brochures, and other secondary sources published by some individual or organization other than the organizations you are investigating. Talk with at least one present employee of each company. Also try to find past employees, who may be able to tell you more than present employees. Try to find people who are or were in jobs similar to the one you seek.

Consider all aspects that are important to you on the job, including whether or not relocation is likely and whether there are opportunities for promotion. In the concluding section, summarize the reasons you have chosen one company over the other.

Case 31. The Concerned Citizen

Look into legislation that you consider unfair to you or to some segment of the population. Write a report about this law, or these laws, and make recommendations for change, with reasons. Remember that you are most convincing when you give specific, definite evidence, not when you emote. Although your mind is made up before you start (you could decide that you are wrong), use an objective approach and wording. Be considerate of your reader. Make photocopies of your report and send to your senators and representatives.

Case 32. Fashion Merchandising

Assume that you have been hired as a buyer or manager for a chain of small stores specializing in misses or junior fashions. Study fashion publications in the field and make recommendations to your supervisor about purchases for the next season. Give special attention to presently fashionable items or styles that should be increased, decreased, or dropped entirely. Present this information as simply as you can, but give sources of your information and the basis for your recommendation.

Case 33. Investment Counseling

Assume that you are an investment counselor. Your friend, Ann Moore, asks your advice about what to do with $75,000 cash that she inherited. She is 42, single, with no dependents. She owns a large townhouse that she bought for $40,000 fifteen years ago. She earns $27,000 a year and has no debts except for mortgage payments of $260 a month. She is happy with her residence and does not plan to move. She has been employed by the federal government for seventeen years.

She is interested in investing the $75,000 for long-term growth. What do you recommend? She must be given specific reasons supported by adequate background information. Present your findings in a letter to Ann.

Case 34. Sales and Marketing

Assume that you are the new sales manager of a company that sells a product that you know well or one about which you can find complete information. Compare this product with its leading competitors. Write a report in which you compare your product with the others. Include strengths and weaknesses. Summarize with recommendations for features to be stressed in sales campaigns. Also include recommendations for improvement of your product.

Case 35.   Feasibility of Implementing Word Processing Center*

Facts: You are the president of (your last name), O'Hara, and Feinstein, a legal corporation, with offices in the central business area of your hometown. Your firm and the firms of O'Hara and Feinstein have recently merged into one legal corporation to provide more and better legal services to the local community. Your company is growing rapidly. There are nine attorneys, including yourself, and five secretaries. Your leased suite of offices covers 2,600 square feet and is located at (you supply the exact address). Your company does not furnish parking space.

Because of the growth of your firm, you, O'Hara, and Feinstein have just concluded a staff meeting where the major topic was whether to install some type of equipment to set up a word processing center for the correspondence of your firm. Lately, the secretaries have fallen behind in finishing letters, reports, depositions, briefs, case reviews, annual reports, and the usual accounting and office documents that are necessary in an office like yours. More and more overtime must be paid and authorized, and Saturday morning work is getting to be a regular occurrence.

You decided at today's meeting to look into the possibility of installing word processing equipment. Both Robert J. O'Hara and James W. Feinstein are interested in this possibility. Data are needed to answer these questions to make a justifiable decision:

1. Should additional secretaries be hired?
2. Will productivity (output) increase with a word processing center?
3. Will operating costs be reduced, increased, or remain the same?
4. What personnel changes would be needed?
5. Should the equipment, if installed, be leased or purchased?
6. What configuration of word processing equipment do many legal firms use?
7. Will special training or orienting be needed? If so, who will provide this training and at what cost to your firm?
8. What will the cost of the equipment be?
9. What kinds of equipment will be needed?

---

* Case written by Dr. Jean W. Vining. Used with permission.

Directions: Your typed report should be presented in acceptable report format and addressed to you, O'Hara, and Feinstein, a Legal Corporation, at the address you supply. Include your name as preparer of the report.

The completed report must contain a cover, title page, letter of transmittal, table of contents, the body describing and transmitting the findings, analysis of findings, sections relative to your investigation, conclusions, and recommendations. A bibliography listing at least four current references not more than five years old should also be included. Optional but appropriate are the authorization letter, a synopsis, and an appendix section. At least two graphics (tables or charts) must be included in the report.

Sources of data might include the following: your college library, local public library, survey of and visits to word processing companies (see the heading entitled Word Processing Equipment and Supplies in your current yellow pages of the telephone directory for a list of possible firms to interview), survey of and visits to local legal firms and to word processing centers in similar industries. You may use all sources to gather your data plus your own ingenuity. Be sure to give references for sources that help you.

Case 36. Reducing Expenses for John Lee and Company's Sales Personnel*

Facts: You are the administrative manager for John Lee and Company, an industrial company that is one of 33 branches located in the Southwest. The home office for John Lee and Company is Dallas, Texas, with regional offices located in Memphis, Houston, New Orleans, Tulsa, and Little Rock. For the last ten years the 135 sales representatives in the 33 branches have been supplied with a company-owned car with total maintenance provided by John Lee and Company. Each representative has paid an annual prorated portion of the liability insurance coverage for his or her company car and has been given a gasoline allowance not to exceed $400 per month. Generally, John Lee and Company has had a policy of replacing the sales representative's car with a new car every 18 to 24 months. Costs have increased rapidly during the last two years and the long-time practice of furnishing sales people with company cars is now being questioned. This policy is also being questioned by many other firms throughout the nation. Possibly management can arrive at a more economical plan without sacrificing sales.

---

* Case written by Dr. Jean W. Vining. Used with permission.

Directions: As administrative manager, investigate the possibility of having your salespeople purchase their own automobiles with your company establishing a reimbursement plan that would include a generous gas mileage allowance, with each salesperson providing total car maintenance. Some of the maintenance expenses could be reimbursed as part of the new plan.

Another alternative for John Lee and Company would be to begin purchasing compact cars that would get increased gas mileage, and the company might also ask each sales representative to drive his or her car longer than the usual 18–24 months before receiving a replacement. Look into what plans similar companies have for meeting the transportation needs of their sales staff. What general procedures do these companies follow? Are structured policies and procedures stated? What kinds of accountability might the company expect from their personnel regarding the use of company vehicles? What are the trends?

When you have gathered your data, write your findings in a clear, concise, readable report (possibly in memorandum format) addressed to the president of your company, Mr. John M. Lee, Jr., whose address is 111 Main Street, Suite 16E, Dallas, Texas 75280.

Be sure to follow recommended report-writing fundamentals and the basic theories of communication that you have learned to convey your data and pose recommendations that are plausible and workable.

Case 37. Corporate Gift Giving as a Goodwill Policy*

Facts: You are the administrative assistant to the president of Delta Manufacturing Company, a manufacturer in the New Orleans area. At this morning's regular staff meeting, you were asked (authorized) to investigate the policy of corporate gift giving. The question to answer is this: Should Delta Manufacturing Company begin the practice of gift giving? The management and the company president, Frank R. Smith, have been thinking about giving presents to your firm's industrial customers, as many of Delta's competitors do. Corporate gift-giving is a commonplace practice by many firms. Your company may want to become involved in this practice if the practice is legal and successful. Your management recognizes that such a policy can cause problems if mismanaged or if implemented haphazardly with no structured ground rules or policies spelled out before implementing the practice.

You are to research this problem. The practice of corporate gift

---

* Case written by Dr. Jean W. Vining. Used with permission.

giving generally consists of a company giving presents to selected officials of those organizations with whom the company does business on a regular basis. Usually the gifts have nominal value (limits which can be spelled out in any guidelines that you decide to map out) and most commonly consist of such items as food items, leather goods, office supplies, leisure items, or tickets for entertainment. These gifts are intended as goodwill gestures—as expressions of appreciation for the client's business. Most company officials look on the practice as ethical as long as the gift values remain low and as long as the gifts are uniformly given to all customers.

Directions: Your typed report should be submitted to Mr. Frank R. Smith, president of Delta Manufacturing Company, 1005 Poydras Street, New Orleans, Louisiana 70130. Your report should include a cover, title page, letter of transmittal, table of contents, and the findings and analyses section presented in the body of the report. You will recommend whether or not the Delta Manufacturing Company should implement a policy of presenting gifts to its customers, along with other recommendations for the policy to be implemented. Or you may decide to recommend against establishing such a policy. If so, give reasons that can be substantiated by the facts and figures presented in your report.

Findings should be justified by verifiable data.

Case 38. Research to Substantiate Recommendations for Change in Employment Testing

This case relates to Case 3. Assume that Ed Amos did not agree with your recommendation about the length of typewriting tests for temporary employees. You decide that you could possibly be wrong. Use secondary sources and interviews with business educators, or questionnaires, in order to find the answer, if there is one. As with all reputable research, do not look only for sources that support your original point of view.

This problem is especially beneficial to students majoring in business education. Use the *Business Education Index, Dissertation Abstracts*, and any other guide to published sources.

Write a report to Mr. Amos, giving your findings and conclusions and recommendations. Include the information and background given in Case 3. You suspect that Mr. Amos does not remember the content of your original report—or that he has lost it. In any event, you should repeat the original information in order for your present report to make sense.

Interview twenty graduates from your college who majored in your area of specialization. Choose ten who graduated ten years ago, and ten who graduated five years ago. Numbers can be changed according to the time available and the specifications of your instructor. Names and addresses of former students will ordinarily be available from the dean's office.

What will you ask these people that will be beneficial to you and to other students who are now preparing for the same career? Consider your questions carefully and draw a questionnaire to guide you in your oral interview, which can be done in person or by telephone.

Present your findings with recommendations in the format suggested by your instructor. You may wish to address your report to the chairperson of the department in which you are majoring, the dean of your college, the president of your college, or to other students in your major field of study.

Case 40

You have decided to open a small retail business in your town or city. For the purpose of this research, assume you have the necessary capital. Decide upon the kind of business according to your real interests and present knowledge. For example, if you like to play tennis, investigate the possibility of starting a tennis shop. If you love books, consider a bookstore, and so on.

The purpose of this report is to determine the location in your town or city to establish your store. Use information from the Bureau of the Census about particular areas in your city. Also consider the location of competing businesses.

A variation of this report is to assume that you are a consultant preparing this preliminary study for some other person.

Prepare the report in the form and arrangement recommended by your instructor.

Case 41

Your aunt, age 72, has asked you to investigate the most recent models of automobiles and to recommend one that she should buy. She wants the least expensive car available, provided it has the following features, ranked in importance in the order listed: safety, ease of handling, comfort, durability, economical fuel consumption, and sporty appearance. She wants a four-door model with room enough for herself and at least three friends.

What is your recommendation? Write a letter to your aunt, carefully explaining the basis for your choice. Perhaps you should attach brochures describing the automobile chosen and two or three leading contenders. Do not rely on brochures alone; use other sources to determine the attributes of the automobiles.

Case 42

What are the leading professional journals in your major field? For example, if you are majoring in accounting, what are the leading accounting journals? Examine at least three recent issues of two of the leading journals; recommend one of the two for other people in your career field. To support your recommendation, include this information:

> Kinds of articles
> Extent and kinds of advertising
> Photographs
> Frequency of publication
> Cost
> Sponsorship (for example, some journals are published by professional organizations.)

You will need to give information about both journals and show clearly the basis of your preference.

Case 43

Does your college have a student chapter of one or more professional organizations for your field?

> If so, when and where do these organizations meet?
> Who are the officers?
> What are the requirements for membership?
> What are the benefits of membership?

Provide this information in memorandum form addressed to your instructor.

Find the volume of the *Census of Population and Housing, 1980* that reports data for the town or city in which your college is located. Determine the number of the census tract in which your college is located. (A map showing census tracts of your city will ordinarily be available for your use in the Government Documents Room of your library.)

1. Write a memorandum to your instructor describing the kinds of information available about your neighborhood as listed in the *Census of Population and Housing, 1980.*
2. Include the following information in the memorandum assigned in Part 1, or write a separate memorandum.
   a. What is the median income of households in the census tract in which your college is located?
   b. What is the mean income for these households?
   c. What is the total number of persons 65 years of age or older in this census tract?
   d. How do the greatest number of people in the census tract earn their living? Use the name of the category as it is listed in the census report.

Case 45

Follow the instructions given for Case 44, but use Bureau of the Census information reported in the *Neighborhood Statistics Program,* as described in the introduction of the long report in Chapter 14. (A *Neighborhood Statistics Program* publication for your town or city may not be available. Ask a reference librarian in your college library.)

Case 46

Examine five recent issues (Monday–Friday) of the *Wall Street Journal.*

Write a memorandum report to your instructor about the number and kinds of graphic aids you found in the five issues. If you find instances in which graphic aids do not conform to the principles given in this textbook, mention these discrepancies in your report. Copies of some or all of the graphic aids will be helpful to your discussion.

Case 47

This case also is based on the examination of five recent issues of the *Wall Street Journal* (Monday–Friday). Analyze the advertisements, considering only large advertisements and not the classified section or advertisements of only a few lines. You are likely to find that a great number of these advertisements are for computers or investments of different kinds. What are other leading categories? Use tables with your written discussion to analyze the advertisements in the five issues.

Case 48

Compare five annual reports. Choose the most recent ones available. Annual reports are ordinarily available in the Reference Room of your library.

1. What are the similarities and differences? Overall, which of the five annual reports do you believe is the most effective? The least effective?
2. Assume that you are a consultant asked to recommend improvements for the report that you consider the least effective. Write a preliminary recommendation of one or two pages to the communication supervisor of the company involved. [Use an assumed name for the supervisor.]

Case 49

Write a report on one of the following subjects. The use of secondary sources is likely to form an important part of your investigation. According to the directions of your instructor, you may wish to add primary sources by interviewing people who, because of their background, education, or work experience, have firsthand knowledge of the subject you are investigating.

1. What a business executive should know in order to communicate effectively with business people in Japan. (Or choose Saudi Arabia, Russia, Mexico, or any other country or part of the world with culture and customs different from those in the United States and Canada.)
2. How _____(name of real or imaginary product) should be promoted in _____(name of country or part of the

world in which culture and customs differ from those in the United States and Canada).

3. Communicating through the use of color.
4. The use and misuse of statistics.
5. The changing English language.
6. Laws that apply to honest advertising.
7. Careers in the field of business communication.
8. How an understanding of kinesics (body language) relates to effective communication for business and the professions.
9. How an understanding of proxemics (communication through the use of personal space) relates to effective communication for business and the professions.
10. Planning meetings and conferences.
11. Cutting the cost of written communication.
12. Effective listening.
13. Increasing job satisfaction through communication.
14. The open office.
15. Interviewing (to obtain a job).
16. Interviewing (to select employees).
17. Parliamentary procedure.
18. Quality circles.
19. Teleconferencing.
20. Special telephone services.
21. Electronic mail.
22. Overcoming job-related stress.
23. Writing sales messages.
24. How to dress for success (men) or how to dress for success (women). (Don't depend only on Molloy's famous books by the same title; use additional sources, preferably more recent ones.)
25. Using a computer to construct charts and graphs.
26. Using a computer for letter writing and other short communications (a form of word processing).
27. An overview of software packages for word processing.
28. An overview of software packages for financial analysis.
29. Differences in word usage and spelling, England and the United States.
30. Techniques for effective television appearances.
31. Regional language and usage (expressions peculiar to one or more sections of the United States).
32. Designing questionnaires.
33. Positive versus negative words. (Include examples, and add other elements of persuasive and diplomatic words and phrases.)

34. Optical scanning methods of computer input.
35. Voice recognition as a method of computer input.
36. Legal considerations that affect written and oral communication within and from a business organization.

Case 50

Combine three or more related topics listed in Case 49. For example, parts *5, 29, 31,* and *33* are concerned with language usage. You could combine these related topics into one report. Other similar topics are suggested in parts *27, 28, 34,* and *35.* Other similar groups can be chosen, or you can combine similar topics of your own with one or more of those shown.

A Brief Guide to English Usage

C

497

This appendix section is of necessity an incomplete guide to the use of the English language. Many comprehensive handbooks on language are available for your use through school and public libraries. Every writer should own one or more reliable and comprehensive handbooks, as well as a large, up-to-date dictionary.

The material chosen for Appendix C includes the most frequent areas of difficulty for college students and business writers.

SENTENCE STRUCTURE

A knowledge of sentence structure is essential to exact use of punctuation and, more important, to the most effective presentation of your thoughts.

As a general guide, use only complete sentences, although at times sentence fragments can be used effectively in sales and advertising writing and other informal material. Only complete sentences should be used in formal writing, which includes many reports. Because you do not know the individual preferences of your readers, you are safer *always* to write in complete sentences.

A commonly accepted definition of a complete sentence is that it has at least one subject and one predicate and that it can stand alone as a complete thought. Sentences are classified as *simple, complex, compound*, and *compound-complex*. These terms are confusing to some readers, including college students, because of the words themselves. For example, a simple sentence is not necessarily direct,

498

short, and uncomplicated; and a complex sentence is often short and easy to read, even though it contains at least two clauses. Remember the distinction between a clause and a phrase: *a clause, but not a phrase, contains a subject and a predicate.*

A *simple sentence* contains only one independent clause and no dependent clauses, although it may contain one or more phrases of several kinds.

A *complex sentence* contains one independent clause and one or more dependent clauses. It may or may not contain phrases.

A *compound sentence* contains at least two independent clauses, with or without phrases, and no dependent clauses.

A *compound-complex sentence* contains at least two independent clauses (like a compound sentence) and at least one dependent clause. In addition, it may contain phrases, but not necessarily so.

As a review of your knowledge of sentence construction, examine the five sentences in the immediately preceding paragraph. Classify each sentence, noting the number and kind of clauses in each before you read the following paragraph.

If you were able quickly and surely to classify each sentence, you should have little trouble with sentence recognition and construction or in applying the rules of punctuation. If you were unsure, further study will be beneficial to you. A complete English handbook, used with Appendix C, will be of more value than Appendix C alone. Because of limited space in this textbook, which includes many other elements of communication, details of language usage cannot be explained in full detail.

Here are the "answers":

Sentence 1. Complex sentence, one main (independent) clause and two dependent (subordinate) clauses. The subject of the main clause is *definition;* the predicate is *is.* Each of the two dependent clauses begins with *that.*

Sentence 2. Simple sentence: *Sentences are classified. . . .*

Sentence 3. Simple sentence: *These terms are confusing. . . .*

Sentence 4. Compound-complex. Subject and predicate, first main clause: *simple sentence* is . . . ; subject and predicate, second main clause: *complex sentence is* . . . ; subject and predicate, dependent clause; *it contains.*

Sentence 5. Compound. First main clause: Subject, *you* (understood); predicate: *remember*; second main clause: *clause contains.*

Further illustrations of types of sentences are given below.

Simple Sentences

I shall return.—*Douglas MacArthur*

Understanding is joyous.—*Carl Sagan* (*Understanding* is used here as a noun and the subject of the sentence.)

Towering genius disdains a beaten path.—*Abraham Lincoln*

England and America are two countries separated by the same language.—*George Bernard Shaw*

The fog comes on little cat feet.—*Carl Sandburg*

Play it again, Sam—Title of film; also adaptation of line from another film, *Casablanca.* (The subject is the understood *you.*)

I hate quotations.—*Ralph Waldo Emerson*

Complex Sentences

When people are least sure, they are often the most dogmatic.—*John Kenneth Galbraith*—(Introductory dependent clause.)

In spite of everything I still believe that people are really good at heart.—*Anne Frank* (Dependent clause begins with *that.*)

He who enters a university walks on hallowed ground.—*James B. Conant* (Here the dependent clause, beginning with *who*, separates the subject and verb of the main clause: *he* and *walks.*)

The future offers very little hope for those who expect that our new mechanical slaves will offer us a world in which we may rest from thinking.—*Norbert Weiner* (This sentence contains one independent clause and three dependent clauses. *Future* and *offers* are the subject and predicate of the main clause. The subjects and predicates of the three dependent clauses are: *who expect, slaves will offer,* and *we may rest.*)

Wit has truth in it; wisecracking is simply calisthenics with words.—
Dorothy Parker

Life was meant to be lived, and curiosity must be kept alive.—*Eleanor Roosevelt*

All animals are equal, but some animals are more equal than others.—
George Orwell

Talk low, talk slow, and don't say too much.—*John Wayne* (Three independent clauses.)

Compound-Complex Sentences

Read over your compositions, and wherever you meet with a passage which you think is particularly fine, strike it out.—*Samuel Johnson* (*You* is the understood subject of both independent clauses; *read* and *strike* are the verbs. In the dependent clauses, *you meet, which is*, and *you think* are the subjects and verbs.)

We can secure other people's approval if we do right and try hard; but our own is worth a hundred of it, and no way has been found of securing that.—*Mark Twain* (Three main clauses and one dependent clause, beginning with *if we do*.)

And so, my fellow Americans, ask not what your country can do for you; ask what you can do for your country.—*John F. Kennedy* (Two independent clauses and two dependent clauses.)

BASIC ERRORS IN SENTENCE CONSTRUCTION

The most conspicuous weaknesses in sentence construction are the following:

1. Fragmentary sentences, although these can at times be used effectively.
2. The comma fault, also called a comma blunder, a comma splice, and a baby comma.
3. A fused sentence, also called a run-on sentence.
4. Nonparallel sentences, or sentences of mixed construction.
5. Sentences with dangling or misplaced modifiers.

A fragmentary sentence, the comma fault, and the fused sentence also can be considered as errors in punctuation. These weak constructions occur, however, because the writer is not sure of what constitutes a sentence. The lack of necessary and wisely chosen punctuation results in these sentence weaknesses.

A *fragmentary sentence* is incomplete in itself; it is usually a phrase or a dependent clause. Ordinarily it should not be punctuated as a complete sentence, as in the following example:

> This information is presented here. Because it is necessary to the understanding of the following pages.

Improve by eliminating the period:

> This information is presented here because it is necessary to the understanding of the following pages.

The *comma fault* occurs when two sentences that are definitely separate have been joined together with a comma. They should be punctuated as two separate sentences, joined with a conjunction, or joined with a semicolon. The choice of the method of connection depends, to a certain extent, upon the desired meaning and emphasis. If the ideas are not related to the degree that they belong in the same sentence, they should be expressed in separate sentences. Avoid using a great many semicolons, as they can result in a choppy effect, just as a great number of short, simple sentences can. Usually one idea is more important than another; in this case, a complex sentence should be used.

Notice the following example of a common fault:

> Children in all cultures are taught to become a part of that culture and to transmit it, perhaps it has been considered dangerous to allow excessive questioning of any particular culture. (Improve by starting a new sentence with *perhaps* or by using a semicolon before *perhaps*.)

This sentence could also be revised in the following way, although the meaning and emphasis are slightly changed:

> Because it has been considered dangerous to allow excessive questioning, children in all cultures are taught to become a part of that culture and to transmit it.

In short and closely related sentences, commas may at times be effectively used to join the clauses of compound sentences, as:

> I came, I saw, I conquered.

> Don't hurry, don't worry.

This construction, however, should be used with discretion and extreme caution, especially by the inexperienced writer. (See the discussion of the use of the semicolon under "Punctuation as an Aid to Readability," later in this appendix.)

A *fused sentence* occurs when two sentences are "run-on" with no separation at all. The sentences should be separated by a period, a semicolon, or a comma and a conjunction.

Nonparallel sentences occur when parallel ideas are not expressed in parallel form. An orderly arrangement is necessary for the immediate recognition of relationships of ideas.

The following sentences are not parallel because of unnecessary shifts from active to passive voice:

Jane wrote the music, and the lyrics were written by Mary Hicks.

The play was well written, and the director did a capable job.

Improved versions of these sentences are:

Jane wrote the music, and Mary Hicks wrote the lyrics.

The play was well written and capably directed.

The following sentence is nonparallel because similar ideas are expressed in differing ways, by use of the infinitive and of the gerund:

Taking the elevator is not so healthful as to climb the stairs. (Improve by changing "to climb" to "climbing.")

The following sentence is nonparallel because a relative clause and an infinitive phrase are used to express similar ideas:

We want a personnel manager who can motivate all workers and to recruit experienced salesmen.

An improved version of this sentence is:

We want a personnel manager who can motivate workers and who can recruit experienced salesmen.

A more concise version is:

We want a personnel manager who can motivate workers and recruit experienced salesmen.

The following phrases are not parallel because two gerunds and one infinitive are used in a sentence in which similar expressions should be of the same form:

Buying supplies, keeping the books, and to answer the telephone—

An improved version is:

Buying supplies, keeping the books, and answering the telephone

The following sentence beginning is not parallel because two phrases are used with a clause:

Government of the people, by the people, and that is for the people—

The following sentences are nonparallel because of a misplaced correlative. (Correlatives are pairs of joining words, such as *either, or; neither, nor; both, and; not only, but also.*)

Either to make a living or a life is not an easy task, if it is done well.

Not only must we be concerned with the initial cost but also with the upkeep.

These sentences can be improved in this way:

To make either a living or a life is not an easy task, if it is done well.

We must be concerned not only with the initial cost but also with the upkeep.

Dangling or misplaced modifiers may consist of adjectives or adverbs; phrases, including participial, infinitive, or prepositional; and clauses. Any modifier is misplaced if it does not exactly and logically qualify (restrict, limit, describe) the word or words that it is intended to qualify.

A modifier is said to dangle when it has no reasonable or logical word to modify, as in this sentence:

Working without a coffee break, the telephone calls were completed before noon.

As this sentence is constructed, the participle *working* seems to modify telephone calls, when obviously it cannot. The modifier here could also be described as all the words that come before the main part of the sentence, "working without a coffee break." The sentence should be improved in this way:

> Working without a coffee break, I completed the telephone calls before noon.

Dangling participles sometimes occur because the writer is too much concerned with avoiding the word *I*. *I* and *we* should be used when they are natural and necessary to the sentence, except for the few kinds of business writing that use only the impersonal tone.

Here are more examples of dangling modifiers:

> When stewed until mushy, put the fruit into the blender.

> Talking with the dean, every problem in the college was mentioned by some student or other.

(Do you suppose that they got around to mentioning the need for further study in sentence structure?)

> Being dark and winding, she could barely see the road.

> Completely renovated two years ago, I was most impressed by the old building.

Many misplaced or dangling modifiers do not distort the meaning, at least upon a second reading. But clarity, even immediate clarity, is not our only goal in writing or speaking. We also want to communicate exactly, precisely, and professionally. Even if an imperfect sentence does not result in an unintentional humorous or preposterous statement, like (or worse than) those above, it is still an inexact, amateurish expression.

Avoid using a great many participial openings, even if they do not dangle. Usually the sentence is more direct and forceful when it opens with the subject-verb combination.

Misplaced modifiers may be in sentence positions other than the beginning, as in the following sentence:

> The woman riding the motorcycle in a red jogging suit is my grandmother. (Misplaced prepositional phrase.)

> In the downtown section, with sirens screaming, we saw the fire truck skid to a stop. (Misplaced prepositional phrase.)

The word *only* is easily misplaced. *Rarely, merely, hardly, just, even*, and other words are also located in various places in the sentence, often not in the best location to refer to the exact word or group of words that it modifies. As a general rule, put closely related words together.

The following sentence contains a misplaced *only*, although this particular construction is often used in conversation and sometimes in writing.

He only received a few dollars for his poem.

In formal writing, and preferably on all occasions, the following construction should be used:

He received only a few dollars for his poem.

Regardless of the formality of the writing, the expression is more exact if the modifier is in the best possible location in relationship to the rest of the sentence. In addition, the placement of *only* or similar words can affect the meaning of the sentence.

Notice how the meaning changes, according to the placement of *only*, in the following sentences:

Only MacArthur said that he would return.
MacArthur only said that he would return.
MacArthur said only that he would return.
MacArthur said that only he would return.
MacArthur said that he only would return.
MacArthur said that he would only return.

In the next to the last sentence, the meaning is unclear because *only* could modify either *he* or *would return*.

PUNCTUATION AS AN AID TO READABILITY

The Apostrophe

1. Use an apostrophe in contractions.

- won't
- it's (it is)
- couldn't
- you're (you are)

(Avoid contractions in formal writing.)

2. Use an apostrophe to indicate the possessive case of nouns and indefinite pronouns.

- Mary's cat
- anybody's guess
- a stone's throw
- a year's experience
- children's clothing
- the student's paper (one student)
- the students' papers (more than one student)
- Mr. Ross's automobile
- The Rosses' automobile (an automobile owned by more than one person named Ross)
- Jefferson Davis's home
- Bob and Mary's house (joint ownership)
- Bob's and Mary's shoes (individual ownership)

(Singular nouns ending in *s* may be followed by the apostrophe alone, as: Dr. Jennings' office.)

3. Use an apostrophe in plurals of lower-case letters and abbreviations followed by periods and—optional—in plurals of capital letters, figures, abbreviations not followed by periods, and words referred to as words.

- c's
- Ph.D's
- B's or Bs
- CPA's or CPAs
- 8's or 8s
- the 1940's or 1940s
- and's or ands
- %'s or %s

(Be consistent in your use of the apostrophe. For example, use *and's* or *ands*, but do not use both in the same paper. According to some English handbooks, *and's* is preferred.)

NOTE: The use of the apostrophe is sometimes described as being an aspect of spelling, not punctuation.

The Comma

1. Use a comma to set off an introductory subordinate clause from the independent statement.

- If Johnny can't write, one of the reasons may be a conditioning based on speed rather than respect for the creative process.

- If you don't like the weather in New England, wait a few minutes.
- Although the ability to type is a requisite to many jobs, it should no more be considered purely vocational than the ability to read or write the English language.
- When in doubt, tell the truth.—Mark Twain (Introductory element with "you are" understood.)

2. Use a comma after introductory participial phrases.

- Thinking that he could complete the work in an hour, he left it until the afternoon.
- Having received the notice of cancellation, we tried to stop shipment.
- Elated over the news of his promotion, he kissed everyone on the third floor.

Distinguish between a participle, which is a verb form used as an adjective, and a gerund, which is a verb form used as a noun. A gerund is also referred to as a verbal noun. In the following sentences the gerund acts as the subject; it should not be followed by a comma:

- Seeing is believing.
- Driving along the Natchez Trace is a memorable experience.

3. Use a comma after introductory infinitive phrases.

- To enter the stacks, go to the admission desk and present your identification card.

An infinitive, like a gerund, is not followed by a comma when it is used as the subject. In the following sentence, both clauses of the compound sentence contain an infinitive used as the subject:

- To err is human; to blame it on someone else is even more human.

4. Use a comma after an introductory sentence element consisting of a long prepositional phrase or of two or more phrases.

- In addition to all the books in the general library, many others are shelved in specialized collections.

5. Use a comma after introductory words and phrases.

- Confidentially, this policy is to be changed.
- Nevertheless, we must continue the usual procedure throughout this month.

6. Use a comma to separate words, phrases, or clauses in a series. A reporter tells who, when, where, why, and how.

- His morning consists of eating breakfast, reading the newspaper, and sitting in the sunshine.
- Go to the end of the hall, turn left, and follow the arrows on the wall.
- He ordered a computer, a dictionary, and an eraser.

7. Use a comma to separate coordinate clauses joined by and, but, for, or, nor, yet.

- Short words are best, and the old ones when short are best of all.—*Winston Churchill*
- All would live long, but none would be old.—*Benjamin Franklin*
- To be good is noble, but to teach others how to be good is nobler—and less trouble.—*Mark Twain*
- The show had no chronological order, nor did it have an intelligent narration.

In short sentences the comma is sometimes omitted, as in:

- I came late and you left early.

8. Use a comma to set off nonrestrictive (nonessential) clauses; do not set off restrictive clauses that come within or at the end of a sentence.

- Our salesmen, who are paid a salary plus commissions, earn from $900 to $2,000 a month. (nonrestrictive)
- Salesmen who exceed their quotas receive an extra bonus. (restrictive)

9. Use a comma to set off parenthetical (nonrestrictive, nonessential) words or phrases.

- He said that, in the first place, he was not interested in our product.
- The sales manager, Mr. Harvey L. Wells, is a friend of the customer's sister.
- The store first opened its doors on Monday, May 13, 1904, in St. Louis, Missouri, on the bank of the Mississippi River.
- The statement is true, perhaps, that our prices could be reduced.

Words that are at times used parenthetically are at other times used adverbially. If a word or phrase can be considered supplemental, interrupting, or explanatory, precede and follow the word or phrase with commas. In the following sentences, *perhaps, however,* and *also* are used as adverbs, and, because of their placement in the sentence, should not be set off by commas:

- It is perhaps true that our prices could be reduced.
- However it happened, it was not according to customary office procedures.
- The second statement is also false.

10. Use a comma to separate adjectives of equal rank if the conjunction is omitted.

- She is an efficient, considerate sales representative.

Do not use commas between adjectives of unequal rank, as in:

- The cold late autumn days are here again.

To check whether a comma is needed, try inserting the word *and.* If the expression now makes sense, use a comma.

11. Use a comma to set off contrasting expressions.

- The world is becoming warmer, not colder.

The Semicolon

1. Use a semicolon between main clauses that are not joined by one of the coordinate conjunctions (and, but, for, or, nor, yet).

- Punctuation is more than little marks to be sprinkled like salt and paper through written words; punctuation determines emphasis and meaning.

2. Use a semicolon between main clauses joined with a conjunctive adverb.

- A readable writing style is simple and direct; consequently, it requires less punctuation than a more formal, complicated style.
- Semicolons are a useful means of expressing meaning through punctuation; nevertheless, a great many long compound sentences such as this one, with the main clauses joined by a semicolon and a conjunctive adverb (*nevertheless*), tend to suggest a rather heavy and formal writing style.

NOTE: The substitution of a comma for a semicolon to separate main clauses, as in sentences constructed like the preceding ones that contain no coordinating conjunction, is considered a serious error in punctuation and sentence construction. (See the preceding section titled "Basic Errors in Sentence Construction.")

3. Use a semicolon to separate items in a series if they are parallel subordinate clauses, or if they are long or contain internal punctuation.

- Those attending included Susan Smith, a college professor; Mark David, a field engineer; Diana Watson, an executive secretary; and Leonard Watson, a credit manager.
- We use language to talk about language; we make statements about statements; and we sing songs about songs.

4. Use a semicolon to separate complete clauses joined by a coordinate conjunction if the semicolon will increase readability when clauses are long or contain internal punctuation.

- The semicolon, which is sometimes overused, indicates a stronger break in thought than that indicated by a comma; but it is not so strong as that indicated by a period and is somewhat different in usage from a colon.

The Colon

1. Use a colon to introduce a series of items.

- The factors to be considered are these: cost, speed, and simplicity.
- Three possible areas of operation could be the source of the loss: shipping, advertising, and collections.

2. Use a colon to introduce long quotations or descriptions.

3. Use a colon after such words as "the following" or "as follows."

The Dash

1. Use a dash to show a sudden change in the structure of a sentence or to indicate emphasis.

- Indeed, it was a long leap from the jungle home of the chimpanzee to our modern civilization—and apparently we didn't quite make it.
- Several items—a stapler, two calendars, and three or more chairs—were lost by the movers.

Do not overuse the dash, especially in formal writing, as it may give a "scatterbrained" appearance.

The Hyphen

1. Use a hyphen to join a compound expression used as a single modifier before a noun.

- Is this an interest-bearing note?
- We need up-to-date equipment.

Omit the hyphen when the first word of the compound is an adverb ending in *ly*. Omit the hyphen when the modifier comes after the noun:

- Is this note interest bearing?

2. Use a hyphen in some compound words in which the hyphen is considered part of the spelling, such as self-control and sister-in-law.

3. Use a hyphen to divide words at the end of a line.

Do not divide words unnecessarily, as many lines ending with hyphens can be distracting. When you must divide to avoid extreme unevenness of typewritten lines, follow these guides:

- Divide only between syllables.
- Do not divide a word with fewer than seven letters.
- Do not separate the following syllables from the remainder of the word:
  a syllable that does not contain a vowel (couldn't)
  a first syllable of only one letter (ecology)
  a last syllable of one or two letters (extremely)
- Do not divide hyphenated words at any place other than at the hyphen. (well-being)
- Divide after a one-letter syllable within a word unless the word contains successive single-letter syllables. (congratulations)
- Try to avoid dividing proper names and numbers.
- Do not divide the last word of a paragraph or the last word on a page.

Parentheses

1. Use parentheses to set off explanatory or nonessential material.

- A choice of commas, dashes, or parentheses (used in pairs) can be used to set off parenthetical material.

You can change the meaning slightly according to your choice of punctuation. Dashes are more emphatic than commas. Parentheses indicate a more definite separation in meaning from the rest of the sentence than commas imply.

Quotation Marks

1. *Use quotation marks to enclose the exact words of a writer or speaker.*

2. *Use quotation marks to enclose titles of songs, magazine and newspaper articles, poems, reports, and other short written works.*

3. *Use quotation marks to define terms.*

4. *Use quotation marks to enclose slang expressions.*

5. *Use quotation marks to enclose words used in an unusual way.*

Quotation marks are used with other marks of punctuation in this way:

- Place commas and periods inside quotation marks.
- Place colons and semicolons outside quotation marks.
- Place question and exclamation marks inside the quotation marks when they refer to the quoted material, outside when they refer to the sentence as a whole.

CAPITALIZATION

1. *Do not capitalize unless there is a definite reason to do so. Some writers capitalize unnecessarily.*

Capitalize	*Do Not Capitalize*
Cost Accounting II (name of specific course)	major in accounting (general subject field)
I am taking a course in French. (proper adjective)	I am taking a course in history. (general subject field, not a proper adjective)
President Carpenter (Title used as part of name)	He is president of his fraternity.
The President (of United States)	Our company has a new president.

West Coast (section of country)

He rode west into the sunset. (direction)

Mother is late. (used as name)

My mother is late.

Mississippi River (part of name)

Mississippi and Tennessee rivers

He said, "We shall proceed." (direct quotation)

He said that we would proceed. (indirect quotation)

Summer Series of Lectures (part of title)

This summer is unusually cool. (Season shown in usual way)

WRITING NUMBERS

1. Spell out numbers one through ten if no larger number appears in the same sentence.

(Another rule for spelling out numbers is to write in words any number that can be expressed in no more than two words—which is, in effect, numbers one through one hundred. In business writing, however, the "through ten" rule is more readable and saves time.)

2. Spell out numbers that represent time when they are used with "o'clock." Use figures with A.M. and P.M.

3. Spell out the smaller number when two numbers come together.

- We ordered sixteen 24-inch mirrors.

4. Spell out amounts of money shown in legal documents; follow with the amount shown in figures.

(Do not use this method of expressing numbers in ordinary business writing.)

5. Use figures, regardless of the expressed quantity, to state:

- dates: April 15, 1978—*not* April 15th
- money: $5, $17.20, 5 cents
- dimensions: 5 feet, 2 inches
- percentages: 5 percent
- page numbers: page 7

6. Spell out numbers at the beginning of sentences.

accommodate
accompanying
acknowledging
acknowledgment
across
advisable
all right
attorneys
bargain
beginning
believe
beneficial
benefited
bulletin
calendar
chargeable
competent
congratulations
controlled
convenience
deficiency
definite
desirable
discrepancy

efficient
embarrassing
enclosed
equipped
exceed
excellent
existence
familiar
feasible
February
forcible
guaranteed
handling
incidentally
indispensable
interfered
introducing
journeys
legible
leisure
management
noticeable
occasion
occurred

occurrence
pamphlet
parallel
permanent
personnel
precede
preceding
preferred
prevalent
privilege
procedure
proceed
quantity
questionnaire
receive
recipient
referred
separate
similar
sincerely
surprise
transferring
traveling
truly

FREQUENTLY CONFUSED OR MISUSED WORDS

accept, except

- *Accept* means "to receive with approval."
- *Except* means "excluding."
- All the employees *except* Mr Jones *accepted* the small gifts.

adapt, adept, adopt

- *Adapt* means "to make suitable or fit," as for a particular use, purpose, or situation.
- *Adept* means "highly skilled, well trained, thoroughly proficient."
- *Adopt* means "to take by free choice into a close relationship, previously not existing."
- With a few minor changes we can *adapt* this room for use as a study.

- Because of his many years of experience, Bill is quite *adept* at newspaper writing.
- The young couple has plans to *adopt* a child within the next year.

advice, advise

- *Advice* is a noun that means a "view, opinion, judgment."
- *Advise* is a verb that means "to give an opinion, inform, consider."
- His *advice* was to think first, then respond with an answer.
- The captain will *advise* the tourists of the risk involved as they board his vessel.

affect, effect

- *Affect* is a verb meaning "to influence."
- *Effect*, used as a verb, means "to bring about." Effect is also a noun, meaning "result."
- The weather *affects* our moods.
- Do you think we could *effect* a change in working hours?
- What will be the *effect* of the change?

all together, altogether

- *All together* means "in one group."
- *Altogether* means "entirely."
- The committee members were *all together* when the vote was taken.
- The committee members were *altogether* in agreement.

already, all ready

- *Already* means "previously."
- *All ready* means "entirely ready."
- The secretary had *already* opened the office.
- The conference room was *all ready* for the meeting.

appraise, apprise

- *Appraise* means "to estimate value."
- *Apprise* means "to inform" or "to advise."

capital, capitol

- *Capital* means the city or town that is the official seat of government.

- *Capitol* is the building that contains the governmental offices. (Often not capitalized when referring to state capitol buildings.)

cite, sight, site

- *Cite* means "to quote."
- *Sight* means "something seen."
- *Site* means "position or location."

complement, compliment

- *Complement* means "to complete."
- *Compliment* means "to praise."

continual, continuous

- A *continual* action implies that the action is often occurring, but is not *continuous,* which means "uninterrupted."

council, counsel

- *Council* is a noun meaning "group of persons delegated to give advice."
- *Counsel* used as a noun means "advice"; used as a verb, counsel means "to give advice."

credible, creditable

- *Credible* means "believable."
- *Creditable* means "worthy of credit."

flaunt, flout

- *Flaunt* means "to parade" or "to display boldly."
- *Flout* means "to treat with scorn."

formally, formerly

- *Formally* means "in a formal manner."
- *Formerly* means "previously."

its, it's

- *Its* is a possessive pronoun.
- *It's* is the contraction of "it is" or "it has."
- The horse lost *its* saddle.
- *It's* difficult to study before breakfast.

lose, loose

- *Lose* is a verb, the opposite of "find."
- *Loose* is an adjective, the opposite of "tight."

moral, morale

- *Moral* pertains to right conduct.
- *Morale* means a mental condition with respect to cheerfulness, confidence, and zeal.

passed, past

- *Passed* is the past tense of pass, as "The two ships passed in the night."
- *Past* means "gone by or elapsed in time," as "in past times," or "in the past."

personal, personnel

- *Personal* means "individual" or "private," as in "my personal opinion."
- *Personnel* means "the persons employed in an organization."

precede, proceed

- *Precede* means "to come before."
- *Proceed* means "to go ahead" or "to continue."

principal, principle

- *Principal* means "the most important." It is also "the amount of a loan."
- *Principle* means "a rule or basic truth."

quiet, quite

- *Quiet* means "not noisy."
- *Quite* means "entirely."
- This room is not *quite quiet.*

sometime, some time

- *Sometime* is a point in time, as "The work will be completed sometime soon."
- *Some time* means "an amount of time," as "This method has not been in effect for some time."

stationary, stationery

- *Stationary* means "not moving."
- *Stationery* is writing paper.

who's, whose

- *Who's* means "who is."
- *Whose* means "of or belonging to a person or persons as possessor or possessors."
- *Who's* going to travel by train?
- *Whose* little black puppy is this?

your, you're

- *Your* means "of or belong to you or yourself."
- *You're* is the contraction for "you are."
- *Your* talent in musical performance is superb.
- *You're* not to pass another vehicle in this lane.

FREQUENTLY OCCURRING GRAMMATICAL ERRORS

Subject—Verb Disagreement

This commonly occurring error is particularly troublesome when dictating. Because words or phrases often come between the subject and the verb, the wrong form of the verb is dictated unthinkingly. Using the wrong form of the verb—as in "the boys is" or "the girl are"—is a serious error, a real error, according to all authorities and handbooks, and to almost everyone who will read your message. In simple constructions like these, the mistake is not likely to occur. In slightly more complicated sentences, it often does occur, as in:

> The logic of good communicators seem to be—

Because the plural word *communicators* immediately precedes the verb, *seem* may creep into the sentence, although in a sentence no more involved than this one there is little reason for the wrong verb form even when dictating. As more words intervene, the subject "gets lost" so that the wrong verb seems to be the appropriate one. One of the principles of good writing, however, is that it be simple and direct; another guide is that the subject and verb be close together. Sentences constructed in this way are likely to include the correct form of the verb.

In the sentence below, the verb is singular to agree with the subject *box*:

The box, together with the baskets, was sent to the shipping room.

The word *baskets* is not part of the subject, but because *baskets* immediately precedes the verb, it seems natural to use *were*. In the following sentence, *were* is the correct verb:

The box and the baskets were sent to the shipping room.

Compare the above sentences with the following:

Neither the box nor the basket was sent to the shipping room.

Neither the box nor the baskets were sent to the shipping room.

The following guideline applies to sentences like the preceding ones: When one subject is singular and the other is plural, the verb agrees with the subject closer to the verb.

The Wrong Case of the Pronoun

Using the wrong case of the pronoun is an error that seems to occur more in speech than in writing. It is especially likely to occur in sentences in which *I* is used incorrectly (instead of *me*) as the object of a verb or preposition. Few persons, regardless of their position or educational background, say something like this:

Me and Jim are friends.

However, many persons say or write:

Jim and he are good friends of Mary and I.

In the preceding sentence, "Mary and *me*" should be used because the pronoun is the object of the preposition *of*. The *I* is just as incorrect as the *me* in "me and Jim," but for some reason the *I* seems to many persons to be more "cultured," more "elegant," more "correct."
Remember these cases of pronouns:

Subjective: I   you he she it we they who   whoever
Possessive: my your his her its our their whose whosoever
Objective: me you him her it us them whom whomever

A pronoun in the subjective case is used:

- as the subject of a main or a subordinate clause;
- as a predicate nominative (as in "it is I," although "it is me" is more frequently heard in conversation) and;
- as a word that is in apposition with another word in the subjective case, as "only three persons attending—Jim, Jeannie, and I." (*I*, as well as *Jim* and *Jeannie*, is in apposition with *persons*, which *is* the subject of the sentence.)

A pronoun in the objective case is used when it is the object of a verb or a preposition or when it is used as an indirect object.

A pronoun modifying a gerund (a verb form used as a noun) is in the possessive case, as in:

We will appreciate your writing us immediately.

Notice the reasons for the choice of words in the following sentences:

- Who is to be the new president? (subject)
- Who do you think will be the new president? (Still the subject of the sentence, not the object *of think*.)
- John Jackson, who is our new president, will be at the meeting. (*Who* is the subject of the subordinate clause. A more concise way to word this sentence is to omit *who is* so that *our new president* is used in apposition with *John Jackson*.)
- *For Whom the Bell Tolls*. (*Whom* is the object of the preposition *for*.)

You will have many other decisions to make during your business career in addition to pondering over the question of whether to use *who* or *whom*. Master the expected usage now and stop worrying about it. (Yes, no doubt you already have more important things to worry about. But this is one problem you can solve with very little effort.)

EXERCISES

Exercise 1. Sentence Structure. State whether each of the following sentences is simple, complex, compound, or compound-complex.

1. The Memphis hotel industry fared well in 1985.
2. Although improvement is forecast in two or three years, *complex*

several unexpected events put the hotel industry to the test.

3. Because the districts are made up of two or three counties each, some farmers believe that the districts should be divided. *complex*

4. One-half of the faculty members expect to use the computer from six to ten hours a month. *Simple*

5. Of the total number of respondents, 70 percent listed letters of recommendation; 63 listed manuscripts; and 51 percent mentioned grant applications. *compound*

6. Fifty respondents state that they will use the word processing center at least once a week. *complex*

7. Demand is off in all segments, and a number of hotel managers are re-evaluating their market strategies.

8. Although humans have a wide range of acceptable working conditions, they will not work efficiently outside these limits of human tolerance.

9. In order to decrease errors, we should duplicate these forms.

10. The clerk who will duplicate the forms is away from the office.

Exercise 2. The ten sentences in Exercise 1 are correctly punctuated according to guides given in Appendix D. State the reason for each mark of punctuation in the ten sentences in Exercise 1.

Exercise 3. Sentence Structure. Improve each sentence and state its weakness.

1. This statement is only one illustration of the ways in which words can have several meanings. As I shall discuss later.

2. I shall also speak of barriers to communication many of these barriers are of our own making.

3. Even secretarial work was not acceptable for many years, Women were said to be too weak, physically, for office work.

4. Knowing that words have differing meanings to various individuals, the word "tree" may remind you of a magnolia, an oak, or a pine.

5. Meaning is in the mind; therefore all communication is imperfect.

6. The expression "walking on air" would not apply either when you are tired or depressed.

7. Verbal communication only transfers about 25 percent of our meaning.

8. Believing the subject to be important, the book was written in a year.

9. Typists can make corrections, move words and paragraphs around, and additions and deletions ~~can be done~~ *make* automatically.

10. I shall relate this discussion of communication to management. And especially toward management in the automobile industry.

11. Women typists were known as "typewriters" in the early years of office work. In addition, they "manned" the heavy machines.

12. The woman at the computer smoking a cigarette is breaking office rules. *by*

13. Playing is better than to work, at least at times.

14. To understand this essential tool of good management.

15. Open communication within an organization saves time, reduces frustration, and much expense is saved because of increased cooperation.

Exercise 4. Apostrophes.   Choose the correct word.

1. (That's, Thats) (someone else's, someone elses) problem.   1. _____

2. (Who's, Whose) going with us?   2. _____

3. (You're, Your) to be congratulated.   3. _____

4. (Your, You're) report is excellent.   4. _____

5. (John's, Johns) car is now paid for.   5. _____

6. Mr. Jones has one (year's, years', years) experience.   6. _____

7. Miss Black has three (year's, years', years) experience.   7. _____

8. This (mans, man's) overcoat is to be returned to him.   8. _____

9. These (boy's, boys') bikes are here.   9. _____

10. Mr. (Johnson's, Johnsons') house is on the corner.   10. _____

11. Mr. (Ross', Ross's, Rosses') store has been there for seventeen years.   11. _____

12. (Jim's and Mary's, Jim and Mary's) family consists of three boys.   12. _____

13. (Jim's and Mary's, Jim and Mary's) personalities are completely different.   13. _____

14. A cat indicates contentment and affection by (its, it's) purring.   14. _____

15. (Its, It's) fortunate that two (companies, company's,   15. _____

16. companys, companies') are building (their,
    they're)   16. _____

17. plants in our city, especially since our own
    (company's,   17. _____

18. companys, companies, companies')
    earnings are decreasing.   18. _____

19. An optional spelling of *employee* is
    employe; perhaps there is a shortage of
    e's.   19. _____

Exercise 5. Commas, Semicolons, and Colons. Insert necessary commas, semicolons, and colons. Some sentences need more than one mark of punctuation, and some are correct as given. Do not use additional periods. If you believe a sentence needs no further punctuation, write "correct" by the sentence.

1. Nonverbal communication includes all messages except written and spoken ones.

2. Nonverbal communication, which consists of many forms, permeates all speech and much of written communication.

3. We can never learn to read a person like a book, fortunately, for we are all too complicated for that.

4. Many people take an overly simplified view of the subject.

5. As we all know, perfect communication cannot be achieved by reading a book.

6. Ruesch and Kees classify human nonverbal communication into three broad categories: sign language, object language and action language.

7. We also communicate by tone of voice, which differs according to our mood and the person with whom we are talking.

8. Much of nonverbal communication is not silent, however, regardless of Hall's title, *The Silent Language*.

9. The slamming of a door is not silent, and it is most expressive.

10. Some communication is silent; nevertheless, it is at times most expressive.

11. We all want to express ourselves and to receive the messages of others.

12. We communicate nonverbally to machines, and they communicate nonverbally to us.

13. We push a button to receive black coffee; the machine responds by supplying the coffee.

14. If we push the wrong button, we will receive coffee with cream.

15. In the United States and the Western European countries, personal distance zones are greater than in Arab countries.

16. Believing that height adds status, a businessman put his desk and chair on a raised platform.

17. We carry with us a kind of invisible bubble that we consider to be our own space.

18. As you interview persons or talk with visitors, your desk becomes a barrier between you.

19. Crossing your arms implies resistance.

20. The pupils of our eyes enlarge when we are looking at something that pleases us; they contract when we are displeased.

21. There are regional differences as well as national differences in nonverbal communication; and people in the South, especially in Georgia, smile more often than those in Maine or New York.

22. Millions of frames are chewed up each year, but people tell the ophthalmologists that the dog chewed them up.

23. Because nonverbal communication is mostly unplanned, it is one of the most sincere forms of communication.

24. The four zones of personal distance are these: intimate, personal, social and public.

25. All communication is imperfect, not entirely accurate or complete.

26. We can improve our communication by becoming aware of what other people are trying to tell us through nonverbal communication.

27. Nonverbal communication should not be taken out of context: the spoken message, the environment and previously established relationships.

28. Authors in the field include Edward T. Hall, who wrote *The Silent Language* and *The Hidden Dimension*; Ray Birdwhistell, author of *Kinesics and Context*; and Flora Davis, who wrote *Inside Intuition*.

29. Perhaps communication can bring us all closer together and actually make possible the often meaningless "Have a nice day."

30. "Verbal" means with words, either written or spoken words.

Exercise 6. Hyphens and Quotation Marks. Use hyphens and quotation marks as needed in the following sentences. All other marks of punctuation are used correctly.

1. A well-written "refusal letter" does not present the refusal in the last sentence.

2. Is this letter well written?
3. Preparations are now being made is an example of the use of the passive voice.
4. The blocked arrangement is one of the most widely used letter styles.
5. The time-saving factor must be kept in mind when choosing a letter style.
6. The new production manager displayed admirable self-control when he was referred to as old fashioned.
7. The expression buzz off was not understood by the teacher.
8. He said, We will survive.
9. The best sales messages do not use high-pressure techniques.
10. Have you read the poem, The Road Not Taken?
11. Another poem by the same author is entitled Mending Wall.
12. The student said, I do not understand.
13. Phrases such as Act today! and Hurry! are not usually effective in the action section of a sales letter.
14. The term resale is not an exact synonym for the term sales promotion.
15. He used this cliché: *out of the clear blue sky.*
16. The teacher made this statement: Personalize the favorable and impersonalize the unfavorable is good letter-writing advice.

Show where each of the following words can be correctly divided at the end of a typewritten line. Some cannot be correctly divided.

17. compound
18. alone
19. elopement
20. stopping
21. stopped
22. no-hitter
23. shouldn't
24. drollery
25. pizzazz
26. plight

Exercise 7. Writing Numbers. Choose the correct word.

1. The graduation was (two, 2) weeks ago on   1. _____
2. (May 8, May 8th) 1982.   2. _____
3. (Seventeen, 17) books are now overdue.   3. _____
4. The cost is only ($5, five dollars, 5 dollars, $5.00).   4. _____
5. The wedding is to be at (5, five) o'clock.   5. _____
6. The wedding is to be at (5, five) P.M.   6. _____
7. Place an order for (11, eleven) (25, twenty-five) pound bags of   7. _____

8. flour.   8. _____
9. The interest rate of (7, seven) percent is
   stated on page   9. _____
10. (4, four) of the sales contract.   10. _____
11. We brought (thirteen, 13) suitcases, (5,
    five) garment   11. _____
12. bags, and 172 boxes of books.   12. _____
13. The hall is (19, nineteen) feet,   13. _____
14. (2, two) inches wide.   14. _____
15. The copies cost (5¢, 5 cents, five cents)
    each.   15. _____

Exercise 8. Spelling.   Check *a*, *b*, *c*, or *d* to indicate a misspelled word. If all four words are correct, check *e*. No group has more than one misspelled word.

1. __a. accommodate
   __b. truely
   __c. occurred
   __d. discrepancy
   __e. all are correct
2. __a. accompanying
   __b. traveling
   __c. occassion
   __d. desirable
   __e. all are correct
3. __a. definate
   __b. acknowledgment
   __c. traveling
   __d. noticeable
   __e. all are correct
4. __a. sincerely
   __b. accross
   __c. management
   __d. leisure
   __e. all are correct
5. __a. similar
   __b. efficient
   __c. embarrassing
   __d. questionnaire
   __e. all are correct
6. __a. seperate
   __b. deficiency
   __c. convenience
   __d. introducing
   __e. all are correct

7. __a. controlled
   __b. congradulations
   __c. interfered
   __d. recipient
   __e. all are correct
8. __a. quantity
   __b. procede
   __c. procedure
   __d. precede
   __e. all are correct
9. __a. advisable
   __b. bargain
   __c. all right
   __d. attorneys
   __e. all are correct
10. __a. believe
    __b. beginning
    __c. February
    __d. receive
    __e. all are correct
11. __a. guaranteed
    __b. handling
    __c. incidentally
    __d. feasable
    __e. all are correct
12. __a. priviledge
    __b. journeys
    __c. companies
    __d. existence
    __e. all are correct

13. __a. efficient
 __b. bulletin
 __c. handling
 __d. guaranteed
 __e. all are correct

14. __a. excellent
 __b. equipped
 __c. exceed
 __d. personel
 __e. all are correct

15. __a. pamphlet
 __b. familar
 __c. excellent
 __d. enclosed
 __e. all are correct

16. __a. benefical
 __b. preferred
 __c. parallel
 __d. occurrence
 __e. all are correct

17. __a. chargeable
 __b. acknowledging
 __c. benefited
 __d. bulletin
 __e. all are correct

18. __a. permanent
 __b. surprise
 __c. calender
 __d. competent
 __e. all are correct

19. __a. discrepancy
 __b. desirable
 __c. indispensible
 __d. referred
 __e. all are correct

20. __a. legible
 __b. deficiency
 __c. preferred
 __d. similiar
 __e. all are correct

Exercise 9. Word Choice

1. All the salesmen (except, accept) Mr. Barnes voted to   1. _____
2. (except, accept) the proposed schedule changes.   2. _____
3. Employees are not permitted to (except, accept) gifts from suppliers.   3. _____
4. Can we (adapt, adopt) the suggested course outline for   4. _____
5. use with the newly (adopted, adapted, adept) textbook?   5. _____
6. Free (advice, advise) is said to be worth as much as it costs.   6. _____
7. What do you (advice, advise) me to do about the situation?   7. _____
8. What do you believe will be the (affect, effect) of the tax increase on inflation?   8. _____
9. To (effect, affect) improvements in employee morale, we should communicate more openly and completely.   9. _____
10. Our emotions are often (affected, effected) adversely by physical or mental fatigue.   10. _____

11. That statement is not (all together, altogether) correct.   11. _____

12. The family will be (all together, altogether) for Christmas.   12. _____

13. We have (already, all ready) made plans for our vacation.   13. _____

14. On Friday, June 1, we will be (already, all ready) to leave for Spain.   14. _____

15. She had the diamond (appraised, apprised).   15. _____

16. I was not (apprised, appraised) of the transfer of the manager.   16. _____

17. My ring is too (lose, loose); I feel I   17. _____

18. shall (lose, loose) it.   18. _____

19. Communication systems that conform to (moral, morale)   19. _____

20. (principles, principals) increase employee (moral,   20. _____

21. morale).   21. _____

22. In (passed, past) years, the test was (passed, past) by a   22. _____

23. higher percentage of high school graduates.   23. _____

24. The (personal, personnel) manager does not discuss her   24. _____

25. family or any other aspect of her (personal, personnel) life.   25. _____

26. The speaker was asked to (precede, proceed) with his   26. _____

27. presentation without delay, as the (preceding, proceeding) speaker had exceeded the time limit.   27. _____

28. (Sometime, Some time) in the future, I hope to spend   28. _____

29. (sometime, some time) in Australia.   29. _____

30. The letterhead (stationary, stationery) is weighted   30. _____

31. down with a brick. It is now (stationary, stationery).   31. _____

32. (Who's Whose) the new man in the group?   32. _____

33. (Who's Whose) yellow sportscar is in my parking space?   33. _____

34. (Your, You're) too unsure of (your,   34. _____

35. you're) ability.   35. _____

36. "With our (compliments, complements)" means in less gracious language that whatever is offered is free.   36. _____

37. The artist was most (complimentary, complementary)   37. _____

38. about our use of (complimentary, complementary) colors.   38. _____

39. The (continual, continuous) interruptions seemed to annoy the speaker.   39. _____

40. After working (continually, continuously) throughout the morning, we spent two hours at lunch.   40. _____

41. The Student (Council, Counsel) includes a few representatives from the Graduate School.   41. _____

42. Faculty (councilors, counselors) advise students about the preparation of class schedules.   42. _____

43. The data should create a (creditable, credible) impression   43. _____

44. if the readers are to be convinced of its (creditability, credibility).   44. _____

45. A bit of rather cynical (council, counsel) is: "If you've   45. _____

46. got it, (flaunt, flout) it."   46. _____

47. (Formerly, Formally), the ceremony was conducted quite   47. _____

48. (formerly, formally); it is now much more casual.   48. _____

49. (Its, It's) a lovely day.   49. _____

50. You can't judge a book by (its, it's) cover.   50. _____

Exercise 10. Word Choice

1. Various estimates from recognized authorities (indicate,   1. _____

2. indicates) that forms of nonverbal communication (make, makes) up as much as 75 percent of the transfer of meaning and emotion in face-to-face interaction.   2. _____

3. A business letter or a report (communicate, communicates) through appearance.   3. _____

4. Business letters and reports (communicate, communicates) through appearance.   4. _____

5. Nonverbal communication, as well as written or spoken words, (is, are) sometimes misinterpreted.   5. _____

6. A cleverly phrased sentence or vivid, descriptive words (is, are) of little value if the message is not based on accurate knowledge.   6. _____

7. The invitation was sent to my husband and (I, me).   7. _____

8. Three members arrived early—Mr. Hames, Mr. Baker, and (I, me).   8. _____

9. It was John and (I, me) who presented the skit.   9. _____

10. (Who, Whom) is the new salesman?   10. _____

11. (Who, Whom) telephoned about the contract?   11. _____

12. (Who, Whom) did you say called?   12. _____

13. Miss Brown, (who, whom) you met in St. Louis, is the new sales representative in Maine.   13. _____

14. Mr. Wilson, (who, whom) I thought would go to Maine, has left our organization.   14. _____

15. Miss Jones taught my sister and (I, me) when we were in the first grade.   15. _____

Additional Reference Sources

REPORT WRITING

Baxter, Carol M. *Business Report Writing: A Practical Approach.* Belmont, Calif.: Kent, 1983.

Bowman, Joel P., and Branchaw, Bernadine P. *Business Report Writing.* New York: Dryden, 1984.

Brown, Leland. *Effective Business Report Writing*, 3rd ed. Englewood Cliffs, N.J.: Prentice-Hall, 1973.

Lesikar, Raymond V. *Report Writing for Business.* 6th ed. Homewood, Ill.: Irwin, 1981.

Lewis, Phillip V. and Baker, William H. *Business Report Writing.* 2d ed. New York: Wiley, 1984.

Moyer, R. et al. *The Research and Report Handbook: For Business Industry, and Government.* New York: Wiley, 1981.

Walker, Melissa. *Writing Research Papers.* New York: Norton, 1984.

TEXTBOOKS

This section lists comprehensive textbooks on written and oral communication that include sections on research and report writing.

Bonner, William H. and Voyles, Jean. *Communicating in Business: Key to Success.* 3rd ed. Houston: Dame Publications, 1983.

Figgins, Ross, Golen, Steven P., and Pearce, C. Glenn. *Business Communication Basics: Application and Technology.* New York: Wiley, 1984.

Haggblade, Berle. *Business Communication.* St. Paul: West, 1982.

Himstreet, William C., and Baty, Wayne Murlin. *Business Communications.* 7th ed. Boston: Kent, 1984.

Huseman, Richard C., Lahiff, James M., and Hatfield, John D. *Business Communication*. Hinsdale, Ill.: Dryden, 1981.

Lesikar, Raymond V. *Basic Business Communication*. Rev. ed. Homewood, Ill.: Irwin, 1982.

————. *Business Communication: Theory and Application*. 5th ed. Homewood, Ill.: Irwin, 1984.

Murphy, Herta A., and Hildebrandt, Herbert W. *Effective Business Communications*. 4th ed. New York: McGraw-Hill, 1984.

Pearce, C. Glenn, Figgins, Ross, and Golen, Steven P. *Principles of Business Communication: Theory, Application and Technology*. New York: Wiley, 1984.

Sigband, Norman B. and Bateman, David N. *Communicating in Business*. Glenview, Ill.: Scott Foresman, 1981.

Treece, Malra. *Communication for Business and the Professions*. 2d ed. Boston: Allyn and Bacon, 1983.

————. *Successful Business Communication*. 2d ed. Boston: Allyn and Bacon, 1984.

Wells, Walter. *Communications in Business*. 3rd ed. Belmont, Calif.: Kent Publishing, 1981.

Wilkensen, C. W., Clarke, Peter B., and Wilkensen, Dorothy C. M. *Communicating Through Letters and Reports*. 8th ed. Homewood, Ill.: Irwin, 1983.

Wolf, Morris Philip, and Kuiper, Shirley. *Effective Communication in Business*. 8th ed. Cincinnati: South-Western, 1984.

RESEARCH METHODS AND TECHNIQUES

Barzun, Jacques, and Fraff, Henry F. *The Modern Researcher*. 3rd ed. New York: Harcourt, Brace & World, 1977.

Berdie, Douglas R. and Anderson, John F. *Questionnaires: Design* and *Use*. Metuchen, N.J.: Scarecrow Press, 1974.

Chase, Stuart. *Guides to Straight Thinking*. New York: Harper, 1956.

Clover, Vernon T. and Balsley, Howard L. *Business Research Methods*. 2d ed. Columbus: Grid, 1979.

Converse, Jean M. and Schuman, Howard. *Conversations at Random: Survey Research as Interviewers See It*. Ann Arbor: University of Michigan; Social Research, 1974.

Deming, W. E. *Sample Design in Business Research*. New York: Wiley, 1960.

Edwards, Allen L. *Techniques of Attitude Scale Construction*. New York: Irvington, 1982.

Emory, C. William. *Business Research Methods*. Rev. ed. Homewood, Ill.: Irwin, 1980.

Erdos, Paul L. *Professional Mail Surveys*. Rev. ed. Melbourne, Fl.: Krieger, 1983.

Huff, Darrell. *How to Lie with Statistics*. New York: Norton, 1954.

Kerlinger, Fred N. *Foundations* of *Behavioral Research*. 2d ed. New York: Holt, Rinehart and Winston, 1973.

Kish, Leslie. *Survey Sampling*. New York: Wiley, 1965.

Spear, Mary Eleanor. *Practical Charting Techniques*. New York: McGraw-Hill, 1969.

BASIC PRINCIPLES OF EFFECTIVE WRITING

Barzun, Jacques. *Simple and Direct.* New York: Harper, 1975.

Bernstein, Theodore M. *The Careful Writer: A Modern Guide to English Usage.* New York: Atheneum, 1965.

————. *Do's, Don't's and Maybe's of the English Language.* New York: New York Times Books, 1982.

————. *Do's Don't's and Maybe's of English Usage.* New York: New York Times Books, 1977.

————. *Watch Your Language.* Great Neck, N.Y.: Channel Press, 1965.

Brusaw, Charles T., Alred, Gerald J., and Oliu, Walter E. *The Business Writer's Handbook.* 2d ed. New York: St. Martin's Press, 1982.

Corder, Jim W. *Handbook of Current English.* 6th ed. Glenview, Ill.: Scott Foresman, 1981.

Ewing, David W. *Writing For Results in Business, Government, the Sciences, and the Professions.* 2d ed. New York: Wiley, 1979.

Fowler, H. W. *A Dictionary of Modern English Usage.* 2d ed. Revised by Sir Ernest Gowers. Oxford: Oxford University Press, 1965.

Hodges, John C. and Whitten, Mary E. *Harbrace College Handbook.* 9th ed. New York; Harcourt Brace Jovanovich, 1982.

Kolb, Harold H., Jr. *A Writer's Guide: The Essential Points.* New York: Harcourt Brace Jovanovich, 1980.

Mascolini, Marcia V., and Freeman, Caryl P. *Objective Writing for Business and Industry.* Reston, Virginia: Reston, 1984.

Sigband, Norman, Bachman, Lois J., and Hipple, Theodore W. *Successful Business English.* Glenview, Ill.: Scott Foresman, 1983.

Strunk, W. and White, E. B. *The Elements of Style.* 3rd ed. New York: Macmillan, 1979.

Zinsser, William. *On Writing Well.* New York: Harper and Row, 1980.

BUSINESS AND PROFESSIONAL SPEAKING

Applebaum, Ronald L. and Anatol, Karl W. E. *Effective Oral Communication for Business and the Professions.* Chicago: SRA, 1982.

Ehninger, Douglas, et al. *Principles and Types of Speech Communication.* 9th ed. Glenview, Ill.: Scott Foresman, 1981.

Holm, James N. *Productive Speaking for Business and the Professions.* Boston: American Press, 1983.

Mudd, Charles S. and Sillars, Malcolm O. *Speech Content and Communication.* 4th ed. New York: Harper and Row, 1980.

Rodman, George R. *Public Speaking: An Introduction to Message Preparation.* 2d ed. New York: Holt, Rinehart, and Winston, 1981.

Samovar, Larry A. and Mills, Jack. *Oral Communication: Message and Response.* 5th ed. Dubuque, Ia.: William C. Brown, 1983.

Tacey, William S. *Business and Professional Speaking.* 4th ed. Dubuque, Ia.: William C. Brown, 1983.

Walter, Otis M. and Scott, Robert L. *Thinking and Speaking: A Guide to Intelligent Oral Communication.* 5th ed. New York: Macmillan, 1984.

Berlo, David. *The Process of Communication*. New York: Holt, Rinehart and Winston, 1960.

Downs, Cal, Linkgukel, Wil, and Berg, David M. *The Organizational Communicator*. New York: Harper & Row, 1977.

Goldhaber, Gerald M. *Organizational Communication*. 3rd ed. Dubuque Ia.: William C. Brown, 1983.

Keltner, John W. *Elements of Interpersonal Communication*. Belmont, Calif.: Wadsworth, 1973.

Koehler, J. W., Anatol, Karl W. E., and Applebaum, Ronald L. *Organizational Communication: Behavioral Perspectives*. 2d ed. New York: Holt, Rinehart, and Winston, 1981.

Rothwell, J. Dan, and Costigan, James I. *Interpersonal Communication*. Columbus: Charles E. Merrill, 1975.

Smeltzer, Larry R. and Waltman, John. *Managerial Communication; A Strategic Approach*. New York: Wiley, 1984.

Timm, Paul R. *Managerial Communication*. Englewood Cliffs, N.J.: Prentice-Hall, 1980.

THE JOB SEARCH

Bolles, Richard Nelson. *What Color Is Your Parachute? A Practice Manual for Job-Hunters and Career Changers*. Rev. ed. Berkeley, Calif.: Ten Speed Press, 1982.

Bostwick, Burdette E. *Finding the Job You've Always Wanted*. 2d ed. New York: Wiley, 1980.

————. *Resume Writing: A Comprehensive How-to-do-it Guide*. 2d ed. New York: Wiley, 1980.

Djeddah, Eli. *Moving Up. How to Get High-Salaried Jobs*. Berkeley, Calif.: Ten Speed Press, 1978.

Donaho, Melvin W. and Meyer, John L. *How to Get the Job You Want*. Englewood Cliffs, N.J.: Prentice-Hall, 1976.

Gootnick, David. *Getting a Better Job*. New York: McGraw-Hill, 1978.

Jackson, Tom. *The Perfect Resume*. New York: Doubleday, 1981.

Index